States, Citizens and the Priva

Recent years have seen a growing role for private military contractors in national and international security. To understand the reasons for this, Elke Krahmann examines changing models of the state, the citizen and the soldier in the UK, the USA and Germany. She focuses on the national differences both with regard to the outsourcing of military services to private companies and their specific consequences for democratic control over the legitimate use of armed force. Tracing developments and debates from the late eighteenth century to the present, she explains the transition from the centralized warfare state of the Cold War era to privatized and fragmented security governance, and the different national attitudes to the privatization of force.

ELKE KRAHMANN is a Senior Lecturer in the Department of Politics at the University of Bristol. Her previous publications include *New Threats and New Actors in International Security* (2005) and *Multilevel Networks in European Foreign Policy* (2003).

States, Citizens and the Privatization of Security

Elke Krahmann

CAMBRIDGE
UNIVERSITY PRESS

CAMBRIDGE UNIVERSITY PRESS
Cambridge, New York, Melbourne, Madrid, Cape Town, Singapore,
São Paulo, Delhi, Dubai, Tokyo

Cambridge University Press
The Edinburgh Building, Cambridge CB2 8RU, UK

Published in the United States of America by Cambridge University Press,
New York

www.cambridge.org
Information on this title: www.cambridge.org/9780521110198

First published 2010

Printed in the United Kingdom at the University Press, Cambridge

A catalogue record for this publication is available from the British Library

Library of Congress Cataloguing in Publication data
Krahmann, Elke.
States, citizens, and the privatization of security / Elke Krahmann.
  p. cm.
Includes bibliographical references and index.
ISBN 978-0-521-11019-8 (hbk.)
ISBN 978-0-521-12519-2 (pbk.)
1. National security–Case studies.   2. Security, International–Case
studies.   3. Contracting out–Case studies.   4. Private military companies–
Case studies.   5. State, The–Case studies.   6. Civil-military relations–
Case studies.   7. Democracy–Case studies.   8. Great Britain–Military
policy.   9. United States–Military policy.   10. Germany–Military
policy.   I. Title. II. Title: States, citizens, and the privatization of security.
UA10.5.K73 2010
355.3′54–dc22
2009042810

ISBN 978-0-521-11019-8 Hardback
ISBN 978-0-521-12519-2 Paperback

Contents

Illustrations

Figures

Tables

Acknowledgements

While researching and writing this book, I have benefited from the financial and intellectual support of many organizations and individuals too numerous to name individually. In particular, I would like to acknowledge the funding I have received from the British Academy, the German Academic Exchange Service and the United States Institute of Peace for various parts of my research ranging from my initial theoretical ideas to interviews conducted in the United Kingdom, the United States and Germany. This research would also not have been possible without the institutional support from the Center for European Studies at Harvard University, the German Historical Institute and the Center for Global and International Studies at the George Washington University in Washington DC, and the Department of Politics at the University of Bristol which permitted me to take several research leaves to focus entirely on this project. My colleagues in Bristol have been a great help before and during the writing stage. My special thanks go to Tim Edmunds who helped me keep up my motivation while he himself was writing his own book and to Richard Little who commented on my proposal for this monograph. I must also mention my wonderful grant administrator, Jean Pretlove, who was not only of great assistance with my funding applications and management, but who also took a very personal interest in my research.

Of course, no comparative empirical research project is possible without the practitioners and experts who are willing to be interviewed about their work. Although not all of their detailed knowledge and interesting experiences could be included within the limited scope of this book, they have provided important background information and deeply influenced my argument concerning the complexity and variance of private military contracting in Western democracies. I would like to thank these individuals from the German and British Ministries of Defence, the US Department of State, the US Department of Defense, the Gesellschaft für Entwicklung, Beschaffung und Betrieb (GEBB), the International Peace Operations Association (IPOA), the British Association of Private Security Companies (BAPSC) and DynCorp for taking the time to talk to me.

In addition, I would like to express my sincere gratitude to the many colleagues who have read and commented upon the preliminary papers presented at national and international conferences and workshops which have formed the foundations of this manuscript. They have offered valuable criticisms and encouragement, and I would not have been able to complete this project without their input. Special thanks go to Deborah Avant, Anna Geis, Carlos Ortiz and Christopher Spearin as well as the two anonymous reviewers for their extensive advice regarding the final manuscript. They have ensured that I have made my argument as clear and consistent as possible, and any remaining deficiencies are my responsibility alone.

Finally, as always, I am grateful to my friends and family for their love and support. To them, I dedicate this book.

Acronyms

AWACS	Airborne Warning and Control System
AWE	Atomic Weapons Establishment
BAE	British Aerospace
BAPSC	British Association of Private Security Companies
BDWS	Bundesverband Deutscher Wach- und Sicherheitsunternehmen
BNFL	British Nuclear Fuels
BSIA	British Security Industry Association
C4ISR	Command, control, communications, computers, intelligence, surveillance and reconnaissance
CBO	Congressional Budget Office
CIS	Communications and Information Systems
CoESS	Confederation of European Security Services
CONDO	Contractors on Deployed Operations
CONLOG	Contract for Logistics Support
CPA	Coalition Provisional Authority
CSC	Computer Sciences Corporation
DARA	Defence Aviation Repair Agency
DFID	Department for International Development
DLA	Defence Logistics Agency
DOD	Department of Defense
ECOWAS	Economic Community of West African States
EDS	Electronic Data Systems
ESG	Elektroniksystem- und Logistik GmbH
EU	European Union
FAIR	Federal Activities Inventory Reform
FTE	Full Time Equivalent
GAO	Government Accountability Office
GDP	Gross domestic product

GEBB	Gesellschaft für Entwicklung, Beschaffung und Betrieb
HDW	Howaldtswerke-Deutsche Werft
IDIQ	Indefinite delivery/indefinite quantity
IPOA	International Peace Operations Association
ISAF	International Security Assistance Force
ISO	International Organization for Standardization
IT	Information technology
KBR	Kellogg, Brown and Root
KINTOP	Krisenreaktionskräfte Interoperabilität
LOGCAP	Logistic Civil Augmentation Program
MBB	Messerschmidt-Bölkow-Blohm
MEJA	Military Extraterritorial Jurisdiction Act
MEO	Most Efficient Organization
MOD	Ministry of Defence
MOU	Memorandum of Understanding
MPRI	Military Professional Resources Inc.
NATO	North Atlantic Treaty Organization
NGO	Non-governmental organization
OMB	Office of Management and Budget
OSCE	Organization for Security and Cooperation in Europe
PFI	Private Finance Initiative
PSC	Public Sector Comparator
RAF	Royal Air Force
ROC	Reconstructions Operations Centres
RO-RO	Roll-on, roll-off
SA	Sturm Abteilung
SALIS	Strategic Airlift Interim Solution
SAS	Special Air Service
SOFA	Status of Forces Agreement
SPOT	Synchronized Predeployment and Operational Tracker
SS	Schutzstaffel
TA	Territorial Army
TAFMIS	Training Administration and Financial Management Information Systems
UCMJ	Uniform Code of Military Justice
UK	United Kingdom

UN	United Nations
UOR	Urgent Operational Requirement
USA	United States of America
VFM	Value for Money
WEU	Western European Union
WIB	War Industries Board
WMD	Weapons of mass destruction

1   Introduction

We have this idealized vision of war as being men in uniform fighting for the political cause of their nation-state. That is actually an anomaly. It describes only the last 300 years.[1] Peter W. Singer

Democratic control over the use of collective force for national and international security has been a problem since the rise of modern democracy in Europe and North America. By the twentieth century, however, the issue finally appeared to have been resolved. Public and parliamentary oversight of national armed forces comprising professional soldiers or citizen-soldiers promised to prevent the abuse of military power by both state and non-state actors. The controversy over the growing role of private military contractors in Western military has to be seen in this context.[2] Ranging from the outsourcing of essential military services for national defence to the proliferation of armed guards shooting at civilians in Afghanistan and Iraq, private contractors have become a new and seemingly unregulated force. Private military companies are the incorporated face of this development. In contrast to the *condottieri* of fourteenth-century Italy and the post-colonial mercenaries of the 1970s, modern private military contractors are registered businesses with headquarters, administrative staff, public relations officers and ISO 9001 certification. These businesses not only supply armed guards, but also technical services across the full spectrum of military and military support functions, such as weapons maintenance and operations, site guarding, training, education, risk analysis, intelligence, transport, supplies, logistics and base

[1] Cited in J. Dao, ' "Outsourced" or "Mercenary," He's No Soldier', *New York Times*, 25 April 2004.
[2] R. Mandel, *Armies without States: The Privatization of Security* (Boulder, CO: Lynne Rienner, 2002); P. W. Singer, *Corporate Warriors. The Rise of the Privatized Military Industry* (Ithaca, NY: Cornell University Press, 2003); D. D. Avant, *The Market for Force. The Consequences of Privatizing Security* (Cambridge: Cambridge University Press, 2005); C. Kinsey, *Corporate Soldiers and International Security. The Rise of Private Military Companies* (London: Routledge, 2006).

1

management. The size of the contemporary private military industry is staggering. In particular, the United Kingdom (UK) and the United States (USA) have outsourced large sections of their national and international security provision to the private sector. By 1996 contractors in the employ of the US Department of Defense (DOD) supplied 25 per cent of base commercial activities, 28 per cent of depot maintenance and 70 per cent of army aviation training for the US armed forces.[3] By 2008 this proportion had more than doubled in key sectors such as management, telecommunications, maintenance and repair.[4] In the UK private military contractors not only conduct the majority of military training and maintenance, but also manage all navy ports and main army garrisons. Even in international military deployments, the scale of private sector involvement has increased massively since the end of the Cold War. While in the former Yugoslavia the ratio of military contractors to US armed forces personnel was one to fifty, in Iraq the DOD employed as many private military contractors as it had troops in the country.[5]

Of course, private armed forces in Europe and North America are not a new phenomenon. But the past 300 years have witnessed their progressive elimination due to the emergence of the state monopoly on the legitimate use of collective force, anti-mercenarism and democracy.[6] According to these norms, the prohibition of the use of military force by private actors and democratic control over the military are essential for public security and international peace. Not by coincidence, the rise of the state monopoly on collective violence occurred simultaneously with the establishment of modern democracy and citizen armies. The centralization of control over collective force within the hands of democratically elected governments and the replacement of mercenaries with citizen-soldiers evolved as key mechanisms for preventing private and collective abuses of military power. The current privatization and outsourcing of military services challenges these mechanisms. It is not

[3] DOD, *Improving the Combat Edge through Outsourcing* (Washington DC, March 1996), p. 8.

[4] Government Accountability Office (GAO), *Defense Budget: Trends in Operation and Maintenance Costs and Support Services Contracting*, GAO-07–631 (Washington DC, May 2007), p. 3; DOD, Agency Reports Fiscal Years 1997–2008.

[5] Congressional Budget Office (CBO), *Contractor's Support of U.S. Operations in Iraq* (Washington DC, August 2008), p. 1.

[6] J. E. Thomson, *Mercenaries, Pirates, and Sovereigns. State-building and Extraterritorial Violence in Early Modern Europe* (Princeton, NJ: Princeton University Press, 1994), p. 27; D. Avant, 'From Mercenary to Citizen Armies: Explaining Change in the Practice of War', *International Organization*, 54, no. 1 (2000), 41–72; S. Percy, *Mercenaries: The History of a Norm in International Relations* (Oxford: Oxford University Press, 2007).

simply a different way of providing security; it has serious implications for the democratic control of the use of armed force.

This book seeks to understand the reasons for and implications of the proliferation of private military force in Europe and North America. It does so from a distinct theoretical perspective, namely the Theory of the Social Contract and the Republican and Liberal models of democratic civil–military relations which have developed on its foundations. This perspective shows that the recent privatization and outsourcing of military force has not merely been driven by functional reasons such as the changing security environment, post-Cold War demands for peace dividends or advancements in military technology, but also has been shaped by ideological ideal models of the democratic state, the citizen and the soldier.[7] Social Contract Theory served as the origin of these ideal models. It contended that the state monopoly on the legitimate use of violence is the condition for security and peace.[8] The advent of modern democracy required that this monopoly had to be brought under the control of the citizens. How this can be best achieved has remained subject to wide contestation. In particular, two competing theories and their associated public ideologies have influenced this debate so far: Republicanism and Liberalism.[9] Republicanism advocates the centralization of the provision of security within the state and national armed forces composed of conscripted citizen-soldiers. Liberalism, which in the following also includes Neoliberalism, suggests the fragmentation and limitation of governmental powers and the political neutrality of professional armed forces. This book demonstrates that Republicanism and Liberalism continue to shape our understanding of the ideal roles and relations of the state, society and the military.[10]

[7] G. Arnold, *Mercenaries: The Scourge of the Third World* (Basingstoke: Macmillan, 1999), p. 173; Singer, *Corporate Warriors*, p. 67; C. Spearin, 'American Hegemony Incorporated: The Importance and Implications of Military Contractors in Iraq', *Contemporary Security Policy*, 24, no. 3 (2003), 28; A. R. Markusen, 'The Case against Privatizing National Security', *Governance*, 16, no. 4 (2003), 477–8; M. Edmonds, 'Defense Privatisation: From State Enterprise to Commercialism', *Cambridge Review of International Affairs*, 13, no. 1 (1999), 114–29; E. Fredland and A. Kendry, 'The Privatisation of Military Force: Economic Virtues, Vices and Government Responsibility', *Cambridge Review of International Affairs*, 13, no. 1 (1998), 147–64.
[8] T. Hobbes, *Leviathan*, edited by R. Tuck (Cambridge: Cambridge University Press, 1991).
[9] J.-J. Rousseau, *The Social Contract and Other Later Writings*, edited by V. Gourvitch (Cambridge: Cambridge University Press, 1997).
[10] E. A. Cohen, *Citizens and Soldiers: The Dilemmas of Military Service* (Ithaca, NY: Cornell University Press, 1995); A. Carter, 'Liberalism and the Obligation to Military Service', *Political Studies*, 46, no. 1 (1998), 68–81; R. C. Snyder, 'The Citizen-Soldier Tradition and Gender Integration of the U.S. Military', *Armed Forces & Society*, 29, no. 2 (2003), 185–204.

Moreover, they provide a suitable basis from which to assess the consequences of the contemporary privatization and outsourcing of military services. In particular, both reveal that the growing role of private military contractors transforms the formal and informal institutions and relations which have ensured democratic control of military force over the past centuries. In order to address the implications of this transformation and the new security demands arising from transnational threats, the book concludes by proposing a reform of Republican and Neoliberal models of civil–military control.

In order to illustrate the importance of Republicanism and Liberalism for the explanation and evaluation of the privatization of military force in Western democracies, the following chapters examine and compare the use of private military contractors in four cases: the UK, the USA, Germany and in international military interventions. These case studies have been selected for several reasons. Firstly, democratic control of the use of military force in the UK, the USA and Germany is particularly important because these countries have some of the largest and most sophisticated armed forces found in Western democracies. How these countries control their militaries has a considerable impact on national and international security. Secondly, all three countries have adopted very divergent attitudes and approaches towards the privatization of military services despite facing similar security challenges and demands. Therefore, they present a theoretical and empirical puzzle, not explained by purely functional arguments concerning the changing security environment. Thirdly, the use of private military contractors in international combat and peacekeeping operations, such as in Iraq, raises particular anxieties regarding democratic control over the legitimate use of military force in international relations. The reluctance of Western governments to deploy private military contractors in conflict zones has reflected these concerns. Even the UK military has proclaimed that it does not 'normally' envisage the involvement of civilian contractor staff in 'non-benign environments', although the praxis proves otherwise.[11]

On the basis of a detailed historical and contemporary investigation of the ideological models of civil–military control in these three Western democracies, this book advances the understanding of private military forces in several ways. Foremost, it demonstrates that the inclusion of ideological factors offers a fuller understanding of how the growing role of private military forces has become possible. These

---

[11] Ministry of Defence (MOD), 'Contractors on Deployed Operations (CONDO)', at: www.aof.mod.uk.

factors also help explain why the scale and form of military privatization has varied significantly among Western democracies. In addition, the book offers a theoretically guided assessment of the consequences of the proliferation of private military contractors for democratic control which not only includes the state, but also the citizens and their parliamentary representations. Finally, this book discusses how existing models of civil–military control might be adapted to the challenges posed by the changing security environment and the growing role of private military forces. In conclusion, this book demonstrates that the transition to private military forces is by no means a uniform, inevitable or functionally driven response to the changing national and international security landscape. It highlights instead the inherently political and ideological nature of the decision to contract out military services to private firms.

Before one can turn to these issues, however, the remainder of this chapter provides an introduction to the main concepts, empirical context and theoretical approach of this book. To do so, the first section examines the distinction between private military contractors and mercenaries. In short, what makes this industry a new phenomenon? The second section discusses the main reasons for the re-emergence of private military forces which have been identified in the literature. The third outlines how ideology offers a complementary explanation, and how it will serve as the theoretical framework for the analysis of the outsourcing and privatization of military services in this book. Nevertheless, the question remains why this development has occurred now. The fourth section answers this question by proposing that repeated ideological changes have occurred during the past three centuries. It identifies two key factors which have contributed to these shifts, namely new security demands and problems of civil–military control. The fifth section argues that the ideal models of democratic control and accountability also serve to assess the implications of the privatization of military services. Finally, the concluding section summarizes the structure of the book.

Private military contractors

Any analysis of the contemporary proliferation of private military contractors in Europe and North America has to begin with a clarification of the differences between contractors and mercenaries. What makes the modern private military industry a new and distinct phenomenon? Although the press all too often conflates private military firms with mercenaries, there are a number of features which differentiate the two. Foremost among these features is the corporate nature of private military companies and their resulting legal status, while mercenaries operate outside the law. The First Additional Protocol to the Geneva Conventions defines mercenaries on the basis of six cumulative characteristics: (1) they are specially recruited locally or abroad in order to fight in an armed conflict; (2) they take a direct part in the hostilities; (3) they are motivated to take part in the hostilities essentially by the desire for private gain and are promised, by or on behalf of a party of the conflict, material compensation substantially in excess of that promised or paid to combatants of similar ranks and functions in the armed forces of that party; (4) they are neither a national of a party to the conflict nor a resident of territory controlled by a party to the conflict; (5) they are not a member of the armed forces of a party to the conflict; and (6) they have not been sent by a state which is not a party to the conflict on official duty as a member of its armed forces.[12] In addition, mercenary forces are, typically, composed on an ad hoc basis and for illicit purposes. They are volatile, dangerous and little concerned with their long-term reputation and compliance with national and international laws.[13] The norm against mercenaries and various efforts to outlaw them, including the Organization of African Union Convention for the Elimination of Mercenarism and the United Nations (UN) International Convention against the Recruitment, Use, Financing and Training of Mercenaries and their exclusion from the safeguards of the Geneva Convention, are responses to the lack of control over mercenaries and the resulting threat to international peace and stability.[14] However, the difficulty of prosecuting mercenaries based on a definition which requires simultaneous evidence for all seven criteria, including the personal motivation of the accused, has not only undermined the widespread endorsement of the UN convention, but also its practical implementation since its coming into force in 2001.

---

[12] Protocol Additional to the Geneva Conventions of 12 August 1949, and Relating to the Protection of Victims of International Armed Conflicts (Protocol I), 8 June 1977, Art. 47, in: *The Geneva Conventions and their Additional Protocols*, at: www.icrc.org.

[13] Percy, *Mercenaries*; Arnold, *Mercenaries*; J. Cilliers and P. Mason (eds.), *Peace, Profit or Plunder? The Privatisation of Security in War-torn African Societies* (Pretoria: Institute for Security Studies, 1999).

[14] African Union, *Convention on the Elimination of Mercenaries in Africa*, CM/817, Annex II, Rev. I (1977); United Nations General Assembly, *International Convention against the Recruitment, Use, Financing and Training of Mercenaries*, A/RES/44/34, 72nd Plenary Meeting, 4 December 1989. For a detailed analysis of the norm against mercenarism see Percy, *Mercenaries*.

By contrast, private military companies are legal businesses with permanent structures, headquarters and management. Although there are still some gaps in the regulation of the industry, private military firms are subject to corporate and contractual law, sector regulations, and national and international legislation in Europe and North America.[15] It is specifically the incorporation of these businesses that has facilitated compliance with public laws and regulations through the assignment of corporate responsibility to private owners or executive boards. The immunity from local criminal prosecution granted to contractor personnel in Iraq has thus not precluded their companies from being charged with fraud or criminal negligence in the USA. High-profile cases have been the corruption charges filed against Custer Battles, the prosecution of Blackwater for negligence by the families of contractors who were killed in Fallujah and the compensation claims made by the relatives of three out of seventeen civilians who were shot by Blackwater employees in September 2007.[16] The effects of business reputation on the share values of firms floated on the stock market, such as L-3 Communications, CSC, CACI and ArmorGroup, also influence the behaviour and considerations of private military contractors. ArmorGroup, for instance, makes a notable effort to distance itself from the mercenary image of the industry by emphasizing regulation and ethical standards, including the Code of Conduct of the International Red Cross and Red Crescent, the US/UK Governments' Voluntary Principles on Security and Human Rights, and its proactive contribution to industry self-regulation.[17] Other companies have suffered the consequences of reputation loss, such as CACI whose share value declined by up to 13 per cent after the US Army began investigations into accusations that some of CACI's employees were implicated in the abuse of inmates at the Iraqi Abu Ghraib prison.[18]

The contemporary private military and security industry is not only distinct from mercenaries; there is also a significant variety within the

---

[15] S. Chesterman and C. Lehnardt (eds.), *From Mercenaries to Market: The Rise and Regulation of Private Military Companies* (Oxford: Oxford University Press, 2007); A. Alexandra, D.-P. Baker and M. Caparini (eds.), *Private Military and Security Companies. Ethics, Policies and Civil-Military Relations* (London: Routledge, 2008); E. Krahmann, 'Regulating Private Military Companies: What Role for the EU?' *Contemporary Security Policy*, 26, no. 1 (2005), 1–23.

[16] C. A. Babcock, 'Contractor Fraud Trial to Begin Tomorrow', *Washington Post*, 13 February 2006; J. Scahill, 'A Very Private War', *Guardian*, 1 August 2007; S. Raghavan and J. White, 'Blackwater Guards Fired at Fleeing Cars, Soldiers Say', *Washington Post*, 12 October 2007.

[17] ArmorGroup, 'Regulation and Ethical Standards', at: www.armorgroup.com.

[18] *BBC*, 'Inquiry into Interrogation Firm', 27 May 2004.

sector. Several authors have attempted to develop typologies of private military and security companies. Peter W. Singer, for instance, distinguishes firms according to the types of services that they provide. According to Singer's tip-of-the-spear typology, 'military provider firms' supply implementation and command, 'military consultant firms' offer advisory and training services and 'military support firms' provide non-lethal aid and assistance.[19] Christopher Kinsey argues that private military and security firms can be differentiated along two axes: the means they use to secure their objective, ranging from lethal to non-lethal, and the object of their protection, ranging from private to public.[20] In practice, these categories more often than not merge into one another. The same firms frequently supply a variety of functions and adapt their services in response to changing customer demands.[21] The services of 'military consultant firm' DynCorp, for instance, range from aviation maintenance, logistics and information technology (IT) support to military training.[22] Even management, risk-consulting and defence procurement companies have significantly expanded their role in the provision of services for the armed forces. The British government support service company Babcock thus oversees the management, maintenance and repair of the UK's four Vanguard-class submarines, which carry its Trident nuclear missiles.[23] Finally, the character of individual companies can transform as the result of mergers and the transnationalization of the industry. Owing to the problems of making categorical distinctions, this book uses the term 'private military companies' for all security and support firms working for national armed forces or international military operations. Rather than referring to particular types of companies or services, the term seeks to highlight that these contractors are replacing uniformed soldiers and form an integral part of contemporary civil–military relations.

The rise of the private military industry

The expanding literature on private military companies has identified a multitude of explanations concerning the causes of the rise of the private military industry.[24] Foremost among them have been functional

---

[19] Singer, *Corporate Warriors*, p. 93.
[20] Kinsey, *Corporate Soldiers and International Security*, p. 10.
[21] Avant, *The Market for Force*, p. 17; Mandel, *Armies without States*, pp. 99–106.
[22] Singer, *Corporate Warriors*, p. 93; DynCorp, at: www.dyn-intl.com.
[23] Babcock, 'Babcock Naval Services', at: www.babcock.co.uk.
[24] Singer, *Corporate Warriors*, pp. 49–70; Kinsey, *Corporate Soldiers and International Security*, pp. 51–7; Avant, *The Market for Force*, pp. 30–8; Alexandra *et al.*, *Private Military and Security Companies*.

Table 1.1. *Armed forces personnel*[25]

Country	1985	1990	1995	2000	2005	2007
USA	2,244,000	2,181,000	1,620,000	1,483,000	1,372,000	1,346,000
UK	334,000	308,000	233,000	218,000	211,000	190,000
Germany	495,000	545,000	352,000	319,000	246,000	247,000

Table 1.2. *Defence spending (per cent of GDP)*[26]

Country	1985–1990 (average)	1990	1995	2000	2005	2007
USA	6	5.3	3.8	3.1	4.1	4
UK	4.5	3.9	3	2.4	2.7	2.3
Germany	3	2.8	1.6	1.5	1.4	1.3

arguments related to changes in the security environment, budgetary pressures and the market forces of supply and demand. The end of the Cold War is, typically, regarded as the starting point of the proliferation of private military firms as it led to massive cuts in national armed forces personnel and military spending on both sides of the Atlantic. As Tables 1.1 and 1.2 indicate, the size of the armed forces and defence budgets in the UK, the USA and Germany are nearly half of what they were at the height of the Cold War in the 1980s.

The reductions in the number of uniformed soldiers have contributed to the expansion of the private military industry in two ways.[27] Firstly, they have supplied a large surplus of ex-military personnel from which private firms have been able to recruit employees with the necessary training and skills. Secondly, the cuts have created new demand for military expertise and personnel after governments in Europe and North America realized in the mid 1990s that their expectations of a peaceful 'new world order' had been premature.[28] Although the

[25] Statistics from NATO, at: www.nato.int/docu/pr/2007/p07–141.pdf. Note: 2007 numbers are estimates, and German armed forces in 1990 are the combined armed forces of East and West Germany after unification.

[26] Statistics from NATO, at: www.nato.int/docu/pr/2007/p07–141.pdf and SIPRI, 'Military Expenditure Database', at: www.sipri.org. Note: 2007 numbers are estimates.

[27] J. L. Taulbee, 'Mercenaries, Private Armies and Security Companies in Contemporary Policy', *International Politics*, 37, no. 4 (2000), 434; Singer, *Corporate Warriors*, p. 67; Spearin, 'American Hegemony Incorporated', 28; Avant, *The Market for Force*, pp. 30–1.

[28] As proclaimed by G. H. W. Bush, 'Toward a New World Order', Speech to Congress, 11 September 1991.

threat of a military attack on Western national territories has disap-
peared, new security threats have emerged from the break-up of the
former Yugoslavia, nuclear proliferation among 'rogue states' and international terrorism. Moreover, the changed relationship with Russia
has unblocked the UN Security Council and has opened the way for
a growing number of multilateral interventions into regional conflicts
which have sprung up partially as the result of the reduction of Soviet or
US support for allies in the developing world. Since Western electorates
have been unwilling to give up their peace dividends for seemingly distant threats, private military contractors have provided governments in
Europe and North America with a way of bolstering their armed forces
without formally increasing their size. In fact, private military companies have offered to even further reduce the number of uniformed
military personnel and, so some governments have argued, the cost
of defence.[29] Finally, private military firms have been at the forefront
of the technological revolution in military affairs which has demanded
highly developed civilian skills in information technology for network-
centric warfare.[30]

However, functional arguments alone cannot account fully for the
proliferation of private military contractors. Among other things, they
fail to explain why there is significant variance in the approach taken by
the European states and North America, despite their common security environment. Within the context of this book, this is represented
by the question of why the UK and the USA have embraced the privatization of military services to a much greater degree than Germany.
Following the logic of the arguments outlined above, the case should
be reversed. Germany has reduced the number of its armed forces personnel to a greater degree than its Anglo-American allies, yet is now
engaging in new missions overseas for which the Bundeswehr has little
expertise or training. Germany was also more directly affected by the
civil war in the former Yugoslavia, is geographically closer to the conflict in Afghanistan and is within direct reach of nuclear 'rogue states'
such as Iran. Lastly, Germany had and still has greater need to mod-
ernize its national armed forces and, thus, for the perceived advanced
technological skills of private military contractors.

29 H. M. Howe, 'Private Security Forces and African Stability: The Case of Executive
   Outcomes', *Journal of Modern African Studies*, 36, no. 2 (1998), 307–31; D. Brooks,
   'Messiahs or Mercenaries? The Future of International Military Services', *International
   Peacekeeping*, 7, no. 4 (2000), 131; Markusen, 'The Case against Privatizing National
   Security', 477–8.
30 P. W. Singer, 'Corporate Warriors: The Rise of the Privatized Military Industry and
   Its Ramifications for International Security', *International Security*, 26, no. 3 (2001–2),
   195.

Ideological factors help us to understand these differences with regard to the decision to outsource military services to private firms. The rise of Neoliberalism has thus been linked to the growth of military contracting in the UK and the USA.[31] What ideology has been embraced by countries which have resisted this move, however, has not been examined so far. Indeed, the literature considers few alternatives to the outsourcing of military services. Instead, many authors seem to believe that it is predetermined by external factors or, at least, that private military companies 'are here to stay' for the foreseeable future.[32] As the next section argues, to fully understand the historical and geographical variability of the roles of the state, the citizen and the soldier in the provision of national and international security, one needs to return to their alternative ideological conceptions which begin with the theory of the Social Contract.

Ideology and civil–military control

Since the seventeenth century, Social Contract Theory has provided the foundations for the state monopoly on the legitimate use of collective violence and the theory of the democratic control of armed force in Western democracies. According to this theory, the origins of the state itself lie in peoples' search for security. Social Contract theorists from Thomas Hobbes to Jean-Jacques Rousseau have argued that citizens give up their right to the private use of force other than in self-defence in return for protection by the state. However, whereas Hobbes wrote under autocratic regimes and accepted that any central authority such as a monarch or despot can have the authority to control the use of collective violence, Rousseau, writing in the wake of the French Revolution, asserted that only a democratic representation of the citizens can legitimately hold control over the collective use of force. Contemporary democratic notions of the state, the citizen and the armed forces and their roles in security still build on Rousseau's theory. However, as Chapter 2 will show in greater detail, even within a democratic frame of reference, the scope of the Social Contract has been subject to debate. What is the appropriate extent of the state's control over the use of armed force, and how can citizens hold both their governments and their militaries accountable? In Europe and North America two ideological traditions have shaped this debate: Republicanism and Liberalism. Both ideologies

---

[31] Singer, *Corporate Warriors*, pp. 66–70; Edmonds, 'Defense Privatisation'; Fredland and Kendry, 'The Privatisation of Military Force'.

[32] J. O. C. Jonah in Chesterman and Lehnardt, *From Mercenaries to Market*, Foreword. See also Singer, *Corporate Warriors*, p. 230; Kinsey, *Corporate Soldiers and International Security*, p. 151.

agree that the roles and relations between the state, the citizen and the soldier are central to ensuring democratic control of and accountability for the collective use of armed force. But Republicanism and Liberalism disagree over the ideal natures of these roles and relations, and the most effective mechanisms of democratic control.[33]

Republicanism departs from the premise that individuals are essentially interdependent and concludes that the community is best placed to ensure the safety of its citizens. The state or government, as the democratic representation of the community, is central to national and international security. The ideal model of the Republican state is that of centralized 'government', i.e. the collective supply of and control over public resources and functions.[34] With regard to security, this ideal model includes the monopoly of the state on the provision of national and international security, the centralized supply of all security-related functions by the state and the armed forces, and the public financing and ownership of and control over the production of the means of collective force ranging from missiles to military services. The Republican ideal of collective security provision is underpinned by the perception of common security interests and norms such as national sovereignty, command and control, and redistribution.[35] The citizens counterbalance the strong powers of the state in security through the combination of two roles: a political role as electors of the government and a military role as citizen-soldiers. These roles permit citizens to exert direct control over the government and the armed forces through their participation in the democratic decision-making process and the implementation of the defence of their community. Moreover, the citizen-soldier contributes to the civilianization of the military and ensures that the armed forces form an integral part of society.[36] The democratic legitimacy of these forces rests on the right and obligation of the citizens to act in collective self-defence.[37] In short, Republicanism believes that mutual interpenetration and integration serves best to ensure the democratic control of the divergent powers and interests of the state, the citizen and the armed forces.

[33] Cohen, *Citizens and Soldiers*; Snyder, 'The Citizen-Soldier Tradition and Gender Integration of the U.S. Military'.
[34] E. Krahmann, 'National, Regional and Global Governance: One Phenomenon or Many?' *Global Governance*, 9, no. 3 (2003), 323–46.
[35] E. Krahmann, 'Conceptualizing Security Governance', *Cooperation and Conflict*, 38, no. 1 (2003), 5–26.
[36] E. A. Cohen, 'Twilight of the Citizen-Soldier', *Parameters*, 31, no. 2 (2001), 24.
[37] Cohen, 'Twilight of the Citizen-Soldier', 23–8; P. Karsten, 'The US Citizen-Soldier's Past, Present, and Likely Future', *Parameters*, 31, no. 2 (2001), 62; M. Kestnbaum, 'Citizenship and Compulsory Military Service: The Revolutionary Origins of Conscription in the United States', *Armed Forces & Society*, 27, no. 1 (2000), 7; R. A. Herrera, 'Self-Governance and the American Citizen as Soldier, 1775–1861', *The Journal of Military History*, 65, no. 1 (2001), 21.

Liberalism, by contrast, sees citizens foremost as autonomous individuals whose interests, rights and freedoms must be protected from undue interference by the state. To achieve this aim, the Liberal model proposes to limit and fragment the functions and powers of the state and the armed forces with regard to the provision of and control over the means and use of collective violence. The Liberal ideal model of the state is that of fragmented 'governance', involving the dispersion of political resources and powers among a multitude of governmental and private actors.[38] In the area of national and international security, the Liberal governance model suggests the geographical and functional fragmentation of security provision among public and private providers at different levels and with divergent expertise. Moreover, it contends that the financing and ownership of and control over the means of violence should be dispersed among multiple actors in order to prevent governmental abuses of power. Underlying the Liberal governance model are norms such as the limitation of state sovereignty, self-government and laissez-faire which see the role of the state in the protection of the right of the citizens to self-determination. The preferred models of the soldier in Liberalism are, therefore, the politically neutral professional soldier or the private military contractor. Both not only offer citizens a personal choice between public and private security providers, but also whether or not to serve in the military. Nevertheless, the ways in which democratic control over both models of the soldier is achieved are quite distinct. The professional soldier is controlled through duty, patriotism, a collective professional ethos, and the separation of the political and military roles of the citizens.[39] Conversely, the private military contractor has no general obligations other than to the employer or contract, is motivated by private gain, is alienated from society and is held accountable through market rather than institutional relations.[40] In summary, the Liberal model argues that the fragmentation, separation and balancing of the control over the means and use of collective force are key to safeguarding the democratic accountability of national and international security.

Arguably, these theoretical ideal models have frequently been transformed by praxis. Many Western democracies include elements

---

[38] Krahmann, 'National, Regional and Global Governance'.

[39] S. P. Huntington, *The Soldier and the State. The Theory and Politics of Civil-Military Relations* (Cambridge, MA: Belknap Press of Harvard University Press, 1957); M. Janowitz, *The Professional Soldier. A Social and Political Portrait* (New York: Free Press, 1960), pp. 218–29; S. C. Sarkesian, J. A. Williams and F. B. Bryant, *Soldiers, Society, and National Security* (Boulder, CO: Lynne Rienner, 1995), pp. 13–15.

[40] Sarkesian *et al.*, *Soldiers, Society, and National Security*, p. 15; S. Crock, T. F. Armistead, A. Bianco and S. Anderson Forest, 'Outsourcing War', *Business Week*, 3849 (15 September 2003), 68–78; J. Burk, 'Patriotism and the All-Volunteer Force', *Journal of Political and Military Sociology*, 12, no. 2 (1984), 229–41; E. Krahmann,

of both Republican government and Liberal governance, and have armed forces composed of professional soldiers as well as citizen-soldiers. However, typically there is one predominant model or ideal. As the following chapters will illustrate, these ideological ideal notions of the state, the citizen and the soldier play a major role in justifying particular versions of civil–military control. Several sets of questions help us to compare qualitatively the influence of Republican and Liberal theories on the institutions and practices of the democratic control over military force in the UK, the USA, Germany and in international interventions in the following case studies. As summarized in Table 1.3, the first question concerns the public expression of Republican or Liberal ideals in government and armed forces publications or speeches. The second set of questions concern the degree to which the financing, ownership and control over military force has been centralized or fragmented among public and private actors in seven dimensions: geography, function, resources, interests, norms, decision-making and implementation. The last question investigates the predominant mechanisms for ensuring the democratic control and accountability of military forces.

Another set of questions serves to compare the predominant model of the soldier in the three countries and in international military operations. This part of the analysis contends that there are three ideal-type conceptions of the soldier representing Republican and Liberal theories, which will be examined in greater detail in Chapter 2: the citizen-soldier, the professional soldier and the private military contractor. They can be distinguished by their answers to four questions: what are the relations of the soldier with the state and society; what is the primary motivation of the soldier; what is the principal identity of the soldier; and how is the democratic control and accountability of the soldier ensured? Since most countries have several types of soldier, the following case studies will focus on the predominant model defined by the highest number of personnel.

While the preceding ideal models help to explain how political ideologies have influenced the institutions and practices of democratic control over the legitimate use of military force, the question remains why the UK, the USA and Germany have favoured different ideologies at various times in their history. The following section suggests that several factors have facilitated shifts from one ideal model to another.

'The New Model Soldier and Civil-Military Relations', in A. Alexandra, D.-P. Baker and M. Caparini (eds.), *Private Military and Security Companies. Ethics, Policies and Civil-Military Relations* (London: Routledge, 2008), pp. 247–65.

Table 1.3. *Framework for the analysis of the model of the state*

Dimension	Questions
Ideology	What is the predominant public ideology espoused by the government and its agencies?
Geographical scope	What is the geographical scope of public and private military service provision? Is it confined to the national level or does it also include international interventions?
Functional scope	What military functions have been outsourced to the private sector? To what extent have particular functions been contracted out?
Resources	What kinds of resources are supplied by the private military sector, e.g. facilities, equipment, services, capital financing? To what extent does a country rely on private resources?
Interests	What is the perception of the citizens' primary interests with regard to the provision of military security?
Norms	What are the underlying norms espoused by the government and its policies?
Decision-making	How does the government decide whether to outsource a military service? To what degree are private firms involved in decision-making processes regarding the supply of military services?
Implementation	How is the provision of private military services implemented, i.e. what types of contracts are used?
Democratic control and accountability	How does the government seek to ensure the democratic control and accountability of private military contractors?

Table 1.4. *Framework for the analysis of the model of the soldier*

Dimension	Questions
Relationships with the state and society	What are the primary relations of the soldier with the state and society?
Motivation	What is the primary motivation of the soldier?
Identity	What is the principal identity of the soldier?
Democratic control and accountability	How are democratic control and accountability ensured?

Causes of ideological change

Functional arguments cannot alone account for the re-emergence of private military forces, but neither can ideology. The primary reason for this puzzle is that both variables are intimately intertwined. Throughout history, changes in national and international security contexts have influenced perceptions as to whether Republican or Liberal models of civil–military relations are best suited for ensuring the democratic control and accountability of the armed forces. In return, ideology has frequently shaped political interpretations of security threats and how best to address them. However, external factors have not been the only causes of ideological transformations in the roles and relations of the state, the citizen and the soldier in Western democracies. Internal problems have also played a major part. In particular, the critique of existing civil–military relations has contributed to growing disillusionment with predominant ideal-type models and demands for change. Three factors appear to account for transitions from one ideological ideal to another: changes in the external security environment, the inconsistent implementation of each model, and the inherent problems with each ideology.

Major changes in the threat environment have been a primary cause of ideological transformations. Frequently, as Chapter 3 will illustrate, shifts from Republican to Liberal models of the state and the soldier have occurred due to transitions from peace to war and vice versa. Major wars such as the Civil War in the USA, the Crimean War and the two World Wars have typically, albeit not always, strengthened support for the Republican ideals of centralized government and the citizen-soldier. Conversely, the absence of major threats to the national homeland has often gone hand in hand with the Liberal model of fragmented security governance and small professional armed forces. This tendency can be explained by the fact that massive threats to national security seem to support the Republican argument that security can best be achieved through centralized collective efforts based on the active participation of the whole population in conscripted citizen armies or nationalized defence industries. During peacetime, common security interests and the need to maintain sizeable armed forces under state control are less obvious and, thus, lend support for the Liberal ideal of limiting and fragmenting the legitimate means of and control over collective force.

A second cause for the transition from one ideology to another has been problems with their practical implementation. The failure of the experiment with conscription during the US Civil War and the shift towards professional armed forces in the UK in 1962 and the USA in 1973, for instance, have been at least partially attributable to inequitable application of the draft and the deployment of citizen-soldiers to fight in conflicts overseas. Since the universality of conscription and the primacy of homeland defence are two of the linchpins of the Republican ideal of the citizen-soldier and democratic control over the armed forces, any doubts in respect of them have disastrous consequences for the model's perceived legitimacy. Typically, two main factors have contributed to the inconsistent implementation of each ideology to the provision of national and international security. One has been the modification of the roles and relations of the state and the soldier due to external changes in the security environment, such as the shift from universal to selective conscription or the use of citizen-soldiers for purposes other than national defence. Another problem has been the mixing of both ideologies. Since Republicanism and Liberalism depart from contradicting ideals and principles, the combination of the two often undermines the inherent logic and practical effectiveness of their competing models of civil–military relations. Thus, the Republican ideals of community and obligation are in direct opposition to the Liberal emphasis on individual rights and freedoms. Similarly, the Republican belief that the integration and mutual interpenetration between the state, the citizen and the armed forces are the best foundations for democratic control and accountability contradicts the Liberal argument that the fragmentation of resources and power and the competition between alternative security providers are the most suitable means. The attempts of the German government to privatize military services within a system that remains largely committed to the Republican ideal of centralized governmental control over the armed forces, as outlined in Chapter 6, are thus creating significant tensions.

Finally, a third reason for the abandonment of one ideal model in favour of another lies in the inherent weaknesses of each ideology, which will be revealed in the following chapters. The widespread perception that private defence contractors had engaged in war profiteering during the First World War, for instance, helped pave the way for a transition towards Republicanism and a nationalization of the UK defence industry during the Second World War. Later, the emergence of a military–industrial complex with closely linked interests between the state and the defence industry in the USA during the 1960s and 1970s led to a critique of the Republican model of centralized state control and contributed to the turn towards the Neoliberal model of fragmented security governance. In both cases, history has demonstrated the limitations of theoretical models of democratic control. It has illustrated that the Liberal ideal of fragmented governance might prevent the abuse of the legitimate use of collective force by the state, but the model is less effective in safeguarding against similar abuses by private firms. The latter is especially likely if the private defence industry gains a disproportionate importance during major conflicts. Conversely, the main weakness of the Republican ideal of centralized state provision of security is its susceptibility to inflating the governmental apparatus and the powers of the executive.

In summary, it can be argued that ideology plays a major part in shaping the roles of the state, the citizen and the soldier with regard to the provision of national and international security. Whether they concern the perceived suitability of competing models of civil–military relations for the existing security environment, the proposition of how the democratic control and accountability of the legitimate use of collective force might best be ensured or the offering of a critique of existing structures, Republicanism and Liberalism have and continue to influence whether and to what degree the provision of security has been monopolized by the state. Moreover, the theoretical and ideological models of civil–military relations provide ideals against which democratic control and accountability of the state and the armed forces generally, and the contemporary privatization of military force in particular, can be evaluated.

Democratic control and accountability

Three main implications arise from the preceding theoretical framework for the assessment of the democratic control and accountability of the armed forces and its private military contractors in the UK, the USA and Germany. The most important implication of this framework is that democratic control is not only a question of the ability of a government to effectively manage and hold private military companies accountable, but it also depends upon the roles and relations of three sets of actors: the state, the citizen and the soldier. Regardless of whether a democracy adopts a Republican or a Liberal model of civil–military relations, it is the triangular relationship between these three actors that has been critical for safeguarding the ultimate sovereignty of citizens with regard to their own security. The substitution of soldiers with private military contractors fundamentally transforms these roles and relations. Private military contractors not only require new mechanisms of democratic control and accountability by the state, but also by the armed forces and the citizens. Moreover, they affect the ability of the citizens to hold their governments accountable if military outsourcing reduces the citizens' level of information about military spending and the numbers of military and military support personnel deployed abroad. This book, therefore, treats the issue of democratic control as a multidimensional problem that includes the state's role in the provision of national and international security and its oversight of private military personnel, the changing roles and functions of the armed forces and their management of private contractors, and citizens' capacity to influence and hold accountable the state and the armed forces for the use of military force.

Another implication is that the debate between Republicanism and Liberalism illustrates that divergent, even contradictory, principles and models can provide equally legitimate and convincing bases for the democratic control of and accountability for the use of collective force in national and international security. Nevertheless, a critique of contemporary democratic civil–military relations can come from multiple directions. Firstly, criticism can arise from the failure of each ideology and model to adequately respond to existing challenges to national and international security. Secondly, the inconsistent implementation of these models in historical and political practice can be critiqued. Thirdly, criticism can identify the inherent flaws and weaknesses of each ideology and model. Over the course of its three parts, this book engages with all three critiques and how they might be addressed. It shows that each of them has played a major part in justifying changes in the roles and relations of the state, the citizen and the soldier since the seventeenth century.

Finally, the preceding framework implies that there is unlikely to be an agreement over how best to achieve and safeguard democratic provision and use of military force since both ideologies depart from different premises. Republicanism perceives individuals as interdependent with their communities and emphasizes their obligations, while Liberalism sees them as autonomous and prioritizes their rights. The choice between each model is always political and always personal. While this author has her own, obvious, preferences, the remainder of this book attempts not to foreclose this choice, but to discuss both models on an equal basis.

Structure of the book

This book is structured in three parts. The first part examines the theoretical and historical developments which have laid the foundations for the contemporary understanding of the roles and relations of the state, the citizen and the soldier within modern democracies. Chapter 2 begins with Social Contract Theory and its elaboration within Republican and Liberal thought. Chapter 3 examines how both ideologies have provided the foundations for changing models of the state and the soldier in Europe and North America during the past three centuries. Having established the ideological and historical context, the second part of the book investigates in four case studies the impact of Republicanism and Liberalism on the privatization and outsourcing of military services and functions in the UK, the USA, Germany and in international deployed operations. The third part of the book returns to the theoretical and ideological debates over the privatization of military force. Drawing on the preceding case studies, Chapter 8 investigates how the Republican and Liberal models of civil–military control may be revised in order to meet the challenges presented by the new security environment and democratic control over the use of armed force. It outlines two alternative models for the future of civil–military relations: Neoliberal security governance and Cosmopolitan Republicanism. As the conclusion highlights, both models have their own dangers, but they hold the promise for improving the democratic control and accountability of national and international security provision in the new millennium.

2   The state monopoly on collective violence and democratic control over military force

Many studies of the contemporary proliferation of private military companies refer to Max Weber's notion that the modern state is defined by the 'monopoly of legitimate physical violence within a certain territory'.[1] Weber, however, sought to define the state and not to explain why the state did, or indeed should, lay claim to the monopoly on the legitimate use of armed force. To fully understand the reasons for and the implications of the contemporary privatization of armed force in Europe and North America, one therefore needs to return to the theoretical and ideological foundations of the relationships between the state, the citizen and the soldier. What are the theoretical origins of the state monopoly on the legitimate use of violence? How did the emergence of modern democracy influence the state's exclusive right to control armed force? And what roles should the citizen and the soldier have in national and international security?

The answers to these questions have been debated over centuries. They begin with the Theory of the Social Contract between the state and its citizens for the provision of collective security. The rights and obligations of the state and the citizens under the terms of the Social Contract have been widely contested, specifically in democratic societies. During the past three centuries, two competing ideologies have been at the heart of this contest: Republicanism and Liberalism. Many theorists and politicians have shaped the debate between these two ideologies, and sometimes they have informed and even merged into one another. Nevertheless, essentially they present divergent ideal models as to how the democratic provision of security is best achieved. To illustrate these differences, this chapter focuses on five key authors who have critically influenced the development of Republicanism and Liberalism over the past centuries.

---

[1] M. Weber, *Political Writings*, edited by P. Lassman and R. Speirs (Cambridge: Cambridge University Press, 1994), pp. 310–11.

This chapter begins by examining the theoretical foundations of these ideologies in the works of two Social Contract theorists: Thomas Hobbes and Jean-Jacques Rousseau. It argues that, while the ideas of Hobbes provide the bases for the state monopoly on collective violence, it was Rousseau who laid the foundations for the understanding of the Social Contract within modern democracy. The second part of this chapter discusses how Republicanism and Liberalism subsequently expanded on Rousseau's ideas of the Social Contract in the eighteenth and nineteenth centuries. In particular, it investigates through the works of James Madison and John Stuart Mill how Republicanism and Liberalism proposed two competing sets of models for the roles and relations of the state, the citizen and the soldier in democratic government. The third part then turns to Milton Friedman, whose Neoliberalism reformulated the Social Contract in the twentieth century. Part Four outlines how this debate between Republicanism and Liberalism has led to the development of competing models of the state and the soldier which will be used as theoretical comparators in the following chapters.

The Social Contract

The key objective of the Social Contract between the citizen and the state is the provision of security. As Hobbes argued, without the Social Contract 'the life of man [is] solitary, poor, nasty, brutish and short'.[2] Unfortunately, human beings are the primary cause of insecurity for each other. Whether conflict is 'in the nature of man', as Hobbes believed, or, according to Rousseau, a result of society, it has been a permanent feature of human interaction.[3] However, the characteristics of this imaginary Social Contract have changed during the centuries. A major step was the difference between the Social Contract between a sovereign and the people as envisaged in Hobbes' *Leviathan* in 1660 and the Social Contract of modern democracy as proposed in Rousseau's *The Social Contract* more than a century later.

Thomas Hobbes

The English scholar and philosopher Thomas Hobbes has been one of the most influential Social Contract theorists. Hobbes developed his ideas on the Social Contract in his famous work *Leviathan*, which

---

[2] T. Hobbes, *Leviathan*, edited by R. Tuck (Cambridge: Cambridge University Press, 1991), p. 89.
[3] *Ibid.*, p. 88; J.-J. Rousseau, *The Social Contract and Other Later Writings*, edited by V. Gourvitch (Cambridge: Cambridge University Press, 1997).

was influenced by his experience of the English Civil War (1642–51). Fleeing from the widespread civil violence that followed the replacement of the monarchy with a parliamentary government, Hobbes reasoned that the only way to protect citizens is to 'erect such a Common Power, as may be able to defend them from the invasion of Forraigners, and the injuries of one another'.[4] Citizens do so by conferring 'all their power and strength upon one Man, or upon one Assembly of men, ... [who] shall Act, or cause to be Acted, in those things which concerne the Common Peace and Safetie'.[5] In short, citizens agree on a Social Contract according to which they give up their natural right to the use of armed force for their private protection and transfer it to a collective authority.[6]

However, the Social Contract does not contribute to human security merely by centralizing the means and use of violence for the purpose of protecting its citizens against each other and foreign invasions. It is not 'the joining together of a small number of men, that gives them this security'.[7] A collective, but still private, provision of security increases the resources which a group of citizens can use for their own protection. However, since there are always individuals or groups who have access to greater force, such an approach can never effectively ensure their safety.[8] The central innovation of the Social Contract is that it prohibits the private use of armed force and invests it in the sovereign. In short, it is the sovereign's *monopoly* on the legitimate use of collective violence that provides security. By giving up their private right to use force under the Social Contract, citizens establish a social environment which permits peaceful interaction by generating the expectation that citizens will not attack each other. As Hobbes argued, 'The nature of War, consisteth not in actual fighting; but in the known disposition thereto, during all the time there is no assurance to the contrary'.[9] Peace and security can thus only be achieved through the mutual and voluntary assurance that citizens will refrain from employing private force to attain their security and interests.[10]

Hobbes recognized that in spite of the voluntary assurance of citizens not to use private force, there might still be distrust as to whether all citizens will comply with it. In these cases, he argued, the assurance is not convincing and the Social Contract is void. To enhance the validity of the mutual assurance of non-violence there must be 'some coërcive Power, to compell men equally to the performance of their Covenants,

[4] Hobbes, *Leviathan*, p. 120.   [5] *Ibid*., p. 120.
[6] *Ibid*., p. 91.   [7] *Ibid*., p. 118.
[8] *Ibid*.   [9] *Ibid*., pp. 88–9.   [10] *Ibid*., p. 92.

by the terrour of some punishment, greater than the benefit they expect by the breach of their Covenant'.[11] Within the domestic realm, the primary objective of the sovereign's monopoly on the use of armed force is thus not the protection of the citizens per se, but the enforcement of the Social Contract. If the sovereign does so successfully, the security of the citizens is a direct consequence of their own behaviour.

In the international realm, however, there exists no peace or security because there is no Social Contract among states: 'the Law of Nations, and the Law of Nature, is the same thing'.[12] Accordingly, 'every Soveraign hath the same Right, in procuring the safety of his People, that any particular man can have, in procuring his own safety'.[13] The sovereign's monopoly on the defence of citizens in international relations appears to be partly a practical, partly a logical consequence of the Social Contract. On the one hand, unity of command under the central authority of the sovereign is necessary for effective national security.[14] On the other hand, the sovereign's role in national defence derives from its monopoly on the control of collective violence within the domestic realm which would be undermined by the existence of armed forces for the purpose of international security not under its control.[15]

As to the form of the 'sovereign' or central authority, however, Hobbes differed significantly from the contemporary understanding. The Social Contract is a covenant between the citizens and a higher, central authority such as a monarch or even a despot who, once the Social Contract is established, cannot be disinvested of his or her powers.[16] Moreover, the sovereign has an independent will which must not be challenged by the citizens, unless they want to breach the Social Contract. Although the sovereign has the obligation to protect the citizens, and citizens are justified in resisting the sovereign authority if it fails to do so, the former decides unilaterally what best ensures the safety of the populous and the common good. The sovereign has 'the Right of making Warre, and Peace with other Nations, and Common-wealths; that is to say, of Judging when it is for the publique good, and how great forces are to be assembled, armed and payd for that end; and to levy money upon the Subjects, to defray the expenses thereof'.[17]

Perhaps because of the distinction between the citizens and the sovereign, Hobbes believed that citizens have no absolute obligation to risk their own life in defence of their country. In fact, he seemed to approve of the hiring of mercenaries when he argued that 'a man that is commanded as a Souldier to fight against the enemy, though his Soveraign

---

[11] *Ibid.*, p. 101.   [12] *Ibid.*, p. 244.   [13] *Ibid.*   [14] *Ibid.*, p. 126.
[15] *Ibid.*   [16] *Ibid.*, pp. 121–2.   [17] *Ibid.*, p. 126.

have Right enough to punish his refusall with death, may neverthelesse in many cases refuse, without Injustice; as when he substituteth a sufficient Souldier in his place'.[18] Only, 'when the Defence of the Commonwealth, requireth at once the help of all that are able to bear Arms, every one is obliged'.[19] Since Hobbes distinguished between the citizens and the sovereign authority, he also failed to discuss in greater detail the problem of control over the armed forces. Although he pointed out that the 'love of Souldiers [for their Commander] ... is a dangerous thing to Sovereign Power', he did not propose how the subversion of the central authority by military feat or the abuse of armed force by the central authority might be prevented.

Writing before the emergence of modern democracy, Hobbes recognized the central role of the state monopoly on violence in ensuring the security of all citizens. However, his interpretation of the Social Contract did not problematize the centralization of military force in the hands of the sovereign. Ultimately, Hobbes believed that citizens pose a greater threat to each other than even the most despotic monarch would pose to them.

Jean-Jacques Rousseau

Over one hundred years after Hobbes, the Genevan philosopher Jean-Jacques Rousseau attempted to address these problems in his work *Of the Social Contract, Principles of Political Right*.[20] Greatly influencing the French Revolution, Rousseau argued in this publication that control over the state and the armed forces has to rest with the citizens. Moreover, he sought to identify a series of mechanisms which can serve to prevent the abuse of political and military power. At the heart of these mechanisms is the democratic notion that the Social Contract is a contract among all citizens rather than between the citizens and a sovereign.

Rousseau agreed with Hobbes that effective security can only be established through collectivizing the means of control over the use of armed force. However, Rousseau pointed out that this raises the question: 'since each man's force and freedom are his primary instruments of self-preservation, how can he commit them without harming himself, and without neglecting the cares he owes himself?'[21] There is always the possibility that the collective force which has been created through the Social Contract is used against the citizens or their interests.

---

[18] *Ibid.*, p. 151.   [19] *Ibid.*, p. 152.
[20] Rousseau, *The Social Contract*.   [21] *Ibid.*, p. 49.

Rousseau's primary concern was to design a Social Contract that prevents the abuse of the sovereign's monopoly on armed force. To do so, he radically reinvented the Social Contract. Specifically, Rousseau argued that the citizen's right to use violence for self-preservation cannot and must not be alienated to a separate sovereign authority or will. Instead, the right and control over armed force is to be invested in the general will of all citizens. The Social Contract is not between the citizen and the sovereign, but among all the citizens who together constitute the 'state': 'This act of association produces a moral and collective body made up of as many members as the assembly has voices, and which receives by this same act its unity, its common *self*, its life and its will. The public person thus formed by the union of all the others... now assumes that of *Republic* or of *body politic*, which its members call *State*.'[22]

According to Rousseau, citizens can assure the legitimacy of the state's use of collective force in two ways. Firstly, by forming the state, the citizens control the collective means of violence. Secondly, by determining the general will, the citizens decide on the use of the means of collective violence: 'Each of us puts his person and all his power in common under the supreme direction of the general will; and in a body we receive each member as an indivisible part of the whole.'[23] But Rousseau proposed a third means for preventing the misuse of the monopoly on collective violence when he argued that national armed forces should consist of citizen militias.[24] 'Regular troops ... are only good for two purposes: to attack and conquer neigbors, or to shackle and enslave Citizens.'[25] Just as citizens make up the state and the general will, they need to constitute their national armed forces in order to ensure their own security. The right and duty of citizens to fight for their country is not merely the means to this end, but derives directly from the Social Contract because 'their very life, which they have dedicated to the State is constantly protected by it, and when they risk it for its defence, what are they doing but returning to it what they have received from it?'[26]

Rousseau's conception of the Social Contract which underlies the ideal of the state monopoly on collective violence within modern democracy thus contains three elements. The first is the citizens' surrender of their natural right to the private use of armed force to the democratic state as their collective representation and means of self-government. The second is the democratic government's reciprocal responsibility for

---

[22] *Ibid.*, pp. 50–1 (emphasis in original).
[23] *Ibid.*, p. 50.   [24] *Ibid.*, p. 234.
[25] *Ibid.*, pp. 233–4.   [26] *Ibid.*, p. 63.

the security of its citizens. The third element is the citizens' control over and contribution to their government and the national armed forces in order to prevent the abuse of the monopoly on collective violence. Nevertheless, the degree to which citizens give up their private rights, the scope of the state's responsibility for the provision of security and other functions, and the particular form of citizens' control over armed force in practice has been subject to contestation. The next section examines how two competing theories, Republicanism and Liberalism, have shaped this debate.

Republicanism and Liberalism

Two theories and their respective ideologies in particular have influenced the controversy over the appropriate roles, rights and responsibilities of the democratic state and the citizen with regard to national and international security since the eighteenth century: Republicanism and Liberalism.[27] At the centre of this debate has been their divergent emphasis on the autonomy or the interdependence of citizens with regard to their own security and welfare. Since citizens are neither fully autonomous nor interdependent, the tension between the degree to which political institutions prioritize one or the other continues to define the relationship between the state and the citizen. Accordingly, the division between Republicanism and Liberalism has never been clear-cut. Both ideologies are best understood as the end points of a continuum with a variety of positions in between. Nevertheless, this book presents the two as distinct ideologies in order to highlight alternative visions of state–societal and civil–military relations. In this reading, the 'liberal understanding of democracy ... emphasizes the rights and choices of the individual, to the exclusion of more republican approaches that emphasize the responsibilities of an active citizenry'.[28]

Rousseau was one of the first modern philosophers to discuss the ideal nature of the relationship between the state and the citizen in the provision of security from a Republican perspective. Already at his time

---

[27] For reviews of this debate see A. Carter, 'Liberalism and the Obligation to Military Service', *Political Studies*, Vol. 46, no. 1 (1998), 68–81; E. A. Cohen, *Citizens and Soldiers. The Dilemmas of Military Service* (Ithaca, NY: Cornell University Press, 1985); J. Burk, 'Theories of Democratic Civil-Military Relations', *Armed Forces & Society*, Vol. 29, no. 1 (2002), 7–29; S. P. Huntington, *The Soldier and the State. The Theory and Politics of Civil-Military Relations* (Cambridge, MA: Belknap Press of Harvard University Press, 1957); R. C. Snyder, *Citizen-Soldiers and Manly Warriors* (Lanham, MD: Rowman & Littlefield, 1999).

[28] Snyder, 'The Citizen-Soldier Tradition and Gender Integration of the U.S. Military', *Armed Forces & Society*, 29, no. 2 (2003), 186.

of writing, however, his views of direct democratic participation were irreconcilably removed from the reality of the emerging nation-state. In particular, the size of most states in Europe and North America challenged Rousseau's notion that the rights of citizens, including their immediate involvement in the deliberation of the common good and the provision of national security, were inalienable.[29] Representative forms of government appeared to be necessary. Yet, if representation was permissible in determining the general will, it could be argued that citizenship and military service were also not necessarily coterminous. How the legitimacy and control of the state and the armed forces could be best maintained under the conditions of representative democracy became a central issue of concern to Republicans and their Liberal challengers. Two key representations of their divergent ideologies are examined below: James Madison's *Federalist Papers* (1787–8) and John Stuart Mill's *On Liberty* (1859) and *Considerations on Representative Government* (1861).

James Madison

Politician, founding father and fourth president of the USA, James Madison has been one of the most influential Republican theorists in the history of Europe and North America. Taking a principal role in the definition of the US constitution and writing his *Federalist Papers* in order to explain the new constitution to US citizens, he not only crucially shaped the translation of Rousseau's democratic Social Contract into political practice, but also inspired public beliefs regarding the appropriate roles and relations of the state, the citizen and the soldier in the USA and Europe.

At the core of Madison's Republicanism was the view that human beings are essentially interdependent.[30] Human beings can only attain security and the fulfilment of other needs through membership of a social and political community. The effective functioning of this political community of interdependent citizens relies on the behaviour of all. Within representative democracy the *direct* link between the state, the citizen and the soldier as outlined in Rousseau's theory of the Social Contract may be weakened. Nevertheless, citizens play a crucial role in the selection and formation of government and in the implementation of policies for the common good, including the provision of national and international security. Because of the separation between the state

---

[29] I. Honohan, *Civic Republicanism* (London: Routledge, 2002), p. 77.
[30] *Ibid.*, p. 1.

and the citizen entailed in representative government, other institutional means have to be devised in order to prevent the abuse of the state's power and monopoly on collective violence. Madison was aware of this when he pointed out that 'in every political institution, a power to advance the public happiness involves a discretion which may be misapplied and abused'.[31]

Madison specifically proposed three means to ensure the legitimacy and control of the state and the armed forces. The first means is the representativeness of government. Fundamental to the Republican model of the democratic state is that 'such a government ... is derived from the great body of society, not from an inconsiderable proportion, or a favoured class of it'.[32] While not all citizens directly participate in government, self-government can be achieved through the equal representation of all. The more representative a government is and the closer it is to self-government, the more likely it is to reflect the general will of a community and the less likely is the abuse of power and violence by the authorities.[33]

The second means for ensuring the control and legitimacy of government is civic virtue.[34] According to Madison, civic virtue facilitates government for the common good. Virtuous citizens actively participate in the deliberation and implementation of the common good; they are dedicated to the public interest and the preservation of the community.[35] In representative democracy, 'the aim of every political constitution is, or ought to be, first, to obtain for rulers men who possess most wisdom to discern, and most virtue to pursue, the common good of society'.[36]

The third means is the mutual obligation between the state and the citizen with regard to national and international security. Citizens have a duty to defend their community through active military service. Partially, this obligation is based on the Social Contract entered into through membership of a political community; partially, it is an aspect of civic virtue. For Madison, like Rousseau, the most appropriate model for democratic armed forces was that of a national militia and the citizen-soldier. However, whereas for Rousseau citizens' participation in the armed forces was a result of their inalienable right to self-defence,

---

[31] J. Madison, *Federalist*, No. 41.
[32] J. Madison, *Federalist*, No. 39.
[33] J. Madison, *Federalist*, No. 46.
[34] M. J. Sandel, 'Liberalism and Republicanism: Friends or Foes? A Reply to Richard Dagger', *The Review of Politics*, 61, no. 2 (1999), 210.
[35] J. P. Geise, 'Republican Ideals and Contemporary Realities', *The Review of Politics*, 46, no. 1, (1984), 23–44; Honohan, *Civic Republicanism*, p. 5.
[36] J. Madison, *Federalist*, No. 57.

for Madison it was a means to control and legitimize the state monopoly on collective violence within a representative democracy.

Standing armies are anathema to the Republican ideal. They represent a division between the armed forces and the community and, thus, undermine the public accountability of the armed forces.[37] Standing armies which do not consist of citizens and are not integrated with their community can also more easily be used for other purposes than the protection of the nation.[38] Citizen-soldiers, conversely, will only be willing to risk their life in self-defence and to protect their community. Madison was convinced that 'besides the advantage of being armed ... the existence of subordinate governments, to which people are attached, and by which the militia officers are appointed, forms a barrier against the enterprises of ambition, more insurmountable than any which a simple government of any form can admit of'.[39]

Republicanism thus advocates the merging of political and military roles through the concept of the citizen-soldier. According to Republicanism, the public monopoly on collective violence is not distinct from politics; it is politics. It is, therefore, erroneous to assume that governmental and military accountability can be ensured through professional neutrality. Rather the government and the armed forces should be as closely representative of and integrated with society as possible.[40] The identity of the state and the armed forces with society assures not only that the actions of the government and the military are supported by the community, but also helps to spread civic virtue through the citizenry by educating them as citizens and as citizen-soldiers.

John Stuart Mill

In the nineteenth century the British philosopher and parliamentarian John Stuart Mill developed the main tenets of classical Liberalism in his seminal work *On Liberty* as well as in the later *Considerations on Representative Government*. Challenging the Republican model of the Social Contract, Mill argued that democratic control over the state and the armed forces is best achieved through limiting their size and powers.

The foundation of Mill's Liberalism is the notion that citizens should be seen as autonomous individuals.[41] Mill's primary concern was with protecting the freedom and rights of the citizen from the demands or

---

[37] Madison, *Federalist*, No. 46.   [38] *Ibid.*   [39] *Ibid.*

[40] R. A. Herrera, 'Self-Governance and the American Citizen as Soldier, 1775–1861', *The Journal of Military History*, 65, no. 1 (2001), 25.

[41] J. S. Mill, *On Liberty with The Subjection of Women and Chapters on Socialism*, edited by S. Collini (Cambridge: Cambridge University Press, 1989), p. 9.

infringements of the state. With regard to military service, this means also protecting the right not to fight. The Liberal view of the relationship between the state and the citizen, and its perception of the appropriate model of the soldier, builds on a single core principle: individual liberty. From this principle follow a number of ideals including freedom of choice, tolerance and the minimum state.

Like Madison, Mill began with the observation that representative democracy is by no means sufficient for preventing the abuse of government.[42] However, unlike the Republicans, Mill's primary apprehension was not with the non-virtuous behaviour of those elected to government, but a more fundamental unease with representative democracy and state power.[43] According to Mill, the belief that democracy enables the self-determination and self-government of citizens is not always correct.[44] Instead, he argued, the democratic state is in danger of being a 'tyranny of the majority'.[45] 'The will of the people ... practically means the will of the most numerous or the most active part of the people; the majority, or those who succeed in making themselves accepted as the majority.'[46]

One solution is to limit the functions and powers of the state. Mill identified three reasons for restricting the interference of a government in the lives of its citizens. The first reason is his contention that citizens are better able to satisfy their needs and interests individually than the state can with its collective measures.[47] The second reason is that it benefits the education of the population to do things for themselves.[48] The third, 'the most cogent reason for restricting the interference of government, is the great evil of adding unnecessarily to its power'.[49] The last reason is the most important. Since no political system provides a perfect safeguard against the abuse of collective power, citizens are only safe from such violations to the degree that they are not subject to the authority of the state.

However, Mill recognized that the state is necessary in order to protect citizens from each other. 'Security of person and property, and equal justice between individuals, are the first needs of society, and the primary ends of governments.'[50] To balance citizens' need for security with a limited state, Mill proposed that the only legitimate function of the state should be the protection of the rights and freedoms of citizens from violation by other citizens: 'the only purpose for which power can be rightfully exercised over any member of a civilised community,

[42] *Ibid.*, pp. 5–9.   [43] *Ibid.*, pp. 8–9.   [44] *Ibid.*, p. 7.   [45] *Ibid.*, p. 8.
[46] *Ibid.*   [47] *Ibid.*, p. 109.   [48] *Ibid.*, p. 109.   [49] *Ibid.*, p. 110.
[50] J. S. Mill, 'Considerations on Representative Government', in *On Liberty and Other Essays*, edited with an introduction by J. Gray (Oxford: Oxford University Press, 1991), p. 421.

against his will, is to prevent harm to others. His own good, either physical or moral, is not a sufficient warrant.'[51] Unlike the Republican state, the Liberal state has no role in the provision of the common good. Indeed, Mill doubted that there can be anything such as a common good which is not merely the interest of a select majority. The state instead provides a legal framework within which citizens can develop self-protection and self-responsibility.[52] Mill was also sceptical of preventative government measures against crime and armed violence because 'the preventive function of government ... is far more liable to be abused, to the prejudice of liberty, than the punitory function'.[53] The government should instead restrict itself to the detection and punishment of any violations of the law.

In addition to limiting the scope of governmental authority, the accountability and legitimacy of the state's control over the collective means of violence can be assured through public scrutiny. In place of citizens' direct involvement in the deliberation and execution of governmental policies as Republicanism proposes, Mill focused on the legitimacy of the results of the political process. He reasoned: 'When the minister ceases to confide in the commander, he dismisses him, and appoints another; but he does not send him instructions when and where to fight. He holds him responsible only for intentions and for results. The people must do the same.'[54]

Unlike Republicans, Mill believed that professional military expertise and advice can be politically neutral. He, therefore, disagreed with the nineteenth-century practice of expecting the Lords of the Admiralty to resign when those who appointed them left office. Conversely, 'The military and naval ministers, therefore, and probably several others, should be provided with a Council, composed, at least in those two departments, of able and experienced professional men. As a means of obtaining the best men for the purpose under every change of administration, that they ought to be permanent.'[55]

The role of citizens with regard to armed force is less clear in Mill's writings. Mill shared Madison's belief that 'every one who receives the protection of society owes a return for the benefit'.[56] However, Mill did not argue in favour of citizens' duty to enlist in the military for the defence of their country. When he contended that all citizens should

[51] Mill, *On Liberty*, p. 13.
[52] Mill, 'Considerations on Representative Government', p. 245.
[53] Mill, *On Liberty*, p. 96.
[54] J. S. Mill, *Dissertations and Discussions: Political, Philosophical, and Historical*, Vol. I (London: Parker, 1859), Appendix.
[55] Mill, 'Considerations on Representative Government', p. 396.
[56] Mill, *On Liberty*, p. 75.

bear their 'share (to be fixed in some equitable principle) of the labour and sacrifices incurred for defending the society or its members from injury or molestation',[57] he included monetary sacrifices such as taxes or the paying for a substitute in order to avoid service in the armed forces. At the same time, Mill's emphasis on the rights and freedoms of citizens, specifically self-protection, seems to be congruent with the right to bear arms enshrined in the US constitution and the basis for defence through militias. The question of a standing army was not addressed by Mill.

Clearer is Mill's opposition to the use of foreign mercenaries because their loyalty lies with the government which hires them and not with the citizens. A despotic government can use mercenaries against its own population: 'Soldiers to whose feelings half or three-fourths of the subjects of the same government are foreigners, will have no more scruple in mowing them down, and no more desire to ask the reason why, than they would have in doing the same thing against declared enemies. An army composed of various nationalities has no other patriotism than devotion to the flag. Such armies have been the executioners of liberty throughout the whole duration of modern history.'[58]

The Liberal relationship between the state, the citizen and the armed forces is thus characterized by the separation and limitation of roles and responsibilities in order to prevent their abuse. The state's control over collective means of violence is restricted to the protection of the life and liberty of its citizens; and citizens ensure the accountability of the exercise of governmental power through indirect rather than direct participation. Public scrutiny of governmental policy and the effectiveness of military actions are preferred over legitimacy derived from the direct involvement of citizens in government and the armed forces. Detection and punishment provide control rather than prevention.

The Republican and Liberal ideals regarding the control of violence outlined above have changed little over time. The core principles espoused by John Stuart Mill and James Madison can still be found in the works of more contemporary authors such as Philip Pettit and Michael Sandel or Friedrich Hayek and John Rawls.[59] Nevertheless, the twentieth century saw a revision and revival of Liberalism. The next

---

[57] *Ibid.*, p. 14, p. 75.
[58] Mill, 'Considerations on Representative Government', p. 429.
[59] P. Pettit, *Republicanism: A Theory of Freedom and Government* (Oxford: Clarendon, 1997); M. J. Sandel, *Democracy's Discontent. America in Search of a Public Philosophy* (Cambridge, MA: Belknap Press of Harvard University Press, 1996); F. Hayek, *The Road to Serfdom* (London: Routledge and Paul Kegan, 1944); J. Rawls, *A Theory of Justice* (Cambridge, MA: Belknap Press of Harvard University Press, 1971).

section discusses how Neoliberalism departed from its predecessor to propose a new model of civil–military control.

Neoliberalism

One of the reasons for the redefinition of Liberalism in the middle of the twentieth century was the perceived overstretch of the modern welfare or 'warfare' state and the growing disillusionment with the Republican model of centralized government. The American economist and Nobel Laureate Milton Friedman addressed the problems of this approach in his book *Capitalism and Freedom* (1962).[60] His work not only provided a major impetus to the formulation of Neoliberalism, but also had a direct influence on US policy through his role as one of President Ronald Reagan's economic advisors.

Neoliberalism proceeds from the same basic principles as classical Liberalism. Its primary concern is with the rights and freedoms of the individual citizen. However, unlike his classical Liberal predecessors, Friedman emphasized the role of capitalism in satisfying the needs of citizens and in limiting the coercive powers of the state. His ideal relationship between the state, the citizen and the soldier is not primarily based on surveillance and punishment of abuses of armed force, but on the availability of free market alternatives to the state. Rather than 'voice', Friedman's Neoliberalism argues that competition between the state and the market provides 'exit' as a strategy for ensuring the control and accountability of military force.

Like classical Liberals, Friedman started from the premise that 'the great threat to freedom is the concentration of power. Government is necessary to preserve our freedom, it is an instrument through which we can exercise our freedom; yet by concentrating power in political hands, it is also a threat to freedom.'[61] He also agreed that two core principles help to prevent the abuse of governmental power: 'the scope of government must be limited'[62] and 'government power must be dispersed'.[63] However, Friedman's Neoliberalism diverges from classical Liberalism in two main respects. The first is the degree to which Friedman advocated the application of these principles to the institutions and practices of the state, citizenship and the armed forces. The second is his emphasis on the role of the free market in preventing the concentration of the means of and control over violence within the state. According to

---

[60] M. Friedman, *Capitalism and Freedom* (Chicago: The University of Chicago Press, 1962).
[61] *Ibid.*, p. 2.   [62] *Ibid.*   [63] *Ibid.*, p. 3.

Friedman, competitive capitalism is 'a necessary condition for political freedom'.[64]

Both aspects merge in Friedman's argument that the outsourcing of public functions to the market serves to limit the scope and powers of government, and the dispersion of capabilities and the competition between the state and the market establishes a balance of power: 'The preservation of freedom requires the elimination of such concentration of power to the fullest possible extent and the dispersal and distribution of whatever power cannot be eliminated – a system of checks and balances. By removing the organization of economic activity from the control of political authority, the market eliminates this source of coercive power.'[65]

The market has another advantage over government: 'To the liberal, the appropriate means (for any ends) are free discussion and voluntary co-operation, which implies that any form of coercion is inappropriate. The ideal is unanimity among responsible individuals achieved on the basis of free and full discussion.'[66] Even representative democracy is unable to approximate the ideal of unanimity. Instead, as Mill had already observed, democracy represents the rule of the majority. The market, on the other hand, 'permits unanimity without conformity; . . . it is a system of effective proportional representation'.[67] In the marketplace, citizens can satisfy their needs through individual choice rather than cooperation.

Friedman agreed that the state's main function is 'to protect our freedom both from the enemies outside our gates and from our fellow-citizens'[68] and that 'there are clearly some matters with respect to which effective proportional representation is impossible. I cannot get the amount of national defense I want and you, a different amount.'[69] However, this does not mean that the ideal of the small state and the balancing role of the market have no role in national and international security. On the contrary, Friedman believed that market principles can suitably be applied to defence. Specifically, he proposed that the 'appropriate free market arrangement [for the armed forces] is volunteer military forces; which is to say, hiring men to serve'.[70] The US practice of peacetime conscription in 1962 was unjustifiable for Friedman[71]: 'Present arrangements are inequitable and arbitrary, seriously interfere with the freedom of your men to shape their lives, and probably are even more costly than the market alternative.'[72]

---

[64] *Ibid.*, p. 4.   [65] *Ibid.*, p. 15, see also p. 3, p. 9.   [66] *Ibid.*, pp. 22–3.
[67] *Ibid.*, p. 23.   [68] *Ibid.*, p. 2.   [69] *Ibid.*, p. 23.
[70] *Ibid.*, p. 36.   [71] *Ibid.*   [72] *Ibid.*

Friedman's propositions can be extended to other aspects of national and international security. Although 'the existence of such indivisible matters – protection of the individual and the nation from coercion are clearly the most basic – ... prevents exclusive reliance on individual action through the market', the principles of the minimal state and the counterbalancing of governmental power with that of the market can help to control the state's monopoly on the legitimate use of armed force.[73] The privatization of national arms industries and the outsourcing of military functions by the national armed forces thus appear to meet Friedman's ideal of dispersing the means of coercion among public and private actors, although he did not give these examples.

While classical Liberalism focuses on citizens' self-help and (constitutional) law in providing limitations to the coercive power of the state, Neoliberalism assigns this role to the free market. It argues that the best means for preventing the abuse of state control over armed force is to establish a competition between the state and the market. The market helps to divide coercive capabilities among multiple companies and between public and private agents and, thereby, prevents a centralization of power which could endanger the rights and freedoms of the citizens.

In summary, Republicanism and Liberalism have proposed competing ideal models of democratic civil–military relations and control over the past three centuries. However, the debate between Republicanism and Liberalism has not only influenced the theoretical conception of how the provision of security could be achieved and controlled within modern democracy. It has also had a direct impact on the institutions and practices related to the democratic provision of national and international security in Europe and North America. In order to provide a conceptual framework for the analysis of these institutions, the following section compares and contrasts the competing models of the state and the soldier which have emerged from these theories.

Competing models of the state and the soldier

As outlined above, Republicanism and Liberalism have played crucial roles in defining the ideal functions and relations of the state, the citizen and the soldier in modern democracies. They have done so primarily by informing political discussions and decision-makers through the presentation of competing models of civil–military relations. In practice, these models have, sometimes, combined aspects of both theories. However, in order to facilitate the following analysis of the impact of

---

[73] *Ibid.*

ideology on the changing roles and relations of the state, the citizen and the soldier, this section outlines the ideal-type models which have served as their templates. Specifically, it focuses on two sets of models and their relations with society. The first is the ideal conception of the role of the state in the provision of national and international security. The second concerns the ideal model of the soldier.

Between centralized government and fragmented governance

Over the past centuries the competing models of the state proposed by Republicanism and Liberalism have been given varying names and individual features depending upon country, policy sector or decade in which they have been applied. In the twentieth century they ranged from Keynesianism, Fordism and the welfare/warfare state on the one hand to Thatcherism, Reaganomics and the regulatory or managerial state on the other.[74] More recently, International Relations Theory has described the distinct Republican and Liberal models of the state as centralized 'government' and fragmented 'governance'.[75] Both can be seen as ideal-types at either end of a continuum that advocates either the centralization or fragmentation of policy-making in order to achieve democratic control. Government in this context should not be confused with the generic term, but refers to models of the centralized state which have their roots in Republican theory. Conversely, governance denotes the non-hierarchical coordination of social relations and the fragmented provision of public services by a multitude of public and private actors as proposed by Liberalism.

With regard to national and international security, the competing ideal-type models of centralized government and fragmented governance can be distinguished in dimensions: (1) the geographical scope of security provision, (2) the distribution of security functions between the state and private companies, (3) the distribution of the resources among public and private providers, (4) the perception of security interests, (5) key norms, (6) the features of the decision-making process, and (7) the implementation of security efforts.[76] Underpinning all these dimensions are the divergent conceptions of Republicanism and

[74] D. Edgerton, *Warfare State. Britain, 1920–1970* (Cambridge: Cambridge University Press, 2006); B. Jessop, 'Post-Fordism and the State', in A. Amin (ed.) *Post Fordism. A Reader* (Oxford: Blackwell, 1994), pp. 251–79.

[75] E. Krahmann, 'National, Regional, and Global Governance: One Phenomenon or Many?' *Global Governance*, 9, no. 3 (2003), 323–46.

[76] E. Krahmann, 'Conceptualizing Security Governance', *Cooperation and Conflict*, 38, no. 1 (2003), 5–26.

Liberalism on how best to ensure the democratic control and accountability of the state and the use of military force.

The Republican ideal-type model of centralized government contends that accountability and control are best achieved through the centralized provision of security within the geographical boundaries of the nation-state. National boundaries circumscribe not only the rights of citizenship, including the participation in the political will-formation process and the defence of the community, but also the obligations of the citizens in terms of mutual responsibility, taxation and other contributions to national defence. In addition, Republican government advocates the centralization of security functions and resources by the state and the armed forces. According to the Republican model of government, security is best achieved and controlled through nationalized defence industries and national armed forces which give the government, and thus the citizens, a direct role in the financing, ownership and provision of national and international security.

Underlying this model is the Republican assumption that citizens are essentially interdependent and that they have common security interests which can only be achieved through collective efforts. From this assumption follows a set of norms which promote the ideal of the strong state as the representation of the common interest. Three norms, in particular, underpin the Republican ideal of centralized government: national sovereignty, command and control, and redistribution.[77] Within the domestic sphere sovereignty relates to the collective self-determination of the citizens through democratically elected governments. In the international arena sovereignty protects democratic government from undue external intervention. Command and control refers to the direct role of the state in the provision of public goods. The Republican government model suggests that the state should command and control national services through public ownership or state agencies. Finally, the Republican notion that many individual needs and interests, security the foremost among them, can only be satisfied by the collective, justifies redistributive policies. The model of centralized government has, therefore, found its highest expression in the welfare state that offers equal access to public services such as education, health and security. Based on these norms, security policy decision-making within the centralized government model is characterized by its hierarchical, democratic and consensual nature.[78] The

---

[77] G. Majone, 'From the Positive to the Regulatory State: Causes and Consequences of Changes in the Mode of Governance', *Journal of Public Policy*, 17, no. 2 (1997), 139–67.

[78] Majone, 'From the Positive to the Regulatory State', 162; B. Jessop, 'Governance Failure', in Gerry Stoker (ed.) *The New Politics of British Local Governance* (Basingstoke: Macmillan, 2000), p. 13.

highest decision-making authority rests with the elected government and is determined through the democratic principles of qualified or absolute majority voting. The norms of command and control further suggest that policy implementation by the government is best centralized, authoritative and, if necessary, coercive, in order to ensure that security policies reflect the interests of the citizens.[79]

The Liberal ideal-type model of fragmented governance is in many ways the polar opposite of centralized government. It builds on the Liberal notion that limiting the role of the state best ensures its democratic control and accountability. Instead of centralization, the governance model contends that the fragmentation of functions, resources, decision-making and policy implementation between the state and the market helps to safeguard democracy. Neoliberalism contends that competition between public and private providers also leads to greater responsiveness to the individual interests of all citizens.

With regard to the provision of security, the Liberal model of fragmented governance can be distinguished from Republican centralized governance along the seven dimensions outlined above. In terms of geographical scope, the governance model prescribes the differentiation of security policy-making and service provision across the local, national and transnational levels.[80] According to Liberalism, the geographical fragmentation of authority facilitates the control of these actors by limiting their influence, and promises greater responsiveness to the diverse interests of citizens who are living in different security environments. In addition, the ideal-type model of fragmented governance envisages the differentiation of security functions and their supply among multiple government agencies, and competing public and private actors.[81] As with geographical fragmentation, Liberalism believes that the centralization of collective services within the state is the prime danger to democratic control, and that the financing, ownership and supply of security resources and functions are best dispersed in order to curtail the power of different actors.[82] Moreover, Neoliberalism contends that competition between the state and the market encourages

[79] H. Aquina and H. Bekke, 'Governance and Interaction: Public Tasks and Private Organisations', in J. Koiman (ed.) *Modern Governance: New Government-Society Interactions* (London: Sage, 1993), p. 160; J. Pierre, 'Introduction: Understanding Governance', in J. Pierre (ed.) *Debating Governance: Authority, Steering, and Democracy* (Oxford: Oxford University Press, 2000), p. 2.

[80] R. A. W. Rhodes, 'Foreword: Governance and Networks', in G. Stoker (ed.) *The New Management of British Local Governance* (Basingstoke: Macmillan, 1999), p. xxxiii.

[81] Majone, 'From the Positive to the Regulatory State', p. 154.

[82] J. Pierre, 'Conclusion: Governance beyond State Strength', in J. Pierre (ed.) *Debating Governance: Authority, Steering, and Democracy* (Oxford: Oxford University Press, 2000), p. 242.

the cost-efficient and effective provision of security functions, and that functional specialization can take advantage of the dispersed resources and expertise required for contemporary security policy-making.[83]

Implicit in the Liberal model of fragmented governance is a belief in the heterogeneous and sometimes conflicting nature of citizens' security interests. Rather than subordinating them to the will of the general public, the Liberal governance model seeks to ensure that citizens can pursue their individual interests as freely as possible. In so far as the political coordination of private security interests is necessary, the governance model argues, it is best left to market forces or to voluntary cooperation among the citizens themselves. Owing to the Liberal focus on individual interests and rights, the guiding norms of the governance model are the limitation of state sovereignty, individual self-government and marketization.[84] Domestically, state sovereignty is limited by restricting the scope of the state and its intervention in the lives of its citizens. According to Liberalism, the main task of the state is the protection of citizens' rights rather than the provision of public services. Internationally, therefore, the governance model is more open to interventions and alternative authorities, such as international private regulatory bodies and private military companies. At the same time, the fragmented governance model prioritizes citizens' right to self-determination. As developed by Friedman, Neoliberal governance contends that citizens' self-determination is best provided for by the market. Political decisions are by definition a representation of the collective interest. The market can respond to individual demands. In security, this means the market can cater to the varying needs of private individuals, households and corporations.

Security policy decision-making and implementation within governance arrangements are accordingly defined by the horizontal dispersion of authority among public and private providers at different levels ranging from national armed forces to transnational military companies. Since resources and expertise are distributed among a variety of actors,

---

[83] J. N. Rosenau, 'Change, Complexity, and Governance in Globalizing Space', in J. Pierre (ed.) *Debating Governance: Authority, Steering, and Democracy* (Oxford: Oxford University Press, 2000), pp. 169–200; A. Cooley and J. Ron, 'The NGO Scramble: Organizational Insecurity and the Political Economy of Transnational Action', *International Security*, 27, no. 1 (2002), 5–39; R. Mandel, *Armies without States. The Privatization of Security* (Boulder, CO: Lynne Rienner, 2002).

[84] K. Walsh (1995) 'Competition and Public Service Delivery', in J. Steward and G. Stoker (eds.) *Local Government in the 1990s* (Basingstoke: Macmillan, 1995), p. 28; B. Jessop, 'The Changing Governance of Welfare: Recent Trends in its Primary Functions, Scale, and Modes of Coordination', *Social Policy & Administration*, 33, no. 4 (1999), 354.

Table 2.1. *Ideal-type models of the state*

	Republicanism	(Neo)Liberalism
Model	*Centralized 'Government'*	*Fragmented 'Governance'*
Geographical scope	National	Local, national, transnational
Functional scope	Centralized provision of security functions by the state and national armed forces	Fragmented provision of security functions by public and private actors
Resources	Centralized financing, ownership and provision of military force by the state and national armed forces	Fragmented financing, ownership and provision of military force by public and private actors
Interests	Common and interdependent national security interests	Diverse national security interests
Norms	National sovereignty, command and control, redistribution	Individual sovereignty, self-responsibility, market choice
Decision-making	Hierarchical, consensus, majority voting	Horizontal, negotiation, self-determination
Implementation	Nationally centralized, authoritative, coercive	Nationally and transnationally fragmented, self-enforced, voluntary
Democratic control and accountability	Citizen participation in government and the armed forces, representativeness of the government and the armed forces of the society, integration of state and society	Limitation and fragmentation of control over military force among public and private actors, parliamentary and legal scrutiny and punishment of abuses of power, market choice and exit option

decision-making frequently has to proceed through negotiation and partnership arrangements. In governance, direct state ownership of the defence industry and command and control over the armed forces is replaced by hands-off steering and the regulation of the private security market. Most crucially, security policies are implemented in a decentralized fashion. Typically, responsibility for the implementation of distinct policies is distributed among public and market actors and compliance with public norms is frequently self-enforced or voluntary.[85]

[85] Walsh, 'Competition and Public Service Delivery', p. 35; Majone, 'From the Positive to the Regulatory State', p. 146.

*Citizen–soldiers, professional soldiers and private
military contractors*

Republican and Liberal theories also offer competing visions of the
roles of the citizen and the soldier in the provision and control of armed
force. For this purpose, they propose three ideal-type models of the
soldier: the citizen-soldier, the professional soldier and the private military contractor. The three models can be distinguished from each other
in four dimensions. The first dimension concerns the ideal relations
between the soldier, the citizen and the state. The second dimension
applies to the soldier's primary motivation, and the third dimension
to his or her predominant identity. Finally, the fourth dimension concerns the question of how to ensure the public control and accountability of the soldier. As the preceding models of the state should be
understood as ideal-types at the ends of an ideological continuum, so
the three models of the soldier presented below should also be viewed
as distinct points on an ideological scale between Republicanism and
Neoliberalism.

The Republican ideal-type model is the citizen-soldier as defined
by four characteristics. The first and most important characteristic is
the relationship of mutual obligation between the citizen-soldier and
the state.[86] The state has the duty to protect its citizens from internal
and external harm, while the citizens are obligated to refrain from the
unilateral use of force and to serve in the defence of the state. Under
the terms of the democratic Social Contract, citizens forego their natural right to use violence to achieve their own security and vest it in
the collective which, with the emergence of nationalism in Europe
and North America, became synonymous with the nation-state.[87] The
conditions and form of Republican military service have varied across
time and space.[88] In Anglo-Saxon countries, for instance, the ideal prevailed that national military service should only be entered into voluntarily. However, implicit in the Republican ideology has always been
the obligation of the citizen to enlist in the military during a national
emergency.[89]

---

[86] E. A. Cohen, 'Twilight of the Citizen-Soldier', *Parameters*, 31, no. 2 (2001), 23–8.

[87] Karsten, 'The US Citizen-Soldier's Past, Present, and Likely Future', p. 62; M.
Kestnbaum, 'Citizenship and Compulsory Military Service: The Revolutionary
Origins of Conscription in the United States', *Armed Forces & Society*, 27, no. 1
(2000), 7.

[88] Kestnbaum, 'Citizenship and Compulsory Military Service', 8.

[89] M. Janowitz, 'The All-Volunteer Military as a "Sociopolitical" Problem', *Social
Problems*, 22, no. 3 (1975), 434.

The second feature of the citizen-soldier is that he or she is essentially motivated by self-defence, albeit at the collective level.[90] Since in modern democracies citizens obtain their security through the existence of the state, the defence of the state equates to their own defence. Yet Republicanism argues that the natural right to self-defence must not be alienated from the citizen. Only the citizen's direct participation in the use of collective force can ensure its democratic control and accountability. Moreover, the citizen-soldier model prevents the abuse of military power in foreign military interventions because it is assumed that citizens will only agree to enlist in the armed forces in the case of a national emergency.

From this follows the third characteristic of the Republican citizen-soldier model, namely the lack of a professional identity. The citizen-soldier, although trained in the use of arms, thinks of his or her service as a civic duty, not as a career. As Eliot A. Cohen writes, 'the true citizen-soldier's identity is fundamentally civilian. ... His participation in military life is temporary and provisional.'[91] According to Republicanism, the civilian and individualist identity of the citizen-soldier contributes to democratic control in several ways. Foremost, it limits the state's ability to maintain large standing armies in peacetime. It also helps to prevent the abuse of the armed forces by the government. Lastly, it provides an opportunity for the education of the citizen in democracy, civic virtue and collective responsibility. The civilian character of the citizen-soldier is particularly visible in the case of local militias, but with the rise of modern democracy it became collectivized at the level of the state in the form of citizen armies.

The fourth characteristic is the merger of social, political and military roles within the Republican concept of the citizen-soldier in order to ensure the accountability and control of the armed forces. Citizen-soldiers do not have to sever their linkages with their family and friends or to develop a new collective identity like professional soldiers, who are expected to shift their primary commitment to a military unit. Neither are citizen-soldiers required to abstain from political engagement. In fact, according to Republican theory, the political activity of citizen-soldiers is encouraged because it is one of the hallmarks of civic virtue and facilitates the integration of and control over the armed forces within the democratic decision-making process.

---

[90] Herrera speaks of 'self-governance'. See Herrera, 'Self-Governance and the American Citizen as Soldier, 1775–1861', 21.
[91] Cohen, 'Twilight of the Citizen-Soldier', 24.

While the citizen-soldier represents almost exclusively Republican ideals, the professional soldier model has been defined by both Republican and Liberal premises to varying degrees in history. From the nineteenth to the late twentieth century, the professional soldier model mixed Republican notions of duty to the state and the military as a self-sacrificing vocation with a Liberal emphasis on a separation of powers and political neutrality.[92] Since the 1980s, however, the rise of Neoliberalism has transformed the model of the professional soldier with the emergence of an 'occupational' view of the soldier which prioritizes rights and financial rewards over the traditional notions of duty and service.[93] Since the occupational model blurs the boundaries between professional soldiers and private military contractors, the following features refer to the traditional ideal of the professional soldier as outlined by Samuel Huntington and Morris Janowitz.[94]

One of the most important features of the traditional professional soldier model is its essentially Republican notion of obligation towards the state or a democratic constitution.[95] Although the professional soldier enters this obligation voluntarily, once accepted, it involves an 'ultimate liability' to sacrifice his or her life in defence of the state.[96] The subjugation of the professional soldier under a military law and judiciary illustrates the professional soldier's special duty towards the state and simultaneously safeguards the democratic control and accountability of the professional armed forces. Professional soldiers who fail to defend their nation are not merely breaching a common law contract but, in essence, they are breaking the Social Contract.

The second characteristic of the professional soldier model is that patriotism is its ideal motivation, expressed as dedication to and willingness to self-sacrifice for the state and society.[97] Professional soldiers do not fight purely for money and, thus, 'transcend "crass commercialism"'.[98] In spite of the turn to Neoliberalism and the emergence of an occupational conception of the military profession, these Republican sentiments can still be found to some degree among the all-volunteer forces

[92] Huntington, *The Soldier and the State*; M. Janowitz, *The Professional Soldier. A Social and Political Portrait* (New York: Free Press, 1960), pp. 218–25.
[93] C. Moskos, 'What Ails the All-Volunteer Force: An Institutional Perspective', *Parameters*, 31, no. 2 (2001), 29–47; see also S. C. Sarkesian, J. A. Williams and F. B. Bryant, *Soldiers, Society, and National Security* (Boulder, CO: Lynne Rienner, 1995), p. 14.
[94] Huntington, *The Soldier and the State*; Janowitz, *The Professional Soldier*.
[95] Huntington, *The Soldier and the State*, pp. 8–18.
[96] Sarkesian *et al.*, *Soldiers, Society, and National Security*, p. 15.
[97] *Ibid.*, p. 13.
[98] Janowitz, *The Professional Soldier*, pp. 228–9.

in the UK and USA.[99] If they are no longer a primary reason for signing up, they are at least instilled into professional soldiers during years of service.

The third characteristic of the professional soldier model is the development of a collective professional identity through extended schooling and training. Both serve to instil democratic norms and standards of operation.[100] Huntington argues that the military profession is a vocation and, thus, distinct from a mere occupation.[101] Specific to a vocation are lengthy formal training, professional standards and a collective occupational consciousness. Since a vocation is based on the Republican ideals of duty and service, it commands 'high esteem, respect, confidence, prestige and, not infrequently, privilege' among ordinary citizens.[102] Professionalism also entails civic virtue through the self-policing of the profession 'through education, selection processes, character inculcation, and ethical codes'.[103] It is a crucial means for ensuring the democratic control and accountability of the armed forces. Professional training teaches soldiers how they should behave in accordance with public norms and punishes those who fail to meet collective standards.

While the professional soldier's relationship with the state and his or her identity and motivation have their roots in Republican ideals, the model also builds on Liberal theory. Specifically, it contends that, in addition to professionalism, the separation of political and military roles is the most suitable means for promoting the democratic control and accountability of the soldier:

A degree of separation (psychological distance) must be maintained between U.S. society and the military profession to ensure military capability and combat effectiveness. ... The political–military dynamics resulting from the role of the profession in politics should ensure nonpoliticization of the profession.[104]

The establishment of a discrete military identity and ethos is instrumental in separating the armed forces from the political process.[105] The physical and geographical distancing of military bases from broader

---

[99] J. Burk, 'Patriotism and the All-Volunteer Force', *Journal of Political and Military Sociology*, 12, no. 2 (1984), 229–41.

[100] Janowitz, *The Professional Soldier*, p. 5.

[101] Huntington, *The Soldier and the State*, p. 11. See also H. Strachan, 'The Civil-Military "Gap" in Britain', *The Journal of Strategic Studies*, 26, no. 2 (2003), 47–8.

[102] C. J. Downes, 'To Be or Not to Be a Profession: The Military Case', *Defense Analysis*, 1, no. 3 (1985), 147–8.

[103] D. M. Snider and G. L. Watkins, 'The Future of Army Professionalism: A Need for Renewal and Redefinition', *Parameters*, 30, no. 3 (2000), 5–20.

[104] Sarkesian *et al.*, *Soldiers, Society, and National Security*, p. 2.

[105] Janowitz, 'The All-Volunteer Military', 439.

society highlights the division between the military and the civilian spheres. Numerous scholars have pointed out that military advice can never be politically neutral and concerns about the social representativeness of professional armies reflect the fact that soldiers participate in the decision-making process by giving advice and carrying out independent manoeuvres. Nevertheless, the professional soldier model emphasizes that the military should not actively seek to influence the public–political debate. The ideal is one of objective advice and submission to the democratically elected authorities.[106] This ideal can specifically be observed in the critique of openly political statements or party affiliations by professional soldiers, such as leading generals in the USA.[107]

Although there appears to be a fine line between professional soldiers who view their work as an occupation like any other and private military contractors, several features distinguish the two ideal models. The origins of these differences can be found in their divergent ideological foundations. The professional soldier model combines Republican obligation with Liberal professionalism and neutrality. By contrast, the private military contractor model fully embraces the Neoliberal principles of individual choice and market competition.

Based on these Neoliberal principles, the primary feature of the private military contractor model is the disconnection between military service and the state. While the citizen-soldier model is defined by mutual obligation and the professional soldier model by unilateral duty, the private military entrepreneur is only bound to the state through a temporary common law contract. The military contractor does not have any ultimate liability to defend the state with his or her life.[108] As of 2009, there was still no legal basis for enforcing any contractual obligations on deployed operations if private military companies feared for the safety of their employees. As the UK Ministry of Defence (MOD) observed: 'Under current legislation, the Military Commander cannot insist that the Contractor or its personnel remain in theatre against their will.'[109] Indeed, several contractors withdrew from the UK operation TELIC in Iraq because of the security risk.[110]

---

[106] B. Abrahamsson, *Military Professionalization and Political Power* (Beverly Hills, CA: Sage, 1972); Janowitz, *The Professional Soldier*, p. 13.
[107] Sarkesian *et al.*, *Soldiers, Society, and National Security*, p. 139.
[108] *Ibid.*, p. 15; S. Crock, T. F. Armistead, A. Bianco, S. A. Forest, 'Outsourcing War', *Business Week*, 3849 (15 September 2003), 68–78.
[109] MOD, 'Contractors on Deployed Operations', *Defence Contracts Bulletin*, 9 April 2003, p. 26.
[110] National Audit Office, *Ministry of Defence: Operation TELIC – United Kingdom Military Operations in Iraq*, Session 2003–4, HC 60 (London: The Stationery Office, 11 December 2003), p. 21.

The second characteristic distinguishing the military contractor model from the professional soldier is profit motivation. While professional soldiers ideally rank patriotism higher than financial rewards, private military contractors have no qualms about the primacy of monetary gain in their choice of employment.[111] Although many private military contractors in Iraq also profess other motives such as trying to help and fighting for democracy and freedom, they admit that the key reason for their being in the region is the high wages that they can earn as military contractors.[112] Contrary to Republicanism, Neoliberalism sees profit motivation as a suitable means for ensuring the democratic control and accountability of private military contractors. Rather than believing that soldiers will honour abstract notions of duty towards the state and society, Neoliberalism contends that profit motivation can be used to encourage the efficiency and effectiveness of private military contractors as well as their responsiveness towards public and private demands.

Thirdly, military contractors lack a distinct professional and collective identity which would ensure their compliance with professional military norms and standards. Due to the differentiation among military functions in contemporary warfare, private military contractors are typically specialists with a particular technical expertise. While professional soldiers are categorized in terms of rank, private military contractors are trained, hired and paid for their individual skills. The military contractor is an expert who provides a particular function from managing base camps to flying unmanned spy planes. Many private military contractors do not even have basic military training. Military contractors also do not develop a collective group identity. Most private military contractors work under short-term contracts of two to six months and for different firms. Since speed of deployment is one of their main advantages, private military companies operate through lists of potential employees who are called up if and when their skills are required. Contractors are typically thrown together with others for a particular operation with little training and preparation. The mixing of different nationalities and backgrounds also inhibits the formation of a collective identity. Some companies offering armed security services,

---

[111] Burk, 'Patriotism and the All-Volunteer Force'; A. Jacobs and S. Romero, 'U.S. Workers, Lured by Money and Idealism, Face Iraqi Reality', *New York Times*, 14 April 2004.

[112] A. E. Cha and J. Spinner, 'Some U.S. Workers Say the Risk Is Too Great', *Washington Post*, 15 April 2004; M. Roig-Franzia, 'Ohioan Gung-Ho, Despite Dangers', *Washington Post*, 2 April 2004; S. McNulty, 'Come to Hell with Halliburton – The Pay's Good', *Financial Times*, 14 June 2004; C. Murphy, 'Iraq's Mercenaries: Riches for Risks', *BBC News Online*, 1 April 2004.

therefore, seek to recruit from certain nations, occupations and even sections of national armed forces in order to improve unit cohesion. From an operational viewpoint, the lack of a common professional and group identity might be a disadvantage. However, Neoliberalism contends that the associated fragmentation of influence and resources can facilitate democratic control and accountability by decreasing the size of the armed forces and mixing civilian and military occupational spheres.

Finally, Neoliberalism favours the alienation of political and military roles within the private military contractor model. Most private military contractors neither work for nor in their home countries. In Iraq private military employees have come from a wide variety of nations with a growing number of contractors recruited from developing countries such as Columbia, Chile, Fiji, Nepal and the Philippines or from Eastern European states such as Croatia, Bosnia, Bulgaria and Ukraine.[113] National citizenship is irrelevant for the military contractor. Most private military companies are happy to recruit anybody who has the necessary expertise. As a consequence, there is a separation of the political and military roles played by the military contractor. According to Neoliberalism, this is an advantage in terms of democratic control and accountability since it facilitates the political neutrality of the soldier. The nationality and citizenship of military contractors have little impact on who gains their services. In return, the political actions of military contractors have no influence on their employers. The military functions of private contractors are commodified and completely divorced from their political persona.

The preceding ideal-type models suggest that distinct civil–military relations in Western democracies are not only a product of divergent security demands and historical developments, but have also been shaped by theoretical and ideological beliefs regarding the most suitable means of democratic control and accountability. However, as Chapter 3 will show, each model has its own theoretical and practical limitations. It is for these and other reasons that the roles and relations of the state, the citizen and the soldier have changed repeatedly in the history of modern democracies.

---

[113] J. Franklin, 'US Contractor Recruits Guards for Iraq in Chile', *Guardian*, 5 March 2004; S. Efron, 'Iraq: Worry Grows as Foreigners Flock to Risky Jobs', *LA Times*, 30 July 2005.

Table 2.2. *Ideal-type models of the soldier*

	Republicanism	Republicanism & Liberalism	Neoliberalism
Model	*Citizen-soldier*	*Professional soldier*	*Private military contractor*
Relationships with the state and society	Reciprocal obligation	Duty	Contract
Motivation	Self-defence	Patriotism	Monetary gain
Identity	Individual-civilian	Collective-professional	Individual-professional
Democratic control and accountability	Combination and integration of political and military roles, political and social representativeness of society	Separation of political and military roles, political neutrality, military professionalism and discipline	Alienation of political and military roles, political neutrality, market pressures, contract law

Conclusion

This chapter has illustrated that the emergence of modern democracy in Europe and North America serves as a central theoretical watershed between the employment of mercenaries in previous centuries and the outsourcing of military services in modern times. Associated with new ideal models of the state, the citizen and the soldier, democracy has led to the establishment of contemporary norms concerning the control and accountability of armed forces and, thus, has contributed to the progressive elimination of mercenarism. Mercenarism could still be justified in terms of Hobbes' understanding of the Social Contract between the citizens and a separate sovereign authority. The contemporary privatization of military force, however, has evolved within the theoretical context of modern democracy which sees control over the use of collective violence as an inalienable right of the citizenry. Nevertheless, as the preceding sections have argued, even under the conditions of the democratic Social Contract there have been competing models of the ideal role and relationships between the state, the citizen and the soldier. Republicanism and Liberalism have played a central role in defining these competing models in terms of centralized government and fragmented governance, and the citizen-soldier, the professional soldier and the private military contractor. The rise and fall of these alternative models and their impact on the institutions and practices of the democratic control over military force in Europe and North America from the emergence of modern democracy in the late eighteenth century until the end of the Cold War will be traced in the following chapter. It illustrates how the ideological debates outlined above can help to explain the changing roles of the state, the citizen and the soldier, and the associated rise of the private military contractor.

3   The transformation of the state and the soldier

Since the establishment of modern democracy in Europe and North America in the late eighteenth century, the competing models of civil–military relations proposed by Republican and Liberal theorists have influenced the institutions and practices by which Western societies have sought to ensure the democratic accountability of the provision of national and international security. The ideal-type models of the state and the soldier outlined in Chapter 2 have played crucial parts in this respect. The ideological and practical definitions of the roles of the state have influenced the degree of its monopoly on the legitimate use of military force and the democratic control of its powers in recent history, while the models of the soldier have defined the roles, responsibilities and relations of the armed forces with the state and society. However, changes in these roles and relations have been a regular feature of past centuries. As argued in the introduction, three factors in particular have influenced when and how these transformations have occurred, namely the emergence of new security threats, the inconsistent implementation of both ideologies and the inherent problems of each ideal-type model.

By analysing these changes in the examples of the UK, the USA and Germany, this chapter illustrates that the contemporary privatization of military services is neither new nor inevitable, but is part of a historical cycle of critique and transformation of the state monopoly on collective violence. It shows how the ideological competition between Republicanism and Liberalism has influenced varying conceptions of the state and the soldier within different security contexts. Specifically, the following analysis is structured into five sections. The first four sections analyse the historical evolution of different forms of civil–military relations. They distinguish between four major periods characterized by particular models of the state and the soldier: the period from the late eighteenth century until the First World War, the period of the two World Wars, the Cold War, and the period from the beginning of the 1980s to the end of the Cold War. The fifth section discusses how the democratic control over and accountability for the provision of national and international security have been key considerations in the shifts from one model to another. The chapter concludes by arguing that sometimes changes in the prevailing ideological models of the state and the soldier have been in response to new threats, while at other times they have been due to a critique and dissatisfaction with the models themselves.

Democracy and security before the First World War

During the eighteenth and nineteenth centuries modern democracy became established in Europe and North America, setting the stage for the development of new forms of civilian control of the armed forces.[1] The bases for these new models of control were laid by the prevailing ideological ideals of the state and the soldier. This section examines in turn how these models have shaped distinct institutions and practices of civil–military control in the UK, the USA and Germany.

In the UK the period before the First World War was characterized by the predominance of a Liberal ideology that favoured controlling the collective use of force by limiting the roles and size of the state, the defence industry and the armed forces. This approach appeared to be particularly suited for a security environment that featured, mostly, localized wars overseas such as the Napoleonic Wars and the Crimean War, as well as colonial wars in India, Burma, China, South Africa, Egypt and Sudan. It controlled the military establishment by radically cutting back the size of the armed forces and the defence budget after each conflict.[2] Moreover, Liberalism coincided with popular beliefs which held the conscription of citizen-soldiers to be anathema to the rights and freedoms of a true Englishman.[3] Instead, the population supported a combination of public and private ownership of an emerging but small armaments industry,

---

[1] C. Barnett, *Britain and Her Army, 1509–1970* (London: Allen Lane The Penguin Press, 1970); B. F. Cooling (ed.) *War, Business, and American Society. Historical Perspectives on the Military-Industrial Complex* (Port Washington, NY: Kennikat Press, 1977); D. Chandler (ed.) *The Oxford History of the British Army* (Oxford: Oxford University Press, 1996); J. M. Brereton, *The British Soldier. A Social History from 1661 to the Present Day* (London: The Bodley Head, 1986); T. S. Langston, *Uneasy Balance: Civil-Military Relations in Peacetime America since 1783* (Baltimore, MD: The Johns Hopkins University Press, 2003); D. R. Segal, *Recruiting for Uncle Sam: Citizenship and Military Manpower Policy* (Lawrence, KS: University Press of Kansas, 1989).

[2] P. Burroughs, 'An Unreformed Army? 1815–1868', in D. Chandler (ed.) *The Oxford History of the British Army* (Oxford: Oxford University Press, 1996), p. 161; Barnett, *Britain and Her Army*, p. 283.

[3] P. Fraser, 'British War Policy and the Crisis of Liberalism in May 1915', *Journal of Modern History*, 54, no. 1 (1982), 2; Barnett, *Britain and Her Army*, p. 257, p. 377.

and a mixture of militia, volunteer and professional armed forces.[4] In the defence industry, democratic control was facilitated by the fragmentation of resources between the state-owned Royal Gunpowder Factory, Royal Small Arms Factory and Royal Arsenal, and a small number of private armaments and ammunition producers, including Armstrong, Vickers and Nobel Dynamite.[5] In the military, the division of the armed forces into several components with distinct models of the soldier constrained their size and influence. On the one side were the navy and the regular army which consisted of professional soldiers under the central control of the government.[6] They made up the bulk of the armed forces and were in charge of controlling the population at home, defending the nation, fighting wars overseas and pacifying the empire.[7] On the other side were the militia and the volunteers, consisting of part-time citizen-soldiers who were raised and managed locally and only liable for homeland defence.[8] In addition, local and private mercenary forces provided further personnel to manage the empire.[9] Throughout the colonies, private contractors performed civilian and military support functions, including transport, cooking, sanitation and taking care of horses and other livestock.[10] Officially, however, the government did not hire mercenaries. Its native volunteer forces were formally part of the UK military and subject to its discipline. The East India Company had its own mercenary force to police the colony, but the company's forces were incorporated into the UK military or disbanded when India was put under governmental control in 1858.[11]

In the second half of the nineteenth century the security environment was largely similar with military conflicts mostly confined to the British colonies. However, the enfranchisement of larger sections of the British population and the rise of Republican notions such as the mutual obligation between the state and its citizens for defence and welfare introduced new ideas as to how the armed forces should be held accountable. In particular, the awakening middle classes began to criticize the weak civilian control over the military, and the separation of the regular army and the militia from society.[12] Democratic control over the armed forces was eventually improved by centralizing political

---

[4] Barnett, *Britain and Her Army*, p. 282.   [5] *Ibid.*, p. 290.
[6] Brereton, *The British Soldier*, p. 47, p. 50.   [7] *Ibid.*, p. 43.
[8] Barnett, *Britain and Her Army*, p. 257.
[9] *Ibid.*, p. 273, pp. 275–6.
[10] E. M. Spiers, *The Late Victorian Army 1868–1902* (Manchester: Manchester University Press, 1992), pp. 293–4.
[11] Burroughs, 'An Unreformed Army?', p. 185.
[12] H. Cunningham, *The Volunteer Force. A Social and Political History 1859–1908* (London: Croom Helm, 1975), p. 11; Burroughs, 'An Unreformed Army?', p. 183.

authority over the military, placing it in the hands of elected civilian representatives. While previously, 'thirteen separate authorities competed with one another for executive control over the various branches of the administration', by the end of the era successive reforms had helped to establish parliamentary authority over the aristocracy-led military and to merge previously independent, and frequently competing, agencies.[13] The creation of a civilian Secretary of State for War in 1854 and the subordination of the military Master-General of the Ordnance under his authority were significant developments in this respect.[14]

The spread of Republican ideas among the middle classes also led to a revival of the citizen-soldier model. Volunteer corps expressed the aspirations of wealthy citizens to play a greater role in the running of the country and the defence of the nation and the empire. The abolition of the purchase system in the 1871 represented an important step towards democratizing the armed forces by opening up new career paths.[15] In practice, however, the need for an independent income replaced purchase as a mechanism that limited access to the officer class, while low pay and voluntary recruitment meant that the soldiers still came from lower classes.[16] Although the end of the nineteenth century saw some centralization of parliamentary control over the British military, the predominance of the Liberal models of the small state and the professional soldier changed very little.[17]

In the USA, by contrast, a mixture of Liberal and Republican ideological principles dominated public conceptions of democratic civil–military relations between 1788 and the First World War. These principles assigned to the state a central, but limited role in the provision of national and international security, and promoted citizen militias as the ideal armed forces.[18] Arguably, the American security environment was different from the UK. It faced, primarily, internal conflicts with Native Americans, border wars with the Spanish and the Civil War, all of which posed a direct threat to homeland security. However, the constitution had already balanced Republican ideals such as civic participation in public government and national defence with Liberal principles such

[13] I. Beckett and J. Gooch, 'Introduction', in I. Beckett and J. Gooch (eds.) *Politicians and Defence. Studies in the Formulation of British Defence Policy 1845–1970* (Manchester: Manchester University Press, 1981), p. VIII. See also Burroughs, 'An Unreformed Army?', p. 171; Barnett, *Britain and Her Army*, p. 309.
[14] Barnett, *Britain and Her Army*, p. 289.
[15] Brereton, *The British Soldier*, p. 76; Barnett, *Britain and Her Army*, p. 241.
[16] Brereton, *The British Soldier*, p. 76–8.
[17] Barnett, *Britain and Her Army*, p. 314. See also Spiers, *The Late Victorian Army 1868–1902*, pp. 180–9; Burroughs, 'An Unreformed Army?' p. 186.
[18] Langston, *Uneasy Balance*, p. 33.

as federalism and a system of institutional checks and balances to ensure the democratic accountability of the use of collective force.[19] In addition, Congress endorsed a mixed ownership of the armaments industry, aiming to divide weapons production between two national armouries at Springfield and Harpers Ferry and private armaments firms.[20] Due to high investment cost and the irregularity of demand determined by small and short conflicts, however, private businesses showed little interest in the manufacture of arms. Instead of having to contain the influence of private armaments producers, the US government had to encourage and subsidize private defence manufacture through the sharing of new technologies developed by its armouries.[21] Both policies significantly strengthened the role of the central government in the governance of the military establishment. In fact, the Ordnance Department and other military agencies 'exercised exclusive control over the selection of contractors and the allocation of contracts' and determined which companies should receive government support.[22]

The same mixture of Liberal and Republican principles also shaped the US armed forces. On the one hand, Liberal ideals accounted for the popular aversion towards a large standing army, and the fragmentation of political control over the militia and the regular forces between the states and the federal government. The latter aimed to prevent the federal government's abuse of military force by forcing it to rely on state loans of militiamen in the case of a national emergency.[23] On the other hand, the belief in the militia system as the prime embodiment of the Republican model of the citizen-soldier 'illustrated what many soldiers believed was the inseparable connection between citizenship and bearing arms on behalf of the Republic'.[24] The Republican principle that armed force must only be used for national self-defence was another rationale for the militia and was enshrined in US law.[25]

---

[19] P. A. C. Koistinen, *The Military-Industrial Complex. A Historical Perspective* (New York: Praeger, 1980), p. 24.

[20] D. R. Beaver, 'The Problem of American Military Supply, 1890–1920', in B. F. Cooling (ed.) *War, Business, and American Society. Historical Perspectives on the Military-Industrial Complex* (Port Washington, NY: Kennikat Press, 1977), p. 77; M. Roe Smith, 'Military Arsenals and Industry before World War I', in: B. F. Cooling (ed.) *War, Business, and American Society. Historical Perspectives on the Military-Industrial Complex* (Port Washington, NY: Kennikat Press, 1977), p. 25.

[21] Roe Smith, 'Military Arsenals and Industry before World War I', pp. 25–31, p. 33; J. Reppy, 'The United States', in N. Ball and M. Leitenberg (eds.) *The Structure of the Defense Industry* (London: Croom Helm, 1983), p. 21.

[22] Roe Smith, 'Military Arsenals and Industry before World War I', p. 42.

[23] Langston, *Uneasy Balance*, p. 33.

[24] R. A. Herrera, 'Self-Governance and the American Citizen as Soldier, 1775–1861', *The Journal of Military History*, 65, no. 1 (2001), 21.

[25] Segal, *Recruiting for Uncle Sam*, p. 24.

Both the limited size of the defence industry and the militia system were very effective in imposing severe restrictions on the democratic use of military force by the federal government. The militias were not only inadequately trained, but also suffered from the reluctance of many citizens to report for service.[26] Large numbers of citizens preferred to risk being fined rather than leave their civilian occupations and families to fight in distant border wars.[27] For the enlisted, service was typically limited to only three months and many citizen-soldiers went home once they had completed their term, irrespective of the progress of a war.[28]

Even the Civil War (1861–5) had little impact on the US models of the state and the soldier. Ownership of the defence industry remained fragmented with armaments production coming one third from the Springfield national armoury after the destruction of Harpers Ferry, and two thirds from other suppliers.[29] Moreover, after the end of the war Congress drastically reduced the defence budget, forcing private armaments producers to return to civilian production or overseas exports.[30] Neither did it spare the national armouries and arsenals, where production came to a 'virtual standstill'.[31]

The main effects of the Civil War were on the Republican ideal of the citizen-soldier because of the government's first and inequitable use of conscription. In particular, its policy to allow the rich to evade enlistment by paying a $300 fee led to violent riots in New York, Massachusetts, Ohio, New Hampshire and Vermont.[32] Although the experiment with the draft was a failure, the government was able to increase its central control over citizen-soldiers with the Enrolment Act of 1863. The Act recognized the federal government's primacy in claiming the military service obligation of its citizens.[33] Nevertheless, after the war the USA returned to the old system of state militias and small national regular forces. Even when the regular armed forces grew to about 100,000 men by 1897, most Americans were certain that 'an active and ideologically sound citizen-soldiery could counterbalance any potential threats posed by ambitious anti-republican regulars'.[34] Indeed, few professional soldiers signed up for more than two terms and, during war, citizen-soldiers in the form of militiamen and volunteers vastly outnumbered

[26] Langston, *Uneasy Balance*, p. 39.
[27] Langston, *Uneasy Balance*, p. 39; Segal, *Recruiting for Uncle Sam*, p. 20.
[28] Segal, *Recruiting for Uncle Sam*, pp. 24–5.
[29] Roe Smith, 'Military Arsenals and Industry before World War I', p. 35.
[30] *Ibid.*, pp. 35–6.   [31] *Ibid.*, p. 38.
[32] Segal, *Recruiting for Uncle Sam*, pp. 25–6.   [33] *Ibid.*, p. 25, p. 43.
[34] Herrera, 'Self-Governance and the American Citizen as Soldier, 1775–1861', 25. See also R. C. Snyder, 'The Citizen-Soldier Tradition and Gender Integration of the U.S. Military', *Armed Forces & Society*, 29, no. 2 (2003), 187.

the regulars.[35] On the whole, the comparatively small size of the defence industry and the standing army ensured that the US government could not engage in war without the mobilization and the democratic support of substantive sections of its population.[36]

In Germany democratic control over the use of armed force was not substantively strengthened until the early twentieth century, thus limiting the comparison with the UK and the USA in terms of its model of democratic civil–military relations. After the unification of Germany under the Prussian king in 1871, the authority over collective means of violence remained firmly within the hands of the emperor and the aristocracy. They used the military not only in border conflicts and the expansion of the empire, but also for the repression of political agitation and strikes among the German citizens. Nevertheless, the monarchy laid the foundations for the relationships been the state, the citizens and the soldier which would define Germany's first democracy between 1919 and 1933. In particular, the industrialization and extensive rearmament before the First World War transformed a largely state-owned armaments sector based on national armouries, munitions factories and workshops into a predominantly private defence industry.[37] Moreover, the empire left Germany with the legacy of an almost purely aristocratic officer corps which strongly supported monarchism.[38] The introduction of general conscription in the nineteenth century brought the model of the citizen-soldier to the rank and file. However, citizens were not conceived as such in terms of Republican ideology, but as politically immature subjects. Rather than increasing the accountability of the armed forces to the broader population, the monarchy used the three years of conscripted military service to instil the ideals of patriotism, loyalty and service to the emperor into the male citizenry. To manifest the absolute control of the monarch over the armed forces, soldiers swore their oaths of allegiance directly to the German emperor.

The period before the First World War thus illustrates the relevance of ideology in determining democratic civil–military relations. Although the UK, the USA and Germany faced different security environments, ideology played an important role in guiding prevailing perceptions about the appropriate roles and relations of the state, the citizen and the soldier in national and international defence. In

---

[35] Herrera. 'Self-Governance and the American Citizen as Soldier, 1775–1861', 27; Segal, *Recruiting for Uncle Sam*, p. 27.

[36] Langston, *Uneasy Balance*, p. 40.

[37] H.-J. Bontrup and N. Zdrowomyslaw, *Die Deutsche Rüstungsindustrie. Vom Kaiserreich bis zur Bundesrepublik* (Heilbronn: Distel Verlag, 1988), p. 51.

[38] W. Hartmann, *Geist und Haltung des Deutschen Soldaten im Wandel der Gesellschaft. Vom Kaiserheer zur Bundeswehr* (Limburg a.d. Lahn: C. A. Starke Verlag, 1998), p. 8.

the USA the Liberal principle of the fragmentation of power and the Republican ideal of the citizen-soldier built on the principles of democratic control contained in the constitution. In the UK the rise of new Republican ideals towards the second half of the nineteenth century contributed to new forms of soldier such as the volunteer corps and the centralization of democratic control within the hands of civilian ministers. In Germany the weakness of democratic institutions following unification prevented the establishment of effective civilian and democratic control over the armed forces along either Republican or Liberal ideals. However, as the next section will illustrate, the legacy of the empire and the First World War shaped the context in which Germany's first democratic government developed its own model of civil–military control.

The World Wars and the centralization of security

While the nineteenth century had already seen the strengthening of Republican beliefs in the responsibility of the state for the welfare of its citizens and the growing popularity of the citizen-soldier model among volunteer corps in the UK, state militias in the USA and conscript forces in Germany, Republicanism did not become a predominant model of civil–military relations until the mid twentieth century. In particular, the unprecedented scale of the threat presented by the two World Wars demonstrated to citizens in Europe and North America the maxim that the security of the individual was inherently bound up with that of the collective. The mobilization of entire populations and economies on both sides of the Atlantic for the purpose of national defence became the most extreme embodiment of the principles of Republican centralized government.

Nevertheless, there was a considerable persistence of ideological beliefs in the face of the new security threats. The centralization of defence industrial production and the turn towards mass conscription during the First World War were, thus, only partial and temporary. After the end of the war all three countries dismantled their national defence industries and substituted citizen-soldiers with professional armies. In the long term, however, the two World Wars laid the foundations for a more durable shift to the Republican ideals of centralized government and citizen armies. One factor in this development was the widespread critique of the Liberal model of fragmented security governance due to the failure of industry to respond to the demands of a major international conflict and accusations of war profiteering. Other factors included the establishment of large and permanent defence industrial sectors and standing armed forces in Europe and North America which seemed to require new mechanisms of democratic control.

The UK entered the First World War as a country dominated by a Liberal ideology and system of democratic security governance. However, the war soon demonstrated that 'Victorian liberal ideas of laissez-faire private enterprise failed to produce efficient war-making'.[39] By 1914 the policy of limited state investment and involvement in national defence had proved a disaster, as demonstrated by a devastating shortfall in ammunitions production. The UK government therefore decided to centralize the resources for and management of the war economy in public hands.[40] By 1917 Lloyd George as Minister of Munitions had 'created a great British armaments industry, much of it in new national factories'.[41]

The persistence of Liberalism also caused politicians to refuse to abandon the principle of volunteering until the second year of the First World War.[42] Instead, the government issued a general call for volunteers. The success of Lord Kitchener's famous appeals was astonishing, and by summer 1915 over two million citizens had signed up for military service.[43] The response demonstrated that Republican ideals were not entirely alien to UK citizens. 'Public school codes of duty, self-sacrifice, and discipline which had permeated every level of society through the education system, youth movements, and Sunday schools, underpinned the patriotic response of many volunteers.'[44] The passing of the Military Service Bill, which conscripted all able-bodied men between 18 and 41 in 1916, seemed to confirm the rise of the Republican model of the citizen-soldier. For the first time in UK history, the defence of their country brought together citizens from all classes and backgrounds.[45]

After the end of the First World War, however, the UK reverted to the Liberal system of democratic control through fragmented governance. The national military industry was dismantled, and public repulsion at the slaughter of over half a million men in the trenches led to a rejection of the conscript system and its immediate abolition.[46] Nevertheless, the

[39] Barnett, *Britain and Her Army*, p. 397.
[40] Fraser, 'British War Policy and the Crisis of Liberalism in May 1915', 18.
[41] Barnett, *Britain and Her Army*, p. 382.
[42] M. Levi, 'The Institution of Conscription', *Social Science History*, 20, no. 1 (1996), 133–67; Barnett, *Britain and Her Army*, p. 367.
[43] Barnett, *Britain and Her Army*, p. 377.
[44] P. Simkins, 'The Four Armies 1914–1918', in: D. Chandler and I. Beckett (eds.) *The Oxford History of the British Army* (Oxford: Oxford University Press, 1996), p. 239.
[45] Brereton, *The British Soldier*, pp. 124–5; Simkins, 'The Four Armies 1914–1918', p. 243.
[46] Barnett, *Britain and Her Army*, pp. 410–15; R. Broad, *Conscription in Britain 1939–1964* (London: Routledge, 2006), p. 243.

experience of the First World War had shifted public conceptions of the state and the soldier towards a more Republican outlook. During the Victorian era, the limited size of the national armed forces and the armaments industry had served to prevent the abuse of military power.[47] With the growth of the armed forces and military industry during the First World War, this model had proven inadequate. Not only had private industry been unresponsive to the needs of the nation, but there was also a public perception that private firms had used the war to make excessive profits.[48] By contrast, the nationalization of armaments production and the centralization of control over the armed forces by the government had ensured that the production and use of the means of collective violence were in the service of the general public.

When rearmament for the Second World War began in 1937, it was therefore in the form of centralized governmental management and ownership. The Ministry of Supply, the Ministry of Aircraft Production and the Admiralty not only acted as consumers of arms, but also controlled the supply of raw materials and related industries.[49] Where the state did not intervene, it nationalized – as it did with the railways, coal mines and iron and steel production – or created new industries to support armaments production. New government-owned factories manufactured nearly half of all weapons required, limiting the role of private businesses.[50]

Moreover, the First World War had demonstrated the Republican belief that the soldier could be 'an ordinary member of society who happened to wear a uniform, his business to preserve freedom'.[51] In fact, the model of the citizen-soldier and the draft had become so widely accepted that the UK government did not again attempt to find its forces through voluntary recruitment at the beginning of the Second World War. On the day that the UK entered the war, Parliament approved the conscription of all men between 20 and 41 in the National Service Act 1939.[52] Even among pacifists a sense of obligation to fight Hitler and

---

[47] C. Trebilcock, 'Legends of the British Armaments Industry 1890–1914: A Revision', *Journal of Contemporary History*, 5, no. 4 (1970), 3–19.

[48] Fraser, 'British War Policy and the Crisis of Liberalism in May 1915', p. 11; Barnett, *Britain and Her Army*, pp. 380–1; H. C. Engelbrecht, 'The Problem of the Munitions Industry', *Annals of the American Academy of Political and Social Science*, 174, no. 1 (1934), 121–5; D. G. Anderson, 'British Rearmament and the "Merchants of Death": The 1935–36 Royal Commission on the Manufacture of and Trade in Armaments', *Journal of Contemporary History*, 29, no. 1 (1994), 5–37.

[49] D. Edgerton, *Warfare State. Britain, 1920–1970* (Cambridge: Cambridge University Press, 2006), p. 73.

[50] *Ibid.*, pp. 77–8.

[51] Brereton, *The British Soldier*, pp. 139–40.

[52] A. Danchev, 'The Army and the Home Front 1939–1945', in D. Chandler and I. Beckett (eds.) *The Oxford History of the British Army* (Oxford: Oxford University Press, 1996), p. 300. In 1941 the age limits were extended to 18–60 years. See *ibid.*, p. 301.

fascism prevailed, resulting in decreasing rates of conscientious objections during the first year of the war.[53]

In the USA the transition from a mixed model of civil–military control to one based purely on Republican principles occurred more slowly, but also more consistently. While in the UK the World Wars brought about the centralization of government in the guise of the nationalization of armaments production and other key industries, Congress resisted the expansion of federal institutions which lacked the experience and personnel for the management of a total war economy on the eve of the First World War.[54] Building on the established combination of Liberal governance and Republican government, it instead endorsed a new form of public–private management: the War Industries Board (WIB). The WIB 'centralized control over a planned economy [which] was established and carried out by representatives of the government, the business community, and the military' together.[55] Government and the armaments industry became increasingly interlinked.[56]

In spite of the traditional predominance of the citizen-soldier, the US government hesitated to introduce mass conscription when it entered the First World War. However, within months Congress had to accept that only mass conscription would be able to meet the personnel requirements of a world war and passed the Selective Service Bill.[57] Learning from its negative experience with the draft in the Civil War, the government sought to ensure this time the consistent application of Republican ideals in order to facilitate the public acceptance of mass conscription. Specifically, it placed the responsibility for the registration of eligible males with local civilian registration boards, which safeguarded public accountability and control over the drafting process, and strictly limited the conditions for exemption from the draft. The approach was successful and, by Armistice in 1919, three million men had been inducted to military service.[58]

After the end of the First World War the US armaments industry contracted, but increasing government interest in the development of new technologies such as aircraft and the renewed outbreak of war in Europe prevented the return to the Liberal practice of controlling the military establishment by limiting its size.[59] For the first time in US history continued government investment in armaments production permitted the emergence of a permanent private defence industry with major companies

[53] Danchev, 'The Army and the Home Front 1939–1945', p. 301.
[54] Koistinen, *The Military-Industrial Complex*, pp. 24–5.   [55] *Ibid.*, p. 8.
[56] Beaver, 'The Problem of American Military Supply', p. 90.
[57] Segal, *Recruiting for Uncle Sam*, p. 28.   [58] *Ibid.*, p. 29.
[59] Reppy, 'The United States', pp. 21–2.

such as Boeing and Grumman. When the USA entered the Second World War, the government perpetuated the system of state–industry cooperation that had evolved. In fact, 'the Second World War massively strengthened the old linkages between American business and the military'.[60]

The period from 1914 to 1945 thus progressively transformed the role of the state in the democratic provision of armed force in the USA. The build-up of the military during the two World Wars put the Liberal system of democratic control through fragmentation increasingly under strain because of the growing power and interpenetration between the federal government, the defence sector and the armed forces. However, the USA did not fully turn towards a Republican model of centralized government of national and international security until the end of the Second World War.[61]

The same applied to the US model of the soldier. In the interwar period the US government demobilized its conscripted armed forces and returned to volunteer recruitment. The First World War seemed to have demonstrated the feasibility of a Republican citizen-army that relied on voluntary enlistment during peacetime, but could count on its citizens to accept mass conscription in the case of a national emergency. After Hitler's invasion of Poland in 1939, US citizens even tolerated peacetime conscription.[62] In preparation for the war, the government reinstated the system of local selective service boards and put the militia, now called the National Guard, under federal authority. During the course of the Second World War, another ten million civilians were inducted and draftees provided two thirds of the US armed forces. Again, the equitability of conscription helped to maintain public support for the citizen-soldier model.[63]

In Germany the imperial monarchist government preserved the private ownership of the armaments industry during the First World War. The management of war supplies was centralized within the Ministry of War and especially the War Materiel Office, but armaments production and related industries involving about forty thousand firms remained in private hands.[64] Close personal relationships between the government and business leaders and the dependence of the war effort on private industry performance increased the influence of the private armaments

---

[60] R. A. Beaumont, 'Quantum Increase: The MIC in the Second World War', in B. F. Cooling (ed.) *War, Business, and American Society. Historical Perspectives on the Military-Industrial Complex* (Port Washington, NY: Kennikat Press, 1977), p. 118.
[61] Koistinen, *The Military-Industrial Complex*, p. 9.
[62] P. Karsten, 'The US Citizen-Soldier's Past, Present, and Likely Future', *Parameters*, 31, no. 2 (2001), 61–73.
[63] Segal, *Recruiting for Uncle Sam*, p. 43.
[64] Bontrup and Zdrowomyslaw, *Die Deutsche Rüstungsindustrie*, p. 92.

sector on the government. The state became a 'self-service counter' for the demands of the private industry. Not only did private armaments firms receive financial support for the conversion from civilian to military production and the building of new production plants, they also forced the government to sign long-term contracts and pay inflated prices.[65] Similarly, the armed forces expanded, but did not change significantly in composition. Mass conscription had been in place since 1814, allowing the government to draft eleven million trained citizen-soldiers to fight in the First World War.[66] Moreover, nationalism and patriotism ensured that there was no widespread opposition to conscription among the German population.

The defeat and abolition of the monarchy in 1919 finally brought the German military under the control of a democratic government. The Weimar Republic, however, was ripped by internal dissent, and the newly formed parliamentary democracy was too weak to exert its authority over the armed forces.[67] The government instead relied on the military to preserve domestic order, which was threatened by infighting between the nationalist and the communist movements. Although the Versailles Treaty imposed strict limitations on the size of the German military and armaments production, the government failed to ensure the democratic accountability of the military sector. Having just emerged from defeat, the government was more concerned with the restoration rather than the containment of the military.

What control there was followed the Liberal model of fragmented governance. Two factors determined the new roles and relations between the German government, the citizens and the armed forces. The first factor was the existence of an influential private defence establishment. The defence industry had become a crucial business and employment sector, and many armaments firms had been able to retain their connections. Most companies were keen to return to the profitable business of military production and safeguarded know-how and machinery by moving to neutral countries such as the Netherlands and Sweden.[68] Instead of using the opportunity to encourage the conversion from military to civilian production to contain the power of private military businesses, the Weimar government planned to rearm Germany as soon as possible and financially supported key industries until the end of Allied controls in the late 1920s.[69]

[65] *Ibid.*, p. 93.
[66] V. R. Berghan, *Der erste Weltkrieg* (Munich: C. H. Beck, 2003), p. 9.
[67] Hartmann, *Geist und Haltung des Deutschen Soldaten im Wandel der Gesellschaft*, p. 62.
[68] Bontrup and Zdrowomyslaw, *Die Deutsche Rüstungsindustrie*, p. 96.
[69] *Ibid.*, p. 99.

In addition, the conditions set in the post-war Treaty of Versailles circumscribed the government's ability to democratize the internal structure and outlook of the armed forces. Among others, these conditions demanded the reduction of Germany's military to 100,000 soldiers, with only 4,000 officers. Since the force limitations made the continuation of conscription based on an equitable citizen-soldier model impossible, they appeared to determine that the new armed forces would be based on professional soldiers. Many of these soldiers and the majority of the officers came from the imperial military and, accordingly, favoured conservative, nationalist and monarchist values.[70]

Unfortunately, rather than facilitating democratic control, the fragmentation of resources between private armaments businesses and professional armed forces increased their independent and anti-democratic powers vis-à-vis a weak government. The Weimar government sought to counter these problems by opening up the access to a career in the professional armed forces to the broader population.[71] But key sections of the electorate, in particular the more progressive elements, remained distrustful of the armed forces.[72] While the new professional military was undoubtedly committed to the principles of duty to the nation, sacrifice and high moral standards, its political neutrality and loyalty to the democratic government were questionable.

In the end, Adolf Hitler's rise to power was not only supported by key armaments firms, but also by the professional military which stood by 'expectant, but cautious'.[73] Many soldiers welcomed Hitler's objective to achieve a 'national renewal' through the rearmament of Germany.[74] As expected, the defence industry prospered under the new fascist regime and its expansionist policies. Private armaments production was tightly controlled by the centralized administration and faced increasing competition from state-owned factories, but the main firms remained privately owned or were restored to private ownership towards the end of the Second World War.[75]

The preparations for the Second World War also saw the reinstallation of universal conscription in 1935.[76] As under the monarchy, this conscript army had little in common with the Republican ideal of the citizen-soldier. Instead of mutual obligation, self-defence and political self-determination through the integration of political and military roles, Hitler's armed forces were characterized by the complete subordination

---

[70] Hartmann, *Geist und Haltung des Deutschen Soldaten im Wandel der Gesellschaft*, p. 63.
[71] *Ibid.*, p. 75.   [72] *Ibid.*, p. 100.
[73] *Ibid.*, p. 112.   [74] *Ibid.*
[75] Bontrup and Zdrowomyslaw, *Die Deutsche Rüstungsindustrie*, pp. 115–16.
[76] Hartmann, *Geist und Haltung des Deutschen Soldaten im Wandel der Gesellschaft*, p. 117.

of the soldier to the fascist leadership and the use of collective means of violence for expansionist wars.[77] Although Hitler formally maintained the separation between the military and his paramilitary Schutzstaffel (SS) and Sturm Abteilung (SA), the armed forces were directly subordinated to Hitler and controlled through his associates in key leadership positions.[78]

The period between 1914 and 1945 thus further illustrates the role of ideology with regard to civil–military relations. It suggests that although major wars may facilitate a conversion towards the Republican models of centralized state control over armaments production and the citizen-soldier which reflect the common security interests of the citizens, this is not always the case. Sometimes particular ideological models can persist despite new security contexts, such as the continuation of a mixed Liberal and Republican model of security governance in the USA. At other times, changes in the models of the state and the soldier lasted only as long as the new security demands, as illustrated by the British return towards the Liberal ideal of the small state and professional armed forces during the interwar period. In addition, this period warns of the inconsistent implementation of particular models of civil–military control as well as their inherent problems. The Liberal ideal of fragmenting the production of defence materiel among public and private producers thus led to problems with war profiteering in the UK and the USA. Moreover, the example of Germany shows how a strong independent defence industry can further weaken an already failing democratic regime if the balance between the state and the market is uneven. The next section examines how the resulting disillusionment with Liberalism and the beginning of the Cold War contributed to making the Republican model of centralized government and conscript armies the predominant ideal in Europe and North America between 1945 and the 1980s.

The Cold War and the warfare state

After the end of the Second World War two factors contributed to a more permanent transition to the Republican model of civil–military relations on both sides of the Atlantic.[79] The first was the beginning of the Cold War and the confrontations in Korea and Vietnam. The second was the rising popularity of the Republican model of the state illustrated by the emergence of Fordism and Keynesianism in the economic and

---

[77] *Ibid.*, pp. 119–22, p. 126.   [78] *Ibid.*, p. 108.
[79] Reppy, 'The United States', p. 22.

financial sectors. While the first factor ensured continued demand for large standing armed forces and armaments production, the latter influenced political decisions on how these new demands would be met.

In the UK the beginning of the Cold War perpetuated the central role of the state in the provision of national and international security. The high demand for armaments and troops to manage the German occupation, the superpower conflict and the increasingly volatile British colonies served as functional reasons.[80] However, it also reflected the degree to which the Republican model of civil–military relations had risen to prominence. The strong state was not only seen as more efficient and effective in providing weapons and soldiers, but also seemed better able to ensure democratic control over an expanded defence establishment than Liberal laissez-faire. The Republican ideals thus served to justify the growth of the British 'warfare state' which functionally intertwined the centralized government of public welfare and national security.[81] High public spending on national defence ensured security and enabled the state to facilitate employment, industrial development and trade. By 1957 40 per cent of all British civil servants worked for the MOD.[82] Moreover, when major private armaments firms failed during the economic recession of the 1970s, the government saved them through nationalization.[83] By the end of the decade the British government owned and managed six main armaments-producing companies and agencies, namely British Aerospace, British Shipbuilders, Rolls-Royce, Short Brothers, British Leyland and Royal Ordnance, with about 390,000 employees.[84] Although the private armaments sector remained sizeable with nearly 400,000 employees across the top nine companies alone, the UK government controlled and managed the private defence industry through its investment, custom and government assistance with armaments exports.[85]

---

[80] A. Farrar-Hockley, 'The Post-War Army 1945–1963', in D. Chandler and I. Beckett (eds.) *The Oxford History of the British Army* (Oxford: Oxford University Press, 1996), p. 316; H. Stanhope, *The Soldiers. An Anatomy of the British Army* (London: Hamish Hamilton, 1979), p. 14.

[81] Edgerton, *Warfare State*, p. 70.   [82] *Ibid.*

[83] A. Pierre, *The Global Politics of Arms Sales* (Princeton, NJ: Princeton University Press, 1982), p. 103.

[84] N. Ball, 'Appendix 1: The United Kingdom', in N. Ball and M. Leitenberg (eds.) *The Structure of the Defense Industry* (London: Croom Helm, 1983), p. 349; Pierre, *The Global Politics of Arms Sales*, p. 102.

[85] Ball, 'Appendix 1: The United Kingdom', p. 349; Pierre, *The Global Politics of Arms Sales*, pp. 103–4; P. Bishop, 'Competition and Collaboration in the Provision of Public Services: The Case of the UK Defence Sector', *Journal of Finance and Management in Public Service*, 3, no. 1 (2003), 15.

Republicanism also provided the ideological basis for the extension of the draft after 1945. Military service as citizen-soldiers had become 'an accepted institution, part of the pattern of British life'.[86] Although there was little direct threat to the UK homeland, Gallup polls indicated strong popular support for military service.[87] However, the popularity of the draft declined progressively over the next years because of the use of citizen-soldiers for purposes other than national defence. The perceived decrease in UK security needs after the end of the Korean War and the dissolution of the empire further undermined the belief in the necessity of universal conscription.[88] A growing proportion of young men 'viewed their compulsory term in the Forces as a sheer waste of time, resenting the interruption in their civilian studies or careers'.[89] When Parliament abolished the draft in favour of professional soldiers in 1962, it was a direct response to the changing security demands. The predominance of Republicanism, however, guaranteed that the state retained its role in the management of the defence economy.

In the USA the transition towards Republican models of the state and the soldier occurred after the end of the Second World War and with the conflicts over Korea and Vietnam. It was facilitated by the general popularity of the Republican ideal of centralized management across different policy sectors ranging from Fordism in economics to Keynesianism in finance. Two developments characterized the centralization of state control over the production and use of military force in the 1950s.[90] The first was the strengthening of public management of the national defence sector by the US government through a number of institutional reorganizations, including the Reorganization Plan No. 6, the Defense Reorganization Act and the expansion of the office of the Secretary of Defence under Robert McNamara.[91] The

---

[86] Barnett, *Britain and Her Army*, p. 487.
[87] Broad, *Conscription in Britain 1939–1964*, p. 110.
[88] F. Myers, 'British Trade Unions and the End of Conscription: The Tripartite Committee of 1950–56', *Journal of Contemporary History*, 31, no. 3 (1996), 511; M. S. Navias, 'Terminating Conscription? The British National Service Controversy 1955–56', *Journal of Contemporary History*, 24, no. 2 (1989), 201.
[89] Brereton, *The British Soldier*, p. 179.
[90] F. J. Cook, 'The Warfare State', *Annals of the American Academy of Political and Social Science*, 351 (1964), 102–9; K. L. Nelson, 'The Warfare State: History of a Concept', in C. W. Pursell, Jr. (ed.) *The Military-Industrial Complex* (New York: Harper & Row, 1972), pp. 15–30; Edgerton, *Warfare State*.
[91] S. Melman, 'Pentagon Capitalism', in C. W. Pursell, Jr. (ed.) *The Military-Industrial Complex* (New York: Harper & Row, 1977), p. 287, p. 294; S. Huntington, 'The Defense Establishment: Vested Interests and the Public Interest', in O. L. Carey (ed.) *The Military-Industrial Complex and U.S. Foreign Policy* (Pullman: Washington State University Press, 1969), p. 8.

second development was the massive expansion of public investment and spending on defence based on the theory of containment outlined in National Security Council Document 68 in 1950.[92] Whereas between 1947 and 1950 defence spending had hovered around 5 per cent of gross domestic product (GDP), after 1951 it more than doubled with averages around 10 per cent.[93] The increased state investment in defence and the military's interest in the exploitation of new technologies soon led to the emergence of private companies predominantly reliant on government contracts and armaments production.[94] Unlike in the UK, these companies remained in private ownership, but this did not necessarily restrict governmental control.[95] As the single customer of the defence industry, the government was able to 'set directly the specifications of the products sold in the market and the rules under which business [was] transacted'.[96] The careful spreading of government contracts across various companies was designed to preserve the ability to expand armaments production quickly in case of war.[97] In addition, the government provided the private industry with state-owned assets such as plants and equipment and subsidized the research, development and production of armaments.[98] By 1969 the value of government-owned property used by the main military contractors exceeded the companies' own investment.[99] To summarize, the government controlled the defence sector by three means: choice of products, investment and intervention in the internal management of

---

[92] M. J. Hogan, *A Cross of Iron. Harry S. Truman and the Origins of the National Security State, 1945–1954* (Cambridge: Cambridge University Press, 1998), pp. 291–305; Koistinen, *The Military-Industrial Complex*, p. 13.

[93] Huntington, 'The Defense Establishment', p. 6; Office of Management and Budget, *Historical Tables, Budget of the United States Government, Fiscal Year 2005* (Washington, DC, 2004), pp. 45–52.

[94] Huntington, 'The Defense Establishment', p. 3, p. 7; Reppy, 'The United States', p. 21, p. 23; M. L. Weidenbaum, 'The Military-Industrial Complex: An Economic Analysis', in O. L. Carey (ed.) *The Military-Industrial Complex and U.S. Foreign Policy* (Pullman: Washington State University Press, 1969), p. 30.

[95] Reppy, 'The United States', p. 23; also Weidenbaum, 'The Military-Industrial Complex', p. 34.

[96] Reppy, 'The United States', p. 25; also Weidenbaum, 'The Military-Industrial Complex', p. 31.

[97] Reppy, 'The United States', p. 28, 31.

[98] *Ibid.*, p. 31; Weidenbaum, 'The Military-Industrial Complex', p. 35; R. E. Lapp, 'The Military-Industrial Complex: 1969', in O. L. Carey (ed.) *The Military-Industrial Complex and U.S. Foreign Policy* (Pullman: Washington State University Press, 1969), p. 44; Melman, *Pentagon Capitalism*, pp. 79–80, pp. 87–92; J. S. Gansler, *The Defense Industry* (Cambridge, MA: MIT Press, 1980), p. 3; M. Pilisuk and T. Hayden, 'Is there a Military-Industrial Complex?', in C. W. Pursell, Jr. (ed.) *The Military-Industrial Complex* (New York: Harper & Row, 1972), p. 54.

[99] Weidenbaum, 'The Military-Industrial Complex', p. 35.

private armaments firms.[100] While the armaments industry remained primarily in private hands, the USA created its own version of the warfare state through the 'semi-nationalized' structure of the military–industrial complex.[101]

The rise of Republicanism in the USA also affected the model of soldier. For the first time in its history the USA adopted mass conscription of citizen-soldiers in the absence of a major threat to its homeland. However, similar to the UK, the increasing inequity of the draft and doubts over the legitimacy of interventions overseas progressively undermined the ideological rationale for the citizen-soldier model up to the 1970s.[102] As personnel needs declined during the course of the Vietnam War and as the baby boom generation reached drafting age, the proportion of eligible men who were enlisted fell from 58 per cent in 1954 to 22 per cent in 1961.[103] Moreover, the deferment of students, which had been introduced to ensure the training of qualified specialists, meant that the poor and African-American citizens disproportionally carried the burdens of conscription and death in Vietnam.[104] The least enfranchised groups of society provided the largest proportion of the national military. Several conferences in 1966 addressed the question of how to reform the system. They controversially debated the Republican and Liberal alternatives of the citizen-soldier and the professional soldier.[105] However, by that time the negative experience of the Vietnam War and the inequity of the conscription system had already discredited Republicanism in the eyes of most citizens. In 1973 the professional soldier superseded the citizen-soldier as the ideal model of the soldier in the USA.

In Germany the ideological outlook also shifted towards Republicanism after the end of the Second World War. Partially this was a consequence of the failure of the Liberal model of democratic

---

[100] Weidenbaum, 'The Military-Industrial Complex', p. 34; Melman, *Pentagon Capitalism*, pp. 37–70; Gansler, *The Defense Industry*, p. 5; J. E. Ullmann, 'The Military Industrial Firm – Private Enterprise Revised', *Policy Analysis*, 29 (9 November 1983).

[101] Weidenbaum, 'The Military-Industrial Complex', p. 34; see also W. Adams, 'The Military-Industrial Complex and the New Industrial State', in: C. W. Pursell, Jr. (ed.) *The Military-Industrial Complex* (New York: Harper & Row, 1972), p. 85.

[102] J. Burk, 'The Military Obligation of Citizens since Vietnam', *Parameters*, 31, no. 2 (2001), 48; Segal, *Recruiting for Uncle Sam*, p. 13.

[103] Burk, 'The Military Obligation of Citizens since Vietnam', 49.

[104] G. Q. Flynn, 'Conscription and Equity in Western Democracies, 1940–75', *Journal of Contemporary History*, 33, no. 1 (1998), 7–8; P. M. Shields, 'The Burden of the Draft: The Vietnam Years', *Journal of Political and Military Sociology*, 9, no. 3 (1981), 215–28; Segal, *Recruiting for Uncle Sam*, p. 35.

[105] Segal, *Recruiting for Uncle Sam*, pp. 35–6.

control under the Weimer Republic; partially it was due to the influence of the occupying powers on the institutional reorganization of German defence. While the UK turned to nationalization and the USA developed its military–industrial complex, Germany's Republican model of national security provision can be described as military corporatism. This model combined a close collaborative relationship between the state and a predominantly private defence industry with mass conscription of citizen-soldiers.

Initially, German state involvement in the armaments sector ceased after the end of the Nazi regime. Allied occupation laws prohibited the manufacture of arms and major private armaments companies such as Krupp temporarily withdrew from the sector.[106] When in 1951 the ban was lifted and the decision was taken to rearm West Germany, it was conducted under Allied control and within the context of a private defence industry. Only in 1955 did a democratic West German government acquire independent control over armaments production and the Bundeswehr. It decided to maintain the predominantly private structure of the industry.[107] In 1977 only five of the top thirty armaments-producing companies in West Germany were fully or partially owned by the federal or state governments, namely Messerschmidt-Bölkow-Blohm (MBB), Vereinigte Flugtechnische Werke-Fokker, Howaldtswerke-Deutsche Werft (HDW), Zahnradfabrik Friedrichshaften and Industrie-anlagenbetriebsgesellschaft München.[108] The defence sector was nevertheless shaped by centralized government intervention and control. A lack of competitive tendering for military contracts, with competitive contracts amounting only to 2–4 per cent, permitted the government to decide which companies would survive in the long term.[109] In addition, the West German government intervened in the defence industry in an attempt to prevent private companies from becoming too dependent upon armaments production.[110] The reform of decision-making structures within the MOD and the Bundeswehr further strengthened central democratic control over the military establishment. Specifically, the German constitution subjected the defence spending and the reformed Bundeswehr to tight parliamentary control.[111]

---

[106] M. Brzoska, 'The Federal Republic of Germany', in N. Ball and M. Leitenberg (eds.) *The Structure of the Defense Industry* (London: Croom Helm, 1983), pp. 111–39.

[107] *Ibid.*, p. 111, 131; Bontrup and Zdrowomyslaw, *Die Deutsche Rüstungsindustrie*, p. 131.

[108] Brzoska, 'The Federal Republic of Germany', p. 126–7.

[109] *Ibid.*, p. 117.

[110] *Ibid.*, p. 129.

[111] M. Küllmer, *The Current State on Civil-Military Relations in Germany*, Paper presented at the First Swiss Summer School on Democratic Governance of Civil-Military Relations, 23–30 August 2003, p. 1.

With regard to its armed forces, the German government decided that the Republican model of the citizen-soldier offered the best insurance against another abuse of military power by undemocratic elements. In concession to the need for military expertise, however, the seed of the new Bundeswehr consisted of 150,000 volunteers, most of whom had previously served in the Reichswehr. The introduction of a universal military service of twelve months for all young men in the following year countered fears that this might lead to a revival of the old military structures.[112] The aim was to create an armed force that was not only socially and politically representative of society, but also fully integrated with it.[113] In addition, the government democratized the internal structure and outlook of the West German armed forces. The new concept of 'Internal Leadership' included ideological education based on the traditional Republican model of the citizen-soldier. This model characterized the new German soldier as a 'citizen in uniform' whose role in the armed forces was defined by civic duty and who combined political and military roles.[114] To emphasize the essentially civilian character of the citizen-soldier, the government modelled the rights of the soldier after civilian law, adjudicated in civilian courts.[115] Another aim of the citizen-soldier model was to ensure that the Bundeswehr would not be used for military aggression.[116] According to the Law of the Soldier, the duty of each soldier pertained only to the defence of West Germany and its democratic constitution.[117]

While in the UK and the USA the use of citizen-soldiers abroad and the increasing inequity of conscription undermined the popular appeal of the model in the 1960s and 1970s, in Germany the Republican ideal of the citizen-soldier remained untainted. A governmental force structure review in 1973 did not rule out a future 'examination of the conversion of the Bundeswehr to an All Volunteer Force', but concluded that the existing security environment precluded any such a move for the time being.[118] The draft had become a 'virtually uncontested'

---

[112] M. Kitchen, *A Military History of Germany from the Eighteenth Century to the Present Day* (London: Weidenfeld and Nicolson, 1975), pp. 337–8.

[113] Kitchen, *A Military History of Germany*, p. 338; K. Longhurst, 'Resisting Change: The Politics of Conscription in Contemporary Germany', in P. Joenniemi (ed.) *The Changing Face of European Conscription* (Aldershot: Ashgate, 2006), p. 87.

[114] Longhurst, 'Resisting Change', p. 87; Kitchen, *A Military History of Germany*, p. 341.

[115] Hartmann, *Geist und Haltung des Deutschen Soldaten im Wandel der Gesellschaft*, p. 215.

[116] Freiherr vom Stein Gesellschaft (ed.) *Der Fahneneid. Die Stellung des Soldaten in Staat und Gesellschaft. Ein Cappenberger Gespräch* (Cologne: Grote, 1970), p. 87.

[117] Hartmann, *Geist und Haltung des Deutschen Soldaten im Wandel der Gesellschaft*, p. 213.

[118] Longhurst, 'Resisting Change', p. 88.

part of the Bundeswehr and the national understanding of the armed forces, and provided up to 200,000 conscripts every year.[119] Although the professional officer corps remained somewhat distinct from German society in terms of social background and political preferences with a clear majority from the upper and middle classes with conservative leanings, conscription helped to alleviate these differences at least among the ranks.[120] Conscripts also provided a bridge between the armed forces and society, both by being educated in civic responsibility and in turn educating their civilian families and friends about the military.

In summary, the Cold War period perhaps demonstrates best the importance of ideology for civil–military relations in the UK, the USA and Germany. Although this period saw the relative decrease of the threat to national security compared to the two World Wars, all three countries strengthened the central role of the state in the management of the defence establishment and continued with the mass conscription of citizen-soldiers. The turn towards Republican models of the state and the soldier is particularly revealing in the USA, which even during the two World Wars had relied on public–private collaboration for the management of its military sector. But the UK and Germany also demonstrate the role of ideological factors, notably their respective disillusionment with Liberal civil–military control mechanisms during the First World War and the Weimar Republic. The next section examines the rise of Neoliberalism at the beginning of the 1980s and its role in the return of private businesses as key players in national and international security.

Neoliberalism and the emergence of security governance in the 1980s

While Republican ideals of civil–military relations predominated during the first decades of the Cold War, by the 1980s Neoliberalism led to the questioning of the efficiency and accountability of centralized government of national and international security in the UK and the USA. Although the period of détente with the Soviet Union had come to an end and the emergence of the Second Cold War would have suggested strong support for the continuation of the warfare state, centralized government was no longer viewed as the most appropriate form of national and international security provision. Neoliberalism promised greater cost efficiency and responsiveness to private interests by

---

[119] *Ibid.*   [120] Kitchen, *A Military History of Germany*, p. 344.

rolling back the state. Rather than a public supply of essential services, it advocated the market as the ideal mechanism for satisfying citizens' needs, including security. In return, Neoliberalism promised to reduce citizens' obligations vis-à-vis the state, including taxation and military service.

In the UK the Conservative Prime Minister Margaret Thatcher (1979–90) made Neoliberalism her election programme, promising to dismantle the British warfare state.[121] Before the election the Conservative Party had expressed its determination to 'sell back into private ownership the recently nationalized aerospace and shipbuilding concerns'.[122] According to the Neoliberal agenda set by the Thatcher government, the privatization and fragmentation of the defence industry would promote increased competition and, thereby, efficiency.[123] The denationalization of the national armaments industry included the privatization of British Aerospace (BAE) and Rolls-Royce, the sale of the Royal Ordnance Factories to Vickers and BAE, and the operation of the Royal Dockyards at Devonport and Rosyth by private contractors.[124] Whereas in 1979 the British military establishment was dominated by state ownership, the 1980s saw the fragmentation of the defence sector between public and private providers.

To ensure the democratic control of the reprivatized industries, the British government initially retained a 'special share' in the companies. However, this did not give the government any role in the 'management, development and profitability of the business'.[125] In addition to privatizing the UK defence industry, the Thatcher government promoted the outsourcing of support services by the armed forces. Key was the administration's market-testing policy which encouraged competition between state and private providers with contracts being awarded to the private sector if it offered better value for money. From 1985 the MOD was required to 'market test' all catering, cleaning, laundry, security-guarding and minor maintenance services, and the policy was later expanded to engineering, supply, training and operations

---

[121] G. Macdonald, 'Reform of UK Defense Procurement and State/Industry Relationships during the 1980s and 1990s', *Defense Analysis*, 15, no. 1 (1999), 3.

[122] M. Bell, 'Defence Industry Privatization: The British Case', *NATO Colloquium*, Brussels, 29–30 June 1994; J. Foreman-Peck, 'The Privatization of Industry in Historical Perspective', *Journal of Law and Society*, 16, no. 1 (1989), 140.

[123] P. Bishop, 'Competition and Collaboration in the Provision of Public Services', 15; W. Walker and P. Gummett, 'Britain and the European Armaments Market', *International Affairs*, 65, no. 3 (1989), 421.

[124] T. Taylor and K. Hayward, *The U.K. Defence Industrial Base* (London: Brassey's, 1989), p. 74.

[125] Bell, 'Defence Industry Privatization: The British Case'.

support.[126] In addition, the government increased competitive tendering, and replaced cost-plus with fixed-price contracts and commercial off-the-shelf procurement.[127] In order to facilitate this, the government abolished the 'buy British' principle and expanded the supplier base to overseas firms.[128] The reforms also transferred decision-making responsibility towards private companies. Rather than directing the development and provision of national defence materiel and services itself, the government adopted a hands-off policy and acted as a customer rather than manager of the defence establishment.[129] The delegation of operational decision-making authority for large-scale projects to prime contractors was aimed at reducing management cost, transfering risk, and increasing economic flexibility.[130]

The rise of Neoliberalism also affected the ideal of the soldier. At first, these changes became apparent in the increased focus on personal freedom, rights and choice, and the emergence of 'nine-to-fiveism', the UK equivalent to the 'occupational' attitudes of professional soldiers in the USA.[131] Later, it resulted in the emergence of a new type of soldier: the private military contractor. Within the context of 'rolling-back' the warfare state, the private military contractor offered a way of implementing Neoliberal principles in the armed forces. Civilian positions were the first to be cut or replaced, reducing the number of civil servants in the MOD by 40 per cent between 1979 and 1990.[132] However, the professional soldier model also increasingly came under pressure. Arguing that private military contractors could provide support functions more cost-efficiently, the UK government progressively relieved professional soldiers of duties such as logistics, management

[126] M. Kaldor, *Rethinking British Defence Policy and its Economic Implications*, Sussex European Institute, Working Paper, no. 8, February 1995, p. 35; E. M. Pint, J. R. Bondawella, J. Cave, R. Hart, D. Keyser, *Public-Private Partnerships Background Papers for the U.S.–U.K. Conference on Military Installations, Assets, Operations and, Services* (Santa Monica, CA: RAND, 2001), p. 8.
[127] Taylor and Hayward, *The U.K. Defence Industrial Base*, pp. 74–6.
[128] Bishop, 'Competition and Collaboration in the Provision of Public Services', 15; Taylor and Hayward, *The U.K. Defence Industrial Base*, p. 74; Macdonald, 'Reform of UK Defense Procurement and State/Industry Relationships during the 1980s and 1990s', 7.
[129] R. Smith, 'Defence Procurement and the Industrial Structure in the U.K.', *International Journal of Industrial Organization*, 8, no 2. (1990), 195; Macdonald, 'Reform of UK Defense Procurement and State/Industry Relationships', 6.
[130] R. Matthews and J. Parker, 'Prime Contracting in Major Defense Contracts', *Defense Analysis*, 15, no. 1 (1999), 28; Walker and Gummett, 'Britain and the European Armaments Market', p. 421.
[131] C. Dandeker, 'The United Kingdom: The Overstretched Military', in C. C. Moskos, J. A. Williams and D. R. Segal (eds.) *The Postmodern Military* (Oxford: Oxford University Press, 2000), p. 43.
[132] *Ibid.*, pp. 35–6.

and training. While the theoretical rationale was that this would allow the professional armed forces to focus on combat operations, the practical implication was that private military contractors took the place of professional soldiers in nearly all other areas of defence.[133]

In the USA the 1970s had already witnessed a growing criticism of Republicanism which had joined military and state interests in the form of a military–industrial complex.[134] The military–industrial complex became synonymous with waste, overspending and bureaucratic overregulation. When Ronald Reagan was elected president in 1981, he stood, like Thatcher, for a Neoliberal ideology which aimed to control the state by cutting back government spending and involvement in the provision of public services. In contradiction to his Neoliberal economic programme, however, Reagan also advocated and implemented one of the largest increases in military investments since the two World Wars. This contradiction has led some authors to consider the 1980s in terms of a resurgence of the warfare state and 'military Keynesianism'.[135] Several observations suggest instead that Reagan's policies 'bridged military eras' and effectively prepared the transformation from the Republican model of centralized government to the Neoliberal ideal of fragmented and marketized security governance in the USA.[136] Although the defence budget increased in percentage of GDP during the first Reagan administration, state spending in other public sectors such as health and education declined significantly.[137] Unlike previous Republican Party presidents, Reagan promoted a change in the conception of the appropriate role of the state in the provision of public goods. According to this model, a small state was good and cutting taxes was a way to reduce its scope and create conditions for the market to step in.

Reagan's Neoliberal policies initially targeted the social services, but by the mid 1980s their logic was increasingly also applied to the military sector. The Competition in Contracting Act 1984 and two subsequent acts in 1986 had a major impact on military procurement by simplifying acquisitions regulations, eliminating military specifications and requiring 'the military services to use competition in contracting

[133] *Ibid.*, pp. 35–6.
[134] Koistinen, *The Military-Industrial Complex*, p. 18.
[135] I. Wallerstein, 'Foes and Friends?' *Foreign Policy*, 90 (1993), 149–50.
[136] G. Schneider and R. Merle, 'Reagan's Defence Buildup Bridged Military Eras', *Washington Post*, 9 June 2004.
[137] M. S. Kamlet, D. C. Mowery and T.-T. Su, 'Upsetting National Priorities? The Reagan Administration's Budgetary Strategy', *The American Political Science Review*, 82, no. 4 (1988), 1294.

in increasing amounts each year'.[138] In addition to promoting a greater reliance on the resources and expertise of private defence contractors for the development, production and provision of military equipment and services, Reagan's reforms expanded the organizational autonomy of private armaments firms and thus their impact on decision-making and security policy implementation.[139]

Reagan also 'rejected the collectivist assumptions of compulsory military service and found that an all-volunteer military force shaped by labour market dynamics was more compatible with its ethic of individualism'.[140] A number of changes within the concept of the professional soldier reflected the growing appeal of a Neoliberal ideology which placed rights over obligations, individualism over the collective, and the market over the state. Most important was the emergence of an 'occupational' view of the military profession among soldiers.[141] As part of this occupational view, motivation for joining the armed forces became increasingly focused on individual and economic benefits such as education, healthcare provisions, pensions, salary, adventure, travel and work experience rather than abstract notions of patriotic duty.[142] The military itself began to adopt a more individualistic, market-oriented approach towards the recruitment and management of its professional soldiers. Recruitment campaigns sounded more like holiday advertisements than campaigns for military enlistment. As a navy advertisement went: 'It's not just a job, it's flight exercise in Hawaii, the Caribbean and Hong Kong.' On the positive side, the Neoliberal concern with individual rights played a major role in the growing recognition of the rights of women and homosexuals, and the status gained by diverse religious groups in the armed forces.[143] Most importantly, as

---

[138] T. L. McNaugher, 'Weapons Procurement. The Futility of Reform', *International Security*, 12, no. 2 (1987), 101. See also S. V. Reeves, *The Ghosts of Acquisition Reform: Past, Present and Future* (Washington DC: The Industrial College of the Armed Forces, National Defence University, 1999), p. 22.

[139] The President's Blue Ribbon Commission on Defense Management, *A Quest for Excellence. Final Report to the President* (Washington DC, June 1986), p. xi; G. Schneider and R. Merle, 'Reagan's Defence Buildup Bridged Military Eras', *Washington Post*, 9 June 2004.

[140] Segal, *Recruiting for Uncle Sam*, p. 16.

[141] C. Moskos, 'What Ails the All-Volunteer Force: An Institutional Perspective', *Parameters*, 31, no. 2 (2001), 29–47; see also S. C. Sarkesian, J. A. Williams and F. B. Bryant, *Soldiers, Society, and National Security* (Boulder, CO: Lynne Rienner, 1995), p. 14.

[142] Segal, *Recruiting for Uncle Sam*, p. 64.

[143] Charles Moskos describes these changes as 'postmodern', but essentially they are based on liberal ideals. See C. C. Moskos, 'Towards a Postmodern Military?' in C. C. Moskos, J. A. Williams and D. R. Segal (eds.) *The Postmodern Military* (Oxford: Oxford University Press, 2000), pp. 3–26.

in the UK, private military contractors increasingly replaced professional soldiers in military support functions.[144] Although the United States Code, Title 10 sets clear limits to the outsourcing of military services, for instance by requiring that at least 60 per cent of depot maintenance had to be performed by Federal employees and by mandating public–private competitions before work in excess of $3 million could be outsourced, the aim was to substitute professional soldiers in all functions that could be provided more cost-efficiently by private military contractors.[145]

In Germany, by contrast, the Republican ideals of the state and the soldier remained relatively popular during the 1980s. Although government ownership declined to minority shares in only two out of the top twenty-seven companies, namely MBB and HDW, the defence industry maintained its close relations with the German government.[146] Competitive tendering continued to be limited and cost-plus contracts common.[147] The government de facto subsidized national armaments firms such as the military dockyards, which had suffered from the economic downturn of the late 1970s, in order to stem large-scale redundancies.[148] Owing to pressure from the industry and from labour organizations, export controls were interpreted more liberally and sales to the developing world increased.[149] In fact, the German government began to actively promote and facilitate armaments exports through public credits and lobbying of other states.[150] Although the government encouraged the conversion from military to civilian production in order to cut excess capacities, it remained committed to a minimum national defence industry to prevent international dependence. Consolidation and international armaments cooperation provided mechanisms for maintaining basic capacities. However, they also increased the mutual dependence and potential for collusion between the government and the industry. Greater efficiency was considered less important than control over the national armaments industry and employment. In the

[144] T. L. McNaugher, 'Weapons Procurement. The Futility of Reform', p. 101. See also Reeves, *The Ghosts of Acquisition Reform*, p. 22.
[145] United States Code, Title 10, Section 2466, cited in DOD, *Improving the Combat Edge Through Outsourcing* (Washington DC: March 1996), p. 15.
[146] Bontrup and Zdrowomyslaw, *Die Deutsche Rüstungsindustrie*, p. 142, p. 146.
[147] Brzoska, 'The Federal Republic of Germany', p. 133.
[148] P. Lock (undated) *Perspektiven der Rüstungsindustrie in Deutschland. Entmythologisierung eines Filzgiganten*, at: www.friedenskooperative.de; M. Brzoska, 'The Erosion of Restraint in West German Arms Transfer Policy', *Journal of Peace Research*, 26, no. 2 (1989), 168.
[149] Pierre, *The Global Politics of Arms Sales*, p. 111.
[150] Brzoska, 'The Erosion of Restraint in West German Arms Transfer Policy', 165.

Bundeswehr an increasing number of young men eligible for conscription chose conscientious objection and civil service over military duty. However, the government and the Bundeswehr continued to insist on the Republican principle of civic obligation.[151] Moreover, a majority of citizens expressed their preference for a conscript army over professional armed forces.

In summary, the 1980s demonstrate how the growing popularity of Neoliberalism can help explain transformations in democratic civil–military relations despite the absence of major changes in the security environment. In no other era has an ideology played such an explicit role in shaping government policies with regard to changes in the models of the state and the soldier and with such radical consequences for the provision of national and international security. Moreover, the persistence of Republican ideals in Germany helps us to understand why its government did not follow the example of its Anglo-American allies.

Civil–military transformations and democratic control

As the preceding analysis has illustrated, changing ideological preferences for particular models of the state and the soldier have stemmed from three factors: transformations in the security environment, problems with the implementation of these models and the internal weaknesses of these ideologies. In this section the last two factors are of particular interest because they concern the democratic control over the use of collective armed force. The analysis has indicated that in historical practice both sets of models have been less successful than each ideology has promised. The introduction of new models or new security challenges has often led to disillusionment and criticism which have ultimately facilitated shifts from one model of civil–military control to another. In order to understand the likely causes of civil–military change as well as the main weaknesses of the Republican and Liberal models of the state, the citizen and the soldier, this section discusses the main issues of democratic control and accountability which have surfaced during the past three centuries.

The most successful period appears to have been the eighteenth and nineteenth centuries when the national security apparatuses and defence production within the newly emerging democracies were limited in size

---

[151] 'Die Wehrpflicht steht für die Bereitschaft der Bürger, persönlich Mitverantwortung für den Schutz ihres Gemeinwesens zu übernehmen', at: www.bundeswehr.de.

and most easily controlled by the government and the citizens. With the growth of national security demands and the military sector in the twentieth century popular democratic control became more difficult. Thus, after the First World War the Liberal ideal of fragmenting the control and ownership of the production of armaments between state agencies and private businesses came under growing critique. Accusations of war profiteering were so pervasive that both the UK and the USA set up government commissions to investigate the behaviour of private firms during the war. In the UK the Royal Commission on the Manufacture of and Trade in Armaments did not have the power to investigate the actions of UK firms, but it provided an important impetus for a public discussion of the advantages and disadvantages of the Liberal model between 1935 and 1939.[152] In this debate large sections of the public and leading political figures, such as the former Minister of Munitions Lloyd George, supported a transition towards the Republican model of centralized state control through the nationalization of the armaments sector in order to prevent future abuses.[153] Although the UK government largely ignored the final report of the Commission, the expression and organization of popular concern about the lack of control over the private armaments sector contributed to the transition from Liberal governance to the Republican model of centralized state control over the military sector. In the USA the mixture of Republican and Liberal governance through the WIB came under similar scrutiny by the Nye Committee. In 1936 the Nye Committee published its results, revealing mismanagement and the growing collusion between businesses and the military. The report specifically criticized the leading role of businessmen in the WIB because 'conflicts of interest were rife, and few safeguards existed to insure that the board operated for the larger public interests'.[154] The Nye Committee concluded that the US model was inadequate to ensure public accountability and control and proposed the nationalization of munitions production and the limitation of profits to 3 per cent in other defence-related sectors.[155] As in the UK, however, the Second World War intervened and major changes were not implemented until the 1950s.[156]

---

[152] For a detailed analysis of the work of the Commission see Anderson, 'British Rearmament and the "Merchants of Death"', 5–37.

[153] *Ibid.*, p. 17–19.

[154] Koistinen, *The Military-Industrial Complex*, p. 10, pp. 11–12.

[155] *Ibid.*, p. 57–8.

[156] E. A. Molander, 'Historical Antecedents of Military-Industrial Criticisms', in B. Franklin Cooling (ed.) *War, Business, and American Society. Historical Perspectives on the Military-Industrial Complex* (Port Washington, NY: Kennikat Press, 1977), p. 184.

The Republican model of centralized state control over the military establishment that was established in the aftermath of the Second World War did not fare much better. By the end of the 1970s the British warfare state and the US military–industrial complex had become synonymous with 'excessive cost, burgeoning military budgets, and scandalous performances'.[157] The 'cosy' relationship between the armed forces and industry was blamed for reducing competition between alternative suppliers and for cost-plus contracting which allowed major firms to negotiate inflated prices.[158] Government efforts to manage and control the private armaments sector created overregulation and stifled innovation.[159] Nationalization, the provision of state-owned assets to private armaments firms and public investments increased the stakes of governments in the performance of the defence industry.[160] Rather than facilitating democratic control over armaments production and exports, governments became sponsors and advocates of their national defence establishments at home and abroad.[161] The ascent of Neoliberalism in the 1980s was a direct response to these problems. It promised to re-establish democratic control, cost efficiency and responsiveness to the demands of the citizens by turning public and private security providers from collaborators into competitors.

The competing Republican and Liberal models of the soldier have also found their limits during the past three centuries. The Republican citizen-soldier has been particularly susceptible to critique because the model proposes universal military service which can only be justified by national emergencies. In addition, the equitable implementation of the citizen-soldier model has always been crucial for its acceptance. Several times in European and North American modern history, the use of conscripts in foreign interventions overseas and the unequal drafting of different segments of society have contributed to undermining public support for the citizen-soldier. The first time was during the American Civil War when violent riots erupted in several Northern states due to a regulation that permitted the rich to avoid the draft by paying a sizeable fee. As a result of the protests, the government refrained from fully enforcing conscription and abolished it immediately after

---

[157] Senator William Proxmire cited in Lapp, 'The Military-Industrial Complex: 1969', p. 42. For the UK, compare Bishop, 'Competition and Collaboration in the Provision of Public Services', p. 15.

[158] Weidenbaum, 'The Military-Industrial Complex', p. 32, p. 36; Lapp, 'The Military-Industrial Complex: 1969', p. 44.

[159] Weidenbaum, 'The Military-Industrial Complex', pp. 36–7.

[160] Ibid., p. 35; Lapp, 'The Military-Industrial Complex: 1969', p. 43.

[161] Gansler, The Defense Industry, p. 26.

the war.[162] In the 1960s and 1970s the UK and the USA faced similar problems when two issues came together. Firstly, there were growing public doubts concerning the legitimacy of military interventions abroad, such as in Britain's former colonies and the US involvement in Vietnam. Secondly, the post-Second World War baby boom generation created a surplus of possible conscripts and forced the armed forces to become more selective in their drafting policies. Together they increasingly discredited the citizen-soldier army in the eyes of the public, with the consequence that the UK abandoned conscription in 1962 and the USA in 1973. The difficulty of maintaining an equitable draft has also not boded well for Germany, which has struggled with high birth rates and declining personnel needs since the 1980s. Ironically, its citizen-army has so far been saved by the growing number of young men who choose civil rather than military service.

The professional soldier model has historically been challenged primarily on the basis of its democratic credentials. In the UK in the nineteenth century the professional soldier model helped to preserve a regular army that was controlled by the aristocracy who mistreated the ranks. The small size of the regular army, the existence of alternative forces in the citizens' militia and volunteers and a well-established democratic political system prevented any abuses of military power. However, growing criticism of the accountability and control of the professional armed forces led to several reforms to increase the civilian authority over the military, and improve the working conditions and access to the officer corps for the lower classes. The German Weimar Republic did not fare as well with its more unified professional armed forces. Dominated by a monarchist officer corps and an antidemocratic outlook, the professional military weakened the democratic government and contributed to Hitler's rise to power. After the end of the Second World War, German rearmament was therefore based on the ideal of the Republican citizen-soldier. The close integration of the military with society and the education of citizen-soldiers in their democratic rights and duties through Internal Leadership became guiding principles for the Bundeswehr.

The role of private contractors employed in military functions by democratic armed forces was too small in the nineteenth and for most of the twentieth century to attract much criticism. Private firms supplied an increasing range of military equipment, but citizen-soldiers or professional soldiers typically filled most civilian and military support roles for all types of military operations. Only during war or in the British

[162] Segal, *Recruiting for Uncle Sam*, pp. 25–6.

colonies did private contractors take over critical services such as logistics or combat support.[163] The limited functional rationale which led to the employment of private auxiliaries in these circumstances meant that private contractors were not considered a distinct model of soldier that might replace citizen-soldiers or professionals. Also the question of democratic control and accountability did not enter public debate. Nevertheless, a range of problems with private contractors emerged. The main problems were profiteering and general unreliability due to the armed forces' lack of control over private military contractors. Profiteering was rife during conflicts when the military depended upon military contractors to meet shortfalls in personnel which were created by the strict limitation of military personnel in peacetime. But private contractors also exploited their position for profit at home, such as by lowering the standards of their services. The poor diet provided by private catering, for instance, led to all UK Army canteens being put under regimental control in 1863.[164] In addition, it was not unusual that the behaviour of private contractors was unsatisfactory or endangered military operations. In fact, 'military authorities periodically despaired of the calibre and motivations of these men, who were not bound by military discipline, sometimes failed to work at the rate or the manner expected of them, and, in some wars, were prone to desert.'[165]

Conclusion

Private military contractors are not new in history, but within the context of modern democracy their re-emergence cannot be fully explained without considering the ideological foundations of this development. In order to be publicly accepted, the proliferation of private military firms has to be legitimized by a model of the state that justifies the devolution of the production and control over armed force to private actors. This chapter has examined how the alternative visions of civil–military relations proposed by Republicanism and Liberalism have influenced varying models of the state, the citizen and the soldier in the UK, the USA and Germany from the eighteenth to the twentieth century. Although the international security environment and national threat perception have determined the demand for security, it has demonstrated that how

[163] Spiers, *The Late Victorian Army 1868–1902*, p. 295.
[164] Brereton, *The British Soldier*, p. 66, p. 68.
[165] Spiers, *The Late Victorian Army 1868–1902*, p. 294.

different countries have responded to this demand has been influenced by the predominant ideological preferences at the time.

Moreover, the preceding analysis has shown that neither set of models is perfect. While the primary objective of both theoretical ideals is to ensure the democratic accountability and control of the production and use of the collective means of violence, historical practice has illustrated the shortcomings of each. The Republican ideal of centralized government has been criticized for overregulation, bureaucratization and cost-expansion. The Liberal model of fragmented and privatized governance has been faulted for unresponsiveness to national security needs and profiteering. Similarly, their competing conceptions of the soldier have their own flaws. The citizen-soldier model frequently lacks the conditions for its consistent implementation through universal conscription and is not suitable for security challenges beyond a state's national borders. The professional soldier has been challenged over its support for democracy and the growing gap between the armed forces and society. Lastly, private contractors have been prone to profiteering and unsatisfactory services. In order to understand what these observations mean for the growing role of private military companies and the democratic control and accountability of the armed forces, the second part of this book examines in detail the changing roles and relations of the state and the soldier in the UK, the USA, Germany and international interventions since the end of the Cold War.

4   United Kingdom: private financing and the management of security

The UK has been one of the first countries to privatize and outsource significant proportions of its national defence establishment since the rise of Neoliberalism in the 1980s. More than two decades later the UK still stands out in terms of the scale to which private businesses are involved in national defence. The UK armed forces have contracted out military and technical support services, the management of military bases and most of its training, and rely on the private financing of military installations and equipment. In fact, the UK government has almost entirely abandoned the notions that there are core functions of the state, excluded, as a matter of principle, from private sector supply, or that there are major differences between professional soldiers and private military contractors. This chapter analyses the scale of military outsourcing and the increasing replacement of professional armed forces with private military contractors in the UK in terms of the dimensions discussed in the preceding chapters. It illustrates that the fragmentation of security provision among public and private providers cannot be fully comprehended without reference to the underlying ideological transformations. These developments have helped present Thatcher's turn to Neoliberalism as the continuation of a Liberal political tradition dating back to the nineteenth century. The expansion of the private military sector under Thatcher's Conservative successor John Major (1990–7) and the New Labour governments of Tony Blair (1997–2007) and Gordon Brown (2007–) has evolved within this shared ideological context, in spite of divergent party-political affiliations. The conviction that the private sector is in most cases superior and more cost-efficient than the state and the armed forces has united all three administrations.[1]

While the rise of the Neoliberal models of the state and the soldier at the beginning of the 1980s occurred independently from any major

[1] T. Taylor, 'Contractor on Deployed Operations and Equipment Support', *Defence Studies*, 4, no. 2 (2004), 185.

changes in the UK security environment, the end of the Cold War has since led to the perception that these models are more suitable for the new security context. Specifically, the end of the Cold War has led to public demands for a peace dividend and cuts in military personnel, supporting the Neoliberal call for a reduction of the public defence establishment and the armed forces. Moreover, Neoliberalism has offered to address the presumed short-term security demands which have arisen from multiple military interventions in the former Yugoslavia, Somalia, Afghanistan and Iraq with the temporary hire of private military contractors rather than an increase in professional soldiers, allowing the UK to 'punch above its weight'.[2]

While the functional reasons for the outsourcing of military services in the UK have been discussed elsewhere, the ideological foundations of the changing roles and relations of the state and the soldier have so far been under-examined.[3] To address this gap, this chapter analyses the evolution in the models of the state, the citizen and the soldier in the UK since 1990. The first section reviews the ideological rationale for this transformation from Thatcherism to New Labour's 'Third Way'; the second section analyses the implementation of these programmes and their impact on the provision of national defence;[4] the third section debates how these changes have affected the model of the professional soldier; finally, the fourth section discusses the consequences of Neoliberal governance and the changing concept of the soldier for the democratic control of the armed forces in the UK.

Thatcherism, the Third Way and the military

The ideological foundations for the outsourcing of a wide range of military services and functions, and the elevation of the private sector to a key financier of armed forces facilities and equipment in the UK can be found in the rise of Neoliberalism. It suggests that private firms can not only supply public services more cost-efficiently and effectively than states, but also are more responsive to the demands of the citizens.[5] The associated transformation of the roles of the state and the soldier from

[2] E. Krahmann, 'United Kingdom: Punching Above Its Weight' in E. J. Kirchner and J. Sperling (eds.) *Global Security Governance. Competing Perceptions of Security in the 21st Century* (London: Routledge, 2007), pp. 93–112; C. Dandeker and L. Freedman, 'The British Armed Services', *The Political Quarterly*, 73, no. 4 (2002), 468.
[3] C. Kinsey, *Corporate Soldiers and International Security: The Rise of Private Military Companies* (London: Routledge, 2006).
[4] The international use of private military contractors by the UK armed forces will be examined in detail in Chapter 7.
[5] Taylor, 'Contractor on Deployed Operations and Equipment Support', 185.

the Republican model of the centralized warfare state to the Neoliberal ideal of fragmented governance began with Thatcher. However, her successors Major and Blair further elaborated upon these Neoliberal models, using them as the basis for an expansion of the private sector contribution to national and international defence.

The overwhelming ideological predominance of Neoliberalism since the 1980s has been a particular feature of the UK, expressed by a nearly unquestioning support for the privatization and fragmentation of security governance among successive governments and, presumably, the majority of citizens. In contrast to the USA and Germany, where governments have continued to debate what constitutes the inherent functions of the state and the armed forces, which should not be outsourced to the private sector, such a discussion has been largely missing in the public and political discourses of the UK. The post-Cold War period has instead seen the normalization of the Neoliberal model of security governance with its preference for the outsourcing and privatization of military functions. Prime Minister John Major made the greatest ideological and practical inroads towards strengthening the contribution of private firms to the supply of public services. In particular, the Major administration introduced two policies which revolutionized the role of the private sector in the UK: the Competing for Quality programme and the Private Finance Initiative (PFI).

In 1991 the Competing for Quality White Paper revised and expanded Thatcher's market-testing programme, which aimed to improve governmental efficiency by requiring competition between in-house and private bidders for service delivery.[6] It differentiated between three sets of services: services that were inappropriate for government and should be eliminated or privatized; services that were unsuitable for government delivery and should be contracted out; and services that were appropriate for government and should be decentralized and subjected to market-testing. In order to encourage the implementation of the Competing for Quality programme, the government set numerical market-testing targets for all departments and agencies.[7] In the MOD this included submitting third and fourth line logistic support to competitive bids with private businesses and the signing of a growing number of prime contracts for facilities management.[8]

[6] HM Treasury, *Competing for Quality: Buying Better Public Services*, Cm 1730 (London: HMSO, 1991). See also E. M. Pint, J. R. Bondawella, J. Cave, R. Hart, D. Keyser, *Public-Private Partnerships: Background Papers for the U.S.–U.K. Conference on Military Installations, Assets, Operations, and Services* (Santa Monica, CA: RAND, 2001), p. 7.

[7] Pint *et al.*, *Public-Private Partnerships*, p. 9.

[8] M. Uttley, 'Private Contractors on Deployed Operations: The United Kingdom Experience', *Defence Studies*, 4, no. 2 (2004), 147.

The PFI, introduced in 1992 and still in place nearly two decades later, has presented an even more radical innovation.[9] The explicit aim of the PFI has been to 'increase private sector involvement in the provision of public services'.[10] To achieve this objective, it proposes the use of private rather than government capital to finance the design, building and operation of armed forces' facilities and equipment. Similar to leasing, the private financiers are remunerated by 'a stream of committed revenue payments for the use of the facilities over the contract period'.[11] However, because of the huge start-up cost of military assets such as bases, ships and aeroplanes, the contract period is typically much longer than in the private sector, covering ten to twenty years, in order to be attractive to private firms. Moreover, depending on the terms of the contract, the facilities or equipment can remain with the private sector rather than being turned over to government ownership. The MOD initially identified six potential areas for the application of PFI: training, equipment, property and accommodation, support services, utilities and IT. Two years later the MOD had signed twenty-two PFI contracts with a total value of £900 million.[12]

In addition to the PFI, the Ministry sought to expand its use of private contractors under standard outsourcing agreements. To do so, the government initiated a comprehensive review of military functions to identify what kind of military support operations could be contracted out to the private sector.[13] One focus was the repair and maintenance of military equipment, which could be transferred back to the manufacturer.[14] Unlike in the USA and Germany, the absence of any constitutional or legal restrictions on the contracting-out of military services eased the privatization of a growing range of armed forces' functions and facilities in the UK.[15]

The election of the New Labour government under Prime Minister Blair in 1997 did not halt the progress of the Neoliberal model of fragmented

[9] Pint *et al.*, *Public-Private Partnerships*, p. 11; M. Spackman, 'Public-Private Partnerships: Lessons from the British Approach', *Economic Systems*, 26, no. 3 (2002), 285.
[10] House of Commons, 'The Private Finance Initiative (PFI)', Research Paper 01/117, 18 December 2001, p. 1.
[11] *Ibid.*, p. 6.
[12] MOD, 'Public Private Partnerships: Changing the Way We Do Business – PFI Guidelines: Introduction', March 2004; D. Parker and K. Hartley, *Transaction Costs, Relational Contracting and Public-Private Partnerships: A Case Study of UK Defence*, 18 April 2001, Centre for Innovation Research, Ashton University, and Centre for Defence Economics, University of York, p. 8.
[13] R. Tieman, 'More MOD Projects May Be Awarded to Private Sector', *Financial Times*, 14 October 1996.
[14] Tieman, 'More MOD Projects May Be Awarded to Private Sector'.
[15] Spackman, 'Public-Private Partnerships', 285.

security governance. On the contrary, the new government stepped up the outsourcing of public services to private firms.[16] To the electorate, the New Labour government presented its policies as non-ideological responses to budgetary constraints.[17] With regard to the armed forces, this meant the transfer of military services to private suppliers 'depending on whichever is better placed to deliver required services at best value'.[18] However, notwithstanding government rhetoric, Blair's Third Way included an ideological commitment to the expansion of the role of the private sector which drew on the Neoliberal model of the state.[19] The Strategic Defence Review of the New Labour government argued that the private sector had played a major role in providing efficiency savings 'whether through market-testing and contracting out, the involvement of private finance or Public/Private Partnership', and concluded that the 'review has demonstrated the scope to achieve yet more'.[20]

What differentiated the Third Way from Thatcherism was a shift in the decision-making and implementation of security policies from an adversarial method that relied on public–private competition towards partnering with the industry. The former had sought to improve cost efficiency and ensure democratic accountability and control over military procurement and service provision by pitching public and private suppliers against each other. The latter suggested that collaboration and long-term contracting could better achieve these objectives. New Labour's public–private partnerships accordingly modified the mechanisms introduced by the Major administration, such as the PFI, contracting-out, market-testing, joint ventures, benchmarking and public–private collaborations.[21] Importantly, the partnering approach permitted 'suppliers to be more closely involved in setting the requirements, allocating risks, and determining key contractual terms and conditions', while previously outsourcing had proceeded on terms defined by the MOD.[22]

The PFI formed the cornerstone of government reform of the armed forces, providing the default solution for all large-scale military

---

[16] Pint *et al.*, *Public-Private Partnerships*, p. 4.
[17] *Ibid.*
[18] MOD, 'Public Private Partnerships: Changing the Way We Do Business'.
[19] S. Driver and L. Martell, *Blair's Britain* (Cambridge: Polity Press, 2002), p. 81, p. 221.
[20] MOD, *Strategic Defence Review. Modern Forces for the Modern World* (London, July 1998), para 170. See also Parker and Hartley, *Transaction Costs, Relational Contracting and Public-Private Partnerships*, p. 8; P. D. Williams, *British Foreign Policy under New Labour, 1997–2005* (Basingstoke: Palgrave, 2005), p. 121.
[21] Pint *et al.*, *Public-Private Partnerships*, p. 13.
[22] *Ibid.*

procurement projects.[23] MOD policy stated 'that for all projects MOD will only consider using its own capital founding resources if PFI has been demonstrated to be unworkable, inappropriate or uneconomic'.[24] The basic ideological assumption was that the PFI would be the superior solution, and the onus was on the armed forces to prove the opposite before government funds could be committed.[25] The certification of the unsuitability of private financing, however, was not straightforward because cost savings were not the primary criterion for the approval of PFI contracts. According to the MOD:

> The final decision on whether or not to proceed with a PFI procurement is made against the key evaluation criterion of whether the PFI approach offers better Value For Money (VFM) than the Public Sector Comparator (PSC). This is not always purely a function of cost. VFM is usually achieved through increased efficiency, and the transfer of certain risks to the private sector.[26]

Since the principle behind the PFI was the transfer of capital investment risks to private financiers, the guidelines practically made PFIs value for money by definitional fiat.[27]

The fact that the UK government did not a priori exclude any military service from consideration for outsourcing or private financing also demonstrated the predominance of Neoliberalism. Although the government accepted that in 'some instances operational imperatives which require front line military maintenance and repair of equipments and systems will probably rule out PFI solutions for most elements of these requirements', such considerations were of a strategic nature rather than based on principle.[28] Apart from armed combat, the New Labour government had no ideological reservations against the privatization of tasks that the USA and Germany considered inherent functions of the state and national armed forces, such as management and oversight. In fact, the MOD proclaimed that its 'pragmatic approach to selecting procurement routes ... can offer the private sector opportunities for far greater involvement than before in the support of equipment and activities close to the "front line"'.[29]

[23] MOD, 'Public Private Partnerships: Changing the Way We Do Business'; MOD, 'Public Private Partnerships (PPP) – An Overview', (2007) at: www.ams.mod.uk/ (discontinued – last accessed 22 August 2007).
[24] MOD, 'Public Private Partnerships: Changing the Way We Do Business'.
[25] MOD, 'Private Finance Initiative', February 2002.
[26] MOD, 'Public Private Partnerships: Changing the Way We Do Business'.
[27] Pint et al., Public-Private Partnerships, p. 25.
[28] MOD, 'Public Private Partnerships: Changing the Way We Do Business'.
[29] MOD, 'The Private Finance Initiative'.

In short, Neoliberalism has provided the rationale and context for the growing role of private military contractors in UK defence policy since the 1980s. The next section examines how successive governments translated the Neoliberal ideal of security governance into military practice, thereby defining the scope and mechanisms of military privatization in the UK.

From warfare state to manager state

Due to the ideological predominance of Neoliberalism, the UK armed forces have become one of the most privatized militaries in Europe and in comparison to North America. According to UK Defence Statistics, in 2006–7 the MOD spent almost half of its £34 billion defence budget on purchases from the private sector, including £2.8 billion on military support services.[30] The scope and peculiarities of the UK approach towards private military contracting can be analysed in terms of the fragmentation of security functions and resources as well as the growing involvement of private firms in security policy decision-making and implementation. The scale and form of UK defence privatization have been defined by three mechanisms: outsourcing, the PFI and government–industry partnering.

Outsourcing

Outsourcing has presented the first and, initially, the most extensively used mechanism for the increase of private sector involvement in the supply of military services in the UK. Under conventional outsourcing arrangements the military has maintained the ownership of a facility or asset, while a private company has taken charge of associated services such as base management or maintenance. In order to facilitate competition and avoid long-term dependencies on the private service provider, the MOD has typically fixed outsourcing contracts to short terms of between five and seven years. The armed forces also signed, initially, most outsourcing contracts with single companies. Due to the growing scale of private military contracting and the increasing complexity of the services provided, however, the MOD has progressively turned towards prime contracting. Under the prime contracting scheme one company takes the overall responsibility for managing the provision of multiple services by a range of subcontractors. Moreover, the duration of the

---

[30] MOD, *UK Defence Statistics 2007*. Figures are roughly similar between 2003–4 and 2005–6, but a direct comparison with data before 2003 is not possible because of changes in UK government accounting procedures.

contracts has been extended. A typical example of contemporary prime contracting has been the Army Training Estate Strategic Partnering project VANGUARD for the supply of almost all non-military support services at 130 training areas and ranges in the UK under a £600 million contract lasting up to fifteen years until 2018.[31]

The Competing for Quality initiative played a crucial role in expanding the outsourcing of public services. After an investigation of '160 areas of business, costing some [£]1.5 billion annually', the Major government concluded that about half of them could be contracted out to the private sector.[32] Since then, the functional scope of military outsourcing contracts has increased steadily. The first services to be outsourced were armed forces estate management, and water and sewage treatment. Later, the MOD progressed towards the contracting-out of maintenance and repair for military equipment such as armoured vehicles, aeroplanes and navy ships.[33] In 2000 a government target to reduce the cost of armed forces support services by 20 per cent led to the outsourcing of additional functions, specifically logistics.[34] A review conducted by the McKinsey consultancy had suggested that the MOD could save up to £140 million in logistics annually by cutting staff numbers and outsourcing these services to the private sector.[35] The last key areas to be outsourced in national defence were military training and IT. In order to illustrate the scale of the growing functional role of private military service providers in the UK, each area is examined in turn below.

The management of armed forces facilities and estates such as navy bases, garrisons and airfields has been one of the largest areas outsourced to the private sector. As of 2008 private contractors ran all three UK naval bases, including the nuclear submarine base and the naval armament depot. Fleet Support operated parts of Portsmouth naval base under a ten-year contract; Devonport Management managed the Devonport Royal Dockyard; and Babcock held a £825 million contract for management, maintenance and repair of the UK's four

---

[31] House of Commons – Defence Committee, *The Work of Defence Estates*, Fifteenth Report, Session 2006–7, HC 535 (London: The Stationery Office, 14 September 2007), p. 31.

[32] J. Stellar, Minister of State for the Armed Forces, 'Public Private Partnerships in Defence', speech delivered at the Defence and PFI Seminar, 14 March 2000.

[33] For a list of MOD outsourcing projects which are in the planning stage or have been approved since 2004 see Hansard, 'Departmental Project Approvals', Written Answers, 30 October 2006, Vol. 451, Session 2006–7, Columns 104W–106W.

[34] K. Done, 'BAE in MOD Deal on Services', *Financial Times*, 21 July 2000.

[35] J. Mcbeth, 'Scots Tanks Crews Who Led Battle for Basra Could Go in Army Cutbacks', *The Scotsman*, 16 June 2003; H. Tomlinson, 'MOD Axe Could Fall on 10,000 Jobs', *Independent on Sunday*, 15 June 2003.

Vanguard-class submarines which carry the Trident nuclear missiles, and for support services at the naval armament depot until 2013.[36] The army's three main garrisons in Aldershot, Catterick and Bordon have also been under private management or have outsourced significant sections of their work. Primary Management has run Aldershot, including the supply of all non-military operations and services, and provided support services at Catterick Garrison in Yorkshire.[37] Finally, the Royal Air Force (RAF) has outsourced the operation of a range of facilities such as at the RAF Strike Command in High Wycombe and RAF Lyneham, where Hunting held a prime contract for station support, including aviation maintenance and services such as catering.[38]

Controversially, the UK government has also contracted out the management of its Atomic Weapons Establishment (AWE) at Aldermaston, which is responsible for the design, manufacture and support of the UK's nuclear warheads.[39] The latest £2.2 billion contract to AWE Management, a joint venture between British Nuclear Fuels (BNFL), Serco and Lockheed Martin, received some publicity because BNFL had previously falsified safety records at its Sellafield nuclear reprocessing plant. However, check-ups by the Nuclear Installations Inspectorate calmed public criticism and in 2003 the government extended the initial ten-year contract with AWE to twenty-five years.[40]

A second important area of private contracting has been the MOD's defence estate programme. Some facilities have been refurbished under PFIs, but the Ministry has also outsourced the management of the design, construction, refurbishment or maintenance of a large number of military estates in public ownership.[41] In 2006 Carillion won one of the largest single defence estates contracts so far awarded. Under the £500 million prime contract, Carillion maintained 8,500 MOD buildings and other assets in the Midlands, the North of England and Wales.[42] In the same year Modern Housing Solutions received a £690

[36] A. Nicoll, 'MOD Aims to Save Pounds 200m by Shifting Warship Repair Work to Private Sector', *Financial Times*, 23 March 2002; A. Nicoll, 'Babcock to Take over Management of Maintenance at Faslane Submarine Base', *Financial Times*, 23 January 2001; D. Wilcock, 'Dockyards New Owner Revealed', *Western Morning News*, 10 May 2007; Babcock, 'Babcock Naval Services', at: www.babcock.co.uk.

[37] R. Hobson, 'When Contractors Bid to Join Forces', *The Times*, 8 April 1997.

[38] A. Nicoll, 'C-17 Lease Plan Reflects Growing Trend', *Financial Times*, 3 September 1998; Hobson, 'When Contractors Bid to Join Forces'.

[39] D. White, 'MOD Trains Its Big Guns on Commercial Target', *Financial Times*, 13 December 1993.

[40] M. Harrison, 'BNFL Consortium Seeks 15-year Extension to Aldermaston Contract', *The Independent*, 21 June 2001.

[41] MOD, 'Elements of PPP in Defence', September 2002.

[42] NN, 'Midlands Support Services and Carillion Land £690m Deal', *Birmingham Post*, 16 November 2006.

million contract for up to ten years to take over the maintenance and upgrading of 45,000 armed forces homes in England and Wales.[43] The refurbishment of armed forces facilities has been a major objective for the government since military personnel and their families have increasingly and publicly campaigned for better housing. Not all contracts have been successful. Military families who had been living for years in declining facilities were disappointed with some contractors, arguing that houses were 'literally falling apart'.[44]

A third area of military outsourcing has been repair and maintenance. The contracting-out of repair functions expanded specifically as a result of the Smart Acquisition programme. The programme aimed to integrate the private production of military equipment with its repair and maintenance under full life-cycle management and costing plans. For services at the Army Base Repair Organization, for example, the MOD signed a partnering arrangement with Vickers Defence Systems in 2001.[45] Other contracts included the maintenance of RAF Haw Fast Jets at RAF Valley by Babcock International and a £947 million contract with BAE for the support of the RAF Tornado fleet.[46] The latter received some criticism, however, because the MOD had shortly before centralized air force repair and maintenance through the creation of the Defence Aviation Repair Agency (DARA), including an investment of £104 million in the construction of a new hangar.[47]

Another growth area for private contracting has been the provision of logistic support for the armed forces. Since 2004 the MOD has contracted out the majority of its logistic support for deployed operations under the Contract for Logistics Support (CONLOG) arrangement with Kellogg, Brown and Root (KBR) as the prime contractor. For the seven years of the CONLOG contract, the Permanent Joint Forces Headquarters could request logistics and infrastructure services to a value of about £12 million annually with additional services for up to £50 million per year depending on demand from international

[43] H. Wallop, 'Companies Were Paid Pounds 70m to Upgrade Army Housing', *Daily Telegraph*, 8 January 2007.

[44] Wallop, 'Companies Were Paid Pounds 70m to Upgrade Army Housing'. See also National Audit Office, *Ministry of Defence: Managing the Defence Estate: Quality and Sustainability*, Session 2006–7, HC 154 (London: The Stationery Office, 23 March 2007); J. Wheatley, 'Growing Army of Soldiers' Wives Go to War over Their Squalid Homes', *The Times*, 5 January 2007.

[45] G. Paloczi-Horvath, 'MOD Plans New Defence Cuts to Follow Election', *The Engineer*, 26 January 2001.

[46] D. Fortson, 'Consortium to Splash Out £5bn in UK's Big Coastguard Sell-Off', *Business & Money*, 18 February 2007; NN, 'A Single Gate to Government: All Loud on the Western Front', *Guardian*, 1 February 2007.

[47] T. Livingstone , 'MPs Reject Claims on Dara', *Western Mail*, 24 March 2006.

deployments. Notably, the contract embedded a small KBR team into the Permanent Joint Forces Headquarters to 'provide planning input for a wide range of operational services', thus directly involving the private contractor in security decision-making.[48]

Military training has been the fifth major area outsourced to commercial suppliers. However, rather than standard outsourcing contracts, the MOD has increasingly used large-scale PFI projects for private training, such as the Defence Training Review and the Military Flight Training Systems contracts. While the first subsumed all non-military training for the three services, the latter merged private military flight training for the army, navy and the RAF. Smaller conventional contracts paved the way for these projects, but other contracts are still in service. In 1997, for instance, the MOD signed a five-year contract with Hunting for armoured vehicles management, maintenance and driving training for the Royal Armoured Corps.[49] Since December 2005 BAE Systems Insyte Broadoak has provided the Maritime Composite Training System at the Maritime Warfare School.

The reverse development has characterized the provision of IT services for the MOD. As will be discussed in detail below, several IT contracts, including the Defence Intelligence Information System, the Defence Electronic Commerce Service and the Records Storage and Management – Hayes PPP project, have been converted from PFIs back into standard outsourcing contracts.[50] Presumably because of the problems encountered with PFIs in the information sector, the MOD has advertised new initiatives such as the Defence Information Infrastructure project from the start as prime contracts. The £4 billion Defence Information Infrastructure contract entails the construction and support of 'a global network of 150,000 desktops for 300,000 military and civilian staff in 2,000 locations' as well as IT training and support for forward deployed headquarters over ten years.[51]

Overall, the track record of conventional outsourcing and prime contracting projects has been positive in terms of applying the Neoliberal principle of market competition in order to facilitate democratic control over the military's contractors. Although some programmes have

---

[48] Halliburton, 'KBR Awarded Contract for CONLOG', Press Release, 3 February 2004.
[49] A. Nicoll, 'Hunting Contract Puts Army in Driving Seat', *Financial Times*, 25 October 1997.
[50] MOD, *UK Defence Statistics 2007*, Table 1.12, footnote 1.
[51] S. Barry, 'Controversial £4bn Defence Deal Could Bring Hi-Tech Jobs to Wales', *Western Mail*, 3 March 2005. See also M. Odell, 'Services Separated by Hotch-Potch System', *Financial Times*, 1 December 2004; S. Pfeifer, 'EDS Trains Big Gun on Defence', *Sunday Telegraph*, 29 July 2007.

encountered problems with contractor management, the short-term and fixed nature of most contracts has generally ensured competition among multiple bidders and has prevented cost overruns. The New Labour government, however, became increasingly concerned about the cost of rebidding for services every three to seven years. Standard outsourcing arrangements were also tightly circumscribed by the size of the defence budget since key assets had to be financed by public investments. To overcome these perceived limitations, the UK government increasingly moved away from the Neoliberal ideal, favouring PFIs and strategic partnering instead.

Private Finance Initiative

Since the Blair government's announcement of the PFI as the MOD's 'first choice method of funding new capital projects', a large number of major contracts with industry have taken this form.[52] By 2008 the MOD had signed at least sixty-one PFI contracts and was planning more. The UK has, thus, been unique compared to the rest of Europe and North America in that the private sector has not only played a significant role in the provision of military services, but also in their capital investment. PFI contracts have covered nearly the entire range of military functions, short of combat, and have increasingly taken private military contracting to the front line. Moreover, in 2000 the government outsourced the identification of further PFI projects and project support to Partnerships UK, a public–private company, which replaced the Treasury Department's PFI Task Force.[53] In spite of some major failures, the government has retained its ideological commitment to the PFI. Among these failures have been the Airfield Support Services Project, the Armoured Vehicles Training Service, the Combined Aerial Target Service, the Defence HF Communications Service and the Defence Stores Management Solution. All of them have been cancelled, and have been either outsourced under standard contracts and partnering agreements or awarded to in-house bidders.[54]

---

[52] MOD, 'What Do You Know About...? The Private Finance Initiative'. Conversely, more recent statements argue that 'there is no predisposition towards either public or private sector' and that the MOD is taking a 'pragmatic' approach. See MOD, 'Public Private Partnerships in the MOD', at: www.mod.uk (discontinued – last accessed 6 June 2004).

[53] Partnerships UK, at: www.partnershipsuk.org.uk; MOD, 'Public Private Partnerships (PPP) – An Overview', at: www.ams.mod.uk/ (discontinued – last accessed 22 August 2007); Spackman, 'Public-Private Partnerships', p. 285.

[54] House of Commons Hansard, 'Armoured Vehicle Training', Written Answers, 27 June 2005, Vol. 435, Session 2005–6, Column 1203W; House of Commons Hansard,

The most significant area for private investments in the armed forces has been the provision of military training. In 2008 the financing of training facilities and services accounted for 28 per cent of PFI projects with an average duration of over thirty years.[55] By 1997, one year after the Blair government announced its intention to make the PFI the cornerstone of its capital investment programme, the MOD awarded two PFI contracts to finance new training facilities. The first was the £20 million contract for simulator-based training at the Hawk Synthetic Training Service at RAF Valley. The second was the £114 million contract for the Medium Support Helicopter Aircrew Training Facility at RAF Benson. Within a decade the range of training facilities and services funded through the PFI covered three armed forces colleges, four flight simulator sites and four RAF flying schools as well as training for fire fighters, defence animals, marine support to range and aircrews, and ASTUTE class submarines.

Beyond the three military colleges, most training used to be outsourced through individual contracts. However, the government has stepped up the scope of the PFI with the consolidation of the private provision of military training under two new large-scale programmes. The first was the Military Flight Training Systems PFI contract with a consortium of Lockheed Martin and VT Group for the training of all RAF, navy and army pilots costing up to £6 billion over twenty-five years, which was signed in 2008.[56] The second was the Defence Training Review rationalization programme which includes all non-military training, including intelligence, engineering, maintenance, communications, IT and languages, across the three services under a single £16 billion twenty-five-year contract for which the Metrix consortium was the preferred bidder.[57]

Most training PFIs have continued without major controversy. However, some projects, including the Joint Services Command and

'Armoured Vehicle Training Services', Written Answers, 21 June 2005, Vol. 436, Session 2005–6, Column 899W; BAE Systems, 'BAE Systems Unveils Innovative CATS Bid', Press Release, 11 September 2003; House of Commons Hansard, 'Combined Aerial Target Service', Written Ministerial Statements, 14 December 2006, Vol. 454, Session 2006–7, Column 94WS; VT Communications, 'Delivering the Defence High Frequency Communications Service (DHFCS) for the Defence Procurement Agency (DPA), at: www.vtplc.com/communications/; MOD, *Annual Report and Accounts 2004–05*, HC 464 (London: The Stationery Office, 28 October 2005), p. 191.

[55] A database of PFI projects can be found at: www.hm-treasury.gov.uk. However, it does not include all PFIs that were listed in earlier databases on the MOD website.

[56] J. Boxwell, 'VT-Lockheed to Lead Pounds 6bn PFI Deal', *Financial Times*, 30 November 2006; Ascent Flight Training, at: www.ascentflighttraining.co.uk.

[57] J. Boxwell, 'Qinetiq Consortium Wins Bulk of £16bn MOD Contract', *Financial Times*, 17 January 2007.

Staff College, the Army Foundation College and the Attack Helicopter (Apache) Training facility, have lagged behind government expectations for various reasons, including delays and subcontractor mismanagement.[58] In these cases the projected savings of privatization have been wiped out by additional cost. Other projects, such as the £16 billion PFI contract for the first part of the Defence Training Review signed in 2007 with the Metrix consortium, have been critiqued for collusion between the government and industry, and disregard for the government's own standard of value for money. Not only did the MOD fail to develop an in-house comparator to the private sector bids, but it was also accused of potential bias towards Metrix because the government held a 19 per cent share of the Metrix consortium partner QinetiQ.[59]

The second most extensive use of the PFI has been to build or refurbish MOD estates with twelve separate contracts as of 2008. Primarily, the Ministry has utilized private capital financing to address the poor standard of family housing. Allenby/Connaught, the largest estates project so far, includes 'a 35-year contract worth £8 billion, to deliver modern living and working accommodation to Aldershot Garrison and the garrisons around Salisbury Plain'.[60] Under the contract with Aspire Defence Limited, a consortium consisting of Carillion Holdings Limited, KBR and HSBC, Allenby/Connaught has provided housing for 20 per cent of the UK Army.[61] The second largest PFI estate contract was for the redevelopment of Colchester Garrison for an estimated £2 billion, followed by the refurbishment of the MOD's main building in London for a projected cost of £1.5 billion.

The most problematic areas so far appear to have been IT and communications with five and six PFI contracts respectively. In the IT sector PFI projects have ranged from the Training Administration and Financial Management Information Systems (TAFMIS) signed with Electronic Data Systems (EDS) in 1996 to the Records Storage and Management 'Hayes' project contract with ProLogis and TNT awarded

[58] National Audit Office, *PFI: Construction Performance*, Session 2002–3, HC 371 (London: The Stationery Office, 5 February 2003), p. 15; NN, 'Cowboy Training Grounds Apache', *Daily Record*, 31 October 2002; S. Penny, 'Training Woes Blight Apache Plans', *Flight International* (5 November 2002), 20; M. Hickley, 'The No-Fly Apache', *Daily Mail*, 31 October 2002; NN, 'Why the Army Is Mothballing Top Helicopters', *Birmingham Post*, 31 October 2002.
[59] A. Roberts, 'PCS Blasts Armed Forces Training Sell-off', *Morning Star*, 18 January 2007; NN, 'Qinetiq Consortium Thought to Have Won MOD Contract', *Daily Telegraph*, 17 January 2007.
[60] House of Commons – Defence Committee, *The Work of Defence Estates*, Fifteenth Report, Session 2006–7, HC 535 (London: The Stationery Office, 14 September 2007), pp. 15–16.
[61] *Ibid*.

in 2003. Three out of five IT PFIs, namely the Defence Intelligence Information System, the Defence Electronic Commerce Service and the Records Storage and Management project, did not run for their full award period, but were converted back into standard outsourcing contracts.[62] In addition, the Armed Forces Personnel Administration Agency's £250 million contract for the Joint Personnel Administration project, a single armed forces pay, personnel and pensions system, with EDS ran into problems. In spite of overspending on the projected budget, it suffered repeated delays 'threatening payments to 300,000 military personnel and 800,000 pensioners'.[63]

In communications, PFI contracts have included Armymail, RAF Mail, the supply of commercial satellite service through INMARSAT, the Defence Fixed Telecommunications Service, the Defence High Frequency Communications Service and, since 2003, two new military satellites under project Skynet 5. Here, too, the results have been mixed. In 2002 Sir Robert Walmsley, Chief of Defence Procurement, argued that the PFI contract for Skynet 5 would be 'more than 5 per cent cheaper than the traditional method under which the MOD owned and operated satellites'.[64] However, other contracts have been criticized, including the £12 million award for RAF Mail where the contractor has been accused of being 'only interested in maximising profits with the minimum of capital outlay' and the Defence Fixed Communications Service, which was characterized by 'a gap between the authority's expectations and the reality of the contract'.[65]

Conversely, with regard to the MOD's seven utilities PFIs the Ministry has consolidated and expanded its use of private contractors. Since 2004 the Aquatrine project has provided water and sewage treatment for the whole of the UK armed forces at over 2,500 sites. Other utility contracts have included the RAF Fylingdales Power Station run by TG Power Ltd and the Field Electrical Power Supplies by Vickers Specialist Engines. Further mergers of separate PFI projects within single schemes have occurred in transport and logistics. In 2001, for example, the MOD decided to consolidate the Army Germany White Fleet contract signed in 1996 and the RAF White Fleet contract of 1997

---

[62] MOD, *UK Defence Statistics 2007*, Table 1.12, footnote 1; N. Mathiason, 'MOD Under Fire Over Training Plans', *The Observer*, 26 March 2006.

[63] D. Black, 'Private Finance Initiative – Saving Private Finance', *Financial Director*, 1 March 2002; G. Cleland, 'MOD Blunders Leave Forces Short of Pay', 12 December 2007; M. Smith and M. Woolf, 'Soldiers Are Cheated In Pay Blunder', *The Times*, 6 December 2007.

[64] A. Nicoll, 'European Space Industry Gets Pounds 2bn MOD Boost under PFI', *Financial Times*, 27 February 2002.

[65] Black, 'Private Finance Initiative – Saving Private Finance'.

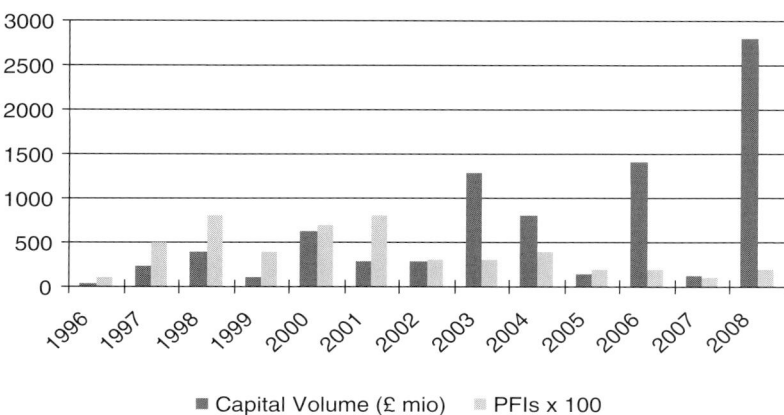

Figure 4.1 MOD PFI projects signed

within the Tri-Service White Fleet project awarded to Lex Defence Management. An earlier attempt at integrating the provision of services across the three services had been made with the Tri-Service Materials Handling Service contract won by Barlow Handling in 2000. One advantage of these projects has been that they have been able to utilize vehicles and services available on the civilian market.

More costly and difficult has been the use of the PFI to fund major equipment projects straddling the divide between transport and logistics and defence procurement, such as the Material Handling Equipment, the Heavy Equipment Transporter, 'C' vehicles, Roll-on Roll-off (RO-RO) Strategic Sea Lift ferries and the Future Strategic Tanker Aircraft projects. The RO-RO project, in particular, encountered early problems due to a delay of the contract negotiations. Rather than fully transferring the capital funding and associated risk for the construction of the ferries to the private contractor, the MOD placed the £80 million order for two ships against future reimbursement by the PFI contractor Andrew Weir in order to ensure the earlier availability of the ships.[66] Similar delays affected the Future Strategic Tanker Aircraft PFI contract for the conversion and servicing of Airbus A330 into air-to-air refuelling aircraft over twenty-seven years, which was signed in 2008 after ten years of negotiations with various bidders.[67]

[66] J. Porter and H. O'Mahoney, 'UK Admits No PFI Contract Yet Signed to Finance MOD Ro-Ros', *Lloyd's List*, 29 May 2002; NN, 'Half-Military, Half-Civilian: The Complex World of the PFI', *Daily Post*, 22 May 2002.
[67] MOD, Defence Factsheet: Future Strategic Tanker Aircraft, at: www.mod.uk.

In summary, the record of PFI contracts has been mixed with regard to the Neoliberal model of democratic control and accountability. On the one hand, they have enabled the UK government to spread the capital investment cost of military procurement and service programmes between public and private investors in line with Neoliberal principles. On the other hand, PFIs have effectively increased the price of military goods and services due to lengthy contract negotiations and the higher profit margin demanded by commercial financiers. Moreover, as illustrated in Figure 4.1, the growing size of individual PFI projects and their long-term duration of up to thirty years have made the government and the armed forces more dependent on single contractors, undermining the competition which lies at the heart of the Neoliberal model of democratic governance.

In order to lower the risk of failure which results from the increased scope and duration of private military contracts, the UK government has sought to facilitate a closer cooperation with industry. The next part discusses how this cooperation has expanded the role of private businesses in the decision-making and implementation of security policies.

Partnering with industry

Partnering with industry has been another mechanism which has further distanced UK national security provision from the Neoliberal ideal of free market competition. In these arrangements 'long-term, high-trust relationships', building on common goals and information-sharing, have replaced the 'control premised on short-lived contracts and dense specifications' which characterized outsourcing under Thatcher and Major.[68] In detail, the MOD's partnering approach has involved changes in four dimensions. The first change has been a transition towards long-term contracts. As noted above, contracts of long duration have always been a primary feature of the PFI. However, where the PFI has proven not to be value for money, the MOD has increasingly also sought long-term partnerships under standard outsourcing contracts. One such example has been the twenty-year Combined Aerial Target Service prime contract with QinetiQ which brought together all existing armed forces target arrangements, including the Mirach service already supplied by QinetiQ under a twenty-five-year long-term partnering agreement, in 2006.[69] The primary aim of long-term contracting has been to provide a framework for the armed forces and industry to work on eliminating

---

[68] T. Entwistle and S. Martin, 'From Competition to Collaboration in Public Service Delivery: A New Agenda for Research', *Public Administration*, 83, no.1 (2005), 237.

[69] MOD 'CATS', at: www.armedforces.co.uk.

problems and cost inefficiencies without the threat of costly contract readvertisements.

The second transformation has been a move away from financial penalties for contractor underperformance to warning notices. Rather than punishing contractors who fail to meet their performance targets, the Ministry has served warning notices in order to give contractors the opportunity to improve their services. Only when these fail to achieve the desired effect, does the Ministry invoke contractual penalties in the form of liquidated damages. However, these penalties apply to no more than 10 per cent of contracts and frequently stay within a low margin of the contract value, sometimes not even covering the additional cost incurred by the government.[70]

Thirdly, the government has sought to encourage contractors to operate more cost-efficiently by offering a share in the gained savings. According to the formal definition provided by the MOD, gain-sharing denotes 'target cost incentive arrangements, whereby a target is identified and contractors have an incentive to beat the target as they share in the cost of the under-run with MOD and get a higher percentage return as profit'.[71] However, again, the application of gain-sharing mechanisms has been limited. In a review of government PFI in 2001, the National Audit Office (NAO) found that only 15 per cent of the surveyed agencies had the right to share in the gains from project refinancing, which presents one of the major sources of increased profits.[72]

Finally, the armed forces have expanded their use of so-called 'integrated project teams' across all forms of defence privatization.[73] The teams consist of a mixture of armed forces and private contractor personnel who jointly provide services such as repair and maintenance at either military or private installations. One example has been the joint teams with prime contractors BAE and Rolls-Royce for the provision of maintenance, repair and overhaul of Tornado and Harrier aircraft in hubs across the UK.[74] Another has been its naval base contract with

---

[70] See for instance, House of Commons – Committee on Public Accounts, *Ministry of Defence: Building an Air Manoeuvre Capability: The Introduction of the Apache Helicopter*, Forty-sixth Report, Session 2002–3, HC 533 (London: The Stationery Office, 15 April 2003), pp. EV22–3.

[71] House of Commons – Defence Committee, *Defence Procurement*, Sixth Report, Session 2003–4, Volume I, HC 572-I (London: The Stationery Office, 2004), p. 16.

[72] National Audit Office, *Managing the Relationship to Secure a Successful Partnership in PFI Projects*, Session 2001–2, HC 375 (London: The Stationery Office, 29 November 2001), p. 4.

[73] J. Spellar, Minister of State for the Armed Forces, 'Focussed Logistics', speech at RUSI, 8 February 2000.

[74] National Audit Office, *Transforming Logistics Support for Fast Jets*, Session 2006–7 HC 825, (London: The Stationery Office, 17 July 2007), pp. 6–7.

Babcock Naval Services at Clyde which has involved 480 Royal Navy personnel and 53 MOD civilians seconded to the company.[75]

Nevertheless, partnering between the armed force and the industry has faced two main problems with regard to democratic control and accountability. Firstly, in some cases the military has not been able to provide the contractual number of qualified uniformed personnel for integrated project teams because of successive personnel reductions since the 1990s. The lack of qualified uniformed personnel has been particularly problematic since it has drawn civilian contractors 'further and further forward in the operational area in the support of their equipment'.[76] Secondly, the expansion of partnering arrangements has increased the dependence of the military on private contractors not only in terms of resources and services, but also with regard to the necessary expertise to evaluate future contracts. The National Audit Office has thus recommended that the MOD should investigate whether 'it has sufficient commercial, cost modelling and project management skills to develop the commercially viable solutions and negotiate contracts, given the increasing complexity and likely volume of industrial logistics support'.[77] Critique was also heard from within the MOD. In 2004 the Chief of Defence Procurement had to admit that partnering with industry had not been very effective because 'government and industry had very different expectations'.[78]

The preceding analysis shows how successive UK governments have transformed the role of the state in national security on the basis of the Neoliberal model of fragmented security governance. The primary features of this transformation have been the progressive expansion of the functional contribution of private contractors from water and sewage treatment to military training and logistics, as well as the growing dependence on private sector resources such as military equipment and services, commercial financing and privately owned facilities. Moreover, while the Conservative government still built upon public–private competition in order to ensure public control over the military establishment, the New Labour government has included the growing involvement of private businesses in the decision-making and implementation process based on long-term partnerships with private

[75] Babcock, 'Babcock Naval Services in Faslane', *Outlook – Babcock Defence Services Magazine* (Winter 2002), p. 4.

[76] P. Smart, 'Support for the Front Line', *RUSI Journal*, 145, no. 1 (2000), 67, cited in Uttley, 'Private Contractors on Deployed Operations', 150.

[77] National Audit Office, *Transforming Logistics Support for Fast Jets*, p. 10.

[78] D. Kirkpatrick, 'Government and Industry: Problematic Partnering', *RUSI Defence Systems*, 7, no. 2 (2004), at: http://rusi.org/go.php?structureID=articles_defence&ref=P4198C021618F9.

Table 4.1. *UK model of the state*

Dimension	UK
Ideology	• Neoliberalism • Conservatives: Thatcherism • New Labour: Third Way
Geographical scope	• National and international
Functional scope	Extensive private sector provision of: • Facility management • Water and sewage • Maintenance and repair • Logistics • Training • IT • Unarmed guarding
Resources	Extensive private provision of: • Equipment • Services • Financing (PFIs) • Estates
Interests	• Cost efficiency
Norms	• Small state • Value for money
Decision-making	• Conservatives: competing for quality, market-testing • New Labour: partnering, gain sharing, integrated project teams
Implementation	• Conservatives: short-term contracting, tight contractual specifications, penalties • New Labour: long-term contracting, warning notices rather than penalties
Democratic control and accountability	• Conservatives: public–private competition • New Labour: public–private partnerships

defence contractors. For the government the issue of democratic control and accountability has moved into the background. Moreover, as the next section will discuss, the consequences of these developments for the model of the professional soldier and its relations with the state and society have been, largely, disregarded.

Dismantling the all-volunteer forces

Since the end of the Cold War, the Neoliberal policies of the UK government have not only transformed the role of the state in national defence, but also have had serious consequences for professional soldiers, their motivation, identity, and roles and relations of accountability and control with the state and society. This section argues that the privatization and outsourcing of military services have affected the professional armed forces in two major ways. The first has been the erosion of the distinction between the professional soldier and the private military contractor. The second has been the growing gulf between the military, society and the political process.

Professionals turned contractors

While in the USA and Germany the question of what are the inherent functions of the government and the armed forces, and the emergence of an occupational self-perception of the soldier, have been controversially debated among the military, politicians and academics, in the UK the armed forces themselves appear to have taken the lead in replacing soldiers with contractors wherever possible and treating professional soldiering like any other occupation.[79] The consequence has been a progressive weakening of the distinction between professional soldiers and private military contractors. Three sets of policies have contributed to this development.

The first has been the failure to engage in a principled debate of what kinds of functions form the core of the military profession and, therefore, must be excluded from consideration for outsourcing to private contractors. For the UK government and the armed forces, the primary criteria for the assessment whether a service should be contracted out to a private commercial supplier have been financial risk transfer, value for money and its potential consequences for military effectiveness. Neither has publicly addressed important questions regarding the ethics of a commercial, profit-oriented supply of military services and the implications of the growing role of private military contractors for democratic control and accountability.

A second set of policies relates to the widespread perception among professional soldiers that the MOD has been breaking its covenant with them by failing to ensure their wellbeing and care within as well as after

---

[79] D. M. Snider and G. L. Watkins, 'The Future of Army Professionalism: A Need for Renewal and Redefinition', *Parameters*, 37, no. 3 (2000), 6; S. Mannitz, 'Weltbürger in Uniform oder dienstbare Kämpfer? Konsequenzen des Auftragswandels für das Soldatenbild der Bundeswehr', in B. Schoch, A. Heinemann-Grüder, J. Hippler, M. Weingardt and R. Munz (eds.) *Friedensgutachten 2007* (Berlin: LIT, 2007), p. 107; G. Kümmel, 'The Winds of Change: The Transition from Armed Forces for Peace to New Missions for the Bundeswehr and Its Impact on Civil-Military Relations', *Journal of Strategic Studies*, 26, no. 2 (2003), 21.

they leave the military.[80] The 'Honour the Covenant' campaign of the Royal British Legion has highlighted missing assistance for professional soldiers in the provision of mental health services, compensation for injury and legal advice.[81] The broken covenant has also concerned the employment conditions within the military and the use of all-volunteer forces by the UK government. A significant number of professional soldiers have left the armed forces because of the persistent work force overstretch and its impact on family life. Moreover, soldiers have felt 'that the work of the Services is no longer valued; [and there is] uncertainty over the future given the current changes in the Forces, and concerns about the quality of equipment'.[82] In particular in the aftermath of the interventions in Afghanistan and Iraq, officers have criticized the UK government's lack of moral and financial support for the armed forces to the point of endangering the lives of professional soldiers.[83]

A third factor has been the military's changed approach towards recruitment and retention, which has increasingly focused on individual and monetary rewards rather than notions such as loyalty and service.[84] The Armed Forces Continuous Attitude Surveys offer an interesting reflection of how the UK military perceives its professional soldiers, their role in society and the political process, and what motivates them.[85] Notable is the instrumentalist approach of the surveys, which primarily seek to establish how the retention of professional soldiers can be improved rather than to investigate what British soldiers think of government and armed forces policies.[86] The fact that the majority of survey questions are about personal job satisfaction, remuneration, family life and rotations suggests that the armed forces themselves have embraced an occupational view of the professional soldier. Moreover, there has been no public study of the attitudes of soldiers towards the privatization and outsourcing of military and support services in the UK. The only sets of questions within the Continuous Attitude Surveys

---

[80] A. Forster, 'Breaking the Covenant: Governance of the British Army in the Twenty-first Century', *International Affairs*, 82, no. 6 (2006), 1043–57; Army, *Soldiering – The Military Covenant*, Army Doctrine Publication Volume 5, February 2000.

[81] Royal British Legion, 'Honour the Covenant', Our Campaign, at: www.britishlegion.org.uk.

[82] National Audit Office, *Ministry of Defence: Recruitment and Retention in the Armed Forces*, Report by the Comptroller and Auditor General, Session 2005–6, HC 1633-I (London: The Stationery Office, 3 November 2006), p. 1.

[83] Forster, 'Breaking the Covenant', 1046.

[84] National Audit Office, *Ministry of Defence: Recruitment and Retention in the Armed Forces*, p. 2.

[85] Armed Forces Continuous Attitude Surveys, at: www.mod.uk.

[86] Some articles seem to suggest such an impact on the morale of professional soldiers in Iraq. See R. Sylvester, 'Army Is a Moral Force', *Daily Telegraph*, 6 March 2006, cited in Forster, 'Breaking the Covenant', 1045.

that refer, albeit indirectly, to the impact that private military contractors have on uniformed personnel are those that investigate disaffection with routine work, multiple deployments and time spent apart from their families. While not mentioned in the survey, the outsourcing of support functions has played a crucial role in increasing such problems because it has limited the number of suitable positions available for soldiers between deployments overseas.[87]

While these policies are undermining the special status of the professional soldier vis-à-vis private military contractors, the MOD has contended that military outsourcing can 'enhance the morale, cohesion, combat effectiveness and ethos of the armed services'.[88] The Ministry has ascribed this to the fact that contractors can relieve military personnel from routine support functions and allow them to focus on tasks which are more intellectually stimulating and personally rewarding. Moreover, the MOD believes that contractors and professional soldiers share a corporate ethos which permits close and mutually beneficial cooperation because most private military personnel are former soldiers. It is thus largely due to the UK government's own policies that many professional soldiers perceive private military contracting not as competition, but as an alternative and increasingly superior career option.

The second most important reason soldiers give for leaving the UK armed forces is better employment prospects in the civilian sector.[89] In fact, a growing number of recruits already join the armed forces with the intention of switching to better-paid positions in the private military sector after they have completed their training and minimum obligatory service.[90] Even for those who remain in the military until the end of their service in their forties, a second career is imperative. Since former Chiefs of Staff such as General Sir Roger Wheeler and the North Atlantic Treaty Organization's (NATO) former Deputy Commander in Chief Lieutenant General Sir Cedric Delves have joined private military companies such as Aegis and Olive Group, the industry has shaken off the mercenary image.[91] Instead, the transition from professional soldier to private contractor has become widely accepted.[92]

---

[87] M. Uttley, *Civilian Contractors on Deployed Military Operations: United Kingdom Policy and Doctrine* (Carlisle, PA: Strategic Studies Institute, September 2005), p. 24.

[88] Uttley, *Civilian Contractors on Deployed Military Operations*, p. 16.

[89] National Audit Office, *Ministry of Defence: Recruitment and Retention in the Armed Forces*, p. 21.

[90] Personal conversations with British soldiers. See also Kinsey, *Corporate Soldiers and International Security*, p. 104.

[91] For a more extensive list see Campaign Against Arms Trade, at: www.caat.org.uk.

[92] Kinsey, *Corporate Soldiers and International Security*, p. 104.

This does not mean that professional soldiers have been uncritical of the government's outsourcing and privatization policies. Being confronted with the contracting-out of many services on a daily basis, professional soldiers have been well aware of its potential negative effects ranging from the decreased quality of catering to the, admittedly rare, withdrawal of private contractors from conflict regions. Armed forces personnel are also wary of the long-term impact of the PFI on the military, both in terms of the commitment of future budgets and the decreased flexibility that long-term contracting involves. However, it has been part of the professional ethos of the UK military not to publicize its criticisms of government policies. The armed forces might be unhappy about the widespread ignorance of the electorate and many parliamentarians on matters concerning the all-volunteer forces; however, the position of political neutrality is ingrained in the very culture of the professional military.[93] Moreover, the government has made it clear to senior officers that it will not permit public criticism of its military policies.[94]

Only recently has the reticence to speak out in public against policies perceived as damaging to the armed forces and to national and international security shown signs of weakening. This willingness has partially been an unintended consequence of the government's own policies. The fading of the dividing line between professional and contractor roles and identities has been leading soldiers to seek similar rights, including parity of pay, a professional association and a public voice. The creation of the Army Rumour Service in 2002 as an informal venue, but also a public forum, for the exchange of opinions online has been one step in this direction. It was followed in 2006 by the constitution of a British Armed Forces Federation as the first representative association of armed forces personnel in the UK.[95] Generally, professional soldiers are 'less willing to "keep quiet" and more willing to challenge authority and press for "test" cases'.[96] They are attempting to address the increasing imbalance of a military covenant that on the one hand demands higher professional standards and limited rights, but on the other hand treats them like the contractors with whom they are increasingly replaced. Giving greater political rights to professional soldiers might be a necessity in the near future due to rulings of the European Court of Human Rights and the

[93] Strachan, H., 'The Civil-Military "Gap" in Britain', *The Journal of Strategic Studies*, 26, no. 2 (2003), 43.
[94] Forster, 'Breaking the Covenant', 1047.
[95] British Armed Forces Federation, at: www.baff.org.uk.
[96] Forster, 'Breaking the Covenant', 1052.

European Court of Justice, but it might also help to reconnect the professional armed forces with UK society.[97]As the next section argues, the need for such reconnection is greater than ever since the privatization and outsourcing of military services in the UK has widened the civil-military 'gap'.

From civil–military 'gap' to 'gulf'

Historically, the gap between the British armed forces and society has its origins in the success of the professional soldier model which has contributed to the near total elimination of the military from the public eye and mind. Based on Liberal principles, UK politicians and the public have perceived democratic control over the collective use of force to be best ensured by delimiting the size of the armed forces and maintaining their separation from the political process. Another reason for the divide between the UK armed forces and the broader population has been the military's difficulty in accepting public and political demands to adjust its own ideals in step with those of society. Instead, the professional armed forces have put forward the argument that their unique functions justify the 'need to be different'.[98]

Ironically, at the same time as the growing number of private military contractors is challenging the professional soldier model, they are widening the gap between the armed forces and the broader population into a 'gulf' by reinforcing these two trends. Contractors not only further reduce the role and visibility of the all-volunteer forces, but also permit the military to distance itself even more from civil society through its growing focus on combat operations. Like all professional armed forces, the UK military has always found it difficult to recruit sufficient numbers of soldiers. The expansion of the private military sector has added to this the attractiveness of a civilian career to already trained military personnel. In 2006 the UK armed forces had a shortfall of 5,170 personnel or nearly 3 per cent against MOD targets.[99] The lack of a military presence and knowledge about the armed forces in society combined with the rise of Neoliberal and postmodern beliefs

---

[97] Strachan, 'The Civil-Military "Gap" in Britain', 55–8. For a more critical view see G. R. Rubin, 'United Kingdom Military Law: Autonomy, Civilianisation, Juridification', *Modern Law Review*, 65, no. 1 (2002), 36–57.

[98] C. Dandeker, 'On "The Need to be Different": Recent Trends in Military Culture', in H. Strachan (ed.) *The British Army. Manpower and Society into the Twenty-First Century* (London: Frank Cass, 2000), pp. 173–87; Dandeker and Freedman, 'The British Armed Services', 465–75; Strachan, 'The Civil-Military "Gap" in Britain', 47.

[99] National Audit Office, *Ministry of Defence: Recruitment and Retention in the Armed Forces*, p. 1.

such as individualism and personal rights have decreased the appeal of a military career.[100]

In addition, media reports of pervasive racism, sexism, homophobia and bullying in the military demonstrate the schism between UK society and the all-volunteer forces. The armed forces' attempts to close this gap have had only limited success. Targets agreed with the Commission for Racial Equality to increase the recruitment of ethnic minorities by 1 per cent each year from 1997 have not been met despite efforts to present the British military as more multicultural.[101] The inclusion of women in the military has progressed from the dissolution of separate female units in 1992 to the opening-up of 70 per cent of all armed forces positions to women in 1998.[102] Yet, only 9 per cent of professional soldiers in the UK are female, demonstrating that the all-volunteer forces are still perceived as primarily a male domain.[103]

The implications of the gulf for the relations of the armed forces with society have been twofold. One has been a growing ignorance of military matters among the population and members of parliament. National and international security policies figure only marginally in elections and everyday politics. Although the British public has a very positive view of the military, in practice it is reluctant to redirect public funds towards defence. Instead, the electorate seems happy to believe government promises that cuts in the armed forces and limited defence expenditures can be combined with multiple international interventions. Both the public and many parliamentarians fail to note that this comes at the cost of an overextended military profession and the growing use of private military contractors.

In addition, the gulf between the military and society has contributed to a pervasive indifference towards military casualties in international interventions among the British population.[104] The electorate perceives the risk of being killed as part of the job, and the number

---

[100] A. Hussain and M. Ishaq, 'Public Attitudes towards a Career in the British Armed Forces', *Defense & Security Analysis*, 21, no. 1 (2005), 79–96.

[101] R. von Zugbach and M. Ishaq, 'Managing Race Relations in the British Army', *Defense Analysis*, 16, no. 2 (2000), 185–202; I. Bellamy, 'Accounting for Army Recruitment: White and Non-white Soldiers and the British Army', *Defence and Peace Economics*, 14, no. 4 (2003), 288.

[102] R. Woodward and T. Winter, *Sexing the Soldier. The Politics of Gender and the Contemporary British Army* (London: Routledge, 2007), pp. 41–2.

[103] The UK is not unique. Most armed forces in Western democracies, whether professional or conscripted, are characterized by their gendered non-representativeness despite anti-discriminatory legislation such as in the European Union. For statistics see Woodward and Winter, *Sexing the Soldier*, p. 17.

[104] Strachan, 'The Civil-Military "Gap" in Britain', 43. See also R. Thornton, 'A Welcome "Revolution"? The British Army and the Changes of the Strategic Defence Review', *Defence Studies*, 3, no. 3 (2003), 56.

Table 4.2. *UK model of the soldier*

Dimension	UK
Relationships with the state and society	• Duty (contractual, temporary) • Broken covenant • Civil–military gulf
Motivation	• Individual and monetary rewards
Identity	• Individual/collective-professional (occupational view)
Democratic control and accountability	• Decreased public knowledge of the military • Lack of public concern over casualties • Decreased commitment of the soldier to society

of deaths in action is not noted with the widespread public reverence observed in the USA. Even the MOD did not initially keep public count of how many soldiers had been injured or killed in Iraq.[105] Incidentally, a significant number of military fatalities were foreign nationals from Commonwealth countries, led by Fiji, Jamaica, South Africa and Zimbabwe, who account for nearly 7,000 soldiers in the UK armed forces.[106]

In summary, the developments above illustrate that the increasing replacement of professional soldiers with private military contractors has serious consequences for the model of the soldier and its connections with state and society in the UK. The most important has been its challenge to the unique motivation, identity and relations of the professional soldier based on the covenant with the state and society. This covenant has contributed to the control and accountability of the professional soldier by offering state support and social recognition in return for a professional dedication to duty, honour and sacrifice. Another consequence has been the widening gulf between the professional armed forces and the citizens, resulting in a lack of electoral knowledge and information about the military, and the weakening of public concern about military casualties. How these developments

---

[105] S. M. Bird, 'UK Statistical Indifference to its Military Casualties in Iraq', *The Lancet*, 367 (4 March 2006), 713–15.
[106] House of Commons Hansard, 'Non-British Commonwealth Armed Forces', Written Answers, 11 July 2006, Vol. 448, Session 2005–6, Column 1798W.

have impacted on the democratic control over the armed forces will be examined in the next section.

The managerial state, private soldiers and democratic control

When the Thatcher government promoted the Neoliberal ideal of the small state and the privatization and outsourcing of military services in the 1980s, one of the key reasons was the disillusionment with the Republican warfare state. In particular, it argued that the growing interconnectedness between the interests of the state, the military and industry had not only undermined efficiency and effectiveness, but also democratic control and accountability. By cutting back the role of the state, Thatcher promised to increase both the quality of public service provision and responsiveness to the wishes of the electorate. As the preceding analysis has shown, successive governments have followed this ideal and thus transformed the roles and relations of the state, the citizen and the soldier in national security. However, the issue of democratic control has re-emerged in different forms because of the inconsistent implementation of Neoliberalism and its inherent limitations. This section discusses three sets of issues and how the UK government has responded to them: decreased public information and scrutiny, growing executive autonomy and the undermining of professional self-regulation of the soldier.

Public information and scrutiny

Theoretically and historically, Liberalism has placed a great emphasis on citizens' ability to scrutinize and to evaluate government actions through the democratic process. Neoliberalism has added to this an emphasis on the choice between competing public and private suppliers of collective services. With regard to democratic control over the legitimate use of military force, both have been combined in the public and parliamentary control over national defence spending. Instead of increasing this control, the outsourcing of military services and the growing role of private military contractors in UK defence appear to have limited electoral and parliamentary information and influence on public spending on defence. Three factors have contributed to this problem.

Firstly, the use of private military contractors and private financing has limited public awareness and information about the true cost of defence. One of the reasons for this has been the absence of centralized public information regarding the number and cost of individual contracts. While the MOD and the Treasury have published basic statistics on PFI projects, so far there has been no such information about standard outsourcing contracts. Moreover, the available public information on private military contracts remains patchy. IT contracts, for instance, have been missing from the Treasury database and many PFI contracts are not included in the defence budget balance sheet. PFI programmes generally make it more difficult for the public and parliamentarians to assess the true cost of defence. Traditional military service provision used publicly financed assets which had to be approved up-front through defence budget allocations. Private financing obscures the total financial commitment made by the government over a lifetime of twenty to thirty years by means of annual instalments. This is even more problematic because spreading the start-up cost of private military services and equipment over several decades does not mean that private financing is more cost-efficient than public borrowing. According to defence economist Keith Hartley, 'governments can always borrow more cheaply than the private sector. If PFI/PPP contracts are to lead to genuine cost savings, the extra financing cost for the private sector must be offset by savings elsewhere on the project.'[107] Where PFI contractors fail to generate efficiency savings, private financing is mere 'intergenerational welfare shifting'.[108] Unfortunately, as the preceding analysis has shown, expected cost efficiencies are not always achieved because of delays or new developments such as changes in military technology or in armed forces demand for particular services.

The second related factor is that long-term contracts have decreased the ability of the electorate and future governments to exit from the commercial provision of military services if these should become too costly, outdated or simply unnecessary. According to Kathy Makin, Director of Widening Smart Acquisition in the MOD:

The length of contracts means that we have to be very sure about the requirement and its enduring nature since, while there is likely to be flexibility for expansion of the scope of some projects, there is unlikely to be much scope for reduction in the requirement except at considerable nugatory cost.[109]

Long-term financial commitments made under PFI and partnering agreements also mean that there is less flexibility within the defence

---

[107] K. Hartley, 'Military Outsourcing: UK Experience', Research Paper, Centre for Defence Economics, University of York (undated), p. 4.

[108] Parker and Hartley, *Transaction Costs, Relational Contracting and Public-Private Partnerships*, p. 4.

[109] K. Makin, 'UK MOD: Raising its Game as a PFI Customer', *RUSI Defence Systems*, 7, no. 1 (2004), 98.

budget. In 2002 the House of Commons Defence Committee had already pointed out the problem that PFIs can commit large parts of the defence budget.[110]

Finally, the New Labour government's partnering approach with industry has decreased the available competition for military contracts and increased the dependence of the armed forces on a small number of companies. The previous Conservative government's hands-off and adversarial method of contracting had focused on policies such as market-testing and public–private competitions, seeking to maintain a basis from which private sector bids could be assessed and, if needed, be replaced by internal military provision. By contrast, the New Labour government has increasingly de-emphasized the need for a public sector comparison to assess the value for money of private contracts. Its partnering mentality has instead facilitated a close cooperation between the MOD and industry. This partnering approach has underrated the differences in rationale between the armed forces and a profit-motivated industry.[111] A MOD assessment of PFI projects thus found that nearly a quarter of contract managers rated the performance of their project only as satisfactory on a four-point scale between 'very good', 'good', 'satisfactory' and 'poor'.[112] In addition, the national and transnational consolidation of the industry due to prime contracting and large-scale PFI has reduced competition among private companies.[113] The New Labour government's strategic partnering policy has effectively supported the creation of national champions.[114] A few companies hold the majority of PFI and prime defence contracts in key sectors either alone or through consortia with smaller businesses, such as EDS and the VT Group in IT, Carillion in estate management, BAE in aerospace, Lex in transport and logistics, and Serco in management. As the following section points out, both the limited public information and influence on defence spending and the close linkages between industry and the government have shifted democratic control and accountability towards the executive.

---

[110] House of Commons – Defence Committee, *Major Procurement Projects*, Fourth Report, Session 2001–2, HC 779 (London: The Stationery Office, July 2002), p. 22.

[111] M. Uttley, 'Public-Private Partnerships in United Kingdom Defence', *RUSI Defence Systems*, 9, no.2 (2006), p. 83.

[112] MOD, *Review of MOD PFI Projects in Construction and Operation* (London, December 2005), p. 9.

[113] R. Matthews and J. Parker, 'Prime Contracting in Major Defense Contracts', *Defense Analysis*, 15, no. 1 (1999), 33.

[114] MOD, *Defence Industrial Strategy: Defence White Paper*, Cm 6697 (London, December 2005), p. 8.

Executive autonomy

The growing executive autonomy with regard to decisions concerning the production and use of military force has two facets. As argued above, private financing and contracting has decreased popular and parliamentary information and control over defence spending. In addition, the replacement of professional soldiers with private contractors has granted the executive greater freedom of manoeuvre with regard to the deployment of military personnel abroad. Both are interconnected in that private military contractors permit governments to engage in major military interventions without having to marshal electoral support for increased defence budgets to keep sufficient numbers of professional soldiers in peacetime. The UK government's willingness to exploit this relationship in the pursuit of its policies has made these developments particularly problematic, since Liberal models of democratic control put a great emphasis on delimiting the use of armed force by containing the size of the military and the defence budget.

This specifically concerns the deployment of soldiers in international conflicts because, once the armed forces are involved in combat, public support has nearly always been unquestioning. In the UK this has been due to a combination of disinterest and patriotism. Disinterest created by the civil–military gap has allowed the government to use its armed forces in conflicts that appear to have no direct relevance to homeland security. Patriotism has ensured that British citizens have rallied behind the government and the armed forces as soon as the latter have been deployed.[115] Historically, this response has been determined by a cultural tradition derived from the experiences of the two World Wars. Under the changed models of the soldier and democratic control over the armed forces, this tradition is outdated and dangerous because it assumes a congruence of the government, the armed forces and society which has been lost during the shift from the Republican warfare state to the Neoliberal models of the state and the soldier. In modern times, as Hugh Stachan argues, such a view of public patriotism presents 'a threat to democracy, freedom of speech and the politics of accountability'.[116] With the growing autonomy of the executive regarding the use of armed force, public scrutiny and debate are more important than ever before. Moreover, as the next section points out, the changing motivation and identity of the professional soldier and the

---

[115] H. Strachan, 'Making Strategy: Civil-Military Relations after Iraq', *Survival*, 48, no. 3 (2006), 73–4.
[116] Strachan, 'Making Strategy: Civil-Military Relations after Iraq', 74.

growing role of private military contractors are challenging the role of professional self-regulation in facilitating the democratic control and accountability of the armed forces.

Professional self-regulation

The UK government's struggle to maintain full control over the increasingly private provision of military services exacerbates the problem of executive autonomy. Owing to the proliferation of private military contractors in proportion to government personnel, the MOD not only finds it difficult to ensure effective contract management, but also cannot count anymore on the professional self-regulation of its civil servants and soldiers to control the actions of its employees on the ground.

That the expanding scope, duration and complexity of private military contracting is creating problems for its management and oversight has been widely noted. In 2005 a MOD Private Finance Unit review of major PFI projects observed that contract management teams in the Defence Logistics Organization and other top-level agencies were under-resourced in terms of personnel and expertise, and frequently not in sufficiently close contact with private contractors to ensure effective supervision.[117] Moreover, major cuts in the civilian workforce of the Defence Equipment and Support Agency from 31,600 in 2005 to 14,900 in 2008 have significantly reduced the number of available project management teams.[118] Rather than reversing its policy of personnel cuts, the government has sought to alleviate the oversight problem through its partnering approach with the industry. However, as noted above, the assumption that the interests of the armed forces and profit-oriented companies can be aligned has proven unrealistic in many cases.

While the issue of contract management concerns the relations of the armed forces with the companies which supply it with military and support services, the lack of professional regulation, standards and identity among contracted personnel adds another dimension to the problem of democratic control and accountability. There are still no specific regulations for private military firms and their employees in the UK. Although the New Labour government approved a law

---

[117] MOD, Private Finance Unit, *Review of MOD PFI Projects in Construction and Operation*, p. 17.

[118] The Defence Equipment and Support Agency was formed in 2007 out of the merger of the Defence Logistics and Defence Procurement Agencies. Defence Analytical Services Agency, *UK Defence Statistics 2005* and *UK Defence Statistics 2008*, at: www.dasa.mod.uk.

for domestic security services in the Private Security Industry Act, armaments and private military firms fall outside its remit.[119] Plans for regulation of private military companies set out in a Green Paper in 2002 have failed due to internal differences among the MOD, the Foreign and Commonwealth Office and the Department of Trade and Industry.[120]

In the place of comprehensive regulations for the emerging private military industry, the government has sought to address the practical issues of control and authority with two policies, namely sponsored reserves and Contractors on Deployed Operations (CONDO). However, as discussed in detail in Chapter 7, both only apply to contractors operating abroad in international interventions. In the national arena, the government has left the issue of professional standards to private sector organizations such as the British Association of Private Security Companies (BAPSC). The association was launched in 2006 and has, so far, only five full members who fulfil the membership criteria modelled on the industry standards set out by the governmental Security Industry Authority.[121]

The preceding analysis shows that the UK government's particular application of the Neoliberal model of civil–military relations and the model's inherent limitations have had important consequences for the relations of accountability and control between the state, the citizen and the soldier. Foremost, the growing role of private military contractors has decreased the ability of citizens and parliaments to control the provision and use of armed force in the UK. While Neoliberalism suggests that the fragmentation of functions and resources contributes to containing the influence of public and private security providers, New Labour's turn towards private financing, long-term contracts and partnering with industry has shifted the balance of power in favour of the executive and the private military sector. The latter is the more problematic since the government and the armed forces have increasingly lacked the ability to compete with and manage its private contractors due to cuts in personnel and expertise. Moreover, the private military industry neither has the professional standards, nor is it subject to government regulations which could replace the self-regulation of the professional soldier who has been

---

[119] Security Industry Authority (SIA), at: www.the-sia.org.uk.
[120] Foreign and Commonwealth Office, *Private Military Companies: Options for Regulation*, HC 577 (London: The Stationery Office, 12 February 2002).
[121] BAPSC, at www.bapsc.org.uk.

bound to the state and society through formal and informal rules of democratic conduct and responsibility.

Conclusion

The UK has been one of the first Western countries to outsource a large range of its national military services. Moreover, through the use of private financing, its armed forces have become reliant on private sector resources and services to a greater scale than most Western democracies. This chapter has illustrated that the rise of Neoliberalism has played an important role in legitimizing the growing contribution of private military contractors to UK security. It has shown that the ostensibly pragmatic approaches of Conservative and New Labour governments towards the privatization and contracting-out of large sections of its defence provision were built upon a vision of the roles of the state, the citizen and the soldier that has clear ideological foundations in Neoliberal thought. Whether under the label of Thatcherism or the Third Way, the ideal has been to convert the state from a provider to a manager of defence, and to cut back the size of the armed forces by outsourcing an ever increasing range of functions to private military businesses. The key objective has been to transform the UK warfare state into a more cost-efficient, responsive and publicly accountable system of democratic governance.

It can be argued that some progress may have been made towards this aim. In this respect, the size of the UK defence budget has been reduced from 3.9 per cent at the end of the Cold War to 2.6 per cent of GDP in 2006, and the number of civilian and uniformed armed forces personnel have been cut from 487,000 to 282,000 between 1990 and 2008. From a historical perspective, these developments seem reminiscent of the limitations that Liberalism placed on the democratic provision and use of military force during the eighteenth and nineteenth centuries. Yet the above analysis questions whether Neoliberalism has indeed improved democratic control and accountability in the UK. The growing role of private military contractors seems to be at the centre of the issue. Rather than merely providing surge capacity in time of national need, the UK government's strategy of long-term contracting through PFI and partnering arrangements has meant that private contractors have become permanent components of the armed forces, thus requiring new mechanisms of control and accountability. Instead of dealing with these issues, the complexity of PFI contracts, off-the-book accounting and the lack of public information about the military have further removed private military contractors from public scrutiny. Moreover, the government's substitution of professional soldiers with private military contractors and the increasingly occupational view of its soldiers have weakened the ability of the armed forces to regulate themselves and have widened the gap between the soldier and society.

5 United States: shrinking the state, outsourcing the soldier

As in the UK, the US armed forces have massively expanded their use of private military contractors since the end of the Cold War. From military logistics, training, maintenance and intelligence analysis to management, the issue of defence privatization in the USA has been well documented. However, little attention has been paid to its origins in the transition from Republican to Neoliberal models of the state, the citizen and the soldier.[1] In the 1980s President Ronald Reagan already introduced the ideological rationale for the outsourcing of military functions to private firms with his advocacy of the 'small state'. Simultaneous increases in defence spending prevented these policies from having a major impact on the composition of the armed forces, but Reagan's successors George Bush (1989–93), Bill Clinton (1993–2001) and George W. Bush (2001–9), have applied Neoliberal principles to the military on a large scale. The end of the superpower confrontation facilitated these reforms because it seemed to usher in a more peaceful 'new world order' which permitted significant cuts in government defence spending and the size of the armed forces. In addition, the Clinton government favoured essentially Neoliberal policies, albeit perhaps not labelling them so, such as cuts in the military budget and the reduction of government debt.[2] US public opinion supported these cuts as part of a major peace dividend. A few years after the end of the Cold War the US government had to revise its security assessment due to the emergence of new threats ranging from the ethnic conflict in the former Yugoslavia, civil wars in Somalia and Rwanda, and international terrorism. In particular, the George W. Bush administration (hereafter the Bush administration) adopted increasingly interventionist security policies, aimed at addressing security threats before they could have a

---

[1] A. Markusen, 'The Case Against Privatizing National Security', *Governance*, 16, no. 4 (2003), 480.
[2] Commission on Roles and Missions of the Armed Forces, *Directions for Defense* (Washington DC: DOD, 1995), p. 3–1.

major impact on the US homeland. However, the growing number and scope of international military interventions conducted by the US military has not lead to a systematic reversal of the post-Cold War reductions in defence spending and military personnel. Instead, the financial pressures of multiple military interventions overseas have increased the pace of Neoliberal reforms and the outsourcing of a growing range of military functions to private contractors. As the result, the US military has been faced with a quandary. On the one hand, the US DOD has had to realize that 'in the future, the U.S. Military will be called on to perform a broader array of missions in more diverse contingency situations than they did in the past while still maintaining a capability for large-scale regional conflicts'.[3] On the other hand, its resources have been increasingly curtailed due to defence budget cuts of nearly 40 per cent and the failure to return regular military spending to Cold War levels in spite of the global 'war on terror' and military interventions in Afghanistan and Iraq.[4]

Together these developments suggest that changes in the international security context after the end of the Cold War offer only a partial explanation for the use of private military contractors in US national defence. Equally important has been the ideological commitment of the Clinton and Bush administrations to Neoliberal models of the state, the citizen and the soldier. These models depart from the premise that private businesses are not only able to supply military and security services more cost-efficiently, but also facilitate democratic control because they are more receptive to the demands of the 'consumer'. This chapter examines the ideological context and practical evolution of the hire of private military contractors in the USA along the dimensions introduced in the preceding chapters. The first section examines the ideological transformation which has redefined the norms, interests and relations of the state and its citizens regarding the provision of US national security. The second section analyses the impact of this ideological shift on the definition of the functions of the state and the military, the distribution of resources, and the growing involvement of private contractors in decision-making and the implementation of security policies. The third section investigates how these changes have affected the model of the soldier and civil–military relations in the USA. Finally, the chapter discusses how these transformations in the roles of and relationships between the state, the citizen and

---

[3] *Ibid.*, p. vii. See also I. K. Garcia-Perez, 'Contractors on the Battlefield in the 21st Century', *Army Logistician*, 31, no. 6 (1999), 40.

[4] DOD, *Improving the Combat Edge through Outsourcing* (Washington DC, March 1996), p. 2.

the soldier impact on democratic control and accountability, and how the US government has responded to these challenges.

Neoliberalism and the armed forces

While in the UK the period after the Second World War saw the nationalization of nearly all areas of defence, the USA never fully abandoned the principle of private military production, leading to the emergence of the military–industrial complex in the 1960s. In 1955 the Eisenhower administration proclaimed: 'It is the general policy of the Federal Government that it will not start or carry on any commercial activity to provide a service or product for its use if such product or service can be procured from private enterprise through ordinary business channels.'[5] Nevertheless, it took until 1966 for the government to introduce specific procedures for comparing public and private sector provisions of goods and services in the Office of Management and Budget (OMB) Circular A-76. Although Circular A-76 was not used extensively at the time, it has laid the foundations for the outsourcing of military services in the USA. Since it is still in use, it merits further examination. In practice, the A-76 process involves five stages. At the first stage the armed forces identify a function which could be outsourced to the private sector. At the second stage they notify Congress of the impending evaluation. At the third, the evaluation stage, the military base responsible for the function develops a statement which outlines the type of work, the work hours and skills required. At the fourth stage the armed forces publicly advertise the statement and invite bids from private companies. At the same time the military develops a competing bid, known as the Most Efficient Organization (MEO). Finally, the military and private sector bids are compared. If a private sector bid is 10 per cent of the personnel cost or $10 million lower than the MEO, the contract is awarded to the private bidder.[6] After the contract ends, the function is again advertised among competing private firms. Notably, rebidding does not, usually, involve another A-76 cost comparison with in-house supply. The A-76 process has, thus, contributed to the progressive expansion of private sector provision of military services.

[5] W. S. Cohen, Secretary of Defense, *Defense Reform Initiative Report* (Washington DC, November 1997), p. 28.
[6] J. W. Lavadour, 'Pitfalls of the A-76 Process. Pressures of a Shrinking Budget: Outsourcing', *Air Force Journal of Logistics*, 25, no. 4 (2001), 3, 40–2; House Armed Services Committee, Military Readiness Subcommittee, *Testimony of David M. Walker, Comptroller General of the United States and Chair of the Commercial Activities Panel* (26 June 2002).

While widely employed by all federal government agencies, the US armed forces have been the largest single user of the A-76 procedure.[7] Moreover, following the rise of Neoliberalism in the 1980s, the extent of the DOD's acquisition of military services from private firms under A-76 procedures has nearly doubled.[8] The ideological imperative to 'roll back the state' bridged the political divide between the Republican and the Democrat Parties and both the Clinton and the Bush administrations progressively applied it to national and international security. When Clinton was elected president in 1993, his objective was to decrease the role of governmental public service provision in favour of the private market. The reforms were headed by Vice-President Al Gore whose National Performance Review sought to identify the potential for reducing the scope of government. In a speech given to a conference on government reform and reinvention Gore summarized the Neoliberal aims of the Clinton administration: 'We are here ... to talk about a subject that lies at the very heart of economic growth and productivity – even basic political legitimacy – for the 21st century: reforming and reinventing government so that it is smaller, smarter and more responsive.'[9] Gore's vision presented a transition from the Republican warfare state to the Neoliberal ideal of fragmenting functions, resources and influence among public and private security providers. It encouraged the self-government of citizens as full partners in the processes of governance and proposed privatization, deregulation and the reduction of taxes and public spending. Gore's Neoliberal model also promised that the democratic control and accountability of public services would be improved by treating citizens as customers.[10]

The Clinton administration's expressed objective was to aggressively pursue the outsourcing and privatization of public services and to introduce new management procedures in those public sectors which could not be privatized.[11] In order to examine how Gore's policies could be applied to the military, the government set up the Commission on Roles and Missions of the Armed Forces. Two years later, the Commission

---

[7] House Armed Services Committee, Military Readiness Subcommittee, *Testimony of David M. Walker.*

[8] Cohen, *Defense Reform Initiative Report*, p. 28; House Armed Services Committee, Military Readiness Subcommittee, *Testimony of Michael W. Wyne, Principal Deputy Under Secretary of Defense for Acquisitions* (June 26, 2002).

[9] 'Gore Pushing Privatization', excerpts from speech on 14 January 1999, *PM (Program Manager)*, 28, no. 2 (1999), 18–22.

[10] *Ibid.*

[11] W. J. Perry, Secretary of Defense, *Annual Report to the President and the Congress 1996* (Washington DC, March 1996), Chapter 6.

published its report, identifying increased competition and efficiency as core elements for improving the government's and the armed forces' provision of national security.[12] The Commission argued that outsourcing and management reforms would help to reduce the cost of defence.[13] Instead of providing all aspects related to the functioning of the armed forces, the Commission proposed that the military should focus on its 'core competencies' and rid itself of 'commercial-type' functions. As the latter, it identified warehousing, weapon system depot maintenance and property management, which could be better and more cheaply supplied by the private sector.[14] The Commission also suggested that the armed forces should directly turn to the private sector for all newly required support functions without going through the A-76 process.[15]

As a first step, the Commission advocated the elimination of restrictive legislation in the United States Code, Title 10 – Armed Forces which prohibited the contracting-out of key military occupations.[16] Among others, the US Code stipulated that federal employees had to perform at least 60 per cent of depot maintenance and prohibited the outsourcing of firefighting and security guard functions.[17] Other restrictions applied to the use of foreign components in the production of military equipment.[18] The Defense Science Board Task Force also criticized the level of Congressional scrutiny of outsourcing and privatization decisions, arguing that 'the current legal environment encourages the politicization of the outsourcing decision process, and thereby complicates, delays and discourages DOD efforts to increase its reliance on private vendors for support services'.[19]

In 1996 the DOD report *Improving the Combat Edge Through Outsourcing* presented an outline of how these policies could be implemented; and one year later Secretary of Defence William S. Cohen's Defense Reform Initiative elaborated the introduction of new management techniques and business practices in the armed forces.[20] Neither

[12] Commission on Roles and Missions of the Armed Forces, *Directions for Defense*, p. ES-2.
[13] *Ibid.*, p. ES-3.
[14] *Ibid.*, p. ES-4, p. ES-6.
[15] *Ibid.*, p. ES-6, p. 3–3.
[16] *Ibid.*, p. ES-6. For a list of the recommended legislative changes see Appendix A of the report.
[17] DOD, *Improving the Combat Edge Through Outsourcing*, p. 15, p. 17.
[18] W. S. Cohen, Secretary of Defense, *Annual Report to the President and Congress* (Washington DC, April 1997), Chapter 13.
[19] Report of the Defense Science Board Task Force on CS&P, August 1996, p. 38a, cited in S. E. Newbold, 'Competitive Sourcing and Privatization: An Essential USAF Strategy', *Air Force Journal of Logistics*, 23, no. 1 (1999), 28–34.
[20] DOD, *Improving the Combat Edge Through Outsourcing*; Cohen, *Defense Reform Initiative Report*, p. i.

of these reports examined whether or when outsourcing and competition between the public and private sectors were more cost-efficient and effective than governmental services; instead they stated the superiority of these measures as a fact.[21] The prime motive for the privatization and outsourcing of military functions was projected savings of about 20 per cent.[22] A second objective was greater effectiveness, and a third aim was improved responsiveness to the needs of the armed forces and the nation.[23] According to the government's Neoliberal convictions, cost efficiency would go hand in hand with increased attention to customer satisfaction.[24]

The flaws in the assumption that public–private competition would automatically and in every area of government lead to substantive cost reductions showed within the first three years of the reforms. In 1999 the House Committee on Armed Services 'noted that prior Department of Defense reform initiatives had not generated the anticipated savings and had created difficulties because of premature budget reductions'.[25] Instead of investing in a comprehensive investigation of the conditions for efficient outsourcing in the military, the Clinton government changed its arguments regarding the advantages of its privatization policies. The Annual Defense Report simply modified the assessment criteria for the success of public–private competition from greater cost efficiency to 'improved performance'.[26] However, contractor performance proved as difficult to evaluate as cost efficiency because service contracts did not always lead to measurable end products.[27] Performance assessment also increased the administrative burden for the DOD since it required the constant monitoring of contract provisions in terms of 'quality of work or product, accessibility, timeliness, accuracy, and customer satisfaction'.[28]

---

[21] DOD, *Improving the Combat Edge Through Outsourcing*, p. 5.

[22] Commission on Roles and Missions of the Armed Forces, *Directions for Defense*, p. ES-6, pp. 3–2–3–3.

[23] *Ibid.*, p. ES-7.

[24] *Ibid.*, p. ES-7, p. 3–26; Perry, *Annual Report to the President and the Congress 1996*, Message of the Secretary of Defense; Cohen, *Defense Reform Initiative Report*, p. iii.

[25] Government Accounting Office (GAO), *Future Years Defense Program: How Savings from Reform Initiatives Affect DOD's 1999–2003 Program*, GAO/NSIAD-99–66 (Washington DC: GAO, February 1999), p. 1.

[26] W. S. Cohen, Secretary of Defense, *Annual Report to the President and Congress 1999* (Washington DC, 1999), Chapter 13.

[27] A. Friar, 'Why Training for Service Contract Management Is Mission Essential', *Defense Acquisition Review*, 39, no. 2 (2004), 268.

[28] J. Cavadias, 'Contract Administration in a Performance-Based Acquisitions Environment Is Serious Business', *Defense Acquisition Review*, 39, no. 3 (2004–5), 326.

By 2001 it had become clear that public–private cost comparisons and outsourcing were not producing the projected military budget savings.[29] Nevertheless, the newly elected Bush administration remained firmly committed to the Neoliberal ideal of increasing the role of private firms in the provision of military services. In order to encourage the armed forces to search for additional outsourcing opportunities and internal efficiency reforms, the government raised the numerical quotas for military positions to be examined through A-76 cost comparisons.[30] In addition, the government advocated partnerships with the industry as a means for reducing management cost. Like the UK, it believed that long-term contracts and stable relations with particular suppliers would generate mutual trust and decrease the need for governmental oversight.

This persistence of the Neoliberal belief that private military contractors are able to supply military equipment and services not only more cost-efficiently but also more democratically, in spite of evidence to the contrary, illustrates the importance of ideology in determining civil–military relations. It confirms that decisions regarding the provision and control of armed force are not defined exclusively by rational and functional arguments. Nevertheless, ideals are transformed in empirical praxis. The next section analyses how successive governments have applied the Neoliberal model of security governance to the armed forces, and how this has transformed the roles and relations of the state and the military in the USA.

Revising the functions of the state and the armed forces

Building on the Neoliberal principle that the democratic control and accountability of the state and the military are best protected by delimiting their functions and resources, the USA has become internationally known for the scale to which it has outsourced national and international security services to private military contractors. In 2008 the US defence budget amounted to $650 billion of which the armed forces spent $315 billion on military equipment and services supplied by private companies.[31] This section assesses the unique features of the transformation of the roles of the state and the armed forces in the USA in terms of three developments. The first concerns the redefinition of what functions are 'inherently governmental' and, thus, affect the state

---

[29] R. H. Graves, 'Seeking Defense Efficiency', *Defense Acquisitions Review*, 36, no. 4 (2001), 51.
[30] Anonymous, 'House Concerned Over Privatization', *Army*, 53, no. 2 (2003), 10.
[31] DOD, *Fiscal Year 2008 Agency Report* (Washington DC, 17 November 2008), p. 108.

monopoly on collective violence; the second concerns the growing number and scope of private military contracts; and the third examines the conversion of the military from a provider to a manager of national defence.

Defining the military core

One of the key factors in the expansion of private military contracting, but also one that distinguishes the USA and Germany most clearly from the UK, has been the debate over what roles and functions are inherently governmental and what can be outsourced to the private sector.[32] Until the mid 1990s the conception of the central functions of the state and the armed forces was fairly broad. The Commission on Roles and Mission of the Armed Forces held the view that governmental core functions included all tasks that 'represent the exercise of sovereign power'.[33] The Commission also recognized that the private market did not supply some types of services and was unlikely to develop the capabilities to do so, making them unsuitable candidates for privatization. Accordingly, the Commission identified only a few select services as areas for private contracting. Most of them pertained to civilian support functions and were provided on US national territory, such as depot maintenance, medical care and family housing.[34] To improve the efficiency of other functions such as military logistics and aviation support, the Commission recommended in-house reforms rather than outsourcing.[35] Finally, the Commission emphasized that an extensive use of private military contractors would necessitate a shift in the role of the armed forces from that of a security provider to a manager. The ability to perform new management and oversight functions would require significant investments and retraining of DOD staff.[36]

A DOD report, published in 1996, was similarly cautious regarding the potential scope of military outsourcing. According to the report, the armed forces would only consider contracting out military services which met three conditions: (1) they did not affect core capabilities, (2) there was a competitive market for these activities, and (3) outsourcing would improve either performance or lower the cost of a service in the

---

[32] Commission on Roles and Missions of the Armed Forces, *Directions for Defense*, p. 3–3; F. Camm, *Expanding Private Production of Defense Services* (Santa Monica, CA: RAND, 1996), p. 3.
[33] Commission on Roles and Missions of the Armed Forces, *Directions for Defense*, p. 3–3.
[34] *Ibid.*, pp. 3–6–3–14.   [35] *Ibid.*, pp. 3–14–3–25.
[36] *Ibid.*, p. 3–3.

context of long-term competition.[37] The DOD reiterated these three conditions in the following year. In fact, the Annual Defense Report 1997 argued: 'Many activities can be best performed by the government entities currently doing the job – because of expertise or technological edge, or for other reasons. In these cases, the Department will retain these capabilities.'[38] The revised supplemental handbook for Circular A-76 of 1996 clearly stated that some technical tasks could not be fully outsourced because of the government's need to retain expertise in these areas as well as for 'reasons of national defense, including military mobilization, security, [and] rotational necessity'.[39]

While the armed forces took a restrictive view of the possible scope of military outsourcing, the Clinton government's interpretation of the Commission's recommendations was different. Secretary of Defence William J. Perry praised the Commission's report as 'far-reaching' in its identification of potential areas for the privatization of military services. He, incorrectly, suggested that the report recommended the wholesale outsourcing of 'education and training, family housing, finance and accounting, data center operations, base infrastructure operations, some elements of medical care, and depot maintenance, as well as direct support of new weapon systems'.[40] Based on this interpretation of the report, Perry and his successor William S. Cohen promised that the DOD would increase its efforts to contract military services out to the private market.[41] Cohen repeated that key to the reform of the US military was a concentration on its core competencies.[42] However, Cohen omitted to elaborate what these core functions were that would be exempt from market competition. The Clinton administration had no clear set of political or even functional criteria to determine what tasks should remain with the government and the armed forces. Instead it passed the responsibility of defining its core functions back to the military. The Federal Activities Inventory Reform (FAIR) Act 1998 required all executive government agencies, including the armed forces, to compile an annual inventory of functions which could be opened up to commercial competition under the A-76 process. However, the Act lacked political guidance on what functions were central to the state

---

[37] DOD, *Improving the Combat Edge Through Outsourcing*, p. 4.
[38] Cohen, *Annual Report to the President and Congress 1999*, Chapter 13.
[39] Office of Management and Budget, *Circular A-76 Revised Supplemental Handbook*, Performance of Commercial Activities (March 1996), p. 35, cited in Newbold, 'Competitive Sourcing and Privatization', 28–34.
[40] Perry, *Annual Report to the President and the Congress 1996*, Chapter 6.
[41] *Ibid.*
[42] Cohen, *Defense Reform Initiative Report*, p. iii.

monopoly on collective violence.[43] By definition, all military services that private companies were willing and able to provide were 'commercial in nature', and the military was pressed to make savings in order to maintain its capabilities in the light of shrinking defence budgets.

By 1999 a consensus appears to have emerged between the government and the armed forces that, apart from the military services legally exempt from outsourcing, the DOD would only exclude tasks which 'directly' contributed to combat or combat support from consideration for privatization.[44] Direct combat support, however, was as difficult to define as the core functions of the military. As Stephen E. Newbold put it, 'the fighter pilot flying combat sorties directly contributes to combat. But what about the in-theatre aircraft maintenance, transporters and supply personnel?'[45] Unsurprisingly, the annual inventories drawn up under the FAIR Act varied considerably between government agencies and even within the DOD. Each service and military unit developed its own interpretations of what to include under 'inherently governmental' and what under 'commercial-type' activities.[46]

Nevertheless, the FAIR Act succeeded in providing the government with a basis for increasing its pressure to expand the use of private suppliers by offering concrete data on the number and types of services which could potentially be outsourced to the private sector. Specifically, the Clinton administration used the data to set central government targets for the number of work positions, also called Full Time Equivalents (FTEs), to be investigated through the A-76 competition process. In 1996 the Defense Reform Initiative set this number to 30,000 positions annually for the next seven years, amounting to a total of 150,000 FTEs subject to assessment by the armed forces by 2003.[47] In order to force the armed forces to make full use of the A-76 process to improve its cost efficiency, the government deduced the projected savings from contracting out these positions in advance from the defence budgets.[48]

The Bush administration adopted an even stricter line on the definition of core military functions in its efforts to increase the private sector provision of national security. In the Annual Defense Report 2002 the

---

[43] W. M. Anderson, J. J. McGuiness and J. S. Spicer, *From Chaos to Clarity: How Current Cost-Based Strategies Are Undermining the Department of Defense* (Fort Belvoir, VA: Defense Acquisitions University Press, September 2001), pp. 4–16.

[44] J. Pulley, 'A Private Worker May Take Your Job', *Air Force Times*, 9 February 1998, p. 11, cited in Newbold, 'Competitive Sourcing and Privatization', 28–34.

[45] Newbold, 'Competitive Sourcing and Privatization'.

[46] GAO, *Defense Management: DOD Faces Challenges Implementing Its Core Competency Approach and A-76 Competitions*, GAO-03–818 (Washington DC, July 2003).

[47] Anderson *et al.*, *From Chaos to Clarity*, pp. 4–13.

[48] *Ibid.*, pp. 4–14.

government criticized the lack of progress made by the armed forces' outsourcing and privatization programs under Clinton: 'Traditionally, "core" has been loosely and imprecisely defined, and too often used as a way of protecting existing arrangements.'[49] To counteract this tendency, the Bush administration raised the target of DOD positions to be submitted to the A-76 procedure to a total of 226,000 FTEs between 2004 and 2009.[50] Although the armed forces repeatedly failed to meet the new targets set by the federal government, by 2005 A-76 competitions had resulted in 'the contracting out of work formerly performed by over 39,000 uniformed and DOD civilian personnel'.[51] The next section discusses the scale of this development and the range of functions which have been outsourced to the private sector.

Military contracting expanded

The Neoliberal redefinition of the core functions of the state and the soldier by the Clinton and Bush administrations has transformed the contributions of private contractors to US national security. Since the size of US military contracting prohibits a detailed analysis of all major programmes, this section examines two developments to illustrate the growing role of private military contractors in national defence. The first concerns the quantitative expansion in the private provision of military services. The second concerns the qualitative extension of the types of functions outsourced to the private sector.

The changing balance between public and private providers has been most noticeable in the growing proportion of military services supplied by private contractors. Already by 1996 the DOD bought '25 percent of base commercial activities, 28 percent of depot maintenance, 10 percent of finance and accounting, 70 percent of Army aviation training, 45 percent of surplus property disposal, and 33 percent of parts distributions' from the private sector.[52] In the following decade the total spending on private military services increased by 146 per cent from $46 to $113 billion.[53] As Figure 5.1 illustrates, the largest increases in commercial service provision have occurred in administration and

---

[49] D. H. Rumsfeld, Secretary of Defense, *Annual Report to the President and Congress 2002* (Washington DC, 2002), Chapter 9.

[50] *Annual Defense Report 2003*, p. 64.

[51] GAO, *Defense Budget: Trends in Operation and Maintenance Costs and Support Services Contracting*, GAO-07–631 (Washington DC, May 2007), p. 19.

[52] DOD, *Improving the Combat Edge Through Outsourcing*, p. 8.

[53] By comparison, the US defence budget expanded by only 85 per cent from $254 to $470 billion. See DOD, Statistical Information Analysis Division, DOD Procurement Reports 1996 and 2006.

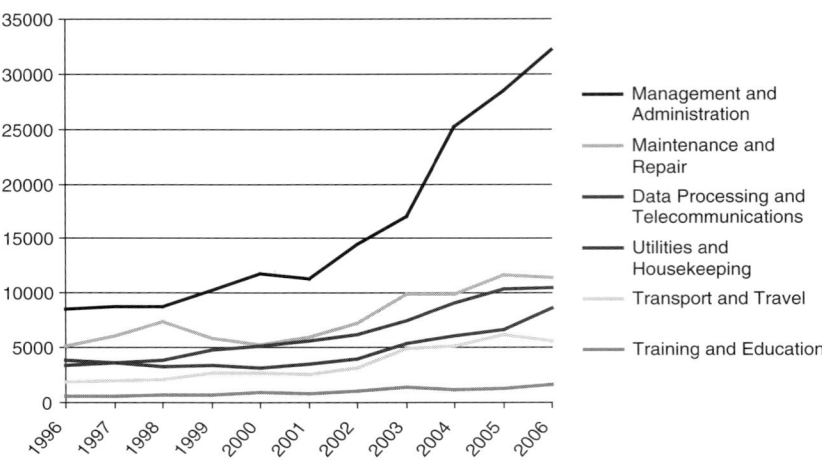

Figure 5.1 DOD military service procurement (million $)

management (277 per cent), transport and travel (190 per cent), train-ing and education (178 per cent), data processing and communications (173 per cent), utilities and housekeeping (154 per cent), and mainten-ance and repair (122 per cent).[54] Some of the expansion of contracts has been the result of the growing proportion of private contracting for particular services such as transport and travel. Other increases have been caused by the growing functional scope of the private sector in the provision of national security. The largest growth areas have included tasks which have been considered inherently governmental functions until the mid 1990s, such as the management of the armed forces and its facilities.

The growing scale of private sector involvement has also been a result of the increasing size and complexity of individual contracts. By the 1990s the armed forces had begun to expand private military contract-ing through the use of indefinite delivery/indefinite quantity (IDIQ) contracts which permit the contracting units to request an indefinite number of services, defined by so-called 'task orders', within a set max-imum budget. Its prime example has been the army's Logistic Civil Augmentation Program (LOGCAP) which has been advertised four times as an IDIQ contract. Typically, about 30 per cent of the largest armed forces contracts, ranging from total life-cycle support for major weapons systems to military research and development, have been

---

[54] Compare GAO, *Defense Budget: Trends in Operation and Maintenance Costs and Support Services Contracting*, p. 3.

awarded on a cost-plus basis.[55] In addition, the US armed forces have turned to outsourcing programmes which not only encompass the provision of services, but also the transfer of funding and ownership to private businesses. Two major programmes have used this approach so far. The first large-scale military procurement programme financed by private capital was the Military Housing Privatization Initiative.[56] The second was the privatization of the US armed forces utilities supplies, including electricity, gas, water, sewage and telecommunication, which are owned, operated and managed by private firms.[57] In contrast to the UK, however, the US government has so far limited its use of private capital funding for military equipment or facilities. While the plans for the extension of private sector financing date back to the Defense Reform Initiative in 1997, the military has used private resources primarily through the leasing of commercial facilities and civilian technologies.[58]

The increasing range of functions outsourced to private military companies has been a second consequence of the application of the Neoliberal model to the armed forces. Like the UK, the US government initially contracted out primarily civilian functions, such as catering and cleaning, or highly specialized technical services, such as the maintenance and training for the Air Force's KC-10 and F-117 aircraft. Over time, however, the pressure on the military to submit more and more positions for consideration for private sector bids has led to a progressive expansion of the number and types of functions delegated to commercial suppliers. This has been facilitated by the fact that public–private competitions according to the A-76 process are not necessary for new or expanded military service requirements or for the continued provision of a function which has already been contracted out. The range of functions defined as commercial rather than governmental thus covers the whole spectrum of the civilian and military tasks of the armed forces, with the exception of large-scale armed combat. It includes utility supplies, medical services, depot maintenance and repair, the lease of equipment and facilities, installation and modification of military technologies, logistics, training, data analysis and processing, information technology, intelligence services, armed guarding and the management

---

[55] L. Mankinson, 'Outsourcing the Pentagon', Center for Public Integrity, 29 September 2004.

[56] GAO, *Military Housing: Better Reporting Needed on the Status of the Privatization Program and the Cost of its Consultants*, GAO-04–111 (Washington DC, October 2003).

[57] R. D. Helwig, 'Privatization of Utility Systems', *The Air Force Comptroller*, 34 (2000), 14–17; GAO, *Defense Infrastructure: Management Issues Requiring Attention in Utility Privatization*, GAO-05–433 (Washington DC, May 2005).

[58] Cohen, *Defense Reform Initiative Report*, Chapter 4.

of government-owned facilities.[59] Since the growing role of military contractors in many of these functions has been examined elsewhere, the following analysis focuses on three types of private military services which have previously been considered inherent functions of the state and the armed forces: armed security-guarding, intelligence analysis and management.[60]

Since the 1980s armed security-guarding has been a core task of the armed forces legally exempted from outsourcing 'because of concerns about the uncertain quality and reliability of private security guard services, base commanders' potential lack of control over contractor personnel, and the right of contractor personnel to strike'.[61] This changed in 2003 when Congress approved a waiver on the legal ban on the private guarding of domestic military bases due to the increased demands on military police and security guards after the terrorist attacks of 11 September 2001. Moreover, the waiver has been extended several times, the most recent extension lasting until 2012. In 2004 a total of 4,300 private security guards worked for the DOD under four contracts in the region of $1.24 billion.[62] To this have been added nearly 13,000 armed security guards deployed by the US armed forces in Iraq and Afghanistan, which do not fall under the legal prohibitions of the United States Code.

While the National Defense Authorization Act for Fiscal Year 2008 has ordered the number of private security guards working for the DOD to be reduced successively to 50 per cent of the personnel employed in 2006, the main criticisms of the programme have not stemmed from the hire of private military contractors for governmental functions, but from Neoliberal cost-efficiency concerns. A Government Accountability Office (GAO) report specifically noted that the DOD had awarded contracts for 46 out of 57 military installations without competition, paying about 25 per cent more than for other contracts.[63] The GAO report also observed that more than sixty private security guards were on record

---

[59] For an overview see GAO, *Defense Budget: Trends in Operation and Maintenance Cost and Support Services Contracting.*

[60] Markusen, 'The Case Against Privatizing National Security'; P. W. Singer, *Corporate Warriors: The Rise of the Privatized Military Industry* (Ithaca, NY: Cornell University Press, 2003); D. D. Avant, *The Market for Force: The Consequences of Privatizing Security* (Cambridge: Cambridge University Press, 2005), pp. 116–39.

[61] GAO, *Contract Security Guards: Army's Guard Program Requires Greater Oversight and Reassessment of Acquisition Approach*, GAO-06–284 (Washington DC, April 2006), p. 6.

[62] T. C. Miller, 'Army Turns to Private Guards', *LA Times*, 12 August 2004. The American unit 'billion' is used throughout this book instead of the European term 'milliard'.

[63] Subcontracting of up to 50 per cent is legally permissible. See GAO, *Contract Security Guards*, p. 3; Miller, 'Army Turns to Private Guards'.

for criminal offences, while others had poor or insufficient training.[64] However, in spite of the problems with the oversight and management of armed security contractors, an army report published in 2006 continued to focus on the question of whether private security guards were more expensive than military personnel, relegating concerns regarding democratic control and accountability to the background.[65]

A similar development has characterized the hiring of private contractors for the direction and control of intelligence and counterintelligence, tasks which the OMB circular A-76 previously defined as inherently governmental.[66] Some of these contracts have hit the newspaper headlines, such as the contract between the Intelligence and Security Command and Titan for interpreters, who were later implicated in the abuse of prisoners at the Abu Ghraib prison in Iraq.[67] Again at Guantánamo Bay, private firms such as Affiliated Computer Systems and Chenega Federal Systems have supplied interrogators and strategic debriefers.[68] The scale of military intelligence contracting has been staggering. According to its former director, 70 per cent of the work at the now defunct Counterintelligence Field Activity unit was conducted by private contractors.[69] In short, intelligence has been transformed from a function of the state and the armed forces to a commercial activity. As will be discussed in detail in Chapter 7, several incidents have illustrated the problems of the growing role of private intelligence contractors. The accusations of torture against private military personnel in Abu Ghraib, for instance, have raised the question of how private contractors, some of whom had not been screened and 35 per cent of whom lacked formal military training as interrogators, could have held positions of military authority.[70]

[64] GAO, *Contract Security Guards*, pp. 3–4.
[65] Deputy Assistant Secretary of the Army, Director for Programs and Strategy, *Contracting Versus Using Department of the Army Civilians to Provide Installation Security* (Washington DC, April 2005), cited in GAO, *Contract Security Guards*, p. 31.
[66] S. Chesterman, '"We Can't Spy … If We Can't Buy!": The Privatization of Intelligence and the Limits of Outsourcing "Inherently Governmental Functions"', *The European Journal of International Law*, 19, NO. 5 (2008), 1071.
[67] G. R. Fay, Investigating Officer, *AR 15–6 Investigation of the Abu Ghraib Detention Facility 205th Military Intelligence Brigade (2004)*, p. 48.
[68] T. Anderson, 'L-3 Cuts Bigger Slice of Govt Pie', *Washington Technology*, 15 May 2006; R. Gowland, 'Privatized Spying – It's All the Rage', *Guardian*, 13 June 2007; G. Witte and R. Merle, 'Contractors Are Cited in Abuses at Guantanamo', *Washington Post*, 4 January 2007.
[69] W. Pincus, 'Increase in Contracting Intelligence Jobs Raises Concerns', *Washington Post*, 20 March 2006. In 2008 the unit was subsumed by the Defense Intelligence Agency.
[70] Fay, *AR 15–6 Investigation of the Abu Ghraib Detention Facility 205th Military Intelligence Brigade (2004)*, p. 50.

The third and largest expansion of the role of private contractors with regard to core government functions concerns the management of the armed forces and its facilities. It illustrates the departure from earlier definitions of inherently governmental tasks as activities related to the definition of the public interest, and to the exertion of political and executive oversight.[71] As noted above, this area has seen an increase of 277 per cent between 1996 and 2006 with contractors employed in tasks such as the drafting of the US defence budget, the preparation of cost estimates for military contract work, and the management and monitoring of other military contractors.[72] The controversial nature of these functions derives from the involvement of private contractors in making political judgments. It is exemplified by the IDIQ contract between the armed forces and Cubic for 'helping to develop DOD policies and procedures, national security strategies, establishing and training foreign military forces and related program management and support'.[73]

As David M. Walker, the Comptroller General of the USA, has argued, the problem with contracting out management and administrative functions is that:

The closer contractor services come to supporting inherently governmental functions, the greater is the risk of their influencing the government's control and accountability for decisions that may be based, in part, on contractor work. This may result in decisions that are not in the best interest of the government, and may increase vulnerability to waste, fraud and abuse.[74]

The use of private contractors in military acquisition functions has raised particular concern because the DOD has frequently lost the capabilities and expertise to design, develop and manage complex acquisition programmes, relying instead on private companies to carry out these responsibilities. The Army's Future Combat System, for example, has been managed by a private company which has identified the necessary requirements of the system, selected the major contractors and subcontractors, and made decisions regarding the cost, schedules and capabilities of the programme.[75] The delegation of acquisition programme

[71] Office of Management and Budget, *Circular A-76 Revised Supplemental Handbook*, p. 35, cited in Newbold, 'Competitive Sourcing and Privatization'.
[72] GAO, *Defense Acquisitions: DOD Needs to Exert Management and Oversight to Better Control Acquisition of Services*, p. 4.
[73] Cubic, 'Cubic Receives Contract to Compete for Wide Range of U.S. Army Force Management Services', Press Release, 3 November 2003.
[74] GAO, *Defense Management: DOD Needs to Reexamine Its Extensive Reliance on Contractors and Continue to Improve Management and Oversight*, GAO-08–572T (Washington DC, 11 March 2008), p. 6.
[75] *Ibid*, p. 8.

design has also meant that the military finds it increasingly difficult to assess the performance of its contractors. As the next section will argue, the outsourcing of a growing range of functions has thus contributed to undermining the ability of the military to act as a manager of national security.

The military as manager

The third development which has characterized the rise of the Neoliberal models of the state and the soldier in the USA has been the progressive transformation of the roles of the military and private businesses with regard to decision-making and the implementation of national defence policies. In practice, this transformation has taken two different forms. Under the Clinton administration the primary objective was to change the armed forces from a supplier to a manager of military services. Drastic cuts among the civilian and military personnel of the DOD forced the armed forces to focus on its supposed core functions and on overseeing the growing number of contractors. Thus, by 2008 only 25,000 contract management personnel were in charge of procurement contracts in the region of $315 billion.[76] However, as in the UK, the simultaneity of management staff reductions and the expansion of private contracting have caused major problems for the democratic control and accountability of private military companies. The central Defence Contract Management Agency has awarded and managed only the largest and most important contracts because of limited resources and personnel. In the majority of cases, individual military bases or depots have selected and supervised their own contractors, despite a lack of qualified personnel.[77] Moreover, the pressure to focus on its core functions has meant for the military a concentration on combat operations and 'contract administration is given the lowest priority and is sometimes viewed as the necessary evil of the business'.[78]

In addition, the shift towards performance-based contracting has significantly increased the managerial and administrative burden of the DOD. In order to assess contractor performance, contracting units within the armed forces not only have had to hire or second additional staff for contract management, but also had to train them in the new procedures.[79] This has been particularly important where, as has been

---

[76] DOD, *Fiscal Year 2008 Agency Report*, p. 108.
[77] *Ibid.*
[78] Cavadias, 'Contract Administration in a Performance-Based Acquisitions Environment Is Serious Business', 326.
[79] Friar, 'Why Training for Service Contract Management Is Mission Essential', 267–77.

increasingly the case, contractor fees depend upon their performance. In these instances, 'the acquisition team cannot comfortably disperse immediately after contract award in the assumption that first-rate contract performance will consistently materialize ... On the contrary, each member of the team must tirelessly work together managing performance from the point of contract award until contract closeout'.[80] The pressure further increased when the Bush administration set a target of expanding performance-based service acquisitions to 40 per cent of all eligible services above $25,000.[81]

To alleviate these problems, in 2003 the Bush administration launched its Strategic Sourcing Initiative which promoted a new method.[82] Similar to the UK's partnering approach, the initiative argued that the military and industry should establish partnerships based on mutual trust rather than control and oversight.[83] Key elements of the new approach have been the consolidation of the DOD's purchasing power through service-wide contracts, the establishment of long-term supplier relationships with business alliances and the use of 'lead systems integrators', i.e. prime contractors that take over the management of major procurement programmes.[84] The government believed that public–private cooperation would 'provide the best of both worlds'.[85] Specifically, it argued that partnerships would help to overcome the problems with the length, complexity and cost of the A-76 process.[86] The consolidation of armed forces acquisition processes has sought to contribute to this aim by moving away from the decentralized system of contracting by the individual services and units towards centralized contract awards and management. This merger has not only sought to achieve economies of scale for the armed forces, but also to ease the management burden and increase public transparency by providing centralized information about private military contracting.[87]

[80]   Cavadias, 'Contract Administration in a Performance-Based Acquisitions Environment Is Serious Business', 326.
[81]   *Ibid.*, 325.
[82]   DOD, Office of the Under Secretary of Defense for Acquisition, Technology and Logistics, *Report to Office of Management and Budget: Implementation of Strategic Sourcing Initiatives* (Washington DC, January 2006), p. 1.
[83]   Camm, *Expanding Private Production of Defense Services*, p. 42.
[84]   DOD, Office of the Under Secretary of Defense for Acquisition, Technology and Logistics, *Report to the Office of Management and Budget: Implementation of Strategic Sourcing Initiatives, Fiscal Year 06 Update* (Washington DC, March 2007).
[85]   S. I. Erwin, 'Brass Ponders Mixed Blessings of Privatization', *National Defense*, 83, no. 544 (1999), 12.
[86]   R. Tiron, 'Public-Private Ventures Could Ease the Pains of Privatization', *National Defense*, 85, no. 570 (2001), 36.
[87]   DOD, *Report to the Office of Management and Budget: Implementation of Strategic Sourcing Initiatives*, p. 35.

While helping to redress the imbalance between the armed forces and the private military industry by consolidating the military's purchasing power and management efforts, the new approach has overlooked the fact that several circumstances make partnering between private companies and the military more difficult than partnering among private businesses. Partnerships in the private sector are typically based on long-term relationships between companies or business alliances. However, such long-term relations run counter to US government procurement rules prohibiting preferential treatment. Partnerships are also not necessarily the cheapest option because they limit full and open competition and are skewed in favour of larger businesses and conglomerates.[88] In fact, the partnership approach further undermines the public–private competition critical for the Neoliberal model of controlling the production and use of military force. The introduction of full life-cycle contracts for weapons systems with a single vendor, often the original manufacturer, as the preferred approach of the Bush administration has, thus, led to increasing the armed forces' dependency on single sources for the support of important weapons systems.[89] The award of large, complex and long-term strategic contracts to business alliances has encouraged additional industry mergers. Finally, partnerships have led to a duplication of infrastructures because companies develop full support systems independently from the resources already available within the armed forces.[90] One of the Defence Logistics Agency's (DLA) responses to duplication has been to become a subcontractor to its own prime contracting companies. In this seemingly absurd set-up, the DLA has sold spare parts to its prime contractors, who then sold them back to the DLA, because the DLA could buy these parts in bulk and, therefore, more cheaply.[91]

In summary, the above illustrates how the Neoliberal model of fragmented security governance has contributed to the growing role of private military contractors in US national defence. This role has been shaped by the redefinition of the core functions of the state and the armed forces, the outsourcing of an increasing number of positions to private businesses, and the turn towards long-term contracting and partnering arrangements with the industry. Significantly, the transformation of the state and the armed forces in the USA has followed similar developments to those in the UK. While initially both governments have

[88] S. P. Ferris and D. M. Keithly, 'Outsourcing the Sinews of War: Contractor Logistics', *Military Review*, 81, no. 5 (2001), 76.
[89] G. L. Starks, 'Public and Private Partnerships in Support of Performance-Based Logistics Initiatives – Lessons Learned from Defense Logistic Agency Partnerships', *Defense Acquisition Review*, 39, no. 3 (2004–5), 305–15.
[90] *Ibid.*, 306.
[91] *Ibid.*, 308.

Table 5.1. *US model of the state*

Dimension	USA
Ideology	• Neoliberalism
Geographical scope	• National, transnational
Functional scope	Extensive private provision of: • Utilities • Medical services • Maintenance and repair • Installation and modification of equipment • Logistics • Training • Data processing and IT • Armed guarding • Intelligence • Management and administration
Resources	Extensive private provision of: • Equipment • Facilities • Services Limited private provision of: • Financing (utilities and housing)
Interests	• 1990–99: Cost efficiency • Since 1999: Improved performance • Customer satisfaction
Norms	• Smarter, smaller, more responsive state
Decision-making	• A-76 public–private competition process • G. W. Bush: Strategic Sourcing Initiative, public–private partnerships, long-term supplier alliances, lead systems integrators
Implementation	• Short to medium-term contracting, penalties • IDIQ contracts • G. W. Bush: Performance-based services acquisition, service-wide contracts, total life-cycle systems management
Democratic control and accountability	• Fragmentation of functions and resources, limited public and Congressional scrutiny, growing dependence on private contractors • Clinton: public–private competitions • G. W. Bush: public–private partnerships

favoured public–private competition and short-term contracts for the provision of military services, since the end of the 1990s these mechanisms have been replaced by public–private partnerships and long-term alliances with leading contractors. However, there have also been major differences. In particular, the tradition of mixing Republican and Liberal principles in the US models of the state and the armed forces has been reflected in a comparatively greater concern over which functions have to be considered inherently governmental and, therefore, excluded from private sector competitions. While in the UK this question has been largely avoided, the US armed forces continue to debate it.[92] The DOD has, therefore, so far refrained from using private financing to the same extent as the UK, despite the large scale of private military contracting. Moreover, US law has retained some regulations which limit or prohibit the use of private military firms in specific functions such as security-guarding, depot maintenance and firefighting. Although some of these were suspended after the terrorist attacks of 11 September 2001, recent policies such as the gradual phasing-out of private security-guarding contracts until 2012 suggest a return to a public provision of key services. As the next section will demonstrate, similar differences can be observed with regard to the US model of the soldier.

Downsizing the professional military

The rise of Neoliberalism in the USA has also contributed to a revision of the professional soldier, and his/her motivation, identity and relationships with the state and society. This section observes the emergence of a new conception of the soldier and its consequences for the democratic control and accountability of the armed forces. It focuses on two developments in particular. The first has been the tension between the traditional ideal of the professional soldier and the rise of Neoliberal beliefs and principles. The second concerns the issue of whether the proliferation of private military contractors contributes to a civilianization of the US military or to a further widening of the civil–military gap.

Challenges to the professional soldier

The strengthening of Neoliberalism under the Clinton and Bush administrations has had both positive and negative consequences for the model of the professional soldier which has defined the US armed forces since 1973. On the one hand, the Neoliberal focus on civil rights has contributed to the democratization of the military. On the other hand, it has put into question the ideals of duty, honour, patriotism and

[92] GAO, *Defense Management: DOD Needs to Reexamine Its Extensive Reliance on Contractors and Continue to Improve Management and Oversight*, p. 5.

professionalism which have been at the heart of military service as a vocation. The Neoliberal emphasis on individual rights has specifically improved the representation and liberties of diverse groups within the armed forces. Often described as features of the 'postmodern military', civil rights have expanded in three main areas: gender equality, religious diversity and homosexuality.[93] While women have been included in the US military since the 1970s, the new Neoliberal policies have advocated the integration of female military personnel into all areas and functions of the armed forces. The introduction of gender-integrated training and mixed-gender units across the three services have been major steps towards this aim, as was the opening-up of some combat roles to women in the early 1990s.[94] In contrast to the UK, women make up 14 per cent of active armed forces personnel, and the professional armed forces' racial representation broadly reflects the composition of US society.[95] Similarly successful has been the extension of religious freedom in the military with the official recognition of a broader range of religious faiths.[96] The least progress has been made towards the equal rights of homosexuals.[97] Although the Clinton administration entered office with the explicit aim to lift the ban on homosexuals in the US military, it failed to gain sufficient support for its plans. The resulting 'Don't Ask, Don't Tell, Don't Pursue' policy has permitted homosexuals to serve in the armed forces if they do not publicize their sexual orientation.[98]

While Neoliberalism has laid the basis for a more representative military, its focus on rights over obligations has at the same time challenged the traditional model of the professional soldier. This challenge ranges from the motivations and identity of the individual soldier to the composition and management of the US armed forces. The ideals of patriotism and duty continue to play an important role for those who join the armed forces, in particular during major armed conflicts. A 2003 survey of male enlistment motivation thus found that 'doing something for our country' outranked all other reasons, whereas in 2001 it had only

[93] C. C. Moskos, 'Towards a Postmodern Military: The United States as a Paradigm', in C. C. Moskos, J. A. Williams and D. R. Segal (eds.) *The Postmodern Military* (Oxford: Oxford University Press, 2000), pp. 14–31.

[94] Moskos, 'Towards a Postmodern Military', p. 22.

[95] Office of the Undersecretary of Defense, Personnel and Readiness, *Population Representation in the Military Services – Fiscal Year 2006*, at: www.defenselink.mil.

[96] Moskos, 'Towards a Postmodern Military', p. 25.

[97] A. Belkin, ' "Don't Ask, Don't Tell": Does the Gay Ban Undermine the Military's Reputation?' *Armed Forces & Society*, 34, no. 2 (2007), 276–91.

[98] Moskos, 'Towards a Postmodern Military', 24–5; E. Kier, 'Homosexuals in the U.S. Military: Open Integration and Combat Effectiveness', *International Security*, 23, no. 2 (1998), 5–39.

been a secondary factor.[99] Military training and service contribute to instilling a professional ethos into the US armed forces. Nevertheless, this ethos has been increasingly difficult to sustain.[100] The change in military recruitment campaigns, illustrated by the army's slogan 'Army of One', reflects the transition towards a Neoliberal outlook. This outlook is concerned with individual objectives and gains such as receiving an education, adventure and being able to see the world.[101] Also the military's self-perception has been changing from a vocation to a business-like organization. As Don M. Snider and Gayle L. Watkins observe, 'the Army has borrowed aspects of human resource systems from corporations, and then wonders why the members of the profession are acting like employees.'[102]

The fact that many soldiers work alongside private contractors on a daily basis has exacerbated the problem of maintaining the identity of the professional soldier. Contractors have become an integral part of military operations to the point that the US Air Force has explicitly included them in its extended 'Air Force family'.[103] The treatment of contractors as soldiers has erased the distinctive status of the military vocation. It has questioned the identity and value of professional soldiers, who are committed to defend their country with their lives, who submit to rigorous training and standards, and who often earn less than their private colleagues.[104] As in the UK, the implicit message that contractors can replace professional soldiers has encouraged many to leave the armed forces for positions in the private military sector.[105] In particular, highly trained and experienced soldiers can earn significantly more in the private marketplace than in the military. Moreover, private contractors have the added bonus of being able to choose the rate and place of their deployment. Many ex-service personnel have,

---

[99] J. Eighmey, 'Why Do Youth Enlist? Identification of Underlying Themes', *Armed Forces & Society*, 32, no. 2 (2006), 307–28.

[100] Eighmey, 'Why Do Youths Enlist?'; T. Woodruff, R. Kelty and D. R. Segal, 'Propensity to Serve and Motivation to Enlist among American Combat Soldiers', *Armed Forces & Society*, 32, no. 3 (2006), 353–66.

[101] Cited in Anderson *et al.*, *From Chaos to Clarity*, pp. 6–10–6–11.

[102] D. M. Snider and G. L. Watkins, 'The Future of Army Professionalism: A Need for Renewal and Redefinition', *Parameters*, 37, no. 3 (2000), 6.

[103] Report of the Secretary of the Air Force, in *US Annual Defense Report 2003*, p. 170.

[104] R. Kelty and D. R. Segal, 'The Civilianization of the US Military: Army and Navy Case Studies of the Effects of Civilian Integration on Military Personnel', in T. Jäger and G. Kümmel (eds.) *Private Military and Security Companies: Chances, Problems, Pitfalls and Prospects* (Wiesbaden: VS Verlag für Sozialwissenschaften, 2007), pp. 213–39; S. J. Zamparelli, 'Competitive Sourcing and Privatization: What Have We Signed Up For?' *Air Force Journal of Logistics*, 23, no. 3 (1999), 12.

[105] *Ibid.*; D. D. Avant, 'Privatizing Military Training', *Foreign Policy in Focus*, 5, no. 17 (2000), 1–3.

indirectly, continued to work for the US armed forces, but they are no longer subject to a common military discipline. Indeed, there is a wide variance among the standards endorsed by private military companies ranging from those with explicit codes of ethics to 'cowboys'. Re-enlistment rates have remained high among soldiers who have been deployed in military operations and have first-hand experience of the benefits of the particular military ethos. However, soldiers engaged in homeland defence and base operations have been less likely to stay in the armed forces because of the weakening of the dividing line between professional soldiers and contractors. The outsourcing of military support functions to private contractors has also decreased the attractiveness of a professional military career for new recruits. Since the armed forces have been asked to focus on their core functions, the range of career options and deployment opportunities for professional soldiers has become narrower and less attractive, whereas the number and variety of jobs offered by private military companies has been increasing.[106] As the next section shows, the consequences of these developments for the relations between the US armed forces and society have been controversially debated.

Closing the civil–military gap or blurring the lines?

The substitution of more than 40,000 US armed forces soldiers with private military contractors has profound implications for civil–military relations.[107] In the USA these implications have variously been perceived as a dangerous 'blurring of the lines' or a beneficial 'closing of the gap' between the military and society.[108] On the one hand, privatization and outsourcing have increased the access to and the role of civilians within the military. Sections of society which have had no motivation to join the armed forces or the reserves now play a direct part in national defence. In short, private contractors have improved the representativeness of the extended armed forces 'family', to paraphrase the US Air Force, and have brought a wider section of society into contact with the armed forces. In some ways this has been closing the divide between the military and civil society. Arguably, this gap

---

[106] Zamparelli, 'Competitive Sourcing and Privatization', 8–19.
[107] GAO, *Defense Budget: Trends in Operation and Maintenance Costs and Support Services Contracting*, p. 19.
[108] M. H. Cooper, 'Private Affair: New Reliance on America's Other Army', *Congressional Quarterly Weekly*, 18 September 2004; P. Feaver and R. H. Kohn (eds.) *Soldiers and Civilians: The Civil-Military Gap and American National Security* (Cambridge, MA: MIT Press, 2001).

has never been as wide as in the UK. Remnants of the Republican citizen-soldier ideal which links the soldier with society exist in the offer of easing the US naturalization process for foreigners who serve or have served in the armed forces. Moreover, this ideal has meant that public displays of support for the armed forces have been commonplace, even among citizens who have no serving family members. US society and the media pay considerable attention to the deaths of their soldiers abroad, and this concern also applies to private military contractors, albeit to a lesser degree.[109]

On the other hand, the growing use of private military contractors has posed serious problems for the existing relations between the soldier, the state and the citizens. Most importantly, the civilianization of the US armed forces has put into question the identity of the professional soldier, which is based on the separation of military and civilian roles. As a professional, the soldier's guiding principles are duty towards the constitution and political neutrality. Social and political integration of the military with society are requirements for the citizen-soldier model, but they do not apply to the same degree to the professional soldier. On the contrary, the identity of the professional soldier draws on an elitist self-image which trades societal status and respect for the willingness to die in defence of the nation. Since the introduction of the all-volunteer forces, the US armed forces have created imaginary and real boundaries between themselves and society which have maintained the elite status of the professional soldier as a vocation. They have ranged from the physical separation of military bases from civilian life to the mental indoctrination of the soldier. As Warren M. Anderson et al. argue, 'From the first day in uniform, military personnel are told that they are part of a proud tradition, that they have accepted a noble calling, and that they have a duty that goes beyond each one of them personally.'[110]

The substitution of uniformed personnel with private military contractors has threatened existing relations between the professional armed forces and society. Foremost, it has questioned the beliefs and identity of the contemporary professional soldier. If private contractors can fill many of the same military positions without making the same commitment, what is the value of the volunteer soldier's oath, training and professional standards? US society has accredited the professional soldier a special status. However, within the armed forces this distinction is being eroded. Private military contractors are operating alongside their uniformed colleagues in national defence and on international

---

[109] D. Avant and L. Sigelman, 'What Does Private Security in Iraq Mean for US Democracy at Home?', Research Paper, January 2008, pp. 31–2.

[110] Anderson et al., From Chaos to Clarity, p. 5–3.

Table 5.2. *US model of the soldier*

Dimension	USA
Relationships with the state and society	• Duty • Civil–military gap decreased by democratization and civilianization of the armed forces
Motivation	• Individual goals and benefits • Patriotism
Identity	• Individual/collective professional (occupational view)
Democratic control and accountability	• Professional neutrality undermined by political lobbying of private military contractors • High public concern over military and contractor casualties

missions. In international military operations contractors have shared the same occupation and accommodation, and have, increasingly, faced the same dangers. In addition, the integration of private military contractors within the daily operations of the armed forces has raised the question of political neutrality and control. While the professional armed forces have been committed to impartial advice and have been prohibited by law from engaging in political activities while on active duty, many private military contractors in the USA have conducted lobbying on a large scale.[111] Thus, between 1998 and 2004 defence contractors spent more than $214 million in campaign contributions and nearly $1.9 billion on Washington lobbyists.[112]

In conclusion, the above demonstrates that the rise of Neoliberalism has resulted in a major transformation of the US model of the soldier since the 1990s. This change has had positive as well as negative consequences for the democratic control and accountability of the armed forces. On the one hand, it has led to a more democratic and representative military. On the other hand, it has challenged the unique collective identity and motivation of the professional soldier and, thus, the armed forces' ability to regulate itself through norms such as duty, honour, sacrifice and political neutrality. Although the gap between the professional soldiers, the state and society have not widened as much as in the

---

[111] DOD, *Directive 1344.10, Subject: Political Activities by Member of the Armed Forces on Active Duty*, 2 August 2004.
[112] L. Makinson, 'Outsourcing the Pentagon', *Center for Public Integrity*, 28 September 2004.

UK where the all volunteer forces believe that the government is breaking its covenant with the soldier, and where society has lost its concern for military casualties, the replacement of professional soldiers with private military contractors is demanding new mechanisms of democratic control and accountability. As the next section will argue, the problems which the outsourcing of military functions to private contractors has created for US democracy apply to both the state and the soldier.

The small state, occupational soldier and democratic control

The question of how to ensure democratic control over the government and the armed forces has been at the heart of both Republican and Liberal theories. The Clinton and Bush administrations' turn to Neoliberalism has not only presented an economic programme, it has also entailed particular models of democratic control and accountability. Specifically, it has conveyed the notion that the latter are most effectively realized by limiting the scope and influence of the government. The related concepts of the small state and lean military, which are focused on their core competencies, have become the ideals of successive US administrations. These administrations have neglected the fact that Neoliberalism does not suggest that restricting and fragmenting the powers of the state per se ensures democratic control. It rather argues that public–private competition is necessary to achieve this aim. The following section discusses how the developments described in the preceding sections have affected US democracy with regard to two issues: the weakening of governmental oversight of the private provision of military services, and the informal and formal control of the new model of the soldier.

Weakening state supervision

One of the key reasons for the weakening of governmental control and oversight of the military establishment since the mid 1990s has been a disregard of the central role of competition for democratic control within Neoliberal theory. Under successive governments, rolling back the state has become an objective in itself, and governments have ignored the lack of evidence for the superior cost efficiency and performance of private contractors in a range of military functions. They have also paid little attention to the challenges to democratic control and accountability that have stemmed from the growing dependence of the armed forces on commercial suppliers. Finally, these governments have neglected the impact of the growing use of private contractors on the predominant model of the soldier and its role in democratic civil–military relations. The result has been the undermining of established mechanisms for control over the armed forces. In terms of the relationship between the government and society, the consequences of uncontrolled privatization and outsourcing have been 'fraud, waste and abuse' as well as decreased democratic accountability.[113] In terms of the link between the armed forces and society, they have been characterized by the circumvention of the formal and informal devices by which the soldier has been subject to democratic norms.

Although one of the key objectives of the Neoliberal reform programme has been to improve the responsiveness of public service provision to the wishes of the citizens, such as greater cost efficiency and improved performance, it has not met initial expectations. In national defence several developments have conspired against the achievement of these aims. Most of them can be linked to the failure of the government to maintain adequate levels of competition between the armed forces and the private military industry, as well as among the leading private military companies. Already in the 1990s the Clinton administration encouraged the consolidation of private armaments and military firms in the USA in order to adapt to the declining defence budgets of the post-Cold War era and take advantage of economies of scale. Within a decade thirty-two armaments producers had consolidated into seven; and forty aerospace firms had merged into five.[114] Moreover, the top US defence and government contractors have acquired many of the most successful private military service companies. Thus, Computer Sciences Corporation (CSC) has bought DynCorp; Northrop Grumman has acquired parts of TRW with its subsidiary Vinnell; and L-3 Communications has bought out Military Professional Resources Inc. (MPRI) and Titan Corp, while MPRI has in turn acquired a host of smaller firms. The most voracious buyer has been Abu Ghraib contractor CACI, which had acquired forty-two defence, IT and intelligence companies by 2008. Under Bush, the preference for prime and sole-source contracting has further facilitated the shrinking of the supplier base by encouraging the formation of consortia and favouring large conglomerates for the provision of integrated product and system support packages. Between 1998 and 2004 only 40 per cent of all DOD

---

[113] GAO, *Contract Management: DOD Vulnerabilities to Contracting Fraud, Waste, and Abuse*, GAO-06–838R (Washington DC, 2006).

[114] Anderson *et al.*, *From Chaos to Clarity*, p. 1–7; K. B. Bowling, 'Candid Voices – Military Readiness: Effects of Outsourcing Repairs', *Air Force Journal of Logistics*, 24, no. 4 (2000), 24–7.

contracts were awarded under 'full and open competition', while 44 per cent of contracts were signed as sole-source contracts.[115]

Another factor has been the Neoliberal liberalization and transnationalization of previously predominantly national defence markets. Historically, the US government has been able to offset the oligopoly power of its main armaments producers by its own position as a monopsy, i.e. sole, buyer of military products and services. Recently, this ability has declined because most companies have significantly expanded the international share of their business. CAE, for example, exports 90 per cent of its business to both commercial and military customers, and Boeing has concluded that 'future training and simulations business in the global military arena depends on foreign government acquisitions of new platforms'.[116]

Both industry consolidation and prime contracting have seemed cost-efficient because they have enabled the generation of economies of scale while maintaining a viable national defence industrial base in the USA. By outsourcing training and maintenance to the producers, the armed forces have also saved making investments in equipment, facilities and technicians. In the long run, however, the lack of competition within the national defence sector and from organic armed forces facilities has created a sellers' market. Where the US armed forces have lacked alternative suppliers, the military has become locked into unfavourable relationships with prime vendors.[117] Rising contract fees and the inability to exclude companies that have been shown to defraud the government from future competitions have been among the consequences of the changing balance between the state and the market.

In addition, the government's pressure to expand the range of services considered for outsourcing to the private sector has contributed to undermining cost efficiency and control. Particularly problematic has been the focus on the definition of core functions as a guide to outsourcing. This approach has implied that all non-core functions of the military are more cost-efficiently provided by private companies. In 1996 a RAND study on DOD outsourcing argued that this is not always the case. The study observed that an in-house provision is preferable for three types of functions. The first type are complex activities which require real-time control because of an uncertain operating environment; the second type are services which require

---

[115] Makinson, 'Outsourcing the Pentagon'.
[116] Anonymous, 'Training and Simulation Industry Profiles', *National Defense*, 84, no. 552 (1999), 43.
[117] Bowling, 'Candid Voices – Military Readiness: Effects of Outsourcing Repairs'.

customized assets; and the third are activities for which performance criteria are hard to specify and contractual failure is difficult
to prove.[118] Many of these conditions have characterized the provision of military services in the post-Cold War era, due to changing
security demand, increasingly complex international interventions
and technological innovations. However, the numerical targets for
A-76 competitions set by the government have created a procurement environment which has de-emphasized the conditions for cost-
efficient outsourcing. Before 1997 DOD A-76 competitions reduced
cost on average by 31 per cent.[119] Since the beginning of the twenty-
first century, similar savings have been more difficult to verify as
the range of new functions subjected to the A-76 has become more
complex and exclusive to the military.[120] A number of studies have
concluded that government estimates of potential savings of 30–50
per cent have been exaggerated.[121]

In addition, the growing administrative burden on the armed forces
has hampered the effective democratic control and accountability
of private military contractors.[122] In 1995 the Commission on Roles
and Missions of the Armed Forces predicted that increased outsourcing would require additional personnel for contract management. It
advised that 'expanding the specialized contracting and oversight skills
will require thorough planning and extensive training'.[123] More than
a decade later, the US military has still not met these requirements.
Contract management remains a high-risk area requiring 'urgent
government action'.[124] The main cause has been the lack of qualified
staff for contractor surveillance.[125] While DOD contract volume has
more than doubled, the number of armed forces contract management

---

[118] Camm, *Expanding Private Production of Defense Services*, p. xi, pp. 26–34.
[119] Cohen, *Defense Reform Initiative Report*, p. 29.
[120] GAO, *Defense Budget: Trends in Operation and Maintenance Costs and Support Services Contracting*, p. 18.
[121] Erwin, 'Brass Ponders Mixed Blessings of Privatization'; GAO, *DOD Competitive Sourcing: Results of A-76 Studies over the Past 5 Years*, GAO-01–20 (Washington DC, December 2001), p. 4; Lavadour, 'Pitfalls of the A-76 Process'; Anderson *et al.*, *From Chaos to Clarity*, p. 4–27.
[122] Anderson *et al.*, *From Chaos to Clarity*, p. 4–28.
[123] Commission on Roles and Missions of the Armed Forces, *Directions for Defense*, p. 3–4.
[124] GAO, *Contract Management: DOD Vulnerabilities to Contracting Fraud, Waste, and Abuse*, p. 2.
[125] GAO, *Contract Security Guards*; GAO, *Contract Management: Guidance Needed to Promote Competition for Defense Task Orders* (Washington DC, 2004); GAO, *Military Operations: DOD's Extensive Use of Logistics Support Contracts Requires Strengthened Oversight* (Washington DC, 2004).

personnel has been significantly reduced since the beginning of the 1990s.[126] The decline of uniformed personnel in technical functions not directly related to combat has exacerbated the problem of monitoring contractor performance. Without their own experts, the armed forces have been less able to assess private military contractor performance and obtain value for money.[127]

The Bush administration's attempt to address the problem of contractor surveillance through partnering with the industry has also faced a number of problems. Rather than re-establishing competition as the core principle of Neoliberal democratic control, public–private partnerships have facilitated the long-term dependence of the armed forces on the private military industry and have further weakened lines of public accountability.[128] According to the GAO, partnering 'can blur the oversight responsibilities between the lead systems integrator and program management officials'.[129] The partnership approach has specifically neglected the fact that the military and industry operate according to different rationales which, if put into a collaborative relationship, tend to undermine cost efficiency and control. A survey conducted by researchers at the US Defence Acquisitions University found that 'mission effectiveness is what DOD's belief system emphasizes and on what they are graded'.[130] Conversely, private industry is primarily concerned with meeting the requests of their customers even, or especially, if these demands increase their contract volume. A partnership approach that encourages collaboration rather than competition between the military and industry is, therefore, likely to lead to an expansion of cost as both actors are more concerned with performance than efficiency. Whether performance has indeed improved through outsourcing remains unclear because the ultimate assessment of contractors has been difficult.[131] Asked to evaluate the measurement of contractor performance, 25 per cent of DOD respondents thought it was not effective and 42 per cent were not sure.[132] Based on their own experience, 73 per cent of soldiers

---

[126] GAO, *Contract Management: DOD Vulnerabilities to Contracting Fraud, Waste, and Abuse*, p. 8.
[127] C. M. Bolton, Jr., 'Providing the Soldier with the Right Stuff', *Army*, 55, no. 10 (2005), 44; Commercial Activities Panel, *Improving the Sourcing Decisions of the Government*, Final Report, April 2002, p. 4.
[128] Camm, *Expanding Private Production of Defense Services*, p. 42.
[129] GAO, *Contract Management: DOD Vulnerabilities to Contracting Fraud, Waste, and Abuse*, p. 7.
[130] Anderson *et al.*, *From Chaos to Clarity*, p. 5–17.
[131] GAO, *Defense Acquisitions: DOD Has Paid Billions in Award and Incentive Fees Regardless of Acquisitions Outcomes* (Washington DC, 2005).
[132] Anderson *et al.*, *From Chaos to Clarity*, p. D-29.

who had worked with private contractors believed that outsourcing had not improved the execution of their mission.[133]

In summary, the preceding problems illustrate that the US government has followed policies which have been inconsistent with Neoliberal principles for ensuring democratic control and accountability. Instead, the government has created conditions where the military has become increasingly dependent upon private military contractors and unable to exert its supervisory function. Under these conditions, the self-regulatory capabilities of the armed forces have been particularly important in order to ensure democratic control and accountability. However, as the following section argues, these too have been challenged by the proliferation of private military contractors.

Civilians or soldiers?

Since existing mechanisms for democratic supervision of the soldier in the USA have been based on the model of the professional soldier, the growing role of private contractors has had a profound impact not only on the democratic control over the armed forces, but also over the individual soldier.[134] Specifically, the professional soldier model has established relations of accountability and control which have relied on the formal norms and standards of professional soldiering as a vocation, and the external division between and strict regulation of political and military roles. The definition of private military contractors as civilians has put both sets of mechanisms into question. The best illustration of the difference between soldiers and contractors is that professional soldiers and citizen-soldiers swear an oath to the US constitution, but private contractors do not. Private military contractors do not recognize any duty to the state, the public or the US constitution beyond the terms of their contract. Moreover, because the military hires contractors for their specialist expertise, there is no collective training or ethos that commits private contractors to the armed forces, its beliefs and mission. Finally, while professional soldiers formally and informally subscribe to political neutrality, private defence contractors can use their wealth and position as employers and taxpayers to influence the political process.[135]

---

[133] Anderson et al., From Chaos to Clarity, p. D-34.
[134] D. Avant, 'Privatizing Military Training: A Challenge to US Army Professionalism', in D. M. Snider and G. L. Watkins (eds.) The Future of The Army Profession (Boston, MA: McGraw-Hill, 2002), pp. 179–96.
[135] Makinson, 'Outsourcing the Pentagon'.

Arguably, the recruitment of private contractors from the ranks of former US soldiers and civilian DOD employees has helped to bridge the professional divide between members of the armed forces and contractors. The wish to serve their country, personal morals and high standards of behaviour remain important to those who have received their education and professional training in the armed forces. However, the availability of former military personnel has been a result of the temporary surplus created by the end of the Cold War. Within the next decade or two, this surplus will shrink and the proportion of ex-service personnel among private military contractors will decline as many will reach retirement age. They will increasingly be replaced by personnel who have no experience of military professionalism. So far, there have been no concerted efforts to offset this trend by establishing publicly endorsed professional training or values among private military contractors working on US territory. Some of the larger private military companies, such as MPRI, DynCorp and Bechtel, proclaim codes of conduct which their employees are expected to follow. However, DynCorp's and Bechtel's over twenty pages long codes of ethics and business conduct merely list guidelines on harassment of co-workers, organizational conflicts of interest and the protection of company assets, while leaving out more sensitive issues such as the use of armed force.[136] Moreover, the effectiveness of internal monitoring and enforcement of company ethics and internal standards of operation remains doubtful. The development of national and international private security industry codes of conduct through company associations, such as the International Peace Operations Association (IPOA) and BAPSC, suffers from similar surveillance and enforcement problems.[137]

In addition, the government is still catching up with the formal regulation of private military contractors employed in national defence. As Chapter 7 will discuss in detail, high-profile cases of contractors abusing armed force in Iraq have led to a strengthening of legislative and executive control over private military staff working within 'operational areas' in declared wars and contingency operations under the Uniform Code of Military Justice. However, the government so far has failed to include national defence in its efforts to increase the control over private contractors.[138] One reason for this omission appears to be

---

[136] DynCorp, at: www.dyn-intl.com; Bechtel, at: www.bechtel.com.
[137] International Peace Operations Association, 'Code of Conduct', at: http://ipoaonline. org; British Association of Private Security Companies, at: www.bapsc.org.uk.
[138] United States Code, Title 10 – Armed Forces.

the comparative lack of public attention paid to the proliferation of private military contractors working on US territory. As of 2009 forty US states had adopted regulations for private security services, including licensing and training requirements, and the US Congress had passed legislation enabling private security firms to check the criminal records of employees. However, most of these regulations pertain only to armed security guards.[139] Large sections of the private military industry are without specific national controls or standards, ranging from military logisticians to interrogators. In addition, variance in the level of state regulation allows private firms to evade regulation by registering in states without any controls such as Mississippi, Alabama or Colorado.[140]

Although the armed forces have developed guidelines for the integration of private contractors within military chains of command, current armed forces guidelines continue to define contractors as civilians.[141] These guidelines stipulate that, outside declared wars and contingency operations, the armed forces can only hold private military personnel accountable through their contracts, and that contractors are subordinate to their contract administrator rather than military commanders. The contract remains the most effective mechanism for controlling private military staff in the USA.[142] However, there are several limitations to contractual control and accountability. Firstly, it places a heavy burden on contract design. Although there are a number of mechanisms which can improve contractor accountability such as including public law values in contracts, specifying training and accreditation requirements, providing for enhanced monitoring, establishing clear performance criteria and providing whistleblower protection, few of them are incorporated into DOD contracts because of insufficient personnel and

---

[139] Testimony of Joseph Ricci, CAE Executive Director, National Association of Security Companies (NASCO) before the House Homeland Security Committee, Hearing on 'The Direction and Viability of Federal Protective Service', 1 May 2007, p. 2. See for instance, Code of Virginia, *Laws Relating to The Regulation of Private Security Services Including Special Conservators of the Peace*, 1 July 2004; California Business and Professions Code, Chapter 11.5. *Private Security Services*; *Act to Permit Reviews of Criminal Records of Applicants for Private Security Employment*, 108th Congress, 1st Session, S 1743, 18 November 2003.

[140] Testimony of Joseph Ricci, p. 2; P. C. Stenning, 'Powers and Accountability of Private Police', *European Journal on Criminal Policy and Research*, 8, no. 3 (2000), 338.

[141] See for instance, Army Regulation 715–9 'Contractors Accompanying the Force', Army Field Manual 3–100.21 'Contractors on the Battlefield' and Army Pamphlet 715–16 'Contractor Deployment Guide'.

[142] L. A. Dickinson, 'Public Law Values in a Privatized World', *The Yale Journal of International Law*, 31, no. 1 (2006), 383–426.

expertise.[143] In fact, research conducted by the GAO and the Center for Public Integrity has indicated that DOD contracts became less rather than more restrictive during the Bush administration. In particular prime, IDIQ and lead systems integrator contracts, which leave the design of subcontracts to the main award-holder, have prevented the use of restrictive contracts to improve governmental control. The Defense Authorization Act of 2007 has sought to address some of these problems by introducing limitations on the use of lead systems integrators.[144] However, contracts have only been as good as the ability of the DOD to monitor and enforce them. As noted above, this ability has been circumscribed by the lack of trained contract managers, insufficient competition among private suppliers and decreasing numbers of in-house experts. Finally, contracts have not been particularly suited to enhancing democratic accountability because they have shifted the burden of democratic scrutiny to the executive at the expense of public transparency. While Congress has to approve the United States Code's armed forces regulations, contracts are designed by the military unit outsourcing a particular service. Contracts are also not usually open to public scrutiny because private military firms can exercise a veto under the Freedom of Information Act concerning confidential commercial information.

The replacement of professional soldiers with private military contractors in US national defence has, thus, created major weaknesses with regard to the democratic control and accountability of the military. While it may have helped to decrease the gap between society and the armed forces, it has undermined established mechanisms of civil–military control such as the professionalism of the armed forces and Congressional oversight. Moreover, Neoliberal alternatives such as industry self-regulation, official legislation and contract management have, so far, been limited due to lack of political interest or investment.

Conclusion

The changing security environment after the end of the Cold War and the 11 September 2001 attacks has served as a key explanation for the growing use of private military contractors by the US armed forces.

---

[143] Dickinson, 'Public Law Values in a Privatized World'.
[144] John Warner National Defense Authorization Act for Fiscal Year 2007, *Public Law* 109–364, 17 October 2006, 109th Congress, 120 STAT. 2217, Title VIII, Subtitle A, Section 807 'Lead Systems Integrators'.

According to this view, the outsourcing of military services to private suppliers has been a response to the unexpected surge in personnel requirements created by the new security demands. This chapter has sought to demonstrate that these arguments only partly account for the growing role of private military contractors in US national defence. Specifically, they fail to explain why the US government has not reversed the cuts in its professional armed forces as it has those in the defence budget. The changing ideological preferences of US governments from Republicanism to Neoliberalism help to explain this puzzle. They illustrate how new ideals and beliefs regarding the democratic control over the provision and use of armed force have contributed to the transformation of the roles and relations of the state, the citizen and the soldier over the past decades. At the core of these ideals has been the Neoliberal conviction that accountability and control are best achieved through the small state. In the military, this has involved nearly halving the number of armed forces personnel and expanding the scope of private sector provision of military services.[145] Moreover, it has gone hand in hand with a redefinition of the inherent functions of the state and the military. In the early 1990s only civilian and technical functions were contracted out to private firms; military outsourcing now involves dangerous, politically critical and mission-essential functions, ranging from armed protection and intelligence analysis to management and supervision. Combat remains the only exclusive function of the US military. However, even this last preserve is increasingly put into question, as Chapter 7 will illustrate.

In addition to providing a deeper understanding of the rationale for military outsourcing, the preceding analysis of the underlying ideological foundations of the rise of private military contractors has also revealed the inherent contradictions of US reforms. It has shown that the fixation on reducing the size of government has proceeded to undermine the competition between the state and the market, which Neoliberal theorists consider essential for maintaining cost efficiency as well as democratic control and accountability. Various government policies under Clinton and Bush have not only strengthened the industry by facilitating the consolidation of defence companies within a few large conglomerates and business alliances, but have also weakened the military by cutting in-house expertise and failing to expand management personnel. Moreover, the substitution of soldiers with contractors has challenged the formal and informal mechanisms by which US society has traditionally controlled the armed forces. A tight net of

---

[145] Anderson *et al.*, *From Chaos to Clarity*, pp. 1–4.

vocational standards and special legislation prevent the undue influence of the military and hold the professional soldier accountable, but
private military contractors on US territory so far lack equally effective
controls. In short, Neoliberalism plays a crucial role in understanding the shift towards private military contracting and its problems.
Moreover, it helps to explain the variation between the US response to
the new security context and that of many European allies. In order to
investigate this variation in greater detail, the next chapter turns to the
outsourcing of military services in Germany.

6   Germany: between public–private partnerships and conscription

The privatization and outsourcing of military services in Germany has gone largely unnoticed, both nationally and internationally. While the scale and scope of military privatization in Germany is considerably smaller than in the UK and the USA, it still ranges from private contracting for military logistics and maintenance to IT services and training. This chapter argues that the persistence of Republican ideals can help us to understand why the privatization and outsourcing of military services to the private sector has not been as extensive in Germany as in its Anglo-American allies, in spite of similar security challenges. Successive German governments under Helmut Kohl (1982–98), Gerhard Schröder (1998–2005) and Angela Merkel (2005–2009) have transformed the roles and relations of the state, the citizen and the soldier according to a mixture of Republican and Neoliberal principles. At the heart of this approach has been the creation of public–private joint ventures for the provision of military services such as the white fleet, clothing stocks, army maintenance and repair, and IT. Moreover, the German government has so far resisted calls for the professionalization of its armed forces and the abandonment of the ideal of the citizen-soldier. Functional arguments cannot fully elucidate these differences because, in comparison with the UK and the USA, the German government has been under particular pressure to reform its provision of national and international security and to generate savings in military spending.[1] Two main factors have contributed to this situation. Firstly, the Bundeswehr, the German armed forces, designed exclusively for territorial defence and for a large-scale ground war in the centre of Europe, has become outdated because of the emergence of new threats and the redefinition of the German constitution to permit out-of-area operations. The latter have required not only a new military structure,

---

[1] G. Portugall, 'Die Bundeswehr und das Privatisierungsmodell der "Öffentlich-Privaten-Partnerschaft" (ÖPP)', in G. Richter (ed.) *Die ökonomische Modernisierung der Bundeswehr: Sachstand, Konzeptionen und Perspektiven* (Wiesbaden: VS Verlag für Sozialwissenschaften, 2007), p. 141.

but also radically different capabilities. Secondly, the reunification with East Germany in 1990 has put a huge financial strain on the federal budget. Large-scale investments have gone into reforming the East German administration, infrastructure and economy, as well as into the move of the federal capital from Bonn to Berlin. At the same time the Maastricht convergence criteria and the Stability and Growth Pact for Euro countries have delimited German government expenditure on defence because these criteria demand that public deficits do not exceed 3 per cent of GDP.[2]

Despite these demands the German government has only slowly expanded its use of private military contractors. While in the UK and the USA lesser pressures have justified the extensive outsourcing of military functions under Neoliberal reform agendas, Germany has not yet completely broken with the Republican ideology that has provided the foundations for the first stable German democracy, and shaped its armed forces and national defence. Since the mid 1990s Neoliberal language and policies have found their way into public administration and sectors such as transport, telecommunications and healthcare. However, significant sections of the German population and the two largest political parties have been sceptical towards a wholesale adoption of the Neoliberal model of the small state, in particular with regards to national and international security. The majority of German citizens and the governing political parties have also, so far, remained committed to the mass conscription of citizen-soldiers to supply its armed forces.[3]

In short, while in the UK and the USA ideology has been a driving force in the privatization of military services, in Germany it has been a restraining factor.[4] The ideological investments made in the Republican models of the state, the citizen and the citizen-soldier as the foundations of German democracy after the Second World War have been immense.[5] As the result, these models have become the unquestioned and, by most accounts, successful bases for the democratic control of the state and the Bundeswehr for more than fifty years. Nevertheless, in Germany the Republican ideal has also increasingly been put into

[2] M. Spackman, 'Public–private Partnerships: Lessons from the British Approach', *Economic Systems*, 26, no. 3 (2002), 289.
[3] I.-J. Werkner, 'Die Wehrpflict – Teil der politischen Kultur der Bundesrepublik Deutschland?' in I.-J. Werkner (ed.) *Die Wehrpflicht und ihre Hintergründe. Sozialwissenschaftliche Beiträge zur aktuellen Debatte* (Wiesbaden: VS Verlag für Sozialwissenschaften, 2004), p. 156; F.-J. Meiers, 'Germany's Defence Choices', *Survival*, 47, no. 1 (2005), 153.
[4] K. Longhurst, 'Why Aren't the Germans Debating the Draft? Path Dependency and the Persistence of Conscription', *German Politics*, 12, no. 2 (2003), 152–3.
[5] Bundesministerium der Verteidigung, *Weissbuch 2006. Zur Sicherheitspolitik Deutschlands und zu Zukunft der Bundeswehr* (Berlin, 25 October 2006).

question. Externally, Germany's commitment to expanding its contributions to UN, NATO or European Union (EU) peacekeeping operations has necessitated expeditionary capabilities and more professional armed forces. Internally, the shrinking of the Bundeswehr has threatened to undermine the equitability of and public support for general conscription, especially among the younger generation. The problem of adapting the traditional Republican conceptions of the citizen-soldier and the warfare state to Germany's changing security conditions has facilitated a transition towards the Neoliberal model of security governance. Yet this model has been transformed in such a way as to provide a bridge between Republican and Neoliberal principles.

As the following sections will argue, the German merger of Republican and Neoliberal ideals contains its own dangers for the democratic control and accountability of the armed forces. This chapter examines the transformation of the roles of the state, the citizen and soldier and its consequences in four sections. The first section analyses the ideological and normative foundations of the reform and privatization of the German military and its relations with the state and society. The second section discusses the privatization of Bundeswehr functions in terms of geography, function, resources, decision-making and the implementation of national defence policies. It pays specific attention to two developments: the Gesellschaft für Entwicklung, Beschaffung und Betrieb (GEBB), a government-owned private company tasked with the development and implementation of Bundeswehr privatization projects, and its role in the creation of military public–private joint ventures; and the Bundeswehr's pilot projects for the outsourcing of military functions. The third section examines the German debate regarding conscription and the challenges to the model of the citizen-soldier. Finally, this chapter discusses how the German government has attempted to safeguard the democratic control and accountability of the armed forces under these transformed conditions.

Reforming the Republican model

One of the reasons for the strength and persistence of the ideological commitment to the Republican models of the state and the soldier can be found in their enshrinement in the West German post-war 'Basic Law', which became the German constitution after reunification.[6] For its mentors, the primary aim of the Basic Law was to ensure democratic

---

[6] G. Richter, 'Privatization in the German Armed Forces' in T. Jäger and G. Kümmel (eds.) *Private Military and Security Companies: Chances, Problems, Pitfalls and Prospects* (Wiesbaden: VS Verlag für Sozialwissenschaften, 2007), pp. 165–76.

control over the military and prevent its reversal into a 'state within the state', as happened during the Weimar Republic, or its abuse by nationalist and fascist forces such as the Nazis. The German constitution, therefore, entails a series of explicit and detailed stipulations for the roles and relations of the state, the citizen and the armed forces in national and international security. Article 87(a) of the German constitution determines the state's monopoly on the right to establish armed forces.[7] In addition, Article 87(b) proscribes a functional and institutional separation between the military organization of the armed forces and the civilian Bundeswehr administration. The latter holds the exclusive authority and responsibility to provide the armed forces with personnel management, material provision and procurement.[8] Moreover, the constitution states that 'the Bundeswehr Administration is conducted by a *federally owned* administrative authority with its own administrative organization'.[9] Legal scholars, therefore, contend that both articles provide clear constitutional guidelines on the prerogative of the government and government institutions to supply national and international security, and a prohibition of unlimited privatization.[10]

In order to further civilianize and safeguard the democratic control of state military institutions, the forefathers of the constitution also favoured the active participation of the citizenry in national defence. The first West German Federal President Theodor Heuss, for instance, asserted that the conscripted citizen-soldier was the 'legitimate child of democracy'.[11] Article 12 of the constitution, therefore, establishes the government's right to conscript males above eighteen years of age to serve in the armed forces or in civilian security functions. In addition to ensuring the democratic accountability of the armed forces, the conscripted soldier is regarded as a bulwark against the abuse of the German armed forces in offensive and expeditionary wars, which are explicitly prohibited in Articles 26 and 87(a). However, the constitution also safeguards the right of conscientious objection to military service.

In spite of these seemingly clear and immutable constitutional guidelines regarding the roles of the state, the citizen and the armed forces, and the resulting legal constraints on the privatization of military

---

[7] Portugall, 'Die Bundeswehr und das Privatisierungsmodell der "Öffentlich-Privaten-Partnershaft" (ÖPP)', pp. 147–8.
[8] Richter, 'Privatization in the German Armed Forces', p. 170.
[9] German Constitution, Article 87(b), 1 (translation and italics by the author).
[10] Cited in Richter, 'Privatization in the German Armed Forces', p. 170.
[11] Cited in H. Dinter, 'Wehrpflicht, Freiwilligenarmee und allgemeine Dienstpflict – Aktuelle Argumentationslinien', in I.-J. Werkner (ed.) *Die Wehrpflicht und ihre Hintergründe. Sozialwissenschaften Beiträge zur aktuellen Debatte* (Wiesbaden: VS Verlag für Sozialwissenschaften, 2004), p. 112.

services, the 1990s saw a revision of the Republican principles underlying the democratic control of the German military. Changing national and international circumstances and the promotion of Neoliberalism by the UK and the USA have led to a questioning of the suitability of the existing models. The Kohl government made the first efforts to reform the Bundeswehr in light of these developments. However, since the government consisted of a coalition between the Conservative CDU/CSU and the Liberal FDP, its attitude towards Neoliberalism was ambivalent. On the one hand, the administration approved the sale of federal government shares in private industries and the formal privatization of the postal and railway systems. In fact, the government changed the constitution in order to permit these privatizations of public services. On the other hand, Kohl's own CDU/CSU party remained faithful to the Republican ideals of community, solidarity and social market capitalism that had been the foundations of the German military corporatism.[12] Due to the resulting compromise, the state became the sole owner of the newly created private rail company and the government decided not to pursue similar privatizations in the defence sector. Rather than changing the constitution to pave the way for the outsourcing of military services, the government maintained its commitment to safeguard the state's role in the materiel supply of the armed forces. In the defence sector the Kohl government preferred internal reforms and progressive adjustments to privatization in order to improve the efficiency of the armed forces and reduce defence spending.[13]

To develop new management techniques and internal reforms suitable for the German system, the Bundeswehr set up a Working Group on Cost Limitation and Rationalization in the Office in 1992.[14] The working group proposed two mechanisms, namely market-testing, and cost and performance responsibility. While market-testing sought to encourage greater efficiency by comparing public and private service provision, cost and performance responsibility aimed to do so by giving armed forces agencies and units greater responsibility and flexibility in the use of their finances and personnel. The cost and performance

---

[12] J. Schmid, 'Mehrfache Desillusionierung und Ambivalenz: Eine sozialpolitische Bilanz', in G. Wewer (ed.) *Bilanz der Ära Kohl: Christlich-liberale Politik in Deutschland 1982–1998* (Opladen: Leske + Budrich, 1998), pp. 91–4.

[13] Bundesministerium der Verteidigung – Org 4 (1998) *Market-Testing – Richtlinie*, p. II (Vorbemerkungen) cited in G. Jaklin, 'Abgrenzung des Market Testing der Bundeswehr zu Outsourcingkonzepten in privatwirtschaftlichen Unternehmen', unpublished paper, Universität der Bundeswehr München, 28 March 2000, p. 8.

[14] Gruppe Aufwandsbegrenzung und Rationalisierung im Betrieb, see Portugall, 'Die Bundeswehr und das Privatisierungsmodell der "Öffentlich-Privaten-Partnershaft" (ÖPP)', pp. 148–9.

responsibility programme included three elements: cost and performance calculation, controlling and the Continuous Improvement
Programme. The latter offered financial rewards to armed forces
employees who suggested new cost-saving strategies.[15]

Although these mechanisms drew on Neoliberal new public management strategies, all were incorporable within the prevailing Republican
ideological and institutional structures of the Bundeswehr. The
Continuous Improvement Programme, for instance, differed only in
some aspects from the improvement proposal process that had been
used by the public administration since 1961.[16] They also conformed to
the Republican ideals of democratic accountability and civilian responsibility by providing armed forces personnel with greater input into and
authority over the management of their units.[17]

Although the German defence sector has always been, predominantly, in private hands and private firms have supplied most of the
Bundeswehr's equipment, the Kohl government and the armed forces
strictly delimited the potential scope for the privatization or outsourcing of military service functions. In 1998 the MOD identified a wide
range of military core functions which would a priori be excluded from
market-testing between the armed forces and the private sector: defence
political functions, military leadership, military intelligence, combat
and local combat support, local support in crisis and conflict environments, military services related to operational and combat capabilities,
military leadership and combat education, logistics and medical services in deployed operations, military minimum capabilities, planning,
personnel management, organization and administration.[18]

[15] L. Wochnik, 'Das kontinuierliche Verbesserungsprogramm (KVP) als Instrument
   der Gestaltung organisatorischen Wandels', in G. Richter (ed.) *Die ökonomische Modernisierung der Bundeswehr: Sachstand, Konzeptionen und Perspektiven*
   (Wiesbaden: VS Verlag für Sozialwissenschaften, 2007), p. 197. See also G. Portugall,
   'Das kontinuierliche Verbesserungsprogramm (KVP) in der Bundeswehr –
   Eine sozialwissenschaftliche Bestandsaufnahme', in G. Richter (ed.) *Die ökonomische Modernisierung der Bundeswehr: Sachstand, Konzeptionen und Perspektiven*
   (Wiesbaden: VS Verlag für Sozialwissenschaften, 2007), pp. 211–32.
[16] Bundesrechnungshof, *Bemerkungen 2006 zur Haushalts- und Wirtschaftsführung des
   Bundes* (Bonn, November 2006), p. 180.
[17] C. Großeholz, 'Die ökonomische Modernisierung der Bundeswehr im Meinungsbild
   der Soldatinnen und Soldaten', in G. Richter (ed.) *Die ökonomische Modernisierung
   der Bundeswehr: Sachstand, Konzeptionen und Perspektiven* (Wiesbaden: VS Verlag für
   Sozialwissenschaften, 2007), pp. 16–17.
[18] Bundesministerium der Verteidigung, OrgStab 4, *Market-Testing Richtlinie (MT-RL) –
   Verfahrensregelung zum marktwirtschaftlichen Vergleich von Leistungen für die Bundeswehr*
   (Bonn, 1998), cited in J. Keller, 'Streitkräfte und ökonomisches Kalkül: Top oder
   Flop? Grundsätzliche Überlegungen zu einer Ökonomisierung der Bundeswehr', in G.
   Richter (ed.) *Die ökonomische Modernisierung der Bundeswehr: Sachstand, Konzeptionen
   und Perspektiven* (Wiesbaden: VS Verlag für Sozialwissenschaften, 2007), p. 56.

Although these stipulations remained formally in place, Kohl's successor Chancellor Schröder favoured a Neoliberal reform of the German state and the armed forces along the lines of the British 'Third Way'.[19] Forced to tone 'down his liberal rhetoric' due to the persistent strength of Republican beliefs within his own party and in German society, Schröder pursued his Neoliberal policies 'by stealth'.[20] For the armed forces Defence Minister Rudolf Scharping took the lead in implementing Schröder's Neoliberal programme by signing Framework Agreement on Innovation, Investment and Efficiency in the Bundeswehr with representatives of major German companies in December 1999.[21] The framework agreement set out three objectives: (1) the use of private innovations in order to increase the portion of the defence budget that could be used to invest in the reform of the Bundeswehr; (2) the use of private investments; and (3) the creation of not a small, but a modern state. As a starting point, the framework agreement identified fourteen pilot projects for collaboration with the private sector, including depot management, IT support, the running of an army combat centre, logistic supply, simulator training, and air force maintenance and repair.[22]

In praxis, the Schröder government lacked clear models of how to implement its promise of greater collaboration with private military companies. The government also distrusted the ability and willingness of civil servants within the MOD to develop privatization and outsourcing projects for the armed forces.[23] Instead it left the details to the new private, but fully government-owned, GEBB and private consultancies. According to the Defence White Paper 2000, the GEBB would be responsible for the definition of the outsourcing pilot projects agreed under the framework agreement and would systematically identify new areas for commercial contracting in the armed forces.[24] Since the GEBB lacked the necessary personnel and expertise, it, like the Schröder administration, extensively relied on private consultants for

[19] Written interview with the Bundesamt für Wehrtechnik und Beschaffung, 3 June 2004.
[20] S. Padgett, 'Political Economy: The German Model under Stress', in S. Padgett, W. E. Paterson and G. Smith (eds.) *Developments in German Politics 3* (Basingstoke: Palgrave, 2003), p. 140.
[21] Bundesministerium der Verteidigung, *Innovation, Investition und Wirtschaftlichkeit in der Bundeswehr*, Rahmenvertrag vom 15. Dezember 1999.
[22] Bundesministerium der Verteidigung, *Die Bundeswehr der Zukunft. Sachstand der Reform*, (Berlin, 15 June 2001).
[23] R. H., 'Das Neueste zum Neuen Flottenmanagement der Bundeswehr', *Bundeswehrkurier*, Ausgabe 1 (2003), p. 2.; J. Bittner and E. Niejahr, 'Die Berater-Republik', *Die Zeit*, 5 February 2004; G. Heinen, 'Auch Struck gab Aufträge an Berger', *Die Welt*, 19 December 2003.
[24] Bundesministerium der Verteidigung, *Neuausrichtung der Bundeswehr: Grobausplanung, Ergebnisse und Entscheidungen* (Berlin, 2000).

the identification, evaluation and design of new privatization and out-sourcing projects.[25] In fact, between 2000 and 2003 the GEBB spent up to 70 per cent of its budget on private consultancies.[26] These consultancies, including Roland Berger Strategy Consultants, KPMG Consulting, CTCon, Ernst & Young (formerly Arthur Andersen), BearingPoint and Kienbaum, acted as key proponents of Neoliberal reforms which they largely copied from the UK, the USA, Australia and New Zealand.[27] According to Dr Günter Crostack, a partner of KPMG Consulting, there was no need to 'reinvent ... the wheel'.[28]

The Defence White Paper also relaxed the Kohl government's restrictive view on the permissible scope for the privatization and out-sourcing of military services. Among the areas newly excluded from the Bundeswehr's core competencies was the management of its white fleet of 100,000 civilian vehicles and military clothing supplies.[29] In addition, the MOD's revised market-testing guidelines selected five new areas as potential candidates for outsourcing, namely repairs and maintenance, depot management and logistics, services, general administration and training.[30] As investigated in greater detail in Chapter 7, the German armed forces also expanded their use of private contractors to support deployed operations such as in Kosovo and Afghanistan due to a lack of expeditionary capabilities.[31] In 2003 the government's Defence Policy Guidelines stated that the key objective was to sustain and improve the military core capabilities of the armed forces and that 'all services and institutions of the Bundeswehr that did not serve this aim would be critically assessed'.[32] Only on the issue of conscription did the Schröder government remain categorically opposed to reform. As

[25] Bittner and Niejahr, 'Die Berater-Republik'.
[26] GEBB, 'g.e.b.b.: Aufgaben und Status', (Cologne, 13 January 2004).
[27] M. Elbe, 'Werte verwerten? Zum Spannungsverhältnis zwischen Führung und Ökonomisierung am Beispiel der Balanced Scorecard', in G. Richter (ed.) *Die ökonomische Modernisierung der Bundeswehr: Sachstand, Konzeptionen und Perspektiven* (Wiesbaden: VS Verlag für Sozialwissenschaften, 2007), p. 44; Deutscher Bundestag, *Antwort der Bundesregierung auf die Kleine Anfrage der Abgeordneten Thomas Kossendey, Paul Brauer, Ulrich Adam, weiterer Abgeordneter und der Fraktion der CDU/CSU*, Drucksache 14/4426 (30 November 2000), p. 6; J. G. Ross, 'Bundeswehr Embraces Defence Reform', *Armed Forces Journal International*, July 2000.
[28] J. G. Ross, 'Bundeswehr Embraces Defence Reform'.
[29] Bundesrechnungshof, *Bemerkungen 2003 zur Haushalts- und Wirtschaftsführung des Bundes* (Bonn, November 2003), p. 218.
[30] Deutscher Bundestag, *Antwort der Bundesregierung auf die Kleine Anfrage der Abgeordneten Thomas Kossendey, Paul Brauer, Ulrich Adam, weiterer Abgeordneter und der Fraktion der CDU/CSU*, pp. 5–6.
[31] Bundesrechnungshof, *Bemerkungen 2006 zur Haushalts- und Wirtschaftsführung des Bundes*, p. 178.
[32] Bundesministerium der Verteidigung, *Verteidigungspolitische Richtlichtlinien für den Geschäftsbereich des Bundesministers der Verteidigung* (Berlin, 21 May 2003), p. 13.

Scharping's successor, Defence Minister Peter Struck, affirmed: 'The draft is and remains for the foreseeable future the best defence model for the specific situation of Germany.'[33]

The formation of a coalition government between the CDU/CSU and the SPD under Chancellor Merkel between 2005 and 2009 did not end the German government's ambivalence towards the Neoliberal models of the state and the soldier. On the one hand, the government passed new legislation to speed up and ease the formation of public–private joint ventures, which maintained a government share in formally private military companies.[34] On the other hand, Defence Minister Franz Josef Jung transferred the ownership and management of the armed forces' public–private joint ventures from the GEBB to the MOD.[35] The transfer suggested a weakening of the role of the GEBB, which had been a driving force in the privatization of the Bundeswehr under the Schröder administration. Moreover, Defence Minister Jung emphasized that, to his mind, 'the effectiveness of the Bundeswehr is the crucial element, not privatization for its own sake'.[36] A pamphlet published by the GEBB in 2007 also expressed greater scepticism of military outsourcing. The pamphlet noted that previously the GEBB had regarded privatization as the best solution to the Bundeswehr's problems, but a critical reassessment had shown that this approach was not always successful. In future, it concluded, the GEBB would consider internal efficiency improvements and cooperative models 'on a par' with privatization.[37]

The new attitude as well as the increased control of the MOD, which has traditionally been concerned with maintaining the internal capabilities of the Bundeswehr, has been illustrated by the renewed focus on 'internal optimization' in key areas such as the armed forces' hospitals and the decision not to outsource the management of the army officer school in Dresden.[38] In principle, however, the German government has remained committed to extending its cooperation with the private sector where suitable. In its Defence White Paper 2006, the MOD proclaimed that 'cooperation with the industry in the provision of services will be pursued to a maximum up to the complete privatization

[33] Cited in Deutscher Bundestag, *Unterrichtung durch den Wehrbeauftragten: Jahresbericht 2004*, Drucksache 15/5000 (15 March 2005), p. 30 (translation by the author).
[34] Gesetz zur Beschleunigung der Umsetzung von Öffentliche Privaten Partnerschaften und zur Verbesserung gesetzlicher Rahmenbedingungen für Öffentlich Private Partnerschaften, 1 September 2005, BGBl, Jg. 2005, Teil I, Nr. 56, 2676.
[35] S. Kersting, 'Jung bremst Privatisierer. Bundeswehr wird wieder Staatsangelegenheit', *Handelsblatt*, 7 July 2006.
[36] Kersting, 'Jung bremst Privatisierer' (translation by the author).
[37] GEBB, *Teamarbeiter*, p. 7.
[38] GEBB, *Das passt perfekt: Die Bundeswehr und die g.e.b.b. – gemeinsam erfolgreich* (Cologne, July 2008).

of tasks which can be supplied more cheaply by the private sector'.[39] It also approved several new projects between 2006 and 2008, including a public–private partnership for the refurbishment of the Fürst Wrede Garrison in Munich, the privatization of logistics and supply chain management, and the outsourcing of IT training.[40]

In short, the Neoliberal promise to increase the efficiency, effectiveness and democratic accountability of the armed forces has also influenced German national defence policy since the 1990s. However, in contrast to the experience of its allies, the strength of Republican ideals related to social market democracy and the citizen-soldier have tempered the transformation of the roles and relations of the state and the soldier. As the next section will argue, this has led to the emergence of new forms of public–private collaboration in the provision of military services for the Bundeswehr.

Public–private collaboration in the Bundeswehr

By all accounts, the Framework Agreement on Innovation, Investment and Efficiency in the Bundeswehr, signed in 1999, marked the beginning of the privatization and outsourcing of military services in Germany.[41] By 2003 nearly 700 private companies had signed up to the agreement.[42] In addition, the framework agreement determined the creation of a government agency, the GEBB, which would develop future privatization and outsourcing projects for the armed forces. Since then the scope and scale of the privatization of military functions and the involvement of private businesses in decision-making and implementation of German national defence has been shaped by two approaches. The first approach has been the creation of public–private joint ventures, commonly referred to as 'public–private partnerships', which cover entire supply areas such as the white fleet, army maintenance and IT. The second approach has been the outsourcing of select military services to private companies, including the fourteen pilot projects identified in the framework agreement with industry and several new initiatives.

---

[39] Bundesministerium der Verteidigung, *Weißbuch 2006*, pp. 84–5.
[40] GEBB, at: www.gebb.de.
[41] Bundesministerium der Verteidigung, *Die Bundeswehr der Zukunft. Sachstand der Reform* (Berlin, 15 June 2001).
[42] 'Innovation, Investition und Wirtschaftlichkeit in der Bundeswehr' Rahmenvertrag zwischen dem Bundesministerium für Verteidigung und der Industrie (15 December 1999).

Public–private partnerships

The creation of public–private joint ventures to supply entire service categories for the Bundeswehr has been the most significant and most innovative development with regard to military privatization in Germany. So far, the government has established public–private joint ventures for four service segments of the Bundeswehr: the white fleet, clothing supplies, army repairs and maintenance, and IT.[43] In all cases the German government tasked the GEBB, itself a fully government-owned private company, with the development and evaluation of potential public–private partnerships. Although the GEBB has been a strong advocate of the privatization of military services, the resulting joint ventures have integrated Republican principles and Neoliberal polices. These joint ventures have combined continued governmental control through full or partial state ownership with a formal privatization and private industry investments. By limiting contract duration with the joint ventures to medium terms to between seven and twelve years, the GEBB has also sought to prevent longer-term dependencies, although it seems unlikely that the Bundeswehr will decide in favour of alternative suppliers at the end of the contract periods due to the significant investments made in the joint ventures. Lastly, the secondment of Bundeswehr personnel, who had previously served at the related armed forces facilities, to the joint ventures has provided a socially acceptable way of decreasing the number of civil servants to the government's post-Cold War target levels and a bridge between military and industry cultures. While the GEBB has typically considered public–private partnerships less flexible and cost-efficient than outsourcing, it has accepted that the German constitution requires the Bundeswehr to preserve its control and coordination function over the private provision of core military services. The GEBB has also agreed that privatization finds its limits where military services of 'strategic relevance' are concerned.[44]

As listed in Table 6.1, the first public–private partnership created on the basis of these principles was the Bundeswehr (Bw) Fuhrpark Service for the management of the German white fleet. The joint venture is owned 75.1 per cent by the German state and 24.9 per cent by

---

[43] A fourth area – estate management – was also considered for privatization, but was eventually withdrawn from the list. The GEBB argued that the management of the Bundeswehr estates was too heterogeneous and strategically too important for a wholesale privatization. Plans by the GEBB to split the estate management into different sections, which would have allowed for the outsourcing of single service elements to private companies, also failed because of their complexity.

[44] 'Public Private Partnership im Bereich des Bundesministeriums der Verteidigung', at: www.bundeswehr.de (last accessed 6 June 2004).

Table 6.1. *Military public–private joint ventures*[45]

Company name	Duration	Estimated cost (billion)	Ownership
Bw Fuhrpark Service	2002–9	€2.8	• 75.1% government • 24.9% Deutsche Bahn
LHBw Bekleidungsgesellschaft	2002–14	€1.7	• 25.1% government • 74.9% consortium of Lion Apparel and Hellmann Worldwide Logistics
Heeresinstandsetzungslogistik GmbH	2005–13	€1.77	• 49% government • 50% consortium of Krauss-Maffei Wegmann, Rheinmetall Landsysteme and Industriewerke Saar
BWI Informationstechnik GmbH (HERKULES)	2006–16	€7.1	• 49.9% government • 50.1% consortium of Siemens Business Services and IBM Deutschland

the Deutsche Bahn AG, the federal state-owned German train company. While formally a private company, the Bw Fuhrpark Service is, thus, practically a public agency. Moreover, the joint venture has taken into account the size and strategic importance of the white fleet by reserving strong intervention rights and options for the German government. Specifically, the arrangement contractually safeguards the steering authority of the government and places representatives of the Bundeswehr on its board.[46]

The second joint venture was the LHBw Bekleidungsgesellschaft which manages the provision of clothing supplies for the Bundeswehr. It has diverged from the Bw Fuhrpark Service model in terms of a majority contribution from the private sector. The semi-privatized company has a government share of only 25.1 per cent, while a consortium of

---

[45] Estimates based on data provided by the Bundesministerium der Verteidigung, *Bundeswehr Plan 2007* (Berlin, 31 March 2006), p. 16.
[46] BMVg, *Die Bundeswehr der Zukunft*, p. 20.

Lion Apparel and the Hellmann Worldwide Logistics own the remaining 74.9 per cent.[47]

With regard to the third public–private partnership, the Heeresinstandsetzungslogistik GmbH, the GEBB again decided in favour of a greater state share in order to protect governmental oversight in the critical area of army maintenance and repair. In this case the German federal state owns 49 per cent of the joint venture, while a holding company of three German firms – Krauss-Maffei Wegmann, Rheinmetall Landsysteme and the Diehl-subsidiary Industriewerke Saar – owns 51 per cent. Despite these safeguards, the Heeresinstandsetzungslogistik GmbH deals only with technically advanced systems, such as tanks, which amount to no more than 6 per cent of all army maintenance and repairs.

The fourth public–private joint venture, entitled project HERKULES, concerns the IT and communications provision of the German armed forces. After nearly seven years of planning and negotiation with two competing consortiums, the government eventually approved the partnership in December 2006.[48] Given the sensitivity of IT and communication networks for the Bundeswehr, the government decided in favour of a similar corporate set-up, but with a federal state share of 49.9 per cent. The ten-year contract worth an estimated €7.1 billion went to a consortium between Siemens Business Services GmbH and IBM Deutschland GmbH, which holds 50.1 per cent of the newly formed BWI Informationstechnik GmbH.[49]

The keeping of a government share in these formally privatized service areas has allowed the German government to combine the Republican ideal of state guarantees and control with the Neoliberal outsourcing of military functions to private suppliers. Nevertheless, the above public–private partnerships have not been without problems. For one, Bundeswehr efforts to safeguard public oversight of the provision of military services have been criticized for undermining the cost efficiency of these projects and, thus, the government's rationale for the privatizations. In 2004 the Federal Accounting Office concluded that the economic success of the GEBB and its joint ventures could not be verified.[50] Rather than providing real savings, the agency contended

---

[47] LHBw Bekleidungsgesellschaft, at: www.lhbw.de (last accessed 17 March 2005).

[48] Bundesamt für Informationsmanagement und Informationstechnik der Bundeswehr, 'Bundeswehr schließt HERKULES-Vertrag', Press Release, 28 December 2006.

[49] For reasons of consistency, the US term 'billion' for a thousand million is used instead of the European 'milliard'.

[50] C. Esser and U. Stoll, 'Bundeswehr-Millionen verschleudert', *Frontal 21 – TV report*, 1 September 2004; H.-J. Leersch, 'Bundeswehr: SPD denkt an Stopp der Privatisierung' *Welt*, 8 September 2004.

that public–private partnerships frequently only transferred expenses into the future. The Bw Fuhrpark Service's policy of replacing the old white fleet with leased vehicles, for instance, lowered the initial investment cost, but was in the long term more expensive than buying new cars.[51] By 2006 the Bw Fuhrpark Service had to accept this fact and asked the government for a loan to buy cars in an attempt to lower its expenses.[52] Notwithstanding these changes, the Bundeswehr Planning Reviews of 2007 and 2008 reported that Bw Fuhrpark Service savings were lower than estimated.[53] In addition, the Federal Accounting Office has argued that the IT reforms managed through the public–private partnership HERKULES could have been nearly €1 billion cheaper if the Bundeswehr had implemented them itself.[54] The origins of the miscalculations of potential savings have been attributed to the GEBB's interest in the creation of the joint ventures because it was, initially, charged with the management of the government share in the companies. According to the Federal Accounting Office, the GEBB's decisions in favour of these public–private partnerships had therefore been skewed by incorrect projections or foregone conclusions.[55] In particular, the GEBB had argued that the public–private partnerships would be able to save money by being freed from costly and time-consuming public procurement procedures. The Higher State Court Düsseldorf discredited this argument in 2003. It ruled that even military service joint ventures with a minority government ownership should be regarded as state agencies, because they did not change the fact these services were in the 'public interest' and according to Article 87(b) of the constitution were therefore the responsibility of the Bundeswehr.[56] Although the government responded to these accusations by transferring the control of its company shares from the GEBB to the MOD in 2006, the continuation of the joint ventures has not been put into

[51] Bundesrechnungshof, *Bemerkungen 2003 zur Haushalts- und Wirtschaftsführung des Bundes*, p. 219.

[52] Bundesministerium der Verteidigung, *Bundeswehrplan 2007* (Berlin: 31 March 2006), p. 17.

[53] *Ibid.*, p. 9.

[54] Focus article, cited in R. Henning , 'Projekt Herkules', *Bundeswehrkurier* (December 2006), p. 12; F. Kuhn, 'Projekt Herkules: Bundeswehr plant Marsch ins aktuelle Jahrhundert', *Spiegel Online*, 28 November 2006.

[55] Bundesrechnungshof, *Bemerkungen 2003 zur Haushalts- und Wirtschaftsführung des Bundes*, p. 165; H.-J. Leersch, 'Kritik an Scharpings Privatisierungsplänen', *Die Welt*, 4 July 2000.

[56] Oberlandesgericht Düsseldorf, Verg 67/02 (30 April 2003); C. Gramm, 'Bekleidungsgesellschaft und öffentliche Vergabe – Zur Entscheidung des OLG Düsseldorf vom 30. April 2003', Unterrichts Blätter der Wehrverwaltung (UBWV), No. 8 (2003), 282.

question. However, no further joint ventures have been planned since that time. Instead, additional outsourcing projects have focused on conventional private military contracting.

Outsourcing projects

In its 1999 framework agreement with industry the German government identified fourteen potential outsourcing projects for future consideration. These covered five functional areas which are examined in detail below: IT, training, logistics, maintenance and facility management. Although the government stipulated that a condition for a decision to contract these military services out to private companies would be a positive conclusion of a prior market-testing assessment, in practice these assessments were not as rigorous as they could have been. Some assessments were based on analyses by private consulting firms, some on the outcome of outsourcing experiments conducted prior to 1999, and some pilot projects were themselves designated as market-testing exercises. Nevertheless, the government insisted that all pilot projects should be considered test cases for the outsourcing of similar services in other Bundeswehr units.[57] The aim was to apply them across 'all suitable areas of the Bundeswehr, if they prove to be more efficient and equally reliable alternatives'.[58]

Unlike the public–private partnerships, the responsibility for the pilot projects rested with the civilian Bundeswehr administration of the Federal Office of Defence Technology and Procurement[59] which has the overall authority to manage all Bundeswehr contracts with industry. Some market-testing exercises progressed faster than others, but by 2007 the majority of the initial fourteen pilot projects had been implemented. Only three pilot projects, including the technical support for radars on the Frigate 124, the running of a simulator for the navy, and the maintenance and training support of the navy's submarine flotilla, had been cancelled because internal reforms proved to be more cost-efficient or because no commercial supplier could be found.

The outsourcing of IT services was a key focus of the framework agreement and five of the pilot projects identified the provision of software and hardware as candidates for private contracting. The projects ranged from the introduction of commercial IT programmes and hardware into the logistic and administrative management of the

[57] Hw, 'Pilotprojekt 9.2', *Streitkräfte*, 38, no. 36 (16 September 2002), 10.
[58] Bundesministerium der Verteidigung, *Bundeswehr 2002 – Sachstand und Perspektiven* (Berlin, 8 April 2002), p. 39.
[59] Bundesamt für Wehrtechnik und Beschaffung.

Bundeswehr and their adjustment to the special needs of the armed forces to the provision of a communications and data network with coverage for the entire armed forces.[60] The latter included several pilot projects which were eventually integrated into the public–private partnership of project HERKULES. The modification and use of standard commercial software and hardware was relatively uncontroversial and successful. Only the pilot study 'Krisenreaktionskräfte Interoperabilität I' (KINTOP I) into the improvement of IT interoperability for the German forces in Kosovo did not meet the Bundeswehr's specifications. Deutsche Telekom AG had won the €14.7 million contract for the study in 2000. However, at the end of the contract one year later the Bundeswehr considered the proposed technical solution unsuitable. The responsible Bundeswehr unit had been able to obtain a better solution by procuring readily available civilian technology from EADS Telecom for only €82,000.[61]

The second major area was the outsourcing of training support across the three Bundeswehr services. The first key pilot project was the management and provision of IT training at the Bundeswehr's information technology competence centres in Koblenz, Dresden and other locations around Germany. The second project was the development and running of flight simulators for the Eurofighter and the NH 90 transport helicopter for the German Air Force. The third was basic flight training at the Technical College of the Air Force in Kaufbeuren, and the fourth was the provision of training simulators and general training for the navy.

While the Bundeswehr considered the IT and simulator projects a success, the basic flight training contract at the Technical College of the Air Force was cancelled in favour of an optimized in-house provision. Also not awarded were the two navy contracts. The differences might be attributed to the fact that IT training capabilities were widely available in the commercial sector and the requirements of the Bundeswehr did not differ markedly from private customers. Moreover, the simulator centres did not threaten the central role of soldiers within Bundeswehr training facilities by using a 'train-the-trainers' approach. Private military companies provided only the initial instructions, built the simulators or managed the facilities.[62] The air force also used the

---

[60] Hellmann, at: www.hellmann.net; dds, 'Streckenermittlung leicht gemacht', *Zoom!*, No. 3 (2004), pp. 8–9.

[61] Bundesrechnungshof, *Bemerkungen 2002 zur Haushalts- und Wirtschaftsführung des Bundes* (Bonn, 2002), pp. 192–3; F. Wiederspahn, 'BOS-Funknetze für Europa', *Funkschau*, 24 (2002), 10–12.

[62] '3. Preis: Pilotenausbildung – Helicopter Flight Training Services GmbH (HFTS)', *Behoerdenspiegel* (2006), at: www.behoerdenspiegel.eu.

'train-the-trainers' approach for the Eurofighter.[63] Unlike the outsourcing of flight training in the UK, EADS Military Aircraft, who built the planes, only trained the first round of Luftwaffe pilots and mechanics, who then replaced the private contractors.[64]

However, the Bundeswehr has also investigated a more permanent and extensive contribution of the private sector to military and flight training. An eighteen-year contract with Helicopter Flight Training Services GmbH for simulator-based training facilities for the NH 90 transport helicopter marks the air force's first PFI.[65] Under the terms of the contract, the consortium financed and built an annex to the Air Force Combat Pilot College in Bückenburg where it manages and maintains several training simulators developed by the company. In addition, Eurocopter has been providing full-systems support for training helicopters, as used at the training college since 2000.[66] While the air force still provides its own trainers in Bückenburg, it has been examining the potential for outsourcing the majority of training services at the Technical College in Kaufbeuren.

In the area of maintenance contracting, the Bundeswehr has developed three key projects. The first was the public–private joint venture Heeresinstandsetzungslogistik GmbH, the second was a pilot project concerning the improvement of turn-around times in the air force and the third was navy fleet maintenance, which has traditionally been conducted by private dockyards. In particular in the first two projects, the Bundeswehr was careful to safeguard governmental control and capabilities. As outlined above, the federal government owns 49 per cent of Heeresinstandsetzungslogistik GmbH and a significant proportion of its staff are Bundeswehr soldiers. Similarly, the air force has been reluctant to use conventional outsourcing schemes for its maintenance.

Owing to experience gathered as part of its pilot project, the air force has remained 'sceptic of "one-stop solutions" which involve the complete outsourcing of functions'.[67] Instead the air force has developed a 'cooperation model' similar to the concept of integrated project teams

---

[63] 'Simulators are go', *ETSNEWS* (2006), at: www.ets-news.com; 'Successful Training of Eurofighter Flight Instructors', *Defense-Aerospace*, 26 February 2004.

[64] EADS, 'Erfolgreiche Ausbildung der Ausbilder', Press Release, 10 December 2003.

[65] Rheinmetall, 'Industriekonsortium erhält Auftrag für Ausbildingszentren für NH90-Piloten', Press Release, 20 January 2005.

[66] R. Kruzenberg, 'Heeresfliegerwaffenschule in Bückenburg erreicht 30.000h-Marke mit dem Schulungshubschrauber EC-135', *JetJournal*, 11 September 2006; M. Walter, 'A Flight Line Maintenance Center', *Rotor Journal*, 55 (2004), 26.

[67] Bundesrechnungshof, *Bemerkungen 2006 zur Haushalts- und Wirtschaftsführung des Bundes* (Bonn, 2006), p. 177–8 or B. Winzig and M. Adler, 'Erste Erfahrungen mit Kooperativen Einrichtungen der Einsatzlogistik Luftwaffe', *Europäische Sicherheit*, 55, no. 2 (2006).

in the UK. As part of the cooperation model soldiers and private military contractors have worked together in maintenance and systems support teams at air force bases or private facilities.[68] The aim of the model has been to allow the air force to retain combat soldiers with the necessary expertise to take over the maintenance of aircraft during deployed operations and to assess private contracts while making use of commercial capacities during peacetime.[69] According to the air force, the collaboration model has thus not been 'outsourcing in its conventional sense'.[70] So far, a range of collaborative contracts have been signed, including contracts for Eurofighter maintenance and a systems support centre at an EADS facility in Manching, and for Eurofighter engine repairs at a MTU Aero Engines site in Munich.[71] Moreover, in 2005 the Bundeswehr extended the cooperative contract with MTU to include engine repairs for Tornado, F-4F Phantom and BO-105 aircraft at an air force site in Erding.[72] In this case, MTU has leased the site and employs sixty civilian staff on secondment from the Bundeswehr.[73] Finally, the Bundeswehr and Eurocopter have set up a joint Systems Support Centre for the maintenance and systems support of Tiger and NH 90 helicopters at the Eurocopter facility in Ottobrunn.[74]

In the area of logistics, the use of private contractors has been shaped by pilot projects focused on improving and centralizing the management of Bundeswehr depots and transports through the introduction of systems used in the commercial sector. The aim of pilot project ZEBEL has been to reorganize the management of the central spare parts depot of the army with modern technologies developed by Elektroniksystem- und Logistik GmbH (ESG). Its partner Schenker Deutschland AG supplies the parts as required to a number of private and four Bundeswehr repair centres.[75] Another project has included

---

[68] Winzig and Adler, 'Erste Erfahrungen mit Kooperativen Einrichtungen der Einsatzlogistik Luftwaffe'.
[69] M. Vetter, '... Tendenzen in der Instandhaltung', *Europäische Sicherheit*, 52, no. 7 (2003).
[70] *Ibid*.
[71] *Ibid*.; Winzig and Adler, 'Erste Erfahrungen mit Kooperativen Einrichtungen der Einsatzlogistik Luftwaffe'; EADS, 'Kooperatives Modell für die gemeinsame Eurofighter-Betreuung durch Luftwaffe und EADS', Press Release, 23 January 2003.
[72] h.b., 'Kooperationsmodell der Luftwaffe mit AUTOFLUG', *Europäische Sicherheit*, 55, no. 10 (2006).
[73] Winzig and Adler, 'Erste Erfahrungen mit Kooperativen Einrichtungen der Einsatzlogistik Luftwaffe'.
[74] *Ibid*.; Eurocopter GmbH, 'Efficient Services for the Tiger and the NH90: The Bundeswehr and Eurocopter set up joint Systems Support Centre in Ottobrunn', Press Release, 7 April 2003.
[75] Schenker Deutschland AG, 'Bundeswehr überträgt für weitere Jahre zentrale Logistikfunktionen und ESG und Schenker', Press Release, 18 March 2005.

the provision of a transport route database and programme. It allows the Bundeswehr Logistics Centre to select centrally the fastest routes and most suitable transport media in response to transport requirements submitted online by military units across Germany. The contracts, signed with Mummert & Partner Consulting and Hellmann Worldwide Logistics in 2001 and taken over by ESG in 2005, have involved the development of the system, while local framework contracts provide additional transport when Bundeswehr capacities are insufficient.[76] Importantly, in order to ensure control over the project and the acquisition of the necessary expertise by the Bundeswehr, a collaborative project team with the armed forces has developed the design of the system.[77]

The smallest number of projects has so far been implemented in the area of Bundeswehr management. The most important pilot project in this area has been the private management of support functions at the Army Combat Training Centre Altmark. The first three-year contract for the Army Combat Training Centre went in 2001 to GÜZ-System-Management Ltd, the second was won by the UK outsourcing giant Serco and SAAB Training Systems in 2003.[78] Under the terms of the contracts, the private firms have managed the support sector and provided select services including fleet support and maintenance, fuelling, cleaning and technical support for training reviews and meetings. Military leadership and the training itself have remained within the remit of the Bundeswehr.[79] In addition, the MOD decided in 2008 to contract out the refurbishment and extension of its Fürst-Wrede garrison in Munich to Hochtief PPP Solutions. Although the garrison will remain in state ownership, the company will fund the improvements in return for a twenty-year management contract, representing Germany's second PFI.[80]

Beyond the pilot projects listed in the framework agreement, the Bundeswehr has investigated outsourcing of two other functions: security-guarding and catering. The former has not received much attention in spite of the potentially controversial nature of outsourcing tasks which require armed personnel. Thus, it comes as a surprise that the Bundeswehr has contracted out the majority of the

[76] Hellmann, at: www.ehellmann.de/; dds, 'Streckenermittlung leicht gemacht', 8–9.
[77] W. Klingenberg, 'Mobilität der Streitkräfte', *Europäische Sicherheit*, 54, no. 10. (2005).
[78] STN Atlas Elektronik was split in 2003 into ATLAS Elektronik GmbH (ATLAS) and Rheinmetall Defence Electronics GmbH (RDE).
[79] Interview with the Bundesamt für Wehrtechnik und Beschaffung, written answers.
[80] Hochtief PPP Solutions, at: www.hochtief-pppsolutions.de.

security-guarding of its premises. In 2006 52 per cent of Bundeswehr establishments were protected by private security guards and another 13 per cent were guarded by both military and private staff. Unlike its US counterpart, the German MOD estimates that the private guarding has been about 49 per cent cheaper than the use of military personnel.[81] The MOD also asserts that the strict national regulations for private security guards in Germany, reinforced by internal Bundeswehr requirements for private security contractors, maintain high standards of control and accountability.

The catering project, on the other hand, has been the best-publicized failure among the Bundeswehr's outsourcing trials. The project was set up as a public–private competition between an internally optimized Bundeswehr provision and the Dussmann Company. As part of the competition, the armed forces contracted Dussmann for the management of thirteen military kitchens in the Munich region between 2005 and 2007. For the duration of the contract, it supplied Dussmann with 230 civilian Bundeswehr staff. In June 2006, however, Dussmann unilaterally withdrew from the contract. According to the company, the 'nearly destructive attitude' of the seconded Bundeswehr personnel, whom the company accused of stealing and handing out excessively large portions, had undermined its profit margins.[82] Dussmann also claimed that the Bundeswehr had not assigned sufficient numbers of personnel to permit the company to fulfil its contract.[83] Even before the start of the competition the planned implementation of the pilot project had been delayed because Dussmann was the only competitor for the award and because of the high cost of Dussmann's offer. Moreover, the MOD had been aware of a 'lack of acceptance among the armed forces' regarding the outsourcing of catering services.[84] The project had gone ahead regardless because the GEBB had estimated that the outsourcing of catering could produce savings of up to 70 per cent.[85]

Together the public–private partnerships and the pilot projects of the Bundeswehr illustrate the determination of the German government to combine the Republican ideal of centralized state control and

[81] Deutscher Bundestag, *Antwort des Parlamentarischen Staatssekretärs Dr. Friedrich Pflüger vom 16. März*, Drucksache 16/1043 (2006), p. 21.
[82] H.-J. Leersch, 'Bundeswehr-Privatisierung auf ganzer Linie gescheitert', *Welt*, 21 June 2006 (translation by the author).
[83] Dussmann-Service, 'Dussmann-Gruppe kündigt Vertrag zum Pilotprojekt Truppenverpflegung', Press Release, 19 June 2006.
[84] H.-J. Leersch, 'Bundeswehr-Modernisierung stockt', *Die Welt*, 2 April 2005.
[85] GEBB, *Daten und Fakten – Das neue Verpflegungsmanagement hat ein hohes Potenzial an Einsparungen durch Rationalisierung* (Cologne, 2003).

Table 6.2. *German model of the state*

Dimension	Germany
Ideology	• Republicanism • Neoliberalism
Geographical scope	• National and international
Functional scope	Public–private joint ventures for: • White fleet management • Clothing supply management • Army heavy maintenance and repair • IT services Limited private provision of: • IT • Training • Logistics • Maintenance and repair • Facility management Extensive private provision of: • Armed guarding
Resources	Limited to extensive private provision of: • Equipment • Services • Facilities • Financing (PFIs: NH 90 flight simulator, Fürst-Wrede garrison)
Interests	• State control • Cost efficiency
Norms	• Not small, but modern state • Effectiveness
Decision-making	• Kohl: Market-testing, cost and performance responsibility • Schröder: Public–private partnerships, collaboration model • Merkel: government shares in joint ventures transferred from GEBB to MOD control
Implementation	• Internal optimization, public–private joint ventures, medium-term contracting, train-the-trainers
Democratic control and accountability	• State shares and management roles in key military service joint ventures • Limited role of private military companies

ownership over the supply of military services with internal and commercial cost-efficiency measures modelled on Neoliberal reforms. In spite of growing international security demands and a tight budgetary policy, this ambition has not noticeably decreased over the past decade. On the contrary, the coalition government under Chancellor Merkel appeared to take a more cautious approach to the privatization and outsourcing of military services than her predecessor Schröder. While the functional scope of the involvement of private military contractors in the supply of services for the Bundeswehr is nearly as wide as that in the UK and the USA, its scale has so far been comparatively limited. In addition, the MOD has sought to protect its control over the private provision of military services through public–private joint ventures, medium-term contract periods, collaborative teams of soldiers and contractors, and the 'train-the-trainers' approach. The issue of state control over the military has remained a primary concern. However, before the final section discusses whether the experiment with mixing Republican and Neoliberal models has been successful in ensuring democratic control and accountability of the Bundeswehr, the next section investigates the practical and ideological challenges to the German model of the citizen-soldier.

The end of Germany's citizen army?

The post-Cold War transformation of the Bundeswehr has also challenged the German model of the conscripted citizen-soldier. Although the German government proclaimed as late as 2008 that conscription remains its 'model of the future', changing national and international circumstances have required the adaptation of the Bundeswehr.[86] The report of the Weizsäcker Commission on Collective Security and the Future of the Bundeswehr in 2000 was a milestone in this process.[87] Although the frequent contention that the report advocated the abolition of conscription is incorrect, it was the most controversial issue within the commission's remit. Six out of twenty-one commission members supported an all-volunteer army based on a force of 220,000 professional soldiers, but the majority of commission members favoured a modification of the old system to create a semi-professional force of 240,000 soldiers with a reduced number of 35,000 conscripts.[88] The

---

[86] Bundesministerium der Verteidigung, *Wehrpflicht – Wehrform mit Zukunft* (Berlin, January 2008).
[87] Kommission 'Gemeinsame Sicherheit und Zukunft der Bundeswehr', *Bericht der Kommission an die Bundesregierung* (Berlin, 23 May 2000).
[88] *Ibid.*, pp. 60–1.

ruling Schröder government disagreed with both proposals. The government advocated the introduction of Neoliberal market policies in other areas, but on the question of the draft it was staunchly committed to the Republican model of the citizen-soldier. In fact, the two largest German political parties, Schröder's SPD and the CDU/CSU in opposition, agreed that an all-volunteer force similar to the UK and the USA was out of the question, as was the reduction of the number of conscripts to 35,000, which would fully undermine the equitability of the draft. Changing security requirements, however, have meant that the government has not been able to maintain the Bundeswehr as it presented itself at the end of the Cold War. This section examines two developments and their implications for the German model of a citizen army. The first has been the massive reduction of the West German military from its Cold War size of 500,000 soldiers, in addition to about 90,000 soldiers from the former East Germany, to a joint force of 250,000 in 2006 and its consequences for the draft. The second has been the changing rationale and functions of the Bundeswehr and its effects on the roles and identity of the German citizen-soldier.

Reform, resizing and the draft

As in the USA during the Vietnam War, the equity of conscription has become a key issue for the continuation of the Republican model of the citizen-soldier in Germany. There are two categories of conscripts: basic conscripts and conscripts who voluntarily serve a longer period, but do not enlist as professional soldiers. In November 2008 about 36,000 conscripts fell into the first category, serving 9 months, while around 23,000 conscripts had signed up for an extended service of up to 23 months. This meant that less than half of all eligible young males in Germany completed any form of military service.[89] A significantly larger proportion of 73,000 young men had opted for the civilian service, which has been transformed since the 1970s from a disparaged option for leftist conscientious objectors to a widely respected contribution to the welfare of the nation.[90] In spite of the already existing injustices due to the decreased size of the Bundeswehr, conscript

---

[89] Bundeswehr, 'Die Stärke der Bundeswehr', at: www.bundeswehr.de; Longhurst, 'Why Aren't the Germans Debating the Draft?', 155.
[90] Bundesamt für den Zivildienst, 'Zivildienstleistende im November', at: www.zivildienst.de; G. Kümmel, 'The Winds of Change: The Transition from Armed Forces for Peace to New Missions for the Bundeswehr and Its Impact on Civil-Military Relations', *Journal of Strategic Studies*, 26, no. 2 (2003), 11; Deutscher Bundestag, *Unterrichtung durch den Wehrbeauftragten, Jahresbericht 2006*, p. 35.

numbers have remained above the targets set by the government.[91]
So as to not undermine the semblance of equitability any further, the
Merkel government decided in 2006 to reverse its decision to cut down
the number of basic conscripts to 32,000 and approved an increase
of draftees for the years 2007 and 2008. From 2009 the government
hoped that the smaller size of eligible age cohorts, due to lower birth
rates, would naturally reduce the number of available conscripts to
meet Germany's declining needs.[92]

Ironically, while the government has been at pains to reduce the
number of conscripts, it has simultaneously been apprehensive about
the long-term recruitment of its professional soldiers. One problem
has been the declining health of young men, which has forced the government to lower the criteria for applicants for the extended service
in order to meet its requirements.[93] In order to deal with these contradicting demands, the outsourcing and privatization projects of the
Bundeswehr have become as much a personnel management tool as a
means by which to improve the cost efficiency of the German armed
forces. On the one hand, the government has used the secondment of
civilian or military Bundeswehr personnel to public–private partnerships to encourage surplus staff to transfer to the private sector. On the
other hand, it has hired additional private military contractors to meet
demand in specialist functions which cannot be filled by professional
or conscripted soldiers.

Given the persisting inequalities of conscription in Germany, it is
surprising that opinion polls conducted between 2005 and 2008 have
consistently observed that between 62 and 82 per cent of citizens favour
the preservation of the draft for the near future.[94] In addition to a historical commitment to the tradition of the 'citizen in uniform', the
dedication to the model of a citizen army appears to rest on the persistence of Republican beliefs among the population at large. These ideals
have put a premium on notions of community, welfare and the reciprocity between rights and obligations, irrespective of whether these

---

[91] Deutscher Bundestag, *Unterrichtung durch den Wehrbeauftragten, Jahresbericht 2006*.
[92] Deutscher Bundestag, *Antwort der Bundesregierung auf die Kleine Anfrage der
Abgeordneten Paul Schäfer, Monika Knoche, Wolfgang Gehrke, weiterer Abgeordneter und
der Fraktion DIE LINKE*, Drucksache 16/5341 (14 May 2007), p. 2.
[93] Deutscher Bundestag, *Unterrichtung durch den Wehrbeauftragten, Jahresbericht 2006*,
p. 35.
[94] Emnid Umfrage zum Meinungsbild der Bevölkerung und der Jugend zur
Sicherheitspolitische Lage in Deutschland 2006; T. Bulmahn, 'Das sicherheits- und
verteidigungspolitische Meinungsbild in Deutschland', *SOWI.NEWS*, no. 1 (2006),
11; T. Bulmahn, *Befölkerungsbefragung 2008: Sicherheits- und verteidigungspolitisches
Meinungsklima in Deutschland* (Strausberg: SOWI, November 2008), p. 38.

are through civil or military service.[95] Both the government and the population also believe that general conscription is the best method for ensuring democratic control over the armed forces. Conscription has indeed been successful in facilitating comparatively close relations between the armed forces and society. In 2007 68 per cent of conscripts considered their military service period as a 'positive experience' and an exceptional 48 per cent of Germans felt well or very well informed about the functions and internal organization of the Bundeswehr.[96] The degree of public trust in the armed forces is only exceeded by that in the public police. Conscription has also facilitated the representativeness of the Bundeswehr with the result that the opinions of soldiers and civilians in Germany have been nearly identical on most issues.[97] This agreement has ranged from the ranking of traditional and non-traditional security issues in order of importance to the role of women in the armed forces. However, soldiers and citizens also agree over the decline of religious and moral values which support the Republican obligation to risk one's life for the community, illustrating that Germany has not been immune from the rise of the Neoliberal focus on individual rights and freedoms.[98] Among the motives for the increasing number of young men who have chosen civilian over military service, cost-benefit considerations have replaced conscientious objection.[99] Moreover, in spite of a preference for citizen-soldiers, almost half of the German population can imagine a shift to professional armed forces.[100] As the next section discusses, the changing security environment has played a major role in the debate over a potential professionalization of the Bundeswehr.

New tasks, new identity?

The changing functions of the Bundeswehr have presented a key challenge to the post-war ideal of the citizen-soldier. The transformation of the Bundeswehr from a purely defensive military to an international intervention force has not only questioned the justification for the draft

[95] See also Werkner, 'Die Wehrpflict – Teil der politischen Kultur der Bundesrepublik Deutschland?'.
[96] S. Löwenstein, 'Soldaten fühlen sich im Stich gelassen', *Frankfurter Allgemeine Zeitung*, 26 April 2007; T. Bulmahn, R. Fiebig and W. Sender, *Sicherheits- und verteidigungspolitisches Meinungsklima in der Bundesrepublik Deutschland* (Strausberg: SOWI, April 2008), p. 90.
[97] Kümmel, 'The Winds of Change', 20–5.
[98] Bulmahn, 'Das sicherheits- und verteidigungspolitische Meinungsbild in Deutschland', 11.
[99] Kümmel, 'The Winds of Change', 13.
[100] Bulmahn, *Befölkerungsbefragung 2008*, p. 39.

provided by Republicanism, it has also undermined the identity and self-perception of the German soldier as a 'citizen in uniform'.[101] The shift from a national defence to an international fighting force has proceeded inexorably since the Federal Constitutional Court ruled in 1994 that Bundeswehr missions out-of-area are permitted by the constitution if conducted as part of multinational operations under international mandates.[102] Nevertheless, it took nearly a decade for the German government to redefine the role of the Bundeswehr. In 2003 the government's new Defence Policy Guidelines concluded that there was no longer a need for a conventional defence of the German territory. Instead, 'conflict prevention and conflict resolution as well as the support of alliance partners, also outside the alliance territory, have moved to the forefront.'[103] To deal with these threats, the government proposed a shift towards 'deployable' armed forces which prioritized international operations over national defence.[104]

Since then, the conditions of Bundeswehr operations have changed in major ways, including the growing number and intensity of international missions from the monitoring of the UN weapons embargo along the coasts of the former Yugoslavia to the leadership of NATO's stabilization force in the north of Afghanistan.[105] Most of these international operations have fitted into the ideal of the soldier as helper in emergencies and as peaceful protector, which has shaped the self-image of German citizen-soldiers and their perception by the German public.[106] For many contemporary Germans, their personal experiences of the armed forces have been determined by national Bundeswehr support missions during the Elbe flood catastrophe and the World Soccer Championship in Germany in 2006. The slogan of the fiftieth anniversary of the Bundeswehr, 'Decidedly for Peace', was clearly within

[101] S. B. Gareis, 'Soldat für den Weltfrieden: Der Wandel der Bundeswehr von der Verteidigungs- zur Einsatzarmee', *SOWI.NEWS*, no. 2 (2005), 1.

[102] A. Geis, 'Der Funktions- und Legitimationswandel der Bundeswehr und das "freundliche Desinteresse" der Bundesbürger', in B. Schoch, A. Heinemann-Grüder, J. Hippler, M. Weingardt und R. Munz (eds.) *Friedensgutachten 2007* (Berlin: LIT, 2007), p. 42.

[103] Bundesministerium der Verteidigung, *Verteidigungspolitische Richtlinien für den Bereich des Bundesministers der Verteidigung* (Berlin, 21 May 2003), p. 19 (translation by the author).

[104] Gareis, 'Soldat für den Weltfrieden', p. 1; S. Mannitz, 'Weltbürger in Uniform oder dienstbare Kämpfer? Konsequenzen des Auftragswandels für das Soldatenbild der Bundeswehr', in B. Schoch, A. Heinemann-Grüder, J. Hippler, M. Weingardt and R. Munz (eds.) *Friedensgutachten 2007* (Berlin: LIT, 2007), pp. 98–109.

[105] Deutscher Bundestag, *Unterrichtung durch den Wehrbeauftragten, Jahresbericht 2006*, p. 9.

[106] Geis, 'Der Funktions- und Legitimationswandel der Bundeswehr und das "freundliche Desinteresse" der Bundesbürger', p. 48.

this tradition.[107] However, the latest international interventions have indicated a shift from peace support towards fighting missions. The largest Bundeswehr contingent so far, involving up to 4,500 soldiers, was deployed with the International Security Assistance Force (ISAF) in Afghanistan. The second largest contingent of 3,600 soldiers was despatched to contain the eruption of violence in Kosovo in March 2004.[108] The danger to Bundeswehr soldiers has thus increased significantly, as has the demand for more robust mandates which permit offensive military operations.[109] In particular with regard to Afghanistan, there has been persistent international pressure for the Bundeswehr to contribute to combat missions.[110] The government has responded by deploying Tornado fighter jets on a reconnaissance mission in 2007 and by despatching a quick reaction force in 2008. The armed forces and the German population have viewed the transition towards international combat missions with scepticism. In the wake of the decision to despatch Tornados to Afghanistan, 57 per cent of the German electorate favoured a total recall of the Bundeswehr mission.[111] The rising danger to Bundeswehr soldiers appeared to be in no way justified by the potential threat to German national security.

Since the stipulations of the constitution, which enshrine the Republican principles that the armed forces may only be used for national defence and that conscription serves as the guarantor against expeditionary wars, have remained, formally, unchanged and unchallenged, the deployment of the Bundeswehr in international operations has led to constant tensions between its traditional roles and identity and contemporary practice. Although no basic conscripts, only 9 per cent of extended service conscripts and 7 per cent of reservist soldiers have been involved in international missions, even the deployment of career soldiers abroad represents a historical transformation.[112] The question of whether the deployment of German soldiers in fighting missions abroad necessitates the abandonment of the Republican model of

[107] Translation by the author.

[108] Deutscher Bundestag, *Unterrichtung durch den Wehrbeauftragten, Jahresbericht 2004* (46. Bericht), Drucksache 15/5000 (15 March 2005), p. 24.

[109] Geis, 'Der Funktions- und Legitimationswandel der Bundeswehr und das "freundliche Desinteresse" der Bundesbürger', p. 48.

[110] Deutscher Bundestag, *Unterrichtung durch den Wehrbeauftragten, Jahresbericht 2006*, p. 10.

[111] C. Ingelfinger, 'Mehrheit der Deutschen für Truppenabzug', *Spiegel Online*, 17 March 2007, cited in R. Glassner and C. Schetter, 'Der deutsche Beitrag zum Aufbau Afghanistans seit 2001: Bundeswehreinsatz und ziviles Engagement', in B. Schoch *et al.* (eds.) *Friedensgutachten 2007* (Berlin: LIT, 2007), p. 64.

[112] Deutscher Bundestag, *Unterrichtung durch den Wehrbeauftragten, Jahresbericht 2006*, p. 42.

the citizen-soldier has been reinforced by the clashes with the principles of Internal Leadership. The Internal Leadership doctrine has sought to protect civilian control over the armed forces by educating conscript and professional soldiers in their democratic rights, and asserts the right of soldiers to question any government decision to use military force and to have these decisions examined in court.[113] This right goes beyond the discussion of the legality of an international intervention, to which the German government is already constitutionally committed. It rather concerns the issue of whether the danger to the life of the soldier as citizen, which the government has the obligation to protect under the Social Contract codified in the constitution, is justified by the operational aims.[114] In addition, soldiers have the right to refuse to carry out orders that contradict their personal conscience.[115]

The case of Major Florian Pfaff exemplifies the disjunction between the Republican ideals that have shaped the identity of the German soldier as a 'citizen in uniform' and the changing functions of the Bundeswehr. In 2003 Major Pfaff refused to be deployed in functions that indirectly supported the intervention in Iraq. He thereby made use of his right, indeed his duty, under the principles of Internal Leadership, to question and refuse any orders that would be incompatible with the German constitution and international human rights law.[116] His argument that the pre-emptive intervention in Iraq was in contravention to international law because it lacked a UN mandate was confirmed by the Federal Administrative Court in 2005. The court reinforced the principle that any military orders that contribute to the undermining of international peace, in particular offensive military operations, may be considered as void.[117]

In response to the growing divergence between traditional ideals and new missions, the Bundeswehr has witnessed a clash of two contradictory cultures. Soldiers educated during the Cold War era have felt the tension most and have complained about the 'total mental reconstruction' of the Bundeswehr's identity and functions.[118] They would like to preserve the model of the citizen-soldier and its Republican ideals. Conversely, the younger generation of soldiers have widely

---

[113] Mannitz, 'Weltbürger in Uniform oder dienstbare Kämpfer?', p. 102.

[114] *Ibid.*, p. 102.

[115] Bundeswehr, 'Befehlsverweigerung statthaft', *Blogspot*, no. 38, 22 June 2005.

[116] Kümmel, 'The Winds of Change', 9.

[117] Deutscher Bundestag, *Antwort der Bundesregierung auf die Kleine Anfrage der Abgeordneten Ulla Jelpke, Oskar Lafontaine, Inge Höger und der Fraktion DIE LINKE*, Drucksache 16/4769 (21 March 2007), p. 1.

[118] Mannitz, 'Weltbürger in Uniform oder dienstbare Kämpfer?' p. 106 (translation by the author).

Table 6.3. *German model of the soldier*

Dimension	Germany
Relationships with the state and society	• Reciprocal obligation • Duty
Motivation	• Self-defence, but growing pressure to accept international deployments
Identity	• Individual-civilian, but increasingly individual-professional (deployment professionals)
Democratic control and accountability	• Civilianization of the armed forces • Social integration of the armed forces with society

accepted their role in international interventions and have moved towards an occupational view of the military such as that espoused by the US and UK armed forces.[119] Although the Bundeswehr leadership has viewed the emergence of these 'deployment professionals' with concern, it has been hard-pressed to reform the conception of the Internal Leadership and the model of the citizen-soldier in ways that are consistent with the Bundeswehr's new functions.[120] The survival of the Republican model seems to depend on whether the traditional ideal of the 'citizen in uniform' can be transformed into that of a world citizen in uniform.[121]

In summary, this section has illustrated that, in contrast to the UK and the USA, the German model of the citizen-soldier is not undermined by an ideological transition towards a new concept of the soldier, but by the seeming unsuitability of this model for the new security environment faced by Germany since the end of the Cold War. Although both government and society continue to value the ideal of a conscript army, the inequity of the draft due to massive personnel reductions and the reconstruction of the Bundeswehr as an interventionist force challenge the ideals and principles underpinning the Republican citizen-soldier. The resulting transformation of the model of the soldier towards professional armed forces and the use of private military contractors in select functions have been largely unobserved by the public. However, as the next section will demonstrate,

---

[119] *Ibid.*, p. 107; Kümmel, 'The Winds of Change', 21.

[120] Mannitz, 'Weltbürger in Uniform oder dienstbare Kämpfer?' p. 107 (translation by the author).

[121] G. Kümmel, 'Eine schwierige Melange – Das Bild des Soldaten der Bundeswehr im Wandel', *IF – Zeitschrift für Innere Führung* (2007).

their implications for the democratic control and accountability of the Bundeswehr have been considerable.

The shareholder state, the citizen-soldier and democratic control

In accordance with its Republican models of the state, the citizen and the soldier, the German government has traditionally sought to ensure the democratic accountability of national defence through two key mechanisms: the state monopoly on the use of military force and the integration of the military into society through the citizen-soldier. The professionalization and privatization of the Bundeswehr present obvious challenges to these mechanisms because of the associated changes of the state and the transformation of the model of the soldier according to Neoliberal conceptions of democratic control. While Republicanism views the decreasing direct role of the state and the citizen in national and international security as a threat to democratic accountability, Neoliberalism suggests that limiting the scope of state involvement in favour of the private market increases the responsiveness of public service provision to the citizens. Against these contradictory ideological rationales, the German government has attempted to find a middle way. Similar to the economic paradigm of social market capitalism which seeks to temper the inequalities of the commercial sector with state regulation, the German government has aimed to develop a new model for its armed forces that combines Neoliberal market efficiency with Republican governmental oversight. This section discusses whether and to what degree this model has been successful. In particular, it examines two issues. The first is the inherent contradictions within the new German models of the state and the armed forces, and their implications for democratic control and accountability. The second concerns their impact on civil-military relations.

Control versus cost efficiency

Although the primary rationale for the privatization and outsourcing of military services in Germany has been to increase funds for a transformation of the Bundeswehr from a purely defensive to a deployable armed force, successive governments have prioritized state control over cost efficiency.[122] In particular, the creation of public–private partnerships with significant government shares has aimed to safeguard public

---

[122] Portugall, 'Die Bundeswehr und das Privatisierungsmodell der "Öffentlich-Privaten-Partnerschaft" (ÖPP)', p. 156.

oversight of the private provision of key military services. According to the Higher State Court Düsseldorf, the control of the German government over these public–private partnerships has manifested itself in four dimensions. Firstly, the government has the right to appoint members to the executive office and the boardroom of the four public–private joint ventures. Secondly, the government has exercised crucial oversight of and has provided direct input into the GEBB's design of the companies. Thirdly, the government has assigned Bundeswehr personnel to the companies on a cost-free basis. Fourthly, there have been a high density of control mechanisms that 'radiate' from the government to the management of the four companies.[123] The court concluded that the government not only wanted to preserve direct control over the provision of military services through the establishment of public–private partnerships, but also was obliged to do so according to Article 87(b) of the constitution.[124]

In addition, the German government has sought to preserve more extensive state involvement in outsourcing projects than has been the case in either the UK or the USA. So far, the Bundeswehr's pilot projects have outsourced only a small range of military functions to private contractors. Moreover, through its 'train-the-trainers' approach and its cooperative model the Bundeswehr has attempted to maintain critical expertise in the outsourced tasks which permit it to assess contractor bids and take over these functions after the end of a project or during deployed operations. The assignment of Bundeswehr soldiers to some pilot projects has also contributed to the integration of contractor and military personnel. Finally, private contractors supplying training services, such as for the NH90 transport helicopter, have to inform the German government about the identity of third-party customers and submit relevant financial agreements for public approval.[125]

These attempts to preserve governmental control over private provision of military services have not prevented serious criticisms of Bundeswehr privatization projects. Foremost, it has been argued that Bundeswehr efforts to safeguard public oversight of the provision of military and military support services have, at least partially, undermined the cost efficiency of its privatizations and, thus, the

---

[123] 'Vergaberecht auch nach Privatisierung öffentlicher Einrichtungen', *BayGTzeitung*, no. 10 (2003).
[124] Gramm, 'Bekleidungsgesellschaft und öffentliche Vergabe – Zur Entscheidung des OLG Düsseldorf vom 30. April 2003', 283.
[125] H.-P. Diedrich, 'The Public–private Partnership for NH90 Simulator-Based Flight Training', *RUSI Defence Systems* (2006), 106.

government's rationale for the reforms. Moreover, the lack of clear lines of accountability and responsibility in public–private partnerships has impeded parliamentary oversight of defence spending.[126] As in the UK and the USA, the actual savings achieved through military service privatization have been difficult to determine because of the complexity of the projects including the amount of government investments and start-up costs, the assignation of public employees to the privatized companies and the use of Bundeswehr facilities and equipment. While the Federal Accounting Office has observed savings of around 30 per cent in some of the conventional outsourcing projects, it has specifically questioned the cost efficiency of public–private partnerships.[127]

The government has sometimes contributed to these problems by failing to ensure sufficient competition among the private companies bidding for military contracts, either because competition was limited to national firms for reasons of national security or because the Bundeswehr had already established contacts with a particular company during the project design phase.[128] The army maintenance public–private partnership Heeresinstandsetzungslogistik GmbH, for instance, was not publicly advertised and relied on an industry study which incorrectly asserted the greater cost efficiency and effectiveness of the model over outsourcing or internal optimization. In the case of the Army Combat Centre, an ongoing market-testing exercise with several private contractors set up in 1997 was stopped prematurely so the project could be included in the framework agreement with industry. Although the project study had not been completed, the government termed the interim results successful and announced the Combat Centre as one of the fourteen pilot projects.[129]

Another factor has been the insufficient reduction of civilian Bundeswehr personnel through secondments to public–private partnerships and private contractors. In the case of the public–private partnerships, the majority of the projected savings have depended on such personnel reductions.[130] They were also supposed to provide

---

[126] Portugall, 'Die Bundeswehr und das Privatisierungsmodell der "Öffentlich-Privaten-Partnerschaft" (ÖPP)', p. 155.

[127] J. Riedle, 'General-Instandhaltung für alle', *Instandhaltung*, no. 2 (2006), 20–1.

[128] Deutscher Bundestag, *Antwort der Bundesregierung auf die Kleine Anfrage der Abgeordneten Thomas Kossendey, Paul Brauer, Ulrich Adam, weiterer Abgeordneter und der Fraktion der CDU/CSU*, p. 5.

[129] Written interview with the Bundesamt für Wehrtechnik und Beschaffung, 3 June 2004; H.-J. Leersch, 'Kritik an Scharpings Privatisierungsplänen', *Die Welt*, 4 July 2000.

[130] Interviews with the GEBB, 4 May 2004.

a socially acceptable mechanism for lowering the number of civilian Bundeswehr employees from over 129,000 in 2004 to 75,000 by 2010. Although companies have encouraged seconded Bundeswehr personnel to accept suitable positions in their own businesses or the private sector in general, Bundeswehr employees have been slow to take advantage of these opportunities. In 2004 the Federal Accounting Office criticized the fact that investments of €3 million in the personnel transfer office of the LHBw Bekleidungsgesellschaft had resulted in 8 transfers and not in 200, as had been estimated in the cost comparison study.[131] The number of transfers has since increased, but the failure of the Dussmann catering contract illustrates the resistance of civilian armed forces personnel to perceived takeovers by private companies.

While the joint ventures have attempted to safeguard centralized governmental control of and democratic accountability for privatized military functions, they have nevertheless been negatively affected. Multiple public and private parties involved in the joint ventures, unclear lines of responsibility and public misinformation have especially impeded the democratic accountability of the partnerships. In fact, the larger the number of actors involved and the more legalized their relations, the more difficult it has become for the German parliament to exert its political authority over the provision of military services.[132] Moreover, conventional outsourcing projects have relied as much on effective contract management for democratic control as in the UK and the USA due to a lack of specific legislation regarding private military companies and their employees. Only private security and policing services have been tightly regulated through the German Trade Code and special legislation for security services.[133] Arguably, the latter has been strengthened in 1999 and in 2002 with additional requirements for training hours, a written and oral test on legal and other issues, sufficient insurance and a range of further standards.[134] Other support services and, as Chapter 7 will outline, private military contractors in international operations have so far not been placed under specific legal controls.

[131] H.-J. Leersch, 'Strucks ehrgeizige Privatisierungspläne drohen zu scheitern' *Welt*, 30 November 2004.

[132] Portugall, 'Die Bundeswehr und das Privatisierungsmodell der "Öffentlich-Privaten-Partnerschaft" (ÖPP)', p. 155.

[133] *Verordnung über das Bewachungsgewerbe vom 7. Dezember 1995* (geändert durch Gesetze vom 16. Juni 1998 (BGBl. 1 5. 1291), vom 10. November 2001 (BGBJ. 1 5.2992) und durch Gesetz zur Änderung des Bewachungsgewerberechts vom 23. Juli 2002 (BGBl. 1 8.2724)), Bonn: Bundesgesetzblatt; Weber, *Vergleichender Überblick*, p. 71.

[134] *Gesetz zur Änderung des Bewachungsgewerberechts vom 23.Juli 2002*, Bonn: Bundesgesetzblatt, I, no. 51 (26 July 2002).

The changing Bundeswehr and civil-military relations

In addition to these weaknesses in the government's accountability and control over military functions, the professionalization and privatization of Bundeswehr functions is transforming the relationship between the soldier and German society. This changing relationship can be observed in the emergence of a gap between the armed forces and the population, and the disillusionment of many soldiers with what is perceived as governmental and societal neglect for their contribution to national and international security. Among the developments examined in the preceding sections, two in particular point to a growing disconnect between the Bundeswehr and society. The first is the declining proportion of conscripts in the Bundeswehr, both due to the transition to a deployable force with a greater proportion of career soldiers and to the growing use of private military contractors. The second is the shift towards a professional military identity among the younger generation of career soldiers. The growing disagreement between soldiers and citizens over the role of the Bundeswehr in international interventions illustrates both developments. While 96 per cent of military and civilian respondents concurred that the primary mission of the Bundeswehr was national defence, 74 per cent of armed forces personnel supported peace enforcement operations, but only 64 per cent of the general population felt the same. The responses to the question of whether Germany should pursue a proactive or a restrained foreign and security policy have mirrored this divergence with 63 per cent of the military favouring an active policy as opposed to 53 per cent of the electorate.[135] Accordingly, only about 10 per cent of soldiers feel supported by the German population in their international missions.[136]

The new civil-military differences have also manifested themselves in the decreasing public interest in the armed forces and concern for the lives of deployed soldiers. As fewer Germans have a direct experience of and personal investment in the armed forces, casualties, in particular among those who have chosen a military career, are becoming acceptable. Although significant sections of the German public continue to oppose military interventions, many citizens witness the deaths of German soldiers with indifference.[137] While the media widely reported the first death of a German soldier in an international peacekeeping

[135] Kümmel, 'The Winds of Change', p. 21.
[136] 'Rundum zufrieden ist nur noch eine Minderheit', *Die Bundeswehr*, no. 5 (2007).
[137] G. Kümmel and N. Leonhard, 'Casualties and Civil-Military Relations: The German Polity between Learning and Indifference', *Armed Forces & Society*, 31, no. 4 (2005), 513–36.

mission and subsequent incidents, the small number of Bundeswehr casualties in recent years may have contributed to the lack of any large-scale public protests.[138] Generally, the view appears to prevail that casualties are an 'inevitable' part of military reality.[139] The complacency of the German population has been encouraged by a lack of knowledge about the armed forces' missions abroad. The majority of the German electorate believes that it does not have sufficient information about international Bundeswehr operations such as in Bosnia and Herzegovina, Kosovo, Afghanistan and the Mediterranean.[140]

The paucity of governmental information and explanations for its security and defence policy decisions and the indifference of the population directly affect the armed forces. The Bundeswehr Inspector General's Commissioner for Education and Training has reported that soldiers increasingly doubt the objectives of their mission in Afghanistan and are 'no longer unconditionally backing the military leadership'.[141] Deployed soldiers believe that 'the efforts [are] too great, the risks too numerous, and the results of reconstruction efforts in the country too small'.[142] The parliamentary Bundeswehr Ombudsman,[143] who acts as a voice for the troops and as an intermediary between the individual soldier, the government and society, has repeatedly made the same observation. In his report of 2004 he noted that many soldiers were very critical of their overseas missions, which frequently showed no tangible results.[144] In 2007 he reiterated that, according to the doctrine of Internal Leadership, the government had the obligation to give soldiers a plausible political and military justification for their deployment.[145] Lacking the support of the electorate, such deployments have been especially difficult to defend.

In addition to the doubts among the armed forces about the governmental rationale and social support for its international missions, Bundeswehr personnel have been apprehensive about the effects of the introduction of Neoliberal new management principles and the privatization of military services on their roles and functions. Generally,

---

[138] *Ibid.*, 520.
[139] *Ibid.*, 524.
[140] Bulmahn, 'Das sicherheits- und verteidigungspolitische Meinungsbild in Deutschland', 8.
[141] Cited in Kümmel and Leonhard, 'Casualties and Civil-Military Relations', 523.
[142] *Ibid.*
[143] Wehrbeauftragter des Deutschen Bundestages.
[144] Deutscher Bundestag, *Unterrichtung durch den Wehrbeauftragten: Jahresbericht 2004* (46. Bericht), Drucksache 15/5000 (15 March 2005), pp. 24–5.
[145] Deutscher Bundestag, *Unterrichtung durch den Wehrbeauftragten: Jahresbericht 2006* (48. Bericht), Drucksache 16/4700 (20 March 2007), p. 12.

German soldiers have viewed the use of business management methods to increase the efficiency of the Bundeswehr in a positive light. In surveys, 68 per cent of officers and 44 per cent of the ranks have welcomed the introduction of new management principles.[146] However, two thirds of soldiers complained that these measures had increased their administrative burden and half of them thought that they led to delays in service provision.[147] Soldiers considered the privatization and outsourcing of the Bundeswehr with even greater scepticism than its internal reforms. Among other matters, 36 per cent believed that military and economic considerations sometimes contradicted each other and 20 per cent stated that both are incompatible. Instead of privatizing, about two thirds of German soldiers contended that the armed forces could improve their efficiency by making better use of military personnel and their expertise.[148] As with internal reforms, the opposition to outsourcing has been growing as more and more personnel have gained firsthand experience of it. Between 2003 and 2005 the percentage of armed forces personnel who supported the privatization of Bundeswehr functions shrank from 24 to 16 per cent. In comparison, the proportion of armed forces personnel who believed that privatization offered no benefits for the taxpayer increased from 50 to 58 per cent, and those who feared that military effectiveness would suffer from 47 to 59 per cent.[149] Under these conditions, the government's continued commitment to expanding the use of private military contractors threatens to weaken the relations between the soldier and the state. Many long-term soldiers feel neglected by the politicians. Less than 2 per cent believe the government supports them sufficiently, and 74 per cent would not recommend a military career to their children or friends.[150] While the government embarked on its privatization measures with the promise to direct cost savings into the reform of the Bundeswehr, most armed forces personnel have seen little positive change. On the contrary, widespread underinvestment in personnel, equipment and facilities has been a key complaint among armed forces personnel.

In summary, the attempt of the German government to combine Republicanism with Neoliberalism through public–private joint ventures and the outsourcing of military services has had direct implications

[146] Großeholz, 'Die ökonomische Modernisierung der Bundeswehr im Meinungsbild der Soldatinnen und Soldaten', p. 23.
[147] *Ibid.*, pp. 27–8.
[148] *Ibid.*, pp. 24–25.
[149] Portugall, 'Die Bundeswehr und das Privatisierungsmodell der "Öffentlich-Privaten-Partnerschaft" (ÖPP)', p. 153.
[150] Löwenstein, 'Soldaten fühlen sich im Stich gelassen'.

for the democratic control and accountability of the Bundeswehr. So far, these consequences have not been as serious as in the UK and the USA because of the limited scale of military privatization and the safeguarding of state control through government shares. However, the planned expansion of private military contracting implied by the government's 'pilot' studies and the transformation of the model of the soldier suggest that these challenges are increasing. In particular, two developments need careful consideration. The first concerns the growing complexity and interconnections between the government, the Bundeswehr, the GEBB and private businesses which inhibit public and parliamentary scrutiny. The second development concerns the first signs of an emerging civil-military gap between German soldiers, the state and society due to the decline of conscription and the new roles and identity of the armed forces.

Conclusion

This chapter has illustrated that it is impossible to fully understand the transformation and privatization of the Bundeswehr and its implications without reference to the persistent German commitment to the Republican models of the state, the citizen and the soldier. The functional and financial pressures for the reform of the Bundeswehr would have suggested that the German government should have been more willing to abandon conscription and to seek to improve the cost efficiency of its defence establishment through measures adopted by its UK and US allies. Yet successive administrations have not only upheld the cherished image of the German 'citizen in uniform', but have also prioritized the preservation of centralized governmental control of the private provision of military services over increased savings. The adherence of the German government, the armed forces and the population to the Republican ideals that have shaped the relations between the state, the citizen and the military during Germany's first stable democracy helps to explain these policy choices.

Nevertheless, the preceding analysis also reveals a slow transformation of the models of the state, the citizen and the soldier in Germany due to the changing national and international security context. External pressures have emerged from the integration of the Bundeswehr with its NATO and EU allies and from the demand for greater participation in international interventions. Internal pressures have included the dissonance between Republican national defence forces and the new definition of national security adopted by Germany in 2003, as well as the growing inequity of the draft. The German government has responded to these developments by attempting to find a middle way between the preservation of Republican principles, such as centralized state control over the provision of security and the citizen-soldier, and the introduction of Neoliberal new public management mechanisms and military outsourcing.

Of course, the German middle way has not been without its own contradictions and pitfalls. The results can be viewed as a combination of either the best or the worst of Republicanism and Neoliberalism. Within the former view, the mixing of the two models has contributed to safeguarding democratic accountability, while at the same time increasing the cost efficiency of the Bundeswehr. Within the latter view, the attempt to combine two competing ideologies is undermining democratic oversight due to unclear lines of accountability and increasing bureaucracy, yet prevents any real savings. It appears likely, therefore, that pressure will rise to decide in favour of one ideology or the other. Before examining how both ideological models might be reformed in order to ensure democratic accountability and control within changing national and international security environments, the next chapter investigates the even greater challenges of using private military contractors in international interventions.

While the outsourcing of national defence to private contractors has
become widely accepted, the use of private military contractors in
deployed military operations has been considered a more controversial issue. Even the UK government has argued that the outsourcing of
military functions should not normally happen in 'non-benign environments'.[1] The reasons for this constraint have been the distinct challenges for the democratic control and accountability of the legitimate
use of collective force presented by the deployment of private military
contractors in international interventions. Despite these objections,
recent operations in the Balkans, Afghanistan and Iraq have moved private military contractors close to or even into combat zones.[2] Multiple
simultaneous interventions have served as primary explanations for the
proliferation of private military contracting in deployed operations.
However, they alone cannot account for the changes and the differences
in UK, US and German policies with regard to private contractors in
military operations abroad. Varying ideological positions have played
a major part in determining the conceptions of the three governments
with regard to the appropriate roles of the state, the armed forces and
private military contractors in international security. These positions
have ranged from the application of the Neoliberal model of the small
state to international affairs, to the reluctance to despatch private military contractors abroad based on Republican conceptions of the legitimate use of collective violence.

Private firms have always provided military surge capacity during
major international conflicts, such as during the First and Second
World Wars. Recent international interventions have deviated from
this practice in four main respects which illustrate the importance of
ideology for understanding the contemporary use of private military

---

[1] MOD, 'Contractors on Deployed Operations (CONDO)', at: www.aof.mod.uk.
[2] GAO, *Rebuilding Iraq: Actions Needed to Improve Use of Private Security Providers*, GAO-
05–737 (Washington DC, July 2005), p. 7, p. 15.

contractors. Firstly, many citizens in Europe and North America have not perceived these interventions to be crucial to their national security. The deployment of private contractors has, thus, not been part of a total societal mobilization, but has rather been a result of the resizing of the state and the armed forces according to the Neoliberal ideal of the small state. Secondly, the scope of UK and US private military contracting in conflict areas has increased significantly. While during the first Gulf War in 1991 the ratio of private contractors to military personnel was not more than 1 to 100, in Iraq the number of private military contractors employed by the US armed forces exceeded that of its uniformed soldiers.[3] Thirdly, despite a blurring of the line between soldiers and contractors on the ground, UK and US national security policies have insisted that there will be no employment of military contractors in combat functions and the German government promised that it would not use private military firms abroad.[4] Lastly, the US military's position that it was not able to and would not attempt to ensure public security in Iraq has illustrated an ideological abrogation of the responsibility of an occupying state for public security under international law.[5] This explicit renunciation of the state monopoly on the legitimate use of collective violence epitomizes a changing conception of the role of the state in international security.

In short, the recent interventions in Iraq and beyond represent a watershed in the transformation of roles of the state, the soldier and democratic society with regard to international security. However, these operations have not been the sole cause of this transformation. They demonstrate the weakening of the Republican ideals of the state monopoly on collective violence and state responsibility for global stability and the changing nature of the international military profession. Private military contractors are now dying for democratic states.[6] Nevertheless, most contractors are neither subject to the same military discipline and international laws, nor do they receive the same societal and governmental support as uniformed soldiers. Finally, contemporary interventions also indicate the growing division between Western governments, their citizens and the armed forces over international military operations and

---

[3] C. Spearin, 'American Hegemony Incorporated: The Importance and Implications of Military Contractors in Iraq', *Contemporary Security Policy*, 24, no. 3 (2003), 28; R. Merle, 'Census Counts 100,000 Contractors in Iraq', *Washington Post*, 5 December 2006.

[4] GAO, *Rebuilding Iraq*, pp. 13–14.

[5] M. Sassoli, 'Legislation and Maintenance of Public Order and Civil Life by Occupying Powers' *The European Journal of International Law*, 16, no. 4 (2005), 663.

[6] J. M. Broder and J. Risen, 'Contractor Deaths in Iraq Soar to Record', *New York Times*, 19 May 2007. For an unofficial headcount see http://icasualties.org/.

peacekeeping missions. They exemplify how the employment of private military contractors can undermine established mechanisms of democratic control and international accountability.

The following sections examine the reasons, practice and implications of the use of private military contractors in deployed operations. The chapter begins by discussing the different ideological contexts for the international use of private military contractors in the UK, the USA and Germany. The chapter then turns to a detailed examination of the scope and form of international private military contracting by these three countries between 2003 and 2008. For reasons of consistency, it focuses on the UK and US interventions in Iraq, while in the case of Germany, which did not participate in the Iraq war, it examines a range of missions from Afghanistan to Kosovo. The third section investigates how the proliferation and deaths of private military contractors in deployed operations have contributed to changing the predominant notion of the soldier in international security. Finally, the fourth section examines the challenges that have arisen from the use of private military contractors for the democratic control and accountability of international interventions, and how the UK, the USA and Germany have responded to them.

The rise of Neoliberalism in international security

Republicanism and Neoliberalism not only propose ideal models of the state, but also particular visions of international relations. Specifically, Republicanism promotes the state monopoly on the legitimate use of force, while Neoliberalism advocates the reduction of state interference in international affairs. The latter has found its particular expression in the concept of security governance, which contends that a diverse range of security providers beyond the state such as non-governmental organizations and private corporations best serve the complex and differentiated security needs and interests of citizens.[7] The ideological turn towards Neoliberalism in the UK, the USA and, to some degree, also in Germany thus suggests that the increasing hire of private military contractors for international interventions has been more than a temporary or functional reaction to the surge in demand for military expertise and personnel created by multiple interventions abroad. It illustrates changing ideological beliefs regarding the role of the state in international relations.

---

[7] E. Krahmann, 'Conceptualising Security Governance', *Cooperation and Conflict*, 38, no. 1 (2003), 5–26.

At the same time as ideology has influenced the transformation of the roles and relations of the state, the citizen and the soldier in the UK, the USA and Germany, it has also affected the international security outlook of the three countries. Characteristic of the Neoliberal perspective has been the differentiation of threat perception and international security policies based on its assumption of individualized and differentiated security needs and interests. Thus, Clinton's National Security Strategies of 1997 and 1999 proclaimed not the existence of common threats to the international community, but the global and selective nature of US national security interests.[8] Moreover, the National Security Strategy of 1997 contended: 'We must always be prepared to act alone, when necessary, or as a leader of an ad hoc coalition that may form around a specific objective.'[9] The UN was conspicuous by its absence from these strategies. Conversely, the US government described private firms and non-governmental organizations as its 'natural allies'.[10] The National Security Strategies published under the Bush administration were in many respects similar.[11] Also the UK government shared many of these assessments in its Strategic Defence Review of 1998 and the Defence White Paper 2003.[12] It agreed that the best way to serve UK national and international security interests was through flexible alliances and a special relationship with the USA.[13] The government concluded that the UK needed 'the flexibility to build coalitions of the willing to deal with specific threats when necessary'.[14]

The Republican conception of security espoused by the German government has shaped a different perception of the post-Cold War international security environment and suitable policies, emphasizing common security interests and the role of international organizations. The German Defence White Paper of 1994 thus focused on the collective regional security challenges emerging from the transformation

[8] White House, *A National Security Strategy for A New Century* (Washington DC, May 1997); White House, *A National Security Strategy for a New Century* (Washington DC, December 1999).

[9] White House, *A National Security Strategy for A New Century* (1997).

[10] White House, *A National Security Strategy for a New Century* (1999), p. 27.

[11] White House, *The National Security Strategy of the United States of America* (Washington DC, September 2002); White House, *The National Security Strategy of the United States of America* (Washington DC, March 2006).

[12] MOD, *Strategic Defence Review* (London: 1998); MOD, *Delivering Security in a Changing World*, Defence White Paper, Cm 6041-I (London: HMSO, 2003).

[13] E. Krahmann, 'United Kingdom: Punching Above Its Weight', in E. J. Kirchner and J. Sperling (eds.) *Global Security Governance. Competing Perceptions of Security in the 21st Century* (London: Routledge, 2007), pp. 93–112.

[14] MOD, *Delivering Security in a Changing World*, p. 5.

of Central and Eastern Europe and the former Soviet Union.[15] The White Paper further proclaimed that five norms and interests served as the foundations of German defence policy: the provision of peace and welfare in Germany, the integration of Europe, the transatlantic partnership with the USA, the creation of a new cooperative security organization with Germany's Eastern neighbours and global respect for international law and human rights.[16] Only in 2003 did the government acknowledge explicitly that international conflict prevention and peacekeeping had replaced national defence as the primary concerns of German security policy.[17] Nevertheless, the new Defence Policy Guidelines and the 2006 White Paper continued to emphasize that Germany's security and defence policies would only be pursued through collective organizations, foremost NATO, the EU, the UN and the Organization for Security and Cooperation in Europe (OSCE).[18] Indeed, the reinterpretation of the German constitution in 1994 required that all foreign military interventions had to proceed within the context of a collective mission.[19]

These differences in the ideological outlook of the UK, the US and German governments have critically influenced their military operations abroad. Thus, with regard to Iraq the UK and the USA made little effort to arrive at a common definition of the threat with their allies. Both administrations insisted that the potential development of weapons of mass destruction in Iraq was a danger to their national security, while the governments of France and Germany believed the threat to be remote. The divergence in threat perception joined disagreements over the norms of international relations between states with a Neoliberal ideology and those countries that favoured Republican principles. The US and UK governments embraced the Neoliberal notion that national sovereignty was limited, especially where the regime concerned was neither democratically elected, nor maintained the human rights of its citizens. An international consensus or the mandate of the UN Security Council, while desirable, was not necessary to provide further legitimacy for the intervention in Iraq. In fact, the repeated refusal of the Security Council to support the intervention proved to

[15] Bundesministerium der Verteidigung, *Weißbuch 1994* (Bonn, 1994), chapter 2.
[16] *Ibid.*, p. 42.
[17] Bundesministerium der Verteidigung, *Verteidigungspolitische Richtlinien für den Bereich des Bundesministers der Verteidigung* (Berlin, 21 May 2003), pp. 8–9.
[18] *Ibid.*; German Ministry of Defence, *White Paper 2006 on German Security Policy and the Future of the Bundeswehr* (Berlin, 2006), pp. 24–49.
[19] Bundesministerium der Verteidigung, *Verteidigungspolitische Richtlinien für den Bereich des Bundesministers der Verteidigung*, p. 12.

the governments of Bush and Blair that a flexible coalition of the willing would better serve their countries' security interests.

The resulting fragmented nature of security governance in Iraq did not, initially, seem to present any major problems. The US government was able to mobilize more than 300,000 troops for the war, including 46,000 soldiers from the UK, 2,000 from Australia and 200 from Poland. However, weaknesses in the flexible coalition led by the USA and the UK emerged in the aftermath of the combat phase. The USA and its allies found it increasingly difficult to provide the resources, personnel and expertise for urban security, peacekeeping and policing operations. The personnel shortage was a result of the limited international support for the intervention, the simultaneous peacekeeping missions in the Balkans and Afghanistan, and the rotation of military personnel every six to twelve months.[20] It was also affected by the international dispute over the necessity and legitimacy of the pre-emptive intervention. The latter reduced the willingness of many countries to deploy peacekeeping troops to Iraq. Although the multinational pacification force subsumed almost forty nations, the number of personnel provided by countries other than the USA and the UK amounted at its maximum only to 20,000 troops, including engineers, military policemen, medical personnel and demining specialists.

However, the use of private military contractors was not merely a consequence of the shortage of international troops. It was the continuation of the Neoliberal policies of the small state at the international level. Already before the intervention US military leaders had projected that it would require up to 500,000 soldiers to occupy and pacify Iraq. In particular, General Eric Shinseki argued that it would take 'a significant ground-force presence to maintain a safe and secure environment, to ensure that people are fed, that water is distributed, all the normal responsibilities that go along with administering a situation like this'.[21] However, Secretary of Defence Rumsfeld insisted that a small force of approximately 100,000 would be sufficient.[22] The Bush administration did not plan to take full responsibility for the provision of public

---

[20] E. Schmitt, 'Army Extending Service for G.I.'s Due in War Zones', *New York Times*, 3 June 2004; J. White, 'Soldiers Facing Extended Tours', *Washington Post*, 3 June 2004; S. Lyall, 'British Seek to Thin Iraq Ranks, Add Afghan Forces', *New York Times*, 15 June 2005.

[21] US Senate Armed Services Committee, Hearing, 25 February 2003.

[22] E. Schmitt, 'Pentagon Contradicts General on Iraq Occupation Force's Size', *New York Times*, 28 February 2003; M. Engel, 'Scorned General's Tactics Proved Right: Profile of the Army Chief Sidelined by Rumsfeld', *Guardian*, 29 March 2003; M. R. Gordon and B. E. Trainor, *Cobra II: The Inside Story of the Invasion and Occupation of Iraq* (New York: Pantheon, 2006).

security and other services. Instead, it determined that private contractors would fulfil many of these functions, including the post-conflict reconstruction of Iraqi infrastructure. In the view of the government, contractors would not only limit the need for Congressional approval to deploy troops, but also help to reduce the financial cost of the occupation. When the security apparatus of the old regime in Iraq collapsed entirely and large-scale sectarian violence erupted, the administration therefore decided not to enlarge the mandate and size of the US military contingent, opening the space for private military companies to become a major force in Iraq. Moreover, in 2006 the US government endorsed the use of 'deadly force' by US security contractors 'when such force reasonably appears necessary to execute their security mission to protect assets/persons, consistent with the terms and conditions contained in their contract or with their job description'.[23] The intervention thus set an important precedent in which the USA refused to accept the responsibility of an occupying power for public order and safety enshrined in Article 43 of the Hague Regulations and, effectively, transferred it to private military contractors.[24] According to the DOD, ensuring the safety of the civilian population was 'not part of the U.S. military's stated mission'.[25]

In Germany, by contrast, Republican ideals, such as the primacy of national defence (until 2003), the state monopoly on collective violence and security management, have delimited both the number of international military interventions by the Bundeswehr and its use of private military contractors in deployed operations. They also explain the refusal of the German government to participate directly in the military intervention in Iraq, and why Germany has had no objections to contributing to the missions in Afghanistan and Kosovo which have been conducted under the authority of NATO and clear UN mandates. They also clarify why all other German missions have been led by either the EU or the UN, including European Union Force in Bosnia and Herzegovina (EUFOR), the UN Observer Mission in Georgia (UNOMOG), the UN–African Union Mission in Darfur (UNAMID), the UN Interim Force in Lebanon (UNIFIL) and the EU Naval Force (NAVFOR) Operation Atalanta in the Gulf of Aden. In addition to conceiving the provision of

---

[23] DOD, Defense Acquisition Regulation System, 252.225–7040 (b) (3) (ii).
[24] Sassoli, 'Legislation and Maintenance of Public Order and Civil Life by Occupying Powers', 663; National Audit Office, *Ministry of Defence: Operation TELIC – United Kingdom Military Operations in Iraq*, Session 2003–4, HC 60 (London: The Stationery Office, 11 December 2003), p. 31.
[25] Sassoli, 'Legislation and Maintenance of Public Order and Civil Life by Occupying Powers', 663.

international security as a collective endeavour, the Republican senti-ments of the German government have posed significant barriers to the employment of private military contractors in operations abroad. As the next section will show, in comparison with the UK and the USA these inhibitions have only been overcome where there have been major gaps in the operational capabilities of the Bundeswehr or where contractors have been hired within a collective organizational framework.

Private military contractors in international operations

The preceding ideological developments and the perceived new security demands help us to understand the growing, but also divergent, use of private contractors in international operations since the late 1990s. In these missions private military forces have filled three main functions. Their first function has been to provide technical and logistic support for Western militaries during combat operations. Their second task has been to support or replace international military personnel in peace-keeping and pacification operations. Their third function has been in the training of military staff in transitional countries and in security sector reform. This section examines in turn the policies of the UK, the USA and Germany with regard to the employment of private military firms in deployed operations.

United Kingdom

The scale of UK private military contracting in deployed military operations has been considerable, although not as extensive as that of the US military. During the combat operation in Iraq, the UK armed forces deployed about 2,000 military contractors to support 46,000 uniformed soldiers. According to the UK Defence Manufacturers Association, over one hundred companies participated in the war with contracts valued in the region of £800 million.[26] During the subsequent pacification operation the ratio of contractors to soldiers increased to about one to two. In 2008 the MOD listed about 2,200 civilian con-tractors in Iraq, while the military contingent had decreased to a size

---

[26] Defence Management Agency (DMA), 'Contractor Support to Deployed Operations (CONDO) 2005', at: www.the-dma.org.uk. For a list of companies deployed as CONDOs in Iraq in 2006 see House of Commons Hansard, 'Iraq Service Medal', Written Answers, Vol. 446, Session 2005–6, 10 May 2006, Columns W300-W303.

of only 4,100 soldiers.[27] Altogether, the supply of military services by private firms already accounts for about 30–40 per cent of UK military operations overseas.[28] One of the reasons for the increased use of private contractors in military operations has been the growing reliance on private maintenance as part of equipment procurement packages and full life-cycle management.[29] Equipment support has been the largest single budget item in the UK's intervention in Iraq with about £200 million per year as compared to between £80–120 million for military personnel between 2004 and 2007.[30] Other costs and support services have added another £110 million to this figure.

Similarly extensive has been the range of operational functions which the UK armed forces have outsourced to the private sector. Key areas of private military support abroad have been catering, accommodation, waste disposal, transport, logistics, mission rehearsal, maintenance and repair, and communications. The list of contracts is too long to cover in detail. However, among the most important contracts have been the in-theatre upgrade of the British Army's FV430 armoured fighting vehicle to desert conditions and the servicing of Royal Air Force Tornado planes in Iraq by BAE Systems. Additional equipment and deployed technical support came from Lockheed Martin for the Desert Hawk and from Thales for the Hermes-450 unmanned aerial vehicles. Real-time intelligence for UK operational forces was secured through a contract with L-3 Communications for the supply and management of the armed forces' Integrated Broadcast Service. Serco provided full mission rehearsal, training and debriefing of helicopter crews for military operations in Afghanistan and Iraq. Finally, KBR was awarded the first CONLOG contract for military logistics, while another IDIQ contract with Supreme Foodservices ensured the global supply of catering for UK forces abroad.[31] In contrast to the USA, one of the tasks

---

[27] House of Commons Hansard, 'Iraq: Peacekeeping Operations', Written Answers, Vol. 483, Session 2007–8, 26 November 2008, Column 1552W.

[28] DMA, 'DMA CONDO Sponsors Group Lunch', Events Announcement (2007), at: www.ndi.org.uk.

[29] MOD, *Operations in Iraq: Lessons for the Future* (London: Directorate General Corporate Communications, 11 December 2003), pp. 43–4.

[30] House of Commons – Defence Committee, *Cost of Military Operations: Spring Supplementary Estimate 2006–07*, Tenth Report, Session 2006–7 (6 March 2007), p. 8.

[31] D. Hencke, 'MOD Plans Raid on Landmine Removal Fund to Keep Tornados Flying in Iraq', *Guardian*, 10 March 2008; Serco, 'Training Military Aircrew for Operational Deployment', Press Release; Lockheed Martin, 'United Kingdom Awards Lockheed Martin $2.65 Million Contract to Enhance Desert Hawk Unmanned Aerial System Capability', Press Release, 23 February 2006; MOD, 'Unmanned Aerial Vehicles On the Lookout Over Iraq', *Defence News*, 27 September 2007; 'L-3 Selected as Prime Contractor for U.K. Intelligence Contract', *Reuters*, 28 February 2008.

which the UK military so far conducts itself is military training in
support of security sector reforms in transitional countries. The training of Iraqi military and police forces in the south east of the country
was, thus, supplied by professional soldiers.[32] The MOD also refrained
from hiring armed security guards in Iraq, although other UK government agencies such as the Department for International Development
(DFID) and the Foreign and Commonwealth Office did.[33] To facilitate
oversight, the Foreign and Commonwealth Office took over responsibility for the security of all civilian UK government staff in Iraq in
2004. Most of its contracts have gone to companies registered in the
UK such as Control Risks and ArmorGroup.[34]

Many of the services contracted by the UK military in Iraq brought
civilian contractor personnel near or into the combat zone. In 2003, for
instance, fifty-one employees of Alvis Vickers were flown into Kuwait
to modify the Challenger 2 tank and other vehicles for desert conditions
while the Iraq war was already in progress. Following UK Contractors
on Deployed Operations (CONDO) regulations, the staff were placed
under military regulations and had to receive basic security training in
preparation for their deployment. According to news reports, the contractors worked heroically, 'only 50 kilometres from the Iraq border,
in a continuous 12-hours-on-six-hours-off shift pattern'.[35] In recognition of the centrality of private military contractors in contemporary
deployed operations and the dangers to which contracted civilians have
been exposed, the employees of thirty-eight companies have been eligible for the MOD Iraq Medal. The awardees have included fifteen
BAE Systems engineers for 'their work at Basra Airport, often while
under rocket and mortar fire'.[36]

Mostly, the UK armed forces have employed private military contractors under separate and short-term contractor logistics support
and Urgent Operational Requirement (UOR) contracts.[37] Since 2004,
however, the MOD has outsourced the provision of the full range of

---

[32] MOD, 'Operations in Iraq: About the UK Mission in Iraq', *Defence Factsheet*, at: www.
   mod.uk.
[33] House of Commons Hansard, 'Private Security Companies (Iraq)', Debates – Oral
   Answers to Questions, Vol. 465, Session 2006–7, 22 October 2007, Columns 1–3;
   House of Commons – Defence Committee, *Sixth Report*, Session 2004–5 (16 March
   2005).
[34] Foreign and Commonwealth Office, *UK Government Use of Security Companies for
   FCO Facilities in Iraq*; 'British Security Workers Killed in Fresh Iraq Violence',
   Sunday Herald, 31 July 2005.
[35] N. N., 'Alvis Vickers Limited, Iron Clad Initiative', *The Manufacturer*, July 2003.
[36] BAE Systems, 'Aviation Week and Space Technology Award Recognizes British
   Bulldog Team', Press Release, 14 November 2008.
[37] MOD, *Operations in Iraq: Lessons for the Future*, p. 43.

military logistics overseas with the exclusion of armed security under the CONLOG contract, based on the example of the US Army's LOGCAP. The first of these contracts was awarded to KBR for a duration of seven years in 2004 and could reach up to £50 million per year.[38] Within the context of this contract, KBR has provided military accommodation, catering and facility management, interpreters and medical services including over one thousand employees in Afghanistan and Iraq as well as numerous subcontractors. Moreover, in order to facilitate coordination between KBR and the military, a contractor team embedded in the Permanent Joint Headquarters has been involved in the planning and decision-making for international operations. The armed forces have also awarded similar 'enabling' IDIQ contracts for global food supplies. In 2006 the latest contract went to Purple Foodservice Solutions, including catering for deployed operations in Bosnia, Afghanistan, Iraq, Germany and the South Atlantic for up to £150 million per annum for a maximum of nine years.[39]

Largely, the UK armed forces have been satisfied with the private provision of military services in Iraq. However, there have also been a number of problems. One has been the refusal of two contractors to deploy in the theatre before the combat operation due to concerns about the proximity to the battlefield. Their anxiety was intensified by the earlier capture of two Kenyan drivers subcontracted to the military's catering supplier.[40] Other problems during the combat phase have been inadequate pre-deployment training, shortages in the provision of equipment for civilian contractors such as nuclear, biological and chemical protection gear and body armour, lack of transport capacity and inadequate legal jurisdiction over contractors.[41] By 2003 the MOD also concluded that 'the level of contractor support required to deliver operational CIS [Communications and Information Systems] capability for deployed operations needs careful consideration'.[42] All these problems were exacerbated by the fact that until 2008 the UK armed forces still had no central register of civilian contractors working for the military in Iraq, although they were in the process of setting one up.[43]

---

[38] M. Uttley, *Contractors on Deployed Operations: United Kingdom Policy and Doctrine* (Darby, PA: Diane Publishing, 2005); MOD, 'MOD Awards New Partnering Deal for Logistic Support', Press Release, 3 February 2004.

[39] Purple Foodservice Solutions, 'Frequently Asked Questions', at: www.purplefood-serviesolutions.com.

[40] National Audit Office, *Ministry of Defence: Operation TELIC*, p. 21.

[41] MOD, *Operations in Iraq: Lessons for the Future*, p. 44.

[42] *Ibid.*, p. 8.

[43] House of Commons Hansard, 'Iraq: Peacekeeping Operations', Written Answers, 4 March 2008, Vol. 472, Session 2007–8, Column 2349W.

United States

The extensive use of private military contractors by the US armed forces in Iraq has been well publicized. From the preparation of Operation Iraqi Freedom private contractors have played a crucial role in supporting the war with technical services and logistics. Following the end of the combat phase in April 2003, the role of private military contractors expanded even further. By 2008 private contractors working for the DOD outnumbered the entire US contingent with approximately 155,000 employees as compared to 140,000 soldiers. The cost of private military support exceeded $76 billion, accounting for 17 per cent of the total US budget spent in Iraq.[44]

The types of in-theatre functions contracted out by the US military have been equally wide-ranging and can, therefore, only be illustrated through select examples. The largest share of armed forces spending on contractor support has been on management and logistic support which amounted to nearly $26 billion, including administration, engineering, construction, maintenance, catering, laundry services and mail delivery.[45] All three services have their own logistics support contracts, but by far the largest have been the US Army's LOGCAP III contract with KBR and the LOGCAP IV contract with DynCorp, Fluor and KBR since 2007.[46] Contrary to original estimates, which envisaged support for 25,000 to 50,000 troops, the volume of the work requested under LOGCAP III quickly expanded.[47] By 2007 KBR had provided services worth $22 billion, and operated more than sixty military camps in Kuwait and Iraq for 200,000 soldiers from the USA and the coalition forces.[48] The massive support operation entailed more than 34,000 private employees, including about 11,000 international KBR staff and 14,000 subcontractor personnel, made available through more than 200 subcontracting companies.[49] Notable has

---

[44] Congressional Budget Office (CBO), *Contractor's Support of U.S. Operations in Iraq*, p. 1.

[45] *Ibid.*, p. 8.

[46] Reuters, 'Halliburton's Role in Iraq – from Meals to Oil', *New York Times*, 12 April 2004.

[47] Statement by Alfred V. Neffgen, Chief Operating Officer, KBR Government Operations, Americas Region Before the Committee on Government Reform, United States House of Representatives, 22 July 2004, p. 3.

[48] Rep. Henry A. Waxman, Ranking Minority Member, Committee on Government Reform, U.S. House of Representatives, 'Fact Sheet: Halliburton's Iraq Contracts Now Worth over $10 Billion', 9 December 2004; C. R. Babcock, 'KBR Gets $72 Million in Bonuses for Iraq Work', *Washington Post*, 11 May 2005; CBO, *Contractor's Support of U.S. Operations in Iraq*, p. 5.

[49] Statement by Alfred V. Neffgen, p. 3.

been the increasing outsourcing of management and administrative services which, as Chapter 5 has argued, have traditionally been considered inherently governmental functions. One of the most controversial items has been the $225 million contract with the British company Serco to 'oversee the performance of other contractors and provide programme management analysis, cost analysis and logistics planning' for the LOGCAP IV.[50]

Maintenance and repair of facilities and equipment, as far as they are not supplied under the LOGCAP contracts, have formed a second major category of private military service provision in Iraq costing over $5 billion.[51] Contractors have been crucial for the maintenance, but also the operation, of the increasingly technically sophisticated equipment and weapons systems of the US forces, such as the unmanned Predator drones, the Global Hawks, the Hellfire missile and the B-2 stealth bombers.[52] One example has been the operation and maintenance of the Hunter unmanned aerial vehicles in the Iraqi theatre by civilian employees of Northrop Grumman.[53] More extensive has been an IDIQ contract between the US Air Force and seven prime contractors for 'intermediate level maintenance and mission-related tasks for coalition aircraft deployed to Iraq and Afghanistan' up to a ceiling value of $10 billion awarded in 2008.[54] The prime contractors have included, among others, L-3 subsidiary Vertex Aerospace which has supplied helicopter maintenance services to the US Army at Camp Taji near Baghdad.

Other functions which have seen the growing use of private military and defence companies have been command, control, communications, computers, intelligence, surveillance, and reconnaissance (C4ISR). Eagan McAllister Associates, for instance, held a contract for up to $56 million for 'critical engineering and related support services directly to fleet and shore units' in Iraq, Afghanistan and elsewhere.[55] As with maintenance, these services have been increasingly supplied through flexible IDIQ contracts which cover national defence and deployed operations, depending on requirements. One of the largest

[50] Serco, 'Serco Selected for $225m US Contract to Oversee Key Defense Spending Programme', Press Release, 21 February 2007; M. Shenwar, 'Cost Analysis Support in Iraq', *Truthout*.

[51] CBO, *Contractor's Support of U.S. Operations in Iraq*, p. 7.

[52] I. Traynor, 'The Privatization of War', *Guardian*, 10 December 2003; W. Welsh, 'Army Extends Lockheeds Hellfire Contract', *Washington Post*, 28 May 2007.

[53] Northrop Grumman, 'Operations, Maintenance and Logistic Support of Unmanned Aerial Systems', *Review Magazine Online*, 2007.

[54] Mississippi Economic Council, 'L-3 Vertex Aerospace Awarded CFT Support Contract', Press Release, 16 July 2008.

[55] DOD, Contracts, No. 515–07, 1 May 2007.

of these contracts has been the Strategic Services Sourcing Contract of the Army Communications-Electronics Life Cycle Management Command signed in 2008 with seven companies – Booz Allen and Hamilton, CSC, CACI, Lockheed Martin, Sensor Technologies, ViaTech, and US Falcon – for a maximum total value of $19 billion.[56] These companies manage a host of subcontractors such as ManTech, which provides 'deployed fielding support, maintenance and repair' of various surveillance systems used in the Iraqi and Afghan theatres.[57]

In addition, the US Intelligence and Security Command has outsourced a significant proportion of its intelligence collection and analysis in Iraq to private contractors. The $650 million contract with Titan for interpreters, some of whom were later implicated in the abuse of prisoners at Abu Ghraib, has been widely reported.[58] Despite the scandal, the army later rewarded the contract to Titan. In 2007 an even larger contract for intelligence support in the region of $4.6 billion went to Global Linguistic Solutions, a joint venture between DynCorp and McNeil Technologies. Under the contract the company planned to employ 6,000 local translators and 1,000 US citizens with security clearance.[59]

Unlike the UK, the US DOD also contracts out most of its military and police training in developing countries.[60] In Iraq contracts worth over $50 million and $48 million were awarded for the training of the military and police forces respectively to DynCorp and Vinnell, as well as MPRI and SAIC as its subcontractors.[61] MPRI also independently obtained prime contracts for the integration of the newly created Iraqi armed forces into the reconstruction process and for plans for the future Iraqi force structure.[62] Owing to delays with the training programme

[56] CSC, 'CSC Wins Army Strategic Services Sourcing Contract to Provide Engineering, Logistics and Business Operations Support', Press Release, 20 March 2006.
[57] 'ManTech Wins $118 Million Army Contract to Provide Logistics and Maintenance Support to . . .', *Reuters*, 19 June 2008.
[58] G. R. Fay, Investigating Officer, *AR 15–6 Investigation of the Abu Ghraib Detention Facility 205th Military Intelligence Brigade* (2004), p. 48.
[59] L-3 Communications, 'L-3 Communications Revises 2007 Financial Guidance For Loss of Linguist Contract', Press Release, 18 December 2006; DynCorp International, 'DynCorp International and McNeil Technologies JV Awarded $4.6 Billion Army Linguistic Services Contract', Press Release, 18 December 2006; 'DynCorp Team Wins Iraq Interpreter Deal', *C4ISR Journal*, 20 December 2006.
[60] D. D. Avant, *The Market for Force. The Consequences of Privatizing Security* (Cambridge: Cambridge University Press, 2005), p. 120–31.
[61] A. Rathmell *et al.*, *Developing Iraq's Security Sector. The Coalition Provisional Authority's Experience* (Santa Monica, CA: RAND, 2005), p. 34; Avant, *The Market for Force*, p. 122.
[62] 'Military Professional Resources Inc.', Center for Public Integrity, at: www.publicintegrity.org.

and unsatisfactory performance of the new forces, however, the military took charge of the training mission in 2004.

Finally, there has been the issue of armed security-guarding. While the controversial contract with Blackwater, whose personnel shot seventeen Iraqi civilians in September 2007, had been with the State Department and not the DOD, the armed forces themselves employed 6,000 armed security guards in 2008.[63] Altogether it has been estimated that between 25,000 and 30,000 armed security contractors have worked for US government agencies and other customers in Iraq. Blackwater first became renowned for defending the Coalition Provisional Authority (CPA) headquarters in Najaf for more than three hours against an attack by Shiite militia members.[64] It was also the employer of the four murdered security guards whose bodies were mutilated and publicly displayed in Fallujah in June 2004.[65] Other companies such as Triple Canopy, Sabre, EOD Technology and SOC-SMG have also supplied armed guards through multiple contracts for security services with the Joint Contracting Command in Baghdad.

The extensive scale and scope of US private military contracting in Iraq have led to repeated problems. The issues which have received the most attention have been overcharging and fraud as well as the lack of governmental and legislative control over private military contractors. The accusations against LOGCAP contractor KBR have been much reported in the media. They have included inflated fuel and catering expenses for up to $150 million, the acceptance of kickbacks from Iraqi subcontractors, the known exposure of US troops in Iraq to contaminated water, and the sexual harassment of employees.[66] However, the case of KBR has been no exception. Several prime contractors, such as L-3, Custer Battles, Titan, CACI, Washington Group International, SAIC and Fluor, have been accused of illegal practices or insufficient accounting, leading to war profiteering.[67] L-3 Vertex Aerospace, for

---

[63] J. Glanz and A. J. Rubin, 'From Errant to Fatal Shot to Hail of Fire to 17 Deaths', *New York Times*, 3 October 2007.

[64] D. Priest, 'Private Guards Repel Attack on U.S. Headquarters', *Washington Post*, 6 April 2004.

[65] The Associated Press, 'Four Contractors Killed in Baghdad Ambush', *New York Times*, 6 June 2004.

[66] GAO, *Military Operations: DOD's Extensive Use of Logistics Support Contracts Requires Strengthened Oversight*, GAO-04–854 (Washington DC, July 2004), p. 27; Statements of James Warren and David Wilson in: Committee of Government Reform, *Contracting and the Rebuilding of Iraq: Part IV* (Washington DC, 22 July 2004); Federal Contractor Misconduct Database, at: www.contractormisconduct.org.

[67] Statement of Mr William H. Reed, Director, Defense Contract Audit Agency, House Committee on Government Reform, 9 June 2004; Statement for the Record of Dr Dov S. Zakheim, Under Secretary of Defense (Comptroller), House Committee on

instance, has submitted 'false and inflated claims' for hours worked at Camp Taji; SAIC has been accused of 'improper and unsupported billing'; and Custer Battles was suspended by the DOD from further contracts because of charging the military for civilian security services at Baghdad airport although no planes were flying.[68] Already by 2004 Pentagon auditors noted that in twenty-two of twenty-four reviewed contracts, the 'DOD cannot be assured that it was either provided the best contracting solution or paid fair and reasonable prices for the goods and services purchased'.[69]

The lack of effective DOD oversight has not only permitted 'fraud, waste and abuse', but has also undermined the democratic control of private military contractors in Iraq.[70] The involvement of private interpreters in the Abu Ghraib prison torture scandal thus revealed that the military had not required its contractors to sign the Interrogation Rules of Engagement.[71] Generally, the military's intelligence staff at Abu Ghraib had little or no guidance and experience with managing private contractors. Since there was no doctrine on 'contract management or command and control of contractors in a wartime environment', military leaders were unclear about the roles of contractors or how to discipline them.[72] The issue of control was even more complex in the case of CACI employees who were lent to the armed forces by the Interior Department and, therefore, exempt from the Military Extraterritorial Jurisdiction Act (MEJA).[73] Questions of control have also emerged with regard to the repeated accusations against armed security guards over shooting at innocent civilians or US armed forces. These accusations have not been confined to Blackwater, but have been fairly commonplace. Aegis guards, for example, have been allegedly involved in drive-by shootings; Zapata Engineering employees have been held by

Government Reform, 11 March 2004; United States District Court – Eastern District of Virginia, *United States Ex Rel. DRC, Inc., Robert J. Isakson and William D. Baldwin v. Custer Battles et al.*, Case No. CV-04–199-A; J. Spinner and M. P. Flaherty, 'U.S. Auditors Criticize Halliburton Subsidiary', *Washington Post*, 12 March 2004; L. Parker, 'Jury Fines Defense Contractor in Iraq $10M', *USA Today*, 10 March 2006.

[68] Federal Contractor Misconduct Database, at: www.contractormisconduct.org; G.Witte, 'Lawmakers Told about Contract Abuse in Iraq', *Washington Post*, 15 February 2005.

[69] J. Spinner, 'Pentagon Faults Supervision of Contracts', *Washington Post*, 25 March 2004.

[70] GAO, *Stabilizing and Rebuilding Iraq: Conditions in Iraq Are Conductive to Fraud, Waste and Abuse*, GAO-07–525T (Washington DC, 23 April 2007).

[71] Fay, *AR 15–6 Investigation of the Abu Ghraib Detention Facility 205th Military Intelligence Brigade*, p. 48.

[72] *Ibid.*, p. 19.

[73] E. McCarthy, 'CACI Contract: From Supplies to Interrogation', *Washington Post*, 17 May 2004.

the armed forces for firing on a Marine observation post; and Triple Canopy contractors have been dismissed for targeting civilians 'for amusement'.[74]

Germany

Contrary to official German policy, which considers the provision of military services during deployed operations to be among the Bundeswehr's core functions, the range of private military contracting by the German armed forces in international missions has also expanded.[75] In particular, the demands of the growing number of out-of-area operations of the Bundeswehr have led to a pragmatic weakening of the ideological resistance to privatizations in international interventions.[76] Not only has the Bundeswehr lacked crucial capabilities for international operations, its small expeditionary forces have also increasingly been overstretched. In order to compensate for these gaps, the Bundeswehr has hired private companies on an ad hoc basis. In addition, the Bundeswehr has relied on collective resources provided by private military contractors employed by other nations or international organizations within multilateral operations. The scale and functional scope of private military contracting, however, have been fairly limited.

One of the most long-standing practices has been the hiring of private military transport capabilities, and this is set to continue at least until the delivery of the first European transport aircraft A400M from 2010. Before 2006 the Bundeswehr typically relied on the direct charter of Antonov aircraft from cargo airlines such as Harvey Lift and Volga-Dnjepr. In 2002, for instance, the Bundeswehr spent €100 million on private airlift as part of its deployment to ISAF in Afghanistan.[77] Additional private transport capabilities have taken the form of sealifts. Private shipping companies have transported Bundeswehr Leopard tanks to Kosovo, and the armed forces have chartered RO-RO vessels

---

[74] D. Hastings, 'Iraq Contractors Accused in Shootings', *Washington Post*, 11 August 2007; S. Rayment, "Trophy" Video Exposes Private Security Contractors Shooting Up Iraqi Drivers', *Daily Telegraph*, 26 November 2005; J. B. White and G. Witte, 'Tension, Confusion between Troops, Contractors in Iraq', *Washington Post*, 10 July 2005.

[75] Deutscher Bundestag, *Antwort der Bundesregierung auf die Große Anfrage der Abgeordneten Dr. Werner Hoyer, Dr. Karl Addicks, Daniel Bahr (Münster), weiterer Abgeordneter und der Fraktion der FDP*, Drucksache 15/5824 (24 June 2005).

[76] G. Kümmel, 'Sicherheit Inc.: Private Sicherheits- und Militärdienstleistler, Bundeswehr und Öffentlichkeit', *SOWI.NEWS*, no. 1 (2007), 3.

[77] Bundesrechnungshof, *Bemerkungen 2006 zur Haushalts- und Wirtschaftsführung des Bundes* (Bonn, November 2006), p. 178.

from the German Sloman Neptun Company for the regular delivery of goods to the Balkans.[78] The European Airlift Centre and the Sealift Coordination Centre, which merged in 2007 into the Movement Coordination Centre Europe, have provided additional solutions to individual charter for NATO member states and the EU. The centres have acted as brokers for residual transport capabilities on commercial aircraft and ships hired by member states. The sealifts are paid by the user on demand, while airlifts are tallied on the basis of 'flight hour equivalents', which can be reimbursed through the reciprocal provision of military airlift capacities to other member states.[79]

Since 2006 the Bundeswehr has consolidated the use of private transport capabilities for international military deployments through two projects: the Secure Commercial Strategic Sea Transport project and the Secure Commercial Strategic Air Transport project.[80] The first has involved collaboration with the Danish armed forces for the supply of two, later three, RO-RO vessels over a five-year period from 2006.[81] The second transport project has been secured through NATO's Strategic Airlift Interim Solution (SALIS) programme. As part of the SALIS programme, NATO's Maintenance and Supply Agency has contracted Ruslan SALIS GmbH to provide air transport for allied and EU troops.[82] Under the SALIS contract, the German armed forces have committed themselves to request 750 flight hours worth in the region of €19 million annually until 2009.[83]

Another gap in the Bundeswehr's deployment capabilities has concerned military satellite facilities. In Kosovo, therefore, Germany had to rely on private capacities, including those from Italian Telecom, to link air force units stationed in Italy with military headquarters in Bonn and Berlin.[84] In addition, the Bundeswehr acquired communications

---

[78] U. Petersohn, 'Die Nutzung privater Militärfirmen durch US-Streitkräfte und Bundeswehr', SWP-Studie, no. 36 (Berlin, December 2006), p. 15; S. Mackensen, 'One Hell of a Haul', *SFOR Informer*, no. 160, 3 April 2003.

[79] Klingenberg, W., 'Mobilität der Streitkräfte', *Europäische Sicherheit*, 54, no. 10 (2005).

[80] Bundesministerium der Verteidigung, *Bundeswehrplan 2008* (Berlin, March 2007), p. 16.

[81] Bundesministerium der Verteidigung, *Bundeswehrplan 2008*, p. 17; K. von Dambrowski, 'Unsere Marine im Einsatz', *Marine Forum*, no. 7, August 2007.

[82] Petersohn, 'Die Nutzung privater Militärfirmen durch US-Streitkräfte und Bundeswehr', p. 15.

[83] Deutscher Bundestag, *Antwort der Bundesregierung auf die Kleine Anfrage der Abgeordneten Jan Mücke, Horst Friedrich (Bayreuth), Patrick Döring, weiterer Abgeordneter und der Fraktion der FDP*, Drucksache 16/2907 (11 October 2006), pp. 2–3; Bundesministerium der Verteidigung, *Bundeswehrplan 2008*, p. 16.

[84] R. Bendradt, 'Informationstechnologie in der Bundeswehr', *Telepolis*, 25 June 2000.

satellite links under the first phase of its satellite communications (SATCOM) project from ND SatCom. The contract supplied commercial Intelsat capabilities which allowed the armed forces to link up with contingents in Somalia, Bosnia and Kosovo.[85] For the future, the German armed forces have decided to buy rather than lease satellite capabilities. Unlike the UK, the German government has concluded that it is preferable to invest in the high start-up cost of acquiring a satellite than to incur the higher total expenses of long-term renting. A €939 million contract with MilSat Services GmbH will provide the German armed forces with two of its own military satellites from 2009. Although the armed forces will own the satellites, MilSat will supply support services ranging from the launch of the satellites to management of the central network over ten years with the option of a seven-and-a-half-year extension.[86]

While the German government has made an effort to reduce its systemic dependence on private contractors for deployed operations in the areas of transport and communications, the growing demand on resources and personnel created by simultaneous operations in the Balkans, Afghanistan and the Democratic Republic of Congo has led to the hiring of private military contractors to fill short-term requirements in a number of functions. In Kosovo local companies built the German field camp and managed its sanitation system.[87] In Kosovo and Macedonia Bundeswehr contingents used local businesses for military vehicle repairs, including 35 framework contracts with local motor firms for about 2,500 repairs per year costing €1.6 million.[88] Finally, since 2006 the Bundeswehr has contracted out the catering for its contingent in Bosnia-Herzegovina.[89] In Afghanistan the Bundeswehr has similarly used private military contractors to fill urgent requirements. Rheinmetall Landsysteme despatched two employees to provide maintenance services for Bundeswehr Wiesel vehicles in Kabul during 2003, an Afghan private security company protects the Bundeswehr

[85] *Spacenewsfeed*, 'ND SatCom Wins Follow-up Order from Bundeswehr', 19 August 2001.
[86] Bundeswehr, '"Relaisstationen"' im Orbit', Press Release, 11 July 2006; P. B. de Selding, 'Germany Forms Public-Private Partnership for Military Satcom', *Space News*, 17 July 2006; SES ASTRA, 'ND SATCOM and EADS equip German armed forces with satellite communication networks', Press Release, 2006.
[87] Petersohn, 'Die Nutzung privater Militärfirmen durch US-Streitkräfte und Bundeswehr', p. 18.
[88] Bundeswehr, 'Bundeswehr als Arbeitgeber für Kfz-Betriebe im Kosovo und Mazedonien', Press Release, 22 July 2002.
[89] Deutscher Bundestag, *Unterrichtung durch den Wehrbeauftragten, Jahresbericht 2006*, Drucksache 16/4700 (20 March 2007), p. 14.

base camp in Faizabad, and the international company Supreme is providing catering services for the Bundeswehr site in Mazar-e-Sharif.[90] In the Democratic Republic of Congo the Bundeswehr did not hire private military contractors itself, but used private firms employed by international organizations. The EU, for instance, contracted a private company to build the German field camps in the Democratic Republic of Congo and to provide laundry services, while NATO's SALIS programme provided transport for the German military contingent.[91]

While the outsourcing of military services within international missions has been primarily driven by temporary requirements, the extent of private contracting illustrates the weakening of the ideological strictures against the use of private military contractors in deployed operations. In 2006 the German government admitted that private companies were supplying the Bundeswehr in deployed operations with a variety of services, including logistics such as catering, laundry, fuel and electricity; transport; maintenance for vehicles, base camp institutions and other materiel; building services; sewage and waste disposal; cleaning of textiles and equipment; and private communications services.[92] Moreover, first steps towards a more systematic and long-term use of private contractors in military interventions have been taken. In 2005 the government signed a two-year pilot contract with Bw Fuhrpark Service for the provision of up to 190 vehicles to the German EUFOR contingent in Bosnia-Herzegovina.[93] This little-noted award presents a radical revision of the mission of the Bw Fuhrpark Service, which had been created with the assumption that the management of the Bundeswehr white fleet was a purely national military service.

Despite the limited degree of outsourcing in German military operations abroad, the hire of private contractors by the Bundeswehr has not been without criticism. In the field, the lack of governmental direction over private military companies has led to complaints from soldiers, who feel that the Bundeswehr leadership is failing in its responsibility

[90] Petersohn, 'Die Nutzung privater Militärfirmen durch US-Streitkräfte und Bundeswehr', pp. 18–19; A. Reimann and S. Weiland, 'Bundeswehr Mandat überdenken', *Der Spiegel*, 7 June 2006; GEBB, *Teamarbeiter* (Cologne: July 2007), p. 25.
[91] Deutscher Bundestag, *Unterrichtung durch den Wehrbeauftragten: Jahresbericht 2006*, p. 14.
[92] Deutscher Bundestag, *Antwort der Bundesregierung auf die Anfrage der Abgeordneten Paul Schäfer (Köln), Wolfgang Gehrcke, Heike Hänsel, weiterer Abgeordneter und der Fraktion DIE LINKE*, Drucksache 16/1296 (26 April 2006), p. 11.
[93] Bw Fuhrpark Service, 'Erweiterte Verantwortung für den Mobilitätsdienstleister der Bundeswehr', Press Release, 23 December 2005; Bw Fuhrpark Service, 'Maßgeschneiderte Mobilitätslösungen für das deutsche EUFOR-Kontingent in Bosnien-Herzegowina', Press Release, 10 March 2006.

Table 7.1. *Models of international security provision*

Dimensions	UK	USA	Germany
Ideology	• Neoliberalism	• Neoliberalism	• Republicanism & Neoliberalism
Geographical scope	• International	• International	• International
Functional scope	Extensive private supply of: • Logistics • Maintenance and repair • Communications	Extensive private supply of: • Logistics • Management • Maintenance and repair • Communications • Intelligence • Armed security guards • Military training	Extensive private supply of: • Transport Limited private supply of: • Logistics • Communications • Maintenance and repair
Resources	Extensive private supply of: • Equipment • Services	Extensive private supply of: • Equipment • Services	Limited private supply of: • Equipment • Services
Interests	• Differentiated national security interests • Cost efficiency	• Differentiated national security interests • Cost efficiency	• Common international security interests
Norms	• Small state	• Small state	• Modern state
Decision-making	• Short-term and UOR contracting • Prime contracting	• Short-term and medium-term contracting • Prime contracting	• Medium-term contracts • Public-private partnerships • Multinational collaboration for contracting
Implementation	• Short-term contracts • IDIQ CONLOG contracts • Total life-cycle support	• IDIQ contracts • Performance-based contracting • Total life-cycle support	• Medium-term and specific contracts • Long-term public-private provision of white fleet

Table 7.1. (Cont.)

Dimensions	UK	USA	Germany
Democratic accountability and control	• Fragmentation of functions and resources • Competition • Contractual control	• Fragmentation of functions and resources • Competition • Contractual control	• Public-private collaboration • Limitation of outsourcing • State ownership of equipment

for their care. In Bosnia-Herzegovina, for instance, soldiers observed the lower quality of the food and the decreased flexibility of the provision following the outsourcing of catering services in 2006.[94] In the Democratic Republic of Congo the Bundeswehr deployment experienced serious delays in the building of their field accommodation. The accommodation was later affected by mould and leaking because the private contractor hired by the EU lacked sufficiently qualified personnel. Soldiers also criticized the EU's contracting of inadequate laundry services.[95]

In comparison, the ideological differences with regard to the ideal models of the state and the armed forces between the UK, the USA and Germany can also be observed in their policies regarding private military contracting in international military operations. While the UK and the USA have significantly expanded the outsourcing of military functions in Iraq, Germany has attempted to restrict it to services for which it does not have sufficient in-house capabilities or resources. The differences between the UK and the USA can be explained by the British MOD's proclamation that contractors should not normally be deployed in conflict environments and the more aggressive application of Neoliberalism to international affairs by the US government. However, this section also notes that these variances in the use of military contractors have been decreasing. All three countries have progressively extended the private military support for their missions abroad. This has not only included the growing number of functions outsourced to the private sector, but also the massive scale of contracting due to the cuts in military and civilian armed forces personnel since the end of the Cold War. The implications of the replacement of uniformed soldiers

[94] Deutscher Bundestag, *Unterrichtung durch den Wehrbeauftragten: Jahresbericht 2006*, p. 14.
[95] *Ibid.*, p. 16.

with private contractors for the model of the soldier in contingency operations will be examined in the next section.

A new international soldier

The Neoliberal transformation of the role of the state in international security has been reflected by similar changes in the model of the soldier. Since the consequences of military outsourcing for the national armed forces in the UK, the USA and Germany have already been discussed in the preceding chapters, this section focuses on the emergence of the private military contractor as a new type of international soldier. It discusses three developments and their implications in particular. The first concerns the competition between professional soldiers and private military contractors in military deployments and its consequences for recruitment and retention. The second question concerns the dissolution of the distinction between soldiers and private military contractors in the operational theatre. The third is the changing status of private military contractors in the eyes of the insurgents, the contracting governments and international law.

Consequences for the professional soldier

The consequences of the growing demand for private military contractors for the model of the professional soldier have emerged as central issues in recent interventions. The news that private security guards in Iraq could earn up to $200,000 per year have threatened an exodus of experienced professional soldiers. This has applied particularly to US Army Green Berets or Navy SEALs who typically earn only about $50,000 in base pay and a $23,000 pension by working for their government, and to the UK Special Air Service (SAS) who earn between £25,000–£80,000 depending on skill and rank.[96] The impact has not simply been on the military's ability to compete with private firms in terms of pay; it has also been one of cost already incurred by the state because the training of a Green Beret takes up to eighteen months and costs, on average, $257,000 per soldier.[97] Even before the Iraq war Pentagon officials and armed forces commanders examined possible strategies for increasing retention among senior soldiers to meet the demand for experienced personnel for overseas operations. Among the options considered were special

---

[96] E. Schmitt and T. Shanker, 'Big Pay Luring Military's Elite to Private Jobs', *New York Times*, 30 March 2004; 'The SAS', *The Observer*, 11 November 2001.
[97] Schmitt and Shanker, 'Big Pay Luring Military's Elite to Private Jobs'.

bonus payments, further education and extended leave to enable military staff to work for a private firm for a short period of time and then return to their old position.[98] In the UK the situation has been very similar. A National Audit Office report on the recruitment and retention of armed forces personnel, published in 2006, noted that the increasing availability of jobs with private companies, combined with the stress of repeated deployments to international operations such as Iraq and Afghanistan, have been key factors reducing the attractiveness of a long-term military career.[99] In Germany, by comparison, the impact of the private military industry on the retention of career soldiers has been negligible. Not only have most professional Bundeswehr soldiers too little experience in international military operations to be attractive applicants for leadership positions in private military companies, but also the size of the industry in Germany is very small. Unsatisfactory working conditions and low pay have played a greater role in the growing disillusionment among German soldiers with their career choice.[100]

In spite of these conditions, several factors have so far helped to prevent a mass departure of professional soldiers in the UK and the USA to private contractors. Foremost, private sector salaries, although very attractive, are not as high as suggested by the media. While former Special Forces members and officers can earn up to $1,000 per day, soldiers from other services and the ranks are more likely to receive between $400 and $500.[101] Private military contractors also rarely earn a full year's salary because of the preference for short-term contracts in the sector.[102] In addition, the number of top earners has necessarily been limited because private military companies seek to make a profit. Most companies have only hired ex-military personnel for leadership positions. In 2007 US citizens made up only twenty per cent of private military contractors who worked for the DOD in Iraq.[103] The majority of contract staff have been from transitional or developing countries where wages are low, such as Bosnia, Croatia, Ukraine, Fiji, the Philippines,

[98] *Ibid.*
[99] National Audit Office, *Ministry of Defence: Recruitment and Retention*, Session 2005–6, HC 1633-I (London: The Stationery Office, 3 November 2006), p. 1.
[100] Deutscher BundeswehrVerband, *Umfrage zur Berufszufriedenheit – Zusatzbericht zur Mitgliederbefragung des Deutschen BundeswehrVerbandes*, Vol. 1 (Passau, 26 April 2007).
[101] D. Priest and M. P. Flaherty, 'Slain Contractors Were in Iraq Working Security Detail', *Washington Post*, 2 April 2004; J. Borger, 'Brutal killing of Americans in Iraq raises questions over security firms', *Guardian*, 2 April 2004; private conversation with a former employee of Global Risk Strategies.
[102] GAO, *Rebuilding Iraq*, p. 36.
[103] CBO, *Contractor's Support of U.S. Operations in Iraq*, p. 9.

Colombia, Chile and South Africa.[104] Finally, the UK and US armed forces have used several measures in order to halt the exodus of trained soldiers. One such measure was the general stop-loss policy installed by the US Army between December 2001 and November 2003, with similar policies implemented by the navy, the air force and the marine corps. The stop-loss prevents military personnel from leaving the armed forces at the end of their contract. After the end of the general stop-loss policy in 2003, unit-specific stop-loss programmes came into effect, which prohibited soldiers from leaving the army during deployment or ninety days before or after deployment.[105] Further policies adopted in December 2004 sought to encourage Special Operations Forces to stay in the military up to and beyond the normal twenty-year retirement period by means of an incentive package including bonuses and lump sum payments between $8,000 and $150,000 for re-enlistment for one and six years respectively.[106] The UK has refrained from stop-loss policies, but it has increased its financial retention incentives for a few select positions that have been considered 'pinch point trades', such as signallers, aircrew, submariners and medical assistants.[107] In addition, the UK military has offered a tax-free allowance of £2,240 for every soldier deployed in Iraq, Afghanistan and Bosnia and permitted 'sabbatical' periods for Special Forces, which they can use to work temporarily in higher-paid positions in the private sector.[108]

Together these factors have helped to limit attrition rates among military personnel. However, they illustrate that competition between professional forces and private military companies poses serious challenges for the future. The transition towards postmodern militaries, with increasing emphasis on personal rights and benefits during the 1990s, has prepared the ground for an occupational view of the military profession in the UK, the USA and Germany. Multiple interventions in Iraq, Afghanistan and elsewhere now provide the opportunity to leave the professional armed forces for the greater freedom and pay of occupations in the private sector. As a former US Special Forces member

[104] J. Franklin, 'US Contractor Recruits Guards for Iraq in Chile', *Guardian*, 5 March 2004; S. Efron, 'Iraq: Worry Grows as Foreigners Flock to Risky Jobs', *LA Times*, 30 July 2005; J. K. Elsea and N. M. Serafino, *Private Security Contractors in Iraq: Background, Legal Status and Other Issues* (Washington DC: CRS Report for Congress, 11 July 2007), p. 4.
[105] GAO, *Rebuilding Iraq*, p. 38.
[106] *Ibid.*, p. 37; A. S. Tyson, 'Military Officers Special Perks in Bid to Retain Special Forces', *Christian Science Monitor*, 21 January 2005.
[107] National Audit Office, *Ministry of Defence: Recruitment and Retention*, pp. 48–50.
[108] T. Edmunds and A. Forster, *Out of Step. The Case for Change in the British Armed Forces* (London: DEMOS, 2007), p. 54.

has argued: 'You can stay in the military if you are patriotic, but then your ideals are outweighing your pocketbook.'[109] For a growing number of professional soldiers and reservists the pocketbook has become more important. Moreover, soldiers have been dissatisfied with the strain on their personal lives due to multiple and successive deployments abroad. By 2006 US military leaders spoke of a 'broken force', and UK General Sir Richard Dannatt, Chief of General Staff, publicly asked his government to pull out of Iraq soon because the UK Armed Forces were nearing breaking point.[110] The German Bundeswehr Ombudsman has also observed that the armed forces have been 'chronically under-resourced' to the point of 'endangering life and limb' of soldiers in Afghanistan.[111] UK, US and German career soldiers have felt abandoned by their governments. While private military contractors appear to have all the equipment that they could ask for, the international intervention forces in Iraq, Afghanistan and beyond often suffer from serious and persistent shortages.[112]

Division between combat and support

A second issue has been the weakening division between soldiers and private military contractors in international interventions. It has raised serious questions regarding the legitimacy, authority and accountability of private military personnel, who are increasingly put in positions of killing or being killed.[113] For much of the twentieth century democratic governments in Europe and North America sought to delegitimize combat operations by private military companies such as Sandline International and Executive Outcomes. Politicians and the military in the UK and the USA maintained that private military contractors had no role to play in international conflicts. They argued that there was a clear dividing line between the core tasks of national armed forces, not considered suitable for outsourcing to the private sector, and support

---

[109] Tyson, 'Military Officers Special Perks in Bid to Retain Special Forces'.

[110] R. Taylor-Norton and T. Branigan, 'Army Chief: British Troops Must Pull Out Of Iraq Soon', *Guardian*, 13 October 2006; S. Sands, 'Sir Richard Dannatt: A Very Honest General', *Daily Mail*, 12 October 2006.

[111] Deutscher Bundestag, *Unterrichtung durch den Wehrbeauftragten, Jahresbericht 2007 (49. Bericht)*, Drucksache 16/8200 (4 March 2008), p. 3, p. 13 (translations by the author).

[112] A. S. Tyson, 'General Says Army Will Need to Grow', *Washington Post*, 15 December 2006; A. S. Tyson, 'Military Is Ill Prepared for Other Conflicts', *Washington Post*, 19 March 2007.

[113] J. D. Michaels, 'Beyond Accountability: The Constitutional, Democratic, and Strategic Problems with Privatizing War', *Washington University Law Quarterly*, 82, no. 3 (2004), 1001–127.

functions, which were. Recent interventions have not only put the validity of this argument into question, they have also signalled a change in the attitude of the UK and US governments with regard to the employment of private military contractors during conflicts.

During the combat phase of the Iraq war private military support staff moved closer to the front line than ever before due to the UK and US armed forces' attempts to free soldiers from support functions for combat activities. In particular, the LOGCAP and CONLOG contracts have provided extensive logistic support within conflict environments. The exposure of private military staff to hostile attacks has been another consequence of the outsourcing of a growing range of deployment support functions to the private sector. While during the 1990s military outsourcing in the US and the UK primarily concerned civilian services such as water treatment and housing management, the new millennium has seen the expansion of the private supply of specialist military tasks such as intelligence and interrogation as well as in-theatre weapons support and maintenance.[114] In many military positions and installations in Iraq, private contractors have worked side by side with military personnel whether in the positions of truck drivers in support convoys or interrogators in Abu Ghraib.

The dissolution of the dividing line between combat and support functions has also been a result of broader changes in warfare.[115] According to US Colonel Bill Gallagher, in contemporary warfare 'there is no front, there is no rear. Soldiers of all specialities will face direct contact with an adversary. They all have to have a common set of combat skills.'[116] In the First and Second World Wars soldiers with specialist functions such as clerks, cooks, truck drivers and communications technicians were usually far from the front line. In contemporary wars, such as Somalia, Afghanistan and Iraq, there has been no front in the traditional sense. Instead, these wars or insurgencies have been characterized by a patchwork of peace and combat zones which have created a new, more complex battlefield.

The inability of the multinational forces to establish peace in Iraq after the official end of the war further contributed to the merging of the roles of combat soldiers and contractors. The persistent insecurity on the ground required the military, government agencies and

---

[114] J. E. Manker, Jr. and K. D. Williams, 'Contractors in Contingency Operations: Panacea or Pain?' *Air Force Journal of Logistics*, 28, no. 3 (2004), 14–16.

[115] *Ibid.*, 16.

[116] Col. Bill Gallagher, commander of the Basic combat training brigade at Fort Benning, GA, in T. Shanker, 'Army Pushes a Sweeping Overhaul of Basic Training', *New York Times*, 4 August 2004.

reconstruction firms to hire private contractors for their own protection. Although private guarding was proclaimed to be purely defensive, the situation in Iraq more often than not required military contractors to carry firearms to protect their clients. In some instances the employees of private military companies have engaged in full-scale battles. In an attack on the CPA headquarters in Najaf, for instance, Blackwater guards fought, allegedly, for more than three hours until relieved by US Special Forces. During the exchange eight Blackwater employees reportedly repelled hundreds of Shiite militiamen armed with rocket-propelled grenades and AK-47s.[117] Complaining about the slowness of the US military's responses to requests for help, Scott Custer, co-director of Custer Battles, admitted that his company had established its own quick reaction force.[118]

The implications of the weakening divisions between contractors and the armed forces for the concept of the soldier and his/her role and position in international security have been considerable. They have presented a challenge to the special statuses of the professional soldier and citizen-soldier as the sole legitimate agents within international conflicts and have raised the question of the difference between private military contractors and mercenaries. In modern democracies the special statuses of professional soldiers and citizen-soldiers have rested on their oaths to defend their country with their lives, the authority to kill for a purpose invested in them by elected parliaments, their submission under strict military discipline and their recognition within international law. Yet in Iraq private military contractors, formally and legally defined as civilians, have increasingly died and killed for Western democracies. The decision of the UK and US governments to replace soldiers on the battlefield with contractors and not to take full responsibility for public security in Iraq has, to some degree, legitimized the role of private military contractors. Further illustration of their new legitimacy is the eligibility of contractors deployed with the UK armed forces in Iraq for the MOD Iraq Campaign Medal, and the US's award of medals to private military contractors.[119]

Neither the US Congress nor the UK Parliament has granted contractors with this legitimacy, nor has it emerged from or complied with

---

[117] D. Priest, 'Private Guards Repel Attack on U.S. Headquarters', *Washington Post*, 6 April 2004.

[118] M. Duffy, 'What Private Armies Take to the Front Lines', *Time Magazine*, 12 April 2004.

[119] House of Commons Hansard, 'Iraq Service Medal', Written Answers, Vol. 446, Session 2005–6, 10 May 2006, Columns W300-W303; B. Murray, 'American, British Civilian Contractors Honored for Work in Iraq', *Stars and Stripes*, 28 June 2006.

the established democratic procedures for military accountability and control in both countries. The formalistic position that, after the official end of the war, private contractors not employed by the coalition forces have been 'normal' security guards working within the confines of Iraqi law has disregarded the factual continuation of the conflict, the actions of security guards and the inability of the CPA and its successors to effectively regulate the huge number of private military personnel in Iraq. Moreover, both the UK and US governments' endorsement of the new roles of private military contractors accounts for the growing perception that these contractors are not mercenaries, but a new type of international soldier.

Lacking the legitimacy and accountability of the professional and citizen-soldier models, however, private military contractors in Iraq have suffered the disregard of their armed forces colleagues and have felt undervalued. Professional soldiers have resented the fact that private military contractors have not been subject to the same standards, yet receive better salaries. Moreover, soldiers have feared that the weakening of the distinction between private contractors and professional soldiers has undermined the collective identity of the armed forces and their special status in national and international society. Conversely, contractors have argued that the coalition forces have treated them without due regard and that governments have not sufficiently recognised their contribution to the pacification of Iraq. These opposing viewpoints illustrate the irony of the merger between both models of the soldier. Professional soldiers have become more concerned with monetary gain whereas traditionally their reward was the superior status of the soldier in the eyes of the public, while contractors, whose primary reward is financial, increasingly seek public acknowledgment.

Changing contractor status

Another consequence of the dissolution of the dividing line between contractors and professional soldiers and citizen-soldiers has been the change in attitude towards military contractor personnel by the enemy and the UK and US militaries. The most important change has been that private contractors have become legitimate targets due to their active involvement in military operations. In Iraq there was initially little evidence for such a view among the insurgents. During the first five months after the official end of the war, contractors were negligible targets, while the strikes against the military quickly rose to 500–800 per month. One cause of the increase in the number of attacks on security contractors was the killing of private guards in Fallujah. The insurgent forces appeared to have hit, almost by accident, upon the sensitivity of private military contractors, both in terms of their greater vulnerability than the multinational forces and their ability to attract media attention. The trigger was the ambush, murder and public mutilation of the four US security guards working for Blackwater in the streets of Fallujah in 2004. Filmed on video tape and transmitted around the globe, it created an international storm of public outrage.[120] Crucially, the outrage was not only directed at the killers, but also at the UK and US governments which had hired the contractors and brought them into the country without sufficient security or controls. Before the incident, the media had paid little attention to the large presence of private military contractors in Iraq. Fallujah brought the issue of private military forces in Iraq onto the front pages of Western newspapers, the main TV channels and radio reports.

As one of these reports noted, the 'employees of security companies ... frequently come under fire from insurgents. When they do, they fire back.'[121] The reports thus confirmed the role of private military contractors as de facto combatants and helped to justify the attacks. They illustrated that the insurgents acted in accord with the Geneva Conventions which stipulate that civilians and contractors accompanying the forces are legitimate military targets if and as long as they directly participate in hostilities.[122] Some authors have argued that the Blackwater contractors who defended the CPA headquarters in Najaf in April 2004 could even be tried as mercenaries under the First Additional Protocol of the Geneva Conventions because they were fighting in what was then still an international conflict or alien occupation.[123] What is certain is that their direct involvement in an armed occupation and pacification loses private military contractors the protection from attack that the Geneva Conventions normally grant civilians and opens them up to criminal charges and potential prosecution by local governments, or in the case of contractors to international military forces by their employing state.

---

[120] J. Gettleman, '4 From U.S. Killed in Abush in Iraq', *New York Times*, 1 April 2004; Priest and Flaherty, 'Slain Contractors Were in Iraq Working Security Detail'; Duffy, 'When Private Armies Take to the Front Lines'.

[121] Priest and Flaherty, 'Slain Contractors Were in Iraq Working Security Detail'.

[122] C. Schaller, 'Private Security and Military Companies under the International Law of Armed Conflict', in T. Jäger and G. Kümmel (eds.) *Private Military and Security Companies. Changes, Problems, Pitfalls and Prospects* (Wiesbaden: VS Verlag für Sozialwissenschaften, 2007), pp. 348–9; E.-C. Gillard, 'Business Goes to War: Private Military/Security Companies and International Humanitarian Law', *International Review of the Red Cross*, 88, no. 863 (2006), 525–72.

[123] I.-I. Drews, 'Private Military Companies: The New Mercenaries? – An International Law Analysis', in T. Jäger and G. Kümmel (eds.) *Private Military and Security Companies. Changes, Problems, Pitfalls and Prospects* (Wiesbaden: VS Verlag für Sozialwissenschaften, 2007), p. 339.

Table 7.2. *Private military contractors in deployed operations*

Dimensions	Iraq and beyond
Relationships with the state and society	• Mutual contractual obligation for service and protection between contractors and the state • Public recognition of contractor service
Motivation	• Monetary gain
Identity	• Individual-professional • De facto combatants
Democratic control and accountability	• Limited market competition • Military and/or civilian law

There is no indication that insurgents in Iraq specifically targeted private contractors after Fallujah, but they stopped making a distinction between contractors and soldiers.[124] Moreover, the insurgents began to take military contractors and security guards hostage, in order to blackmail their governments into leaving the country.[125]

The abduction and public killing of military support staff by the Iraqi insurgents in turn brought about an important change in the relationship between the international armed forces and the contractors. From the start of the rebuilding effort, the multinational coalition forces insisted that private contractors were responsible for their own security. Emergency military rescue teams helped in the event of an acute attack, but did not always respond immediately.[126] Following the events in Fallujah, the military had to rethink its position vis-à-vis contractors. If the international coalition continued to disregard the protection of private contractors, this could seriously delay the reconstruction effort either because construction firms could not afford the increasing cost of private security or because their staff refused to stay in the country. Before the attack reconstruction workers had already been wary of the conditions in Iraq.[127]

Faced with these consequences, the US authorities in Iraq decided that the murder of the four Blackwater security guards in Fallujah

---

[124] Iraq Coalition Casualties, *Contractors – A Partial List*, at: http://icasualties.org; GAO, *Rebuilding Iraq*, p. 10.

[125] *Sydney Morning Herald*, 'List of Hostages in Iraq', 16 April 2004; C. Freeman and B. Johnston, 'Italian Hostages "Sitting Ducks" After US Troops Disarmed Them', *Daily Telegraph*, 2 May 2004.

[126] Duffy, 'When Private Armies Take to the Front Lines'; GAO, *Rebuilding Iraq*, p. 19.

[127] J. Chaffin, 'Rising Violence Damps Contractors' Enthusiasm', *Financial Times*, 2 April 2004.

'would not go unpunished'.[128] The planning for Operation Vigilant Resolve began immediately, and within days US Marine forces began a three-week siege on Fallujah, resulting in the deaths of 126 US soldiers and approximately 600 Iraqi insurgents.[129] Coalition Special Forces also took a more active role in rescuing kidnapped contractors, including three Italian security guards in June 2004 and an American military catering contractor in September 2005.[130] In practice, private military contractors have become an integral part of international military forces, whose civilian protection under international conventions and laws has been undermined by their involvement in military conflicts. While this situation cried out for a reform of the legal context within which military contractors were working, the coalition governments did not take major steps in this direction until 2006. In the meantime, professional soldiers had to carry the burden of being responsible for the security of private contractors over whom they had little control.

Democratic control in international missions

Although both Republicanism and Neoliberalism have clear conceptions of how to ensure the democratic control and accountability of the use of collective violence in international security, four major problems have emerged from the recent transformations of the roles of the state and the soldier in deployed operations. Foremost has been the question of the legitimacy, accountability and control of private military contractors in conflicts. The second issue has been the complexity and inconsistency of national and international legislation with regard to civilian contractors. The third problem has been the re-emergence of war profiteering in Iraq and Afghanistan. Finally, contemporary military interventions have been characterized by a lack of civil-military coordination. As this section shows, each of these problems has affected the UK, the USA and Germany to varying degrees due to their different approaches towards contractors in deployed operations.

---

[128] N. Pelham, S. Davoudi and J. Chaffin, 'US Army Promises Punishment After Fallujah Killings', *Financial Times*, 1 April 2004.

[129] R. Sanchez, *Coalition Provisional Authority Briefing*, 8 April 2004, at: www.defenselink. mil; 'US Death Toll in August Is Third Highest', *Washington Post*, 1 September 2005; L. Marlow, 'Siege of Fallujah Lifts with Iraqi Death Toll at over 600', *Irish Times*, 16 April 2004; Associated Press, 'Four Contractors Killed in Baghdad Ambush', *New York Times*, 6 June 2004.

[130] 'Special Forces Free Iraq Hostages', *BBC News*, 8 June, 2004; E. Knickmeyer, 'U.S. Forces Free American Hostage in Iraq', *Washington Post*, 8 September 2005; GAO, *Rebuilding Iraq*, p. 19.

Legitimacy, accountability and control

The controversy over the legitimacy, accountability and control of private military contractors in contingency operations has three main dimensions. The first concerns the question of whether the replacement of national soldiers with international contractors has undermined the democratic safeguards against the abuse of military power in international affairs. The second dimension concerns the issue of whether their employment, in particular in what used to be core military functions such as armed security, has been sufficiently approved through national and international democratic processes. Finally, the third applies to the legitimacy and authority of the private military contractor as a new type of soldier.

As has been argued above, the UK and the US governments' growing reliance on private contractors for military support can be seen as part of a shift towards Neoliberal security governance. However, while Neoliberalism believes that the shrinking of the state and standing national armed forces prevents military adventurism and the abuse of military power by the state, the availability of international private military contractors has allowed government executives in the UK and the USA to become more independent of their legislatures and electorates. In the UK this autonomy has been demonstrated by the government's disregard for the 'biggest anti-war demonstration ever held in Britain and worldwide' which brought one million people onto the streets of London in the wake of the Iraq intervention.[131] Similarly, the 155,000 contractors employed by the US armed forces have allowed the Bush administration to significantly expand its military operation in Iraq without having to ask Congress for the approval of additional troops.[132] In Germany, also, the availability of private contractors for deployed operations holds the potential of circumventing the Law on Parliamentary Participation in the Decision to Use Armed Force Abroad, although the government has not yet made much use of this option.[133]

In addition, private military contractors have helped to limit popular protests at the use of citizen-soldiers in deployed operations. In the USA the massive call-up of Reserves and National Guards for the Iraq

---

[131] E. MacAskill and M. White, 'Blair to Defy Anti-War Protests', *Guardian*, 17 February 2003.

[132] D. D. Avant, 'Privatizing Military Training', *Foreign Policy in Focus*, 5, no. 17, (2000), 2; D. Avant and L. Sigelman, 'What Does Private Security in Iraq Mean for US Democracy at Home?', Research Paper, January 2008.

[133] Gesetz über die parlamentarische Beteiligung bei der Entscheidung über den Einsatz bewaffneter Streitkräfte im Ausland (Parlamentsbeteiligungsgesetz) vom 18. März 2005, Bundesgesetzblatt I, p. 775.

war was particularly controversial because their ultimate rationale and primary task is US territorial defence and not international interventions. Among others, their deployment created major problems for the morale, recruitment and retention of Reservists and National Guards, most of whom had not signed up with the expectation that they might be sent abroad on foreign missions.[134] The Iraq war also led to a significant outflow of volunteers from the Territorial Army (TA) in the UK. Within months of the intervention, the number of reservists leaving the TA more than quadrupled, reducing the TA to its lowest strength since 1907.[135] The German Bundeswehr has so far avoided these problems by only deploying basic conscripts and reservists who have volunteered for international service.[136] However, the shortage of extended service conscripts and professional soldiers might facilitate the hiring of private military contractors in future international missions.

The lack of institutional democratic consent to contractors' participation in military operations has exacerbated concerns about the legitimacy of the increased role of private military contractors. Not only have the UK Parliament, the US Congress and the German Bundestag not directly approved the use of contractors abroad, they also have little information about the number and functions of private military contractors hired by their own militaries. The USA has attempted to address this problem through the creation of a DOD-wide database called the Synchronized Predeployment and Operational Tracker (SPOT) in 2006, while the UK government was still attempting to set up a similar contractor database in 2008.[137] Germany has made no such efforts yet, given the limited number of its contractors abroad. However, the diversity of Bundeswehr contracting arrangements with some private military personnel employed by public–private joint ventures, some by private companies and others by international organizations such as the UN, hold potential dangers for public and parliamentary oversight.

---

[134] B. Graham, 'Pentagon To Shrink Iraq Force', *Washington Post*, 7 November 2003.
[135] M. Smith, 'War Blamed as 6,000 Quit Territorial Army', *Sunday Times*, 30 October 2005.
[136] Bundesministerium der Verteidigung, *The Bundeswehr Reservist Concept* (Berlin, 10 September 2003), p. 17, point 1410.
[137] GAO, *Military Operations: High-Level DOD Action Needed to Address Long-standing Problems with Management and Oversight of Contractors Supporting Deployed Operations*, GAO-07–145 (Washington DC, December 2006), pp. 14–20; GAO, *Stabilizing and Rebuilding Iraq: Conditions in Iraq Are Conductive to Fraud, Waste and Abuse*, GAO-07–525T (Washington DC, 23 April 2007), p. 11.

Regulation and legislation

In addition to public scrutiny and control, regulation and legislation play crucial roles in ensuring the democratic accountability of private military contractors according to Neoliberalism. They are particularly important because the Neoliberal models of the state and the soldier essentially favour the punishment of misconduct over preventative mechanisms such as civic virtue and the integration of the armed forces with society. In contemporary international interventions, however, questions over the applicability of national and international laws, the responsibility to prosecute and gaps in existing regulations have hampered the legislative control over private military contractors. In particular in Iraq, repeated incidents of private security guards engaging in fights with insurgents and contractor killings of civilians have brought these issues to the fore.[138] The UK and US governments have sought to avoid them by emphasizing the civilian status of private contractors under national and international law. However, in practice both governments have accepted that contractors will engage in 'defensive operations'.[139]

In Iraq the issue of contractor regulation was played out in two arenas. The first concerned the formal control of private military contractors within the military chain of command and their relations with military officers. The second was the regulation of private military companies and their employees under national and international law. During the course of the Iraq intervention both changed significantly. The UK military has sought to define its control over private military suppliers in international missions through its CONDO regulations.[140] The aim of CONDO has been to 'enhance the MOD's capability by providing commercial support to operations directly from the UK industrial base, throughout the Line of Communication and *as far forward as possible*'.[141] During the Iraq war the CONDO regulations, which had been developed to clarify the conditions for the employment of contractors in overseas bases, proved to be not entirely satisfactory.[142] Thus, in 2004 the

[138] S. Fainaru, 'Iraq Contractors Face Growing Parallel War', *Washington Post*, 16 June 2007; S. Fainaru and S. al-Izzi, 'U.S. Security Contractors Open Fire in Baghdad', *Washington Post*, 27 May 2007.

[139] Fainaru, 'Iraq Contractors Face Growing Parallel War'.

[140] Headquarters – Department of the Army, *Contractors on the Battlefield*, Field Manual No. 3–100.21 (Washington DC: Headquarters – Department of the Army, 3 January 2003).

[141] A. Higginson, 'Contractors on Deployed Operations', *MOD Defence Contracts Bulletin*, 9 April 2003, 24 (emphasis added).

[142] MOD, 'Contractors Support to Operations', at: www.ams.mod.uk.

MOD concluded that there was still 'inadequate legal jurisdiction'.[143]A key and continuing limitation has been that CONDO only applies to contractors directly employed by the armed forces, discounting sub-contractors or private security guards working for other UK government agencies such as the Foreign Office.[144] Moreover, the armed forces cannot require CONDO contractors and their personnel to remain within theatre against their will.[145] Other problems have affected the implementation of the training and security requirements stipulated in the CONDO policy guidelines, including 'the availability of only limited advice on visa requirements, shortfalls in pre-deployment training and transport to theatre, and the issue of ID cards and protective equipment'.[146] Although the regulations have decreed the inclusion of deployed contractors under the Service Discipline Acts, the MOD has so far favoured 'a pragmatic approach' and stated that it prefers the company to take any disciplinary action.[147] While the regulations also place contractors under Service Law for criminal offences that cannot be pursued by local civilian courts due to Status of Forces Agreements (SOFA) or Memorandums of Understanding (MOU), there have so far been no publicized cases in which Service Law has been applied to CONDO staff.

Tighter regulations apply to the so-called 'sponsored reserves' defined in the Reserve Forces Act (Part V) in 1996. Sponsored reserves are private military contractors in deployed operations who have voluntarily enrolled with the reserve forces. They receive regular training with the reserve forces, have no right to appeal against a call-out and, when serving with the armed forces, are subject to the Service Discipline Acts and Service regulations. Problematically, sponsored reserves further increase the autonomy of the executive since their call-out period can be extended beyond the normal maximum of nine months in agreement between the reservist and the employer. So far sponsored reserves have involved over 340 contractor personnel in several existing and future areas of employment, including in the RAF Mobile Meteorological Unit, as engineering support for the BAE 125 aircraft, in the operation and maintenance of the army's Heavy Equipment Transporters, as crew on the navy's six RO-RO ferries, on two navy hydrographic

---

[143] MOD, *Operations in Iraq: Lessons for the Future*, p. 44.
[144] *Ibid.*
[145] MOD, *Contractors on Deployed Operations (CONDO): Processes and Requirements*, Defence Standard 05–129, Issue 3, 1 May 2008, p. 31; Higginson, 'Contractors on Deployed Operations', 26.
[146] MOD, *Operations in Iraq: Lessons for the Future*, p. 44.
[147] MOD, Contractors on Deployed Operations (CONDO), p. 9, p. 31.

and oceanographic survey vessels, as air and ground crew of the Future Strategic Tanker Aircraft, and in the maintenance of the Rapier Field Air Defence System.[148]

Due to multiple, unclear and changing regulations, the US armed forces faced even greater uncertainty regarding the control over private military contractors. At the beginning of the Iraq war each of the three services had their own rules for contractors deployed in theatre. The army had the most extensive set of regulations with three separate directives, while the navy and the air force had only limited guidelines.[149] Inter-service rules for logistics contractors set out in Joint Publication 4–0 Doctrine for Logistics Support of Joint Operations provided another layer of regulations.[150] In 2004 the DOD attempted to introduce a general department-wide policy with regard to all types of private military contractors.[151] The DOD also published a supplement to the Federal Acquisitions Regulations entitled 'Contractors Accompanying a Deployed Force', which focused on contractual issues, including command structure and the carrying of weapons.[152] In Iraq, however, the new guidelines caused as much confusion as clarity. Few military commanders had time to familiarize themselves with the multiple and changing rules.[153] Moreover, the regulations did not place private military contractors under the military chain of command. The primary authority over private contractors remained their own company and the designated DOD contracting official. Since these officials were not normally in the theatre themselves or were stationed in another location, contractors were frequently managed by representatives who were unsure about their authority.[154]

The MEJA, which had been approved in 2000, also provided no clear regulation. Although it stipulates that contractors employed by

---

[148] 'Sponsored Reserves', at: www.mod.uk (last accessed 17 March 2005); MOD, *Operations in Iraq: Lessons for the Future*, paras. 4.22, 5.3.

[149] GAO, *Military Operations: Contractors Provide Vital Services to Deployed Forces but Are Not Adequately Addressed in DOD Plans*, GAO-03–695 (Washington DC, June 2003), pp. 22–4.

[150] Joint Publication 4–0 *Doctrine for Logistic Support of Joint Operations*, 6 April 2000.

[151] Statement of the Honorable Michael W. Wynne Acting Under Secretary of Defense (Acqustion, Technology, and Logistics) before the United States House Committee on Armed Services (Washington DC, 24 June 2004), p. 6; GAO, *Rebuilding Iraq*, p. 11.

[152] Statement of the Honorable Michael W. Wynne, p. 7.

[153] GAO, *Military Operations: Contractors Provide Vital Services*, pp. 22–3; Statement of the Honorable Michael W. Wynne, pp. 6–7; GAO, *Rebuilding Iraq*, p. 11.

[154] GAO, *Military Operations: High-Level DOD Action Needed to Address Long-standing Problems with Management and Oversight of Contractors Supporting Deployed Operations*, GAO-07–145 (Washington DC, December 2006), p. 23.

the DOD abroad can be prosecuted under US civilian law for offences punishable with more than one year's imprisonment, the difficulty and cost of obtaining information concerning contractor crimes overseas has meant that US courts have so far invoked the Act only once.[155] Moreover, efforts to extend the Act to cover all US contractors have failed. In 2006 Congress therefore approved a major amendment to the National Defense Authorization Act of Fiscal Year 2007.[156] This amendment placed all civilians accompanying the armed forces in declared wars or 'contingency operations' under the Uniform Code of Military Justice (UCMJ).[157] In contrast to the UK, initial doubts as to the willingness of the US armed forces to apply military law to civilian contractors have been discredited by the first court martial of a contractor in May 2008.[158] The contractor, who worked as a translator for Titan, was convicted of stabbing another contractor during a fight and was sentenced to five months in jail.[159] Theoretically, the amendment permits the prosecution of private military contractors deployed by the armed forces for all offences against the UCMJ, including those that are not punishable under civilian law. However, the DOD has issued a memorandum which clarifies that the UCMJ will only be used when US federal criminal courts are reluctant to prosecute civilian law offences or where 'the person's conduct is adverse to a *significant military interest* of the United States'.[160]

The UK CONDO and US UMCJ regulations have gone some way towards clarifying the legal status of their private military contractors in deployed operations. However, the application of local and international laws to contract staff overseas has been and remains controversial. In most instances deployed armed forces and accompanying contractors have been exempted from prosecution under foreign

---

[155] P. W. Singer, 'The Law Catches Up to Private Militaries, Embeds', *DefenseTech*, 3 January 2007; W. Matthews, 'Contractor Crackdown', *Armed Forces Journal*, February 2007; G. Witte, 'New Law Could Subject Civilians to Military Trial', *Washington Post*, 15 January 2007.

[156] Singer, 'The Law Catches Up to Private Militaries, Embeds'; N. Hodge, 'Revised US Law Spotlights Role of Contractors on the Battlefield', *Jane's Defence Weekly*, 10 January 2007.

[157] John Warner National Defense Authorization Act for Fiscal Year 2007, *Public Law* 109–364, 17 October 2006, 109th Congress, 120 STAT. 2217.

[158] S. Fidler and D. Sevastopulo, 'Civilian Workers Could Face Court Martial', *Financial Times*, 10 January 2007.

[159] Multi-National Corps Iraq, 'Civilian Contractor Convicted at a Court-Martial', Press Release, 23 June 2008.

[160] Secretary of Defense, *Memorandum, Subject: UCMJ Jurisdiction Over DOD Civilian Employees, DOD Contractor Personnel, and Other Persons Serving With or Accompanying the Armed Forces Overseas During Declared Wars and in Contingency Operations* (Washington DC: Pentagon, 10 March 2008) (emphasis added).

national laws through SOFAs. Unlike in Afghanistan, there was no SOFA in Iraq. Instead the CPA and, later, the new Iraqi government unilaterally granted immunity to all soldiers and contractors working for the multinational coalition forces until 2008.[161] In addition, CPA Memorandum Number 17, subsequently adopted into Iraqi law, established a registration and licensing regime for private security companies under the authority of the Iraqi Ministry of Interior. The regulation required all employees of private security companies to undergo vetting including for mental and physical fitness, respect for human rights, security and background checks, as well as operations and weapons training. Although all contractors working for the multinational coalition were required to obtain a licence, their legal immunity meant that not all international firms made the effort.[162] Moreover, the Ministry of Interior was considered incapable of enforcing the regulation. In 2008 the Iraqi government finally decided to end the immunity of coalition contractors and to place them on an equal footing with other private military firms operating in the country. The absence of a working legal system in many intervention countries combined with SOFAs, however, normally put the onus of contractor prosecution on the contracting governments.

War profiteering in a new guise

The third major problem has been war profiteering. Preventing excessive private profits and contractor fraud within a Liberal model of the state and the armed forces has by no means been new. Accusations of war profiteering were widespread in the USA and the UK during the First World War, when both countries largely relied on private industry to support their war efforts. Compared to the outsourcing of national defence, international conflicts have always been more susceptible to contractors overcharging governments because of the demand for speed and flexibility, and increased governmental dependence on private businesses. Moreover, during a war the military usually lacks sufficient personnel to supervise contractors. Both factors have also applied to the joint UK and US operation in Iraq and have led to recurrent problems related to ensuring the cost efficiency of private military services. Neither the military nor private clients have had the time or personnel to competitively award contracts, vet companies or fix contract

---

[161] Coalition Provisional Authority Order Number 17 (Revised), *Status of the Coalition Provisional Authority, MNF-Iraq, Certain Missions and Personnel in Iraq.*

[162] S. Fainaru and S. al-Izzi, 'U.S. Security Contractors Open Fire in Iraq', *Washington Post*, 27 May 2007.

specifications. Especially in the early summer of 2003, the UK and US armed forces rushed to obtain private support as it became clear that the war had not ended but was turning into a prolonged occupation. During these first months the majority of UK and US military contracts were awarded on a non-competitive basis.[163] Competition among contracting firms improved somewhat during the course of the intervention, but full and open competition remained rare. Reputation, established relations and the preference of UK and US governments for national companies contributed to limiting competitive pressures on major contractors such as KBR, Vinnell and DynCorp. In fact, smaller private military companies felt forced out of the market.

The extensive use of flexible IDIQ contracts by the US armed forces and, since 2004, by the UK military has been another problem.[164] Normally, these contracts require that the task orders, i.e. the services to be provided, are specified as quickly and as exactly as possible in order to operate cost-efficiently because there are few incentives to prevent overprovision by the contractor.[165] However, due to the constantly changing requirements in Iraq, this was not always possible. Moreover, where task orders had been defined early on, they frequently required changing later at additional expense. But it was not only contractors who abused flexible and open-ended contracts; there were also instances of army officers using contractor rather than military personnel to complete tasks not covered by the contract because of the need for speed or a lack of troops.[166] In one of these cases the army requested KBR to build housing because its own units would be unable to complete the accommodation before the arrival of the division.[167] Even more controversial was the hiring of KBR for the development of a contingency plan for the reconstruction of the Iraqi oil infrastructure prior to the invasion – a reconstruction contract subsequently awarded to KBR itself.[168] Safeguards against contractor abuse, such as the US Federal Acquisition Regulation which proscribes that only up to 85 per cent of contract cost could be reimbursed until all task orders have

---

[163] GAO, *Military Operations: DOD's Extensive Use of Logistics Support Contracts Requires Strengthened Oversight*, p. 8.

[164] *Ibid.*, p. 8.

[165] *Ibid.*, Highlights.

[166] GAO, *Contract Management: Contracting for Iraq Reconstruction and for Global Logistic Support*, GAO-04–869T (Washington DC, 15 June 2004), p. 5.

[167] GAO, *Military Operations: DOD's Extensive Use of Logistics Support Contracts Requires Strengthened Oversight*, p. 4.

[168] GAO, *Contract Management: Contracting for Iraq Reconstruction and for Global Logistic Support*, pp. 5–6. Normally, it is not permitted for a contractor that develops a project plan to subsequently bid for it. See CorpWatch, *Houston, We Still Have a Problem. An Alternative Report on Halliburton* (May 2005), p. 4.

been defined, were frequently ignored.[169] The US Army was especially reluctant to withhold payments until task orders had been definitized because it feared this would endanger the provision of crucial military services in Iraq.[170] In deviation from US government procurement rules, the army thus decided not to delay payments to KBR for LOGCAP services in spite of Defence Contract Audit Agency reports that KBR lacked sufficient controls in its subcontracts and allegations of overcharging.[171]

Another long-term problem in international deployments has concerned contract management and supervision. The DOD had already lacked sufficient contracting staff in its operation in the Balkans. In Iraq the pressure on contract management further increased due to the growing number and complexity of contracts. The difficulties were exacerbated by the small number of contract oversight teams in the country and the inadequate training of military personnel responsible for monitoring contracts.[172] As a result, US Army investigators opened nearly fifty criminal probes into contractors employed in Iraq and the global 'war on terror' ranging from 'high-dollar fraud to conspiracy to bribery and bid rigging'.[173] Moreover, contractor management and surveillance improved only marginally during the intervention. In June 2004 the Defence Contract Audit Agency had only twenty-eight auditors to manage more than eighty prime contracts and hundreds of subcontracts in the value of up to $34.6 billion.[174] By 2007 these personnel shortages had still not been addressed because of alternative commitments and a lack of staff within the main armed forces' contracting agencies.[175] As a LOGCAP contracting official reported, he simply did not have the time or personnel to supervise the provision of services at the twenty-seven installations under his control during his six-month tour in Iraq.[176]

---

[169] Statement for the Record of Dr Dov S. Zakheim, Under Secretary of Defense (Comptroller), House Committee on Government Reform, 11 March 2004.

[170] E. Eckholm, 'No Cut in Halliburton Payments', *New York Times*, 4 February 2005; Reuters, 'US Army Won't Withhold Payment to Halliburton', *New York Times*, 2 February 2005.

[171] Defense Contract Audit Agency, *Audit Report No. 3311–2002K11010001* (Houston, 13 May 2004).

[172] GAO, *Military Operations: DOD's Extensive Use of Logistics Support Contracts Requires Strengthened Oversight*, p. 4.

[173] J. Heilprin, 'U.S. Army Probes War Contractor Fraud', *Associated Press*, 27 January 2007.

[174] Statement of Mr William H. Reed, Director, Defense Contract Audit Agency, House Committee on Government Reform, 9 June 2004.

[175] GAO, *Military Operations: High-Level DOD Action Needed*, p. 21.

[176] *Ibid.*, p. 22.

In summary, although Neoliberalism suggests several mechanisms to counteract war profiteering and facilitate democratic oversight of private military contractors, such as competition, contractual penalties, and management and surveillance of contractors, the UK and US governments failed to consistently apply these measures in Iraq. In what was essentially a war, the armed forces were more concerned with the speed and quality of military support services than their cost efficiency. Rather than punishing companies such as KBR for fraud, the military accredited them very good or excellent performance.[177] Even where overcharging was confirmed, the armed forces only reduced invoices to match the approximate real cost. The general lesson for private military contractors was that if auditors did not discover a company defrauding it, the company would receive full payments; if discovered, it would merely have to refund the excess charges without the fear of further consequences.

Lack of private-military coordination

Lastly, the Iraq war significantly expanded the complexity of private-military coordination. In previous wars private contractors had largely remained behind the lines. In Iraq the military and private contractors worked side by side within a conflict environment. The fact that the coalition forces did not have a formal command and control relationship with private security contractors employed by other actors, unless they entered a military facility, complicated the collaboration between the military and private security firms.[178] While contractors deployed with the UK and US military forces were subject to military rules of engagement, private security guards working for civilian government agencies or private businesses at first only had informal contacts 'based on personal relationships' with the coalition commanders.[179] The degree of cooperation varied widely because of the reliance on informal and personal contacts between the military and the contractors. Some private firms and commanders were interested in and amenable to the idea of improved coordination, others were not.[180] Where voluntary cooperation worked, information exchanges helped to avoid private guards being caught between the lines. However, failure was equally frequent. Officers of the US 2nd Armored Cavalry Regiment thus reported an

---

[177] C. R. Babcock, 'KBR Gets $72 Million in Bonuses for Iraq Work', *Washington Post*, 11 May 2005.
[178] GAO, *Rebuilding Iraq*, pp. 20–1.
[179] *Ibid.*, p. 22.   [180] *Ibid.*, p. 22.

instance in which 'security providers escorted the CAP administrator into an area of operation without the squadron's knowledge and while the squadron was conducting an operation in Najaf ... a fire fight broke out at the CPA administrator's location and the squadron had to send in troops to rescue the CAP administrator and his party'.[181] Sometimes coordination and cooperation between the military and the private security contractors broke down completely. In May 2005, for instance, nineteen Zapata Engineering guards fired at US Marines. According to the military, the security contractors were in trucks and sport-utility vehicles when they started shooting at an armed forces observation post. The same Zapata team later shot at another post. The marines stopped the private security guards and held them in custody for three days. The Zapata employees in turn accused the marines of mistreatment during the arrest and their time in custody.[182] The reverse situation of 'blue on white' incidents in which the multinational forces fired at private security teams were more typical, especially when contractors approached military convoys and checkpoints.[183] Between January and May 2005 the multinational forces counted twenty incidents, with the actual number of likely cases being much higher because contractors had stopped reporting them. The high number of blue on white fire was attributed to 'the military's concerns over insurgents using vehicle-borne improvised explosive devices' and was not alleviated by recognized procedures for passing checkpoints and convoys.[184]

One of the assumptions of the Neoliberal model of fragmented governance is that multiple actors are best able to coordinate and negotiate their collaboration without government intervention. Iraq illustrated that, in contingency operations, the fog of war, complexity, speed, lethality, divergent rationales and competing interests seriously inhibit voluntary cooperation between the military and private contractors. The US government, therefore, proposed to hire a private company to facilitate the exchange of crucial information about troop and private contractor movements in the battlefield. In 2004 the CAP Project and Contracting Office set about institutionalizing this formal, though still voluntary, scheme. The plans envisaged the establishment of Reconstructions Operations Centres (ROCs) in each of the eighteen Iraqi governorates to analyse and disseminate relevant security information to private security companies working in the area. The contract with the Department of the Army was awarded to Aegis and signed in

[181] *Ibid.*, p. 22.
[182] G. Witte, 'Contractors Deny They Shot at Marines, Allege Mistreatment', *Washington Post*, 10 June 2005.
[183] GAO, *Rebuilding Iraq*, pp. 26–7.   [184] *Ibid.*, p. 27.

May 2004. It required Aegis to 'work in conjunction with the appropriate military and civil authorities to establish a primary threat assessment and interpretation cell, which is capable of managing and disseminating information. This primary cell is required to convey expeditiously all information that may affect the security of reconstruction private and sub-contractors . . .'[185]

Operational from October 2004, the primary ROC in Baghdad was open to civilian government agencies, non-governmental organizations (NGOs) and private security contractors working in Iraq. In addition, Aegis established six regional ROCs in Basra, Diwaniyah, Fallujah, Tikrit, Mosul and Camp Victory after it convinced the managing Project and Contracting Office that ROCs aligned with the Major Subordinate Commands and Gulf Region Division deployment were more suited to the task than eighteen centres in each of the governorates.[186] The ROCs provided a number of services ranging from unclassified intelligence information and exchange with private security companies, port of emergency calls for military assistance and medical support, and communication between the military and contractors, which were difficult because of the lack of radio interoperability.[187] The ROC also sought to help improve military knowledge of contractor movement and in turn offered information about military convoys, which private contractors could track in real time.[188]

The response to the ROCs was generally positive. Although private security providers noted that they rarely called for emergency quick reaction forces because insurgent attacks were mostly of short duration, one contractor who did contact the ROC for help received military support within fifteen minutes.[189] However, several problems remained because the project did not consider the fundamental differences between military and private contractor rationales and modes of operation. The armed forces frequently continued to view private security contractors as an obstacle or additional burden on their scarce resources, such as when soldiers had to come to their rescue, while private contractors believed the military targeted them without provocation. A ROC analysis thus found that the number of blue on white fire incidents did not decrease as much as expected. The situation only improved after the multinational corps issued clear procedures for

---

[185] Office of the Special Inspector General for Iraq Reconstruction, *Audit Report: Compliance with Contract No. W911S0–04–C-0003 Awarded to Aegis Defence Services Limited* (20 April 2005), p. 6.
[186] *Ibid.*, p.22.   [187] GAO, *Rebuilding Iraq*, pp. 25–6.
[188] *Ibid.*, p. 26.   [189] *Ibid.*, p. 25.

private security contractors approaching military convoys and check-points where most of the incidents had occurred.[190] What was needed, according to the military, was a greater awareness among soldiers of how to handle contractors and their incorporation into the training and standards of the military. In short, the government would only be able to use contractors effectively on the battlefield if they could be assimilated within the existing roles and relations of the armed forces.

Conclusion

The Iraq war has been widely cited to explain the growth of the role of the private military industry in international interventions. In particular, these explanations refer to the demands for additional military and security personnel created by the unexpected deterioration of public security after the collapse of Saddam Hussein's regime, the lack of international military support for the operation and rotational requirements due to the length of the conflict. What these arguments fail to consider is how the UK and US governments came to be in this situation, and why they chose to rely on private military contractors, while other countries such as Germany primarily rely on national soldiers. This chapter has suggested that both questions can only be fully answered by taking into consideration the ideological preference of the UK and the USA for the Neoliberal model of fragmented security governance based on market mechanisms and the private supply of military and security services, while Germany still subscribes to the Republican ideal of limiting the role of private contractors in national defence and deployed operations. It has argued that recent interventions illustrate the British and American extension of the Neoliberal models of the state and the soldier to the international level. The Iraq war has typified this transformation in several respects, ranging from the differentiated perception of national security interests, the preference for flexible coalitions of the willing, the limitation of Iraqi national sovereignty and the reliance on private military contractors for fragmented security policy decision-making and implementation.

Although the UK and US governments have sponsored the growing role of private contractors in global interventions, they have been surprisingly unprepared for some of its consequences. The Iraq war has specifically demonstrated the failure of both governments to fully consider the implications of the privatization of security governance for military operations and the democratic control over the legitimate use

---

[190] *Ibid.*, p. 27.

of collective violence in international relations. Some of these implications have already been discussed with regard to the employment of private military contractors in national defence. The conditions characteristic of deployed military operations have exacerbated them. In particular, the proliferation and increasing authority of private military contractors with regard to public security in Iraq have further undermined the model of the professional soldier, while furnishing private military contractors with additional legitimacy. The emergence of an occupational view of the military profession has contributed to declining recruitment and retention among the national armed forces, but recent interventions have provided increasing opportunity and normative sanctions for alternative military careers in the better-paying and more flexible private sector. However, the new role of private military contractors has also changed their own status. Initially disregarded, contractors have become equal and legitimate targets of insurgent attacks alongside professional armed forces. Both the growing contribution of private contractors to the military operation and public security and the involvement of contractors in hostilities have demonstrated that the traditional hierarchical and centralized modes of operation and decision-making are unsuited to the increasingly complex interdependence between public and private security providers. Nevertheless, neither the armed forces nor the governments which have facilitated this transformation have prepared new models for the emerging fragmented structure of security governance.

The UK and the US governments have also spent little effort on considering and developing the formal and informal institutional structures and relations required for effective and democratically accountable security governance within their Neoliberal framework. While the two governments have pressed ahead with the privatization and outsourcing of military services in international security, they failed to recognize that existing mechanisms of democratic accountability and control did not match the newly evolving fragmented governance arrangements. In Iraq the democratic oversight of the private use of violence and the provision of military services was, therefore, seriously incapacitated. Private military contractors permitted the UK and US governments to circumvent popular protest and congressional and parliamentary control over the deployment of national soldiers for the intervention in Iraq. In addition, many contractors operated outside the military chain of command and national or international laws and regulations. Finally, the armed forces were insufficiently staffed and trained to fulfil their new contractor management and surveillance functions. The largely reactive responses of the UK and US administrations to the immediate problems in Iraq have also failed to reconsider Neoliberal principles of democratic control and accountability. The reflexive reactions have been to try to expand existing regulations to cover private contractors and to seek to reduce the management burden on the armed forces by promoting partnerships with industry.

The resulting arrangements meet neither Republican nor Neoliberal ideals. In fact, the UK and the US governments have moved further away from the Neoliberal model of the democratic state and the armed forces. Instead of limiting the size and powers of the state, the use of private military contractors has permitted both governments to effectively double their military contingents without making legislative approval necessary. In the place of competition between public and private security providers, the requirements of speed and flexibility during a military operation have created a free-for-all for private contractors who are frequently hired on a sole-source basis and who operate with little government supervision.

In addition, the outsourcing of a large part of public security provision to private companies has brought about a fundamental change in the roles of and relations between private military contractors, the contracting governments and their armed forces. Since the former directly and extensively contribute to the provision of security in deployed operations, private contractors have not only become more extensively involved in information and intelligence exchanges, they have effectively become an integral part of military operations. The dividing line between private military staff and professional soldiers has thus been eroded and established mechanisms of democratic control over international interventions have been undermined. The general implications of this erosion for the relationship between the state, the citizen and the soldier within contemporary democracy will be explored in the next chapter.

8   The future of democratic security: contractorization or cosmopolitanism?

As the preceding chapters have illustrated, the roles of and relations between the state, the citizen and the soldier in Western democracies have repeatedly transformed due to changing internal and external circumstances during the past three centuries. Internally, the competition between Republicanism and Liberalism has offered diverging models for the democratic control over the use of collective force. Externally, varying threats and security challenges, ranging from the two World Wars to transnational terrorism, have presented different demands on national armed forces. Both internal and external factors have been inextricably linked. Changes in the international security environment have led to reformulations of Republican and Liberal theories, while revisions of both ideologies have in turn influenced interpretations of national and international security demands and how best to respond to them within the framework of modern democracy. However, these transformations have not been unproblematic. The preceding case studies of civil-military relations in the UK, the USA, Germany and contemporary international interventions have demonstrated that the theoretical models presented by Republicanism and Neoliberalism have become corrupted in the process of their adaptation to the contemporary security environment and the political praxis, including the transnationalization of the private military industry, the growing dependence of governments on private contractors, and the weakening of public oversight and parliamentary control.

This chapter discusses how the Republican and Neoliberal models might be reformed in order to address these challenges in the future. To do so, it returns to the two factors which have served as the evaluative standards and primary reasons for changes in civil-military relations over the past three centuries: the suitability of different models of the state and the soldier for particular security environments and democratic control over the use of armed force. This chapter contains three sections. The first section analyses the changed security perception in the UK, the USA and Germany and outlines how the transformations presented in the preceding case studies have failed to meet both the security objectives and the Neoliberal and Republican standards of democratic control set by these three governments. The second section discusses how these Republican and Neoliberal models of the state may be revised to improve the effectiveness and democratic control of the UK, US and German armed forces in the new millennium. It presents two competing ideological visions for the future of national and international security within modern democracy: Neoliberal security governance and Cosmopolitan Republican government. The third section proposes two models of the soldier which would be congruent with these visions, namely the transnational private military contractor and the cosmopolitan citizen-soldier. The chapter concludes by arguing that neither revision can meet all possible challenges, but they suggest how democratic control over the changing military forces in Western democracies might be adapted to the changing security environment in a consistent and comprehensive manner.

New security challenges and civil-military relations

Changes in the external security environment have been among the primary explanations for the privatization and outsourcing of military services in Europe and North America. However, external factors cannot fully explain the related transformations of the models of the state, the citizen and the soldier, nor does privatization necessarily seem the most appropriate and democratic response to the changing security context. The following section discusses the key features of the new security environment and the problems with contemporary policy responses in the UK, the USA and Germany.

The changing security environment

Although the end of the Cold War has been a watershed in the evolution of the national and international security environments of European and North American democracies, the security context has by no means remained stable. Instead threat perception has shifted from civil war to transnational terrorism and from rogue states to environmental degradation. The expectation of a more stable and peaceful 'new world order' after the end of the superpower conflict and the dissolution of the Warsaw Pact did not last long. The break-up of Yugoslavia in the early 1990s suggested that civil wars and ethnic conflicts on the outskirts of the enlarging EU would pose new threats to national security, including from refugee flows, transnational crime and uncontrolled weapons transfers. Governments in Europe and North America also seemed prepared to

Table 8.1. *Government threat perception in the 1990s*[1]

UK – Strategic Defence Review 1998	USA – National Security Strategy 1999	Germany – Defence White Paper 1994
1. Civil war	1. Rogue and failed states	1. Failure of democracy in Eastern Europe and the Russian Federation
2. Rogue states	2. Terrorism, drug trade, arms trafficking, organized crime, migration	2. Civil war
3. WMD		3. Ethnic conflict
4. Organized crime		4. Conflicts and instability in developing countries
5. Terrorism	3. WMD	5. Environmental degradation
6. Information technology	4. Failed states	6. Migration
7. Environmental degradation	5. Foreign intelligence	7. Armaments proliferation
	6. Environmental and health threats	8. WMD

accept greater international responsibility for peacekeeping and peace-making, as illustrated by the interventions in Somalia and Haiti. Yet despite massive cuts in their national armed forces in response to the decreased threat from the Soviet Union, national security strategies in Europe and North America changed little and only slowly. The US government's National Security Strategies of 1997 and 1999 were still largely concerned with traditional security threats, and the UK government did not see the need for a Strategic Defence Review until 1998.[2] Germany, in fact, only modified its security rationale in 2003 when the Defence Policy Guidelines recognized that conflict prevention and resolution abroad had superseded the need for a conventional defence of German territory.[3]

Common to the first reformulations of Western defence strategies after the end of the Cold War was the preservation of a fairly traditional outlook, which largely focused on military security threats and considered nation-states as primary adversaries, albeit now in the guise of rogue and failed states, as Table 8.1 indicates.[4] The strategies

[1] MOD, *Strategic Defence Review. Modern Forces for the Modern World* (London, July 1998), para. 78; White House, *A National Security Strategy for a New Century* (1999), pp. 2–3; Bundesministerium der Verteidigung, *Weißbuch 1994* (Bonn, 1994), pp. 30–5.

[2] White House, *A National Security Strategy for a New Century* (Washington DC: May 1997); White House, *A National Security Strategy for a New Century* (Washington DC: December 1999); J. Sperling and L. Tossutti, *National Threat Perception: Survey Results from the United States*, Garnet Working Paper No. 18.11 (May 2007), p. 25.

[3] Bundesministerium der Verteidigung, *Verteidigungspolitische Richtlinien für den Bereich des Bundesministers der Verteidigung* (Berlin, 21 May 2003), p. 19.

[4] Sperling and Tossutti, *National Threat Perception: Survey Results from the United States*, p. 25.

Table 8.2. *Elite threat perception in 2006*[5]

UK	USA	Germany
1. Terrorism	1. Terrorism	1. Terrorism
2. Environmental degradation	2. Macro-economic instability	2. Environmental degradation
3. Natural disasters		3. Cyber attack
4. Macro-economic instability	3. Biological and chemical attack	4. Macro-economic instability
5. Narcotics trafficking	4. Environmental degradation	5. Migratory pressures
6. Biological and chemical attack	5. Nuclear and radiological attack	6. Natural disasters
7. Migratory pressures	6. Conventional war	7. Narcotics trafficking
	7. Cyber attack	

mentioned non-military security concerns, such as environmental degradation, only as secondary threats. Military means and the armed forces remained central to national and international security.[6] Although peacekeeping and humanitarian aid were already becoming key functions of the armed forces, militaries such as that of the UK 'continued to focus their structure, doctrine and ethos around more traditional ideas of warfare'.[7] In the USA the emphasis on combat operations and war fighting was even stronger. Even the German Bundeswehr, which had disavowed foreign military interventions after the Second World War, was concerned with developing a new force structure suitable for military support operations abroad.

After the terrorist attacks of 11 September 2001 threat perception in Europe and North America changed again. As Table 8.2 illustrates, non-state threats led by terrorism, environmental degradation and macro-economic instability have become top security priorities in the views of governments and national security policy elites. Other new security issues have included concerns over immigration and energy security. In spite of this transition, many governments have continued to focus on military means when it comes to national and international

---

[5] Data from Sperling and Tossutti, *National Threat Perception: Survey Results from the United States*, p. 25; Krahmann, *National Threat Perception: Survey Results from the UK*; Gimesi *et al.*, *National Threat Perception: Survey Results from Germany*, p. 10.

[6] MOD, *Strategic Defence Review*, Cm 3999 (London: The Stationery Office, 1998), para. 78.

[7] A. Dorman, 'The United Kingdom', in L. Elliott and G. Cheeseman (eds.) *Forces for Good: Cosmopolitan Militaries in the Twenty-first Century* (Manchester: Manchester University Press, 2004), p. 237.

security. The UK and the USA especially have 'returned to a greater emphasis on war-fighting tasks' as part of the 'war on terror'.[8]

Despite their diversity, the new security threats have three character-istics in common. Firstly, they are not caused by national armed forces. Secondly, the dangers are transnational or global. Thirdly, they are non-existential, i.e., they threaten the Western 'way of life' rather than state and societal survival.[9] As a consequence, many of the new threats fall outside the traditional Westphalian conception of national and inter-national security based on the state monopoly on collective violence. An outcome of the association of the Social Contract with the nation-state, the Westphalian model legitimized the sovereign and later democratic use of armed force by the state to protect its citizens internally and against other states externally. As the Social Contract sought to eliminate or at least control the threat of violence from citizens against each other, so the Westphalian system aimed to pacify international relations by recogniz-ing the state as the sole sovereign and legitimate military power in world politics. Contemporary security issues challenge this model because they derive from the use of violence by non-state actors such as warlords, ter-rorists and criminals. Moreover, many contemporary security concerns are not related to the unregulated use of violence. Environmental prob-lems, economic crises and energy shortages are rather the unintended consequences of legal, social and economic interaction.

Since most of the perceived threats to democracies in Europe and North America do not emanate from states but from non-state actors, they typically affect citizens across national boundaries. Globalization has increased social and economic interconnectedness and interdependence, bringing with it greater vulnerability and new potential for conflict.[10] The elimination of trade barriers and the merging of financial markets have created an economic system where national or regional crises have global repercussions. Although people still cross borders less easily than goods do, international traffic has multiplied, facilitating migration and the spread of infectious diseases. Knowledge and information flows around global communication networks have given rise to greater awareness of inequalities and have opened up new avenues for criminals and terrorists

---

[8] *Ibid.*, p. 243.
[9] Even WMD rarely figure as an existential threat in Western threat perception other than in terms of a terrorist use of chemical, biological or nuclear devices.
[10] P. Cerny, 'Neomedievalism, Civil War and the New Security Dilemma: Globalisation as Durable Disorder', *Civil Wars*, 1, no. 1 (1998), 36–64; E. Krahmann, 'From State to Non-state Actors: The Emergence of Security Governance', in E. Krahmann (ed.) *New Threats and New Actors in International Sec*urity (New York: Palgrave, 2005), pp. 3–19; B. Zangl and M. Zürn, 'The Effects of Denationalization on Security in the OECD World', *Global Society*, 13, no. 2 (1999), 139–61.

to target societies. The scale of economic industrialization has moved beyond localized pollution to threaten the global environment. Western democracies have difficulties in addressing these new security threats unilaterally within their sovereign territories. Whether terrorist attacks, climate change or economic instability, many current security concerns require subnational, transnational and global collaboration with other state and non-state actors in order to be effective.[11]

Finally, the majority of threats faced by citizens in Europe and North America are non-existential. During the Cold War era a potential military exchange between NATO and Warsaw Pact members threatened the nuclear annihilation of Central Europe. Now governments and citizens agree that existing security issues are more likely to endanger their lifestyles than their lives. Terrorist attacks and the use of weapons of mass destruction (WMD) are unlikely to cause massive casualties among Western populations and are feared primarily because of their potential impact on economic stability and the Western 'way of life'.[12] The events of 11 September 2001 have been a case in point. Although the attack caused 2,981 deaths, the highest number of terrorist casualties in a single incident at the time of writing, this number was marginal compared to the 42,643 US citizens who died in traffic-related incidents that year.[13] However, the terrorist attacks had major repercussions on the financial markets and, thus, the US and world economy, while the traffic accidents did not.

The changing nature of contemporary security concerns seems to demand the modification of national and international security policies. Foremost, it questions the utility of military force as the primary means for maintaining peace and security. Traditionally trained and equipped to fight each other, national armed forces struggle to adapt to new tasks, such as combating terrorism, managing conflicts and providing relief in humanitarian emergencies.[14] The variability and complexity of these

---

[11] U. Beck, 'The Terrorist Threat: World Risk Society Revisited', *Theory, Culture & Society*, 19, no. 4 (2002), 39–55; The Commission on Global Governance, *Our Global Neighborhood* (Oxford: Oxford University Press, 1995).

[12] M. Clarke, 'Memorandum Submitted on the Foreign and Security Policy Aspects of the Strategic Defence Review', *Eighth Report: The Strategic Defence Review, Volume II – Minutes of Evidence & Memoranda*, HC 138-I (London: The Stationery Office, 10 September 1998).

[13] National Commission on Terrorist Attacks Upon the United States, *The 9/11 Commission Report*, Executive Summary (Washington DC: Government Printing Office, 22 July 2004); US Bureau of Transportation Statistics, *National Transportation Statistics* (2005).

[14] C. C. Moskos, J. A. Williams and D. R. Segal, 'Armed Forces after the Cold War', in C. C. Moskos, J. A. Williams and D. R. Segal (eds.) *The Postmodern Military. Armed Forces after the Cold War* (Oxford: Oxford University Press, 2000), p. 3.

tasks, as well as their civilian rather than military characteristics, distinguish them from war-fighting. Modern soldiers as often safeguard the distribution of humanitarian aid, resettle refugees and eradicate poppy fields as they deploy to fight an armed enemy. In spite of national security strategies which rank non-military threats above others, national militaries very much remain fighting forces. In fact, the outsourcing of non-core functions to private contractors has strengthened the military's focus on combat operations. Unsurprisingly, political elites in the UK, the USA and Germany regard the military as the least suitable instrument for addressing contemporary security threats after police and intelligence cooperation, economic aid, diplomacy, special operations and other mechanisms.[15] Moreover, 'Anglo-Western society has also come to view their militaries in a different light since the end of the Cold War. The legitimacy of public authority, spending priorities, and professional military autonomy has faced increasing scrutiny and doubt.'[16]

Beyond questioning the utility of military forces for the protection of citizens in Western democracies, the transnational character of contemporary security threats challenges the state monopoly on the legitimate use of violence and the foundations of the Social Contract itself. If citizens perceive their states and armed forces to be no longer capable of supplying effective security, they may turn to alternative providers such as private security firms or international organizations. In Europe and North America this has been happening on a large scale. In the UK the turnover of the private security industry nearly quadrupled between 1990 and 2005.[17] In the USA spending on private security has been nearly twice as high as that for public law enforcement, and private security officers have outnumbered public police in the region of three to one.[18]

The non-existential nature of most contemporary security problems decreases citizens' willingness to accept large military budgets and to contribute personally to national defence. Often described as a postmodern condition, citizens no longer view their security exclusively in

---

[15] Sperling and Tossutti, *National Threat Perception: Survey Results from the United States*; E. Krahmann, *National Threat Perception: Survey Results from the UK*, Garnet Working Paper No. 18.10 (May 2007); T. Gimesi *et al.*, *National Threat Perception: Survey Results from Germany*, Garnet Working Paper No. 18.6 (May 2007).

[16] H. J. Bondy, 'Postmodernism and the Source of Military Strength in the Anglo West', *Armed Forces & Society*, 31, no. 1 (2004), 32.

[17] British Security Industry Association (BSIA), *Members Turnover Statistics*, at: www.bsia.co.uk.

[18] D. L. Altheide and R. S. Michalowski, 'Fear in the News: A Discourse of Control', *The Sociological Quarterly*, 40, no. 3 (1999), 481.

terms of their state and national armed forces.[19] Instead, citizens are concerned about increasingly diverse, complex and, seemingly, distant sets of security issues which appear to leave room for personal interpretations and differences. According to Ipsos MORI surveys, UK citizens are as worried about crime, healthcare and migration as they are about defence.[20] In Germany 60 per cent of the population feel threatened by cuts in social services, 56 per cent by economic instability, 41 per cent by crime and 29 per cent by conflicts abroad. Only 25 per cent of Germans perceive a personal threat from a terrorist attack and 14 per cent from a military attack against German territory.[21]

The increasing diversity of threat perception offers greater freedom of manoeuvre when deciding which security threats to address and which to ignore. In the absence of direct dangers to the national territory, military operations have become 'wars of choice'.[22] However, since the benefits of international interventions for national security are not clear, the new wars of choice are subject to greater political controversy. The US government learned this lesson in Somalia where it decided to abandon its mission after the killing of eighteen American soldiers in an abortive attempt to arrest warlord Mohammed Farah Aidid. In Germany only a minority of 34 per cent of citizens believe that their country should always help other nations in conflicts and crises. Conversely, 20 per cent say it depends on the situation and 43 per cent are principally against an interventionist security policy.[23] The further away a conflict, the less likely citizens are to support a military intervention.[24] More than in previous conflicts, wars of choice raise questions about the cost and benefits of interventions, the legitimacy of using military force, public support and democratic control and accountability.[25] Nevertheless, national policies in the UK, the USA and Germany have only partially adapted to these developments.

---

[19] Moskos *et al.*, 'Armed Forces after the Cold War', p. 4; B. Booth, M. Kestnbaum and D. R. Segal, 'Are Post-Cold War Militaries Postmodern?' *Armed Forces & Society*, 27, no. 3 (2001), 338.

[20] Ipsos MORI, *Long Term Monitor: Most Important Issues Facing Britain Today* (2007), at: www.ipsos-mori.com.

[21] T. Bulmahn, 'Das sicherheits- und verteidigungspolitische Meinungsbild in Deutschland', *SOWI.NEWS*, no. 1 (2006), 2.

[22] R. Haas, 'Wars of Choice', *Washington Post*, 23 November 2003. See also C. Dandeker and L. Freedman, 'The British Armed Services', *The Political Quarterly*, 73, no. 4 (2002), 467.

[23] Bulmahn, 'Das sicherheits- und verteidigungspolitische Meinungsbild in Deutschland', p. 3.

[24] *Ibid.*, p. 9.

[25] A. Forster, 'Breaking the Covenant: Governance of the British Army in the Twenty-first Century', *International Affairs*, 82, no. 6 (2006), 1045.

Transformations in civil-military relations

Despite the changes in the national and international environments, Western armed forces have become more rather than less focused on combat fighting since the end of the Cold War. The privatization of military support functions has played a major role in this transformation. However, its implications for civil-military relations and democratic control over the use of collective violence have been neglected. As the experiences in the UK, the USA, Germany and international interventions examined in the preceding case studies have illustrated, problems for democratic control and accountability derive from the modification of the roles and relations of the state and the soldier. With regard to the democratic control of the state, these problems occur in three areas: public information and parliamentary scrutiny, executive autonomy, and collusion between the government, the armed forces and industry.

One of the foremost problems of recent transformations in civil-military relations has been the negative impact of military outsourcing and privatization on public information and parliamentary control over defence spending and the use of armed force in deployed operations. In the UK and the USA both have declined because of off-the-book accounting of PFIs, the lock-in of future budgets due to long-term contracting and the confidentiality of government-industry contracts. While Neoliberalism asserts that competition between states and markets enhances electoral and parliamentary control over military expenditure, the privatization of military services has thus gone hand in hand with limiting the ability of electorates to scrutinize defence spending. Even in Germany, which has sought to protect centralized and democratic control over the defence establishment through government shares in formally private defence firms and by restricting the scope for the outsourcing of military services, the lack of clear lines of oversight and accountability in public-private joint ventures has obstructed electoral and parliamentary oversight.

Secondly, in spite of divergent ideological models of the state, the privatization of military services has expanded the autonomy of government executives vis-à-vis the legislative with regard to the armed forces and their use in the UK, the USA and Germany. This problem arises from the ability of the executives and the armed forces in all three countries to independently determine the outsourcing of military tasks.[26]

---

[26] D. Avant and L. Sigelman, 'What Does Private Security in Iraq Mean for US Democracy at Home?', Research Paper, January 2008, pp. 15–17.

This ability not only limits the role of parliaments in deciding what types of functions are contracted out to private firms, but also allows the executives to circumvent parliamentary approval for the deployment of soldiers abroad. The considerable executive autonomy gained by using private military contractors is made more problematic by cuts in civil and military service personnel which have reduced the executives' own ability to monitor the growing number of private contractors employed in national and international security.

Thirdly, persistent government preferences for national firms, the consolidation of the defence industry, and the expansion of sole-source contracting and public-private partnerships in the UK, the USA and Germany have decreased competition and increased the influence of private firms irrespective of whether these countries have embraced Neoliberal or Republican models of the state. Rather than facilitating citizens' control over the provision and use of military force through the fragmentation of political power, the outsourcing of military services has augmented the power of the private military industry. Moreover, the dependence of national armed forces on a shrinking number of transnational defence corporations has restricted their ability to punish or exclude from future contracts businesses which fail to meet established cost-efficiency targets or which overcharge the military. In Germany this dependence has even been formalized through the creation of public-private joint ventures such as the Bw Fuhrpark Services GmbH and the Heeresinstandsetzungslogistik GmbH, which have united government and industry interests in a corporate format.

While the problems created by the transformation of the state have been similar in the UK, the USA and Germany, they have diverged significantly with regard to the soldier. In the UK and the USA internal factors related to the transition from the model of the professional soldier to the private military contractor have presented the primary challenge to democratic control of the armed forces. In Germany the main challenge has arisen from external factors linked to the changing functions of the Bundeswehr and its consequences for the Republican ideal of the citizen-soldier. In the UK and the USA three problems have affected democratic control of the armed forces and the soldier. The first has been the weakening of the ethos of the professional soldier who puts duty over rights and perceives his or her work as a vocation rather than a mere occupation. This fading of the professional ethos and identity of the all-volunteer forces has contributed to the undermining of the democratic character of the military by weakening the self-regulatory capabilities of the military. It has diminished the degree to which professional military standards, such as duty, honour, sacrifice and political neutrality, have been able to prevent soldiers and the armed forces from behaving contrary to public norms and expectations.

Another problem has been the perceived betrayal of the covenant between the state, society and the professional armed forces. The covenant, which promised a special social status and government care for those who promised to risk their lives to protect other citizens, has been a key part of the professional armed force's commitment to the defence of the democratic state. However, declining job security, narrowing career options, worsening working and living conditions, and increasing deployments have created the impression that the state no longer keeps its side of the bargain. These problems have been exacerbated by the fact that many professional soldiers in the UK and the USA work alongside private military contractors who have significantly better pay and employment conditions than they do, and at less risk to their personal lives. As a consequence, professional soldiers have found their loyalty towards the democratic state and their societies increasingly stretched and have left the armed forces in considerable numbers.

The widening gap between citizens and the armed forces has also been problematic. Partially due to the increasing professionalization and contractorization of the military, which have permitted the UK and US armed forces to focus on combat functions and become even more distant from civilian society, a pervasive lack of public knowledge and interest in the military has been generated. Since professional soldiers are bound by the notion of political neutrality, the democratic process has thus become skewed in favour of the executive and private military companies who freely lobby government bodies and parliament.

Whereas in the UK and the USA the concerns over the democratic control of the soldier have originated in the transition from professional soldiers to contractors, in Germany the main problems have stemmed from the perceived unsuitability of the Republican model of the citizen-soldier for the new security environment. Specifically, the citizen-soldier model has posed two problems for existing mechanisms of democratic oversight and the use of the German armed forces: the inequality of conscription, and international collaboration and deployments outside Germany. The growing inequality of conscription has presented the most serious challenge to the democratic control of the Bundeswehr because of the central role of the draft in integrating the military with German society. According to the Republican citizen-soldier model, civil-military integration ensures civilian control over the armed forces, facilitates the congruence of soldiers' norms with those of the society, and contributes to public knowledge about security and defence policies. The legitimacy of the duty of citizens to serve as citizen-soldiers, however, rests on its universal application.[27] The shrinking of the Bundeswehr in response to the decreased military threat to the national territory has, thus, created significant problems for conscription. Only the growing number of young men who opt for civilian rather than military service has saved the model so far.

The second concern for the democratic control of the Bundeswehr has come from the pressures to professionalize the German armed forces in order to contribute to multinational operations. Since most of the new security threats require international collaboration in order to be effectively addressed, the German government has placed a considerable emphasis on multilateral missions. Moreover, the German constitution stipulates that Bundeswehr missions out of area are only permissible if conducted under the auspices of an international organization such as the UN, the EU or NATO. Both developments have been problematic because they have contradicted the traditional Republican ideal that governments cannot legitimately deploy citizen-soldiers for missions other than national defence. The citizen-soldier model of the Bundeswehr has also not been integrated easily with the professional armed forces of most of Germany's allies in Europe and North America. The professionalization of the Bundeswehr, however, would necessitate a fundamental rethinking of the mechanisms for democratic control of the armed forces which have so far rested on the identity of the 'citizen in uniform'.

Together these developments illustrate that recent adjustments to the changing security environment in Europe and North America have not been successful. Raising the question of how both Neoliberal and Republican theory might be revised in order to safeguard democratic control over the armed forces in the new millennium, the following two sections return to the ideal models of the state and the soldier.

Revisiting the role of the state

Rather than presenting fixed ideals, Republican and Liberal models of the democratic provision of national and international security have evolved over time to meet new practical and normative demands. The first major change in both models occurred during the eighteenth century with the emergence of representative democracy, in order to accommodate the growing size of self-governing communities with the rise of the democratic nation-state. The second key change happened during

---

[27] Although women are a notable exception from the draft, recent changes have improved the access of women to positions within the Bundeswehr.

the twentieth century as a result of the crisis in public service provision caused by the overstretch of the warfare state and transnational interdependence. The changing nature of security threats faced by Europe and North America and the problems with democratic control observed above challenge these ideologies again to adapt to new circumstances. This section examines recent developments in Neoliberal and Republican theories and their practical application to the role of the state in contemporary national and international security.

Neoliberal security governance

The basic tenets of the Neoliberal model rest on the fundamental belief in the superiority of the market, and the democratic credentials of fragmented and limited state power. Nevertheless, this book has argued that the Neoliberal policies adopted by the UK and the USA have not been entirely successful in meeting the problems posed by the new security environment and internal democracy. To address both issues requires a more fundamental reassessment of the Neoliberal models of the state, the citizen and the soldier. Contemporary theoretical and empirical literature proposes three mechanisms as the basis for a revision of Neoliberalism: competitive federalism, fiscal control and private standard-setting. Together they seek to improve democratic control by returning to the fundamental tenets of the Neoliberal governance model.

Foremost among these mechanisms is a promotion of competitive federalism as the ideal model of Neoliberal democratic governance.[28] Nobel Prize winner James Buchanan has developed the theory of competitive federalism in detail. According to Buchanan, 'The theory of competitive federalism emphasizes the prospects for exit, both internal and external, as constraints on political control over the individual.'[29] Similar to the market in goods, where decreasing demand leads to reductions in supply, 'exit' in the democratic system refers to the ability of citizens to opt out of and withdraw the funding for disagreeable policies and, thereby, influence political decision-making beyond the electoral process. Since states and local governments cannot afford to risk losing citizens and their tax revenue due to unpopular policies, the exit option exerts a continuous disciplining function over democratic

---

[28] A. Harmes, 'Neoliberalism and Multilevel Governance', *Review of International Political Economy*, 13, no. 5 (2006), 735. See also Y. Qian and B. R. Weingast, 'Federalism as a Commitment to Preserving Market Incentives', *Journal of Economic Perspectives*, 11, no. 4 (1997), 83–92.

[29] J. M. Buchanan, 'Federalism and Individual Sovereignty', *Cato Journal*, 15, nos. 2–3 (1995), 260.

governance. Competitive federalism aims to increase the potential for exit by creating political structures which emulate those of the market. The primary feature of these structures is that they allow citizens to choose between competing regulatory bodies as well as public and private service providers. Their secondary feature is the ability of citizens to exert direct control over the use of fiscal resources and to withhold funding from services or policies they do not want.

In order to maximize the democratic self-determination and fiscal control of citizens, competitive federalism seeks to make the units of political decision-making and public service provision as large as necessary and as small as possible. This augments democratic governance because individual interests and preferences are more likely to correspond among small and homogenous groups of citizens than among large and diverse units.[30] Presented with the challenge of increasing transnational interdependence, Neoliberal authors argue that expanding the scope of governance units which enhance market and political choices and limiting those that inhibit self-determination can help to establish competitive federalism.[31] Market-enabling structures are laws and institutions which permit exit by allowing the free movement of citizens as well as goods, capital and firms across unit boundaries. Market-inhibiting arrangements are those that impose collective restrictions, such as industry and labour regulations, and collectively financed public services, such as national healthcare, pensions and security.[32]

At a minimum, the application of competitive federalism to the provision of national and international security suggests that key to improving democratic accountability is the restoration of competition. This entails the reinvigoration of the competition between public and private providers of military services and the publication of relevant data to permit citizens to scrutinize public spending and make informed choices about the allocation of their taxes. Moreover, competition needs to be improved within the private military industry by avoiding long-term contracting and partnering arrangements which contribute to the creation of national champions and military-industrial complexes and by abandoning the preferential treatment of national firms. At a maximum, competitive federalism advocates increasing the ability of citizens to choose individually and directly among public and private security providers at the national, transnational and global levels. This involves creating market-enabling structures for the supply of military

---

[30] *Ibid.*, p. 263.
[31] Harmes, 'Neoliberalism and Multilevel Governance', pp. 735–7.
[32] *Ibid.*, p. 736.

security services at the international level and restricting compulsory security provision to the subsidiary levels.

Practical examples of competitive federalism include the facilitation of a free trade in military goods and services among NATO and EU member states through the privatization of national defence companies, the harmonization of national standards and common export regulations. Moreover, with regard to private security and policing services the EU has established the mutual recognition of national licences to enable private firms to supply their services in other member states.[33] The interest of citizens in Europe and North America in personally selecting their security providers appears to be illustrated by the exponential increase in private spending for commercial security services during the past decades, while popular demand for a peace dividend has led to declines in national defence budgets from Cold War levels.[34] With the heightened priority of non-state threats such as terrorism, crime and infectious diseases which target individual citizens rather than states, collective defence seems to be replaceable by more personal risk management in accordance with Neoliberal ideals. In addition to their individual and direct employment of private security providers at the national level, citizens are also expressing their preferences for international security provision through market behaviour. Private donations provide an important source of funding for the growing role of non-governmental organizations and charities in managing transnational security concerns such as refugee flows or HIV/AIDS. Moreover, private transnational corporations are hiring their own security firms in order to be able to access critical resources and markets in conflict regions.

The Neoliberal model also emphasizes the contribution of private standard-setting and industry self-regulation to democratic control in globalizing political, economic and security environments.[35] The ideal of self-regulation is by no means new within Neoliberal thought. However, the democratic potential of private regulation and standards seems particularly relevant in a context where actors outside state borders and national policy-making structures affect citizens' interests and security concerns. Self-regulation can not only help to overcome the difficulty of national governments to agree on transnational regimes,

[33] E. Krahmann, 'Regulating Military and Security Services in the European Union', in A. Bryden and M. Caparini (eds.) *Private Actors and Security Governance* (Münster: LIT, 2006), p. 203.
[34] British Security Industry Association (BSIA), *Members Turnover Statistics*.
[35] N. Gunningham and J. Rees, 'Industry Self-Regulation: An Institutional Perspective', *Law & Policy*, 19, no. 4 (1997), 364; D. Held, 'Law of States, Law of Peoples: Three Models of Sovereignty', *Legal Theory*, 8, no. 1 (2002), 5–17.

but also conforms with the democratic ideal of competitive federalism by delegating market-inhibiting policy decisions to subsidiary actors. The democratic value of self-regulation and private standard-setting is based on two features. Self-regulation can claim to be the result of direct and conscious deliberation among the businesses involved, which are subsequently subjected to these standards.[36] In addition, self-regulation and private standard-setting typically evolve in response to citizens' concerns about industry practices and, thus, also reflect the interests of the public.[37]

Appropriate institutional structures and government policies can strengthen the democratic potential of self-regulation and private standard-setting. Market pressures deriving from citizens' demand and consumption serve as its primary method for ensuring compliance with public expectations. In this context, industry associations can play an important role in transmitting citizens' expectations by acting as a sounding board and publicizing industry codes of conduct and best practices against which the performance of individual businesses can be measured. Notably, 'an industry's public commitment to such principles can generate new expectations of accountability, both inside and outside the industry.'[38] The public shaming of firms which fail to conform to industry standards works not only because of professional socialization, but also because it has a direct impact on a company's share value, sales and profits.

While Neoliberalism favours self-regulation at subsidiary levels, states remain important for the setting of the conditions which enable and support private industry standards. Among others, states can create a positive environment for self-regulation by eliminating policies which limit national and international competition among businesses. Governments can also assist private sector regulation by themselves acting as responsible consumers of private services. This includes buying from the best suppliers rather than from national champions and excluding from public contracts companies which fail to comply with industry best practice. More directly, governments can publicly endorse particular self-regulation schemes.[39]

The internationalization of the laws of war, criminal responsibility and humanitarian rights provide some examples for the emergence of enabling laws at the global level. Deborah Avant notes: 'Individual

---

[36] Gunningham and Rees, 'Industry Self-Regulation', p. 377.
[37] Ibid., p. 379.   [38] Ibid., p. 383.
[39] Ibid., p. 401.

military personnel cannot escape criminal responsibility for actions that violate international law by citing civilian orders. This can be cited as a budding *international* standard for military professionals.'[40] Restrictive national and transnational standards of professional conduct, in particular in the private policing sector, complement international laws. In Europe and North America there are thus numerous national and international industry associations such as the British Security Industry Association (BSIA), the Bundesverband Deutscher Wach- und Sicherheitsunternehmen e.V. (BDWS) and the Confederation of European Security Services (CoESS). Most European governments have implemented national regulations on private security companies, but industry associations play a crucial role in implementing these regulations by offering the required training or by handing out licences.[41] Private military companies are also increasingly developing individual and industry-wide codes of conduct within collective associations such as IPOA and BAPSC. Although so far their efforts have had only limited success, both associations seek to gain greater credibility for their private standards by seeking recognition from governments and NGOs. BAPSC, in particular, has hoped to receive UK government accreditation since the government has been unable to agree on a national regulation of private military firms following the publication of its advisory Green Paper in 2002. The US-based IPOA has, alternatively, investigated the willingness of NGOs to act as external and independent monitors of its code of conduct in order to increase the accountability and transparency of its members.

A revised Neoliberalism thus aims to address the problems of democratic control over national and international security posed externally by the changing character of contemporary security threats and internally by the lack of public information and parliamentary scrutiny, government-industry collusion and increased executive autonomy. The ideal of competitive federalism answers to the demands of the non-military, transnational and non-existential nature of contemporary security threats through a system of multilevel governance at the local, national, regional and global levels. Based on the principle of subsidiarity, this system offers to improve democratic control and accountability by addressing threats at their appropriate levels and by encouraging the transnational self-regulation of the security sector. In

[40] D. D. Avant, *The Market for Force. The Consequences of Privatizing Security* (Cambridge: Cambridge University Press, 2005), p. 52.
[41] Confederation of European Security Services (CoEss), *Panoramic Overview of Private Security Industry in the 25 Member States of the European Union* (2004), at: www. coess.org.

addition, the fundamental tenets of Neoliberalism suggest that offering citizens a choice between competing security providers may eliminate, or at least improve, the democratic weaknesses in current policy-making arrangements.

Cosmopolitan Republican government

In the light of a growing critique of Neoliberalism, Republican theory has experienced an academic revival.[42] Building on this revival, leading scholars, such as Jürgen Habermas and Ulrich Beck, have developed what might be termed Cosmopolitan Republicanism as an alternative to Neoliberalism.[43] They suggest that several cosmopolitan modifications of the Republican model of government may help to overcome many of the problems faced by Western democracies, including global interdependence and transnational security challenges and how to effectively and democratically address them.[44] These adjustments include: the broadening of citizenship, political community and the Social Contract from the national to the regional or even global levels; the reform of international organizations; the strengthening of solidarity and democratic participation through the promotion of civic virtue and civil society; and the strengthening of international law and courts.

At the heart of the Cosmopolitan Republican model of democracy is the enlargement of the scope of the Social Contract from national to regional or global communities.[45] This requires a shift in the definition of community from its current ethnic and national foci to a conception based on interdependence and equal access to a collective deliberative

---

[42] I. Honohan, *Civic Republicanism* (London: Routledge, 2002); P. Pettit, *Republicanism: A Theory of Freedom and Government* (Oxford: Clarendon, 1997); J. Maynor, *Republicanism in a Modern World* (Cambridge: Polity Press, 2003).

[43] U. Beck, 'The Cosmopolitan Perspective: Sociology of the Second Age of Modernity', *British Journal of Sociology*, 51, no.1 (2000), 79–105; J. Habermas, *The Inclusion of the Other* (Cambridge: Polity Press, 1999); J. Habermas, *The Postnational Constellation* (Cambridge: Polity Press, 2001). David Held is another key representative of Cosmopolitan theory. However, his Cosmopolitanism, unlike that of Beck and Habermas, originates in a Liberal concern with rights rather than in the Republican ideals of community and obligation. See, for instance, D. Held, *Democracy and the Global Order: From the Nation State to Cosmopolitan Governance* (Oxford: Polity Press, 1995), p. 15.

[44] R. Chung, 'The Cosmopolitan Scope of Republican Citizenship', *Critical Review of International Social and Political Philosophy*, 6, no. 1 (2003), 135–54; L. Elliott, 'Cosmopolitan Ethics and Militaries as ' "Forces for Good" ', in L. Elliott and G. Cheeseman (eds.) *Forces for Good: Cosmopolitan Militaries in the Twenty-first Century* (Manchester: Manchester University Press, 2004), p. 18.

[45] Beck, 'The Cosmopolitan Perspective', p. 90; J. Bohman, 'Republican Cosmopolitanism', *The Journal of Political Philosophy*, 12, no. 2 (2004), 336–52.

political process. The first involves the recognition of common threats and
the inability of nation-states to address them unilaterally. As Habermas
argues, transnational and global dangers such as environmental degradation, nuclear proliferation, terrorism and crime have 'long since united
the world into an involuntary community of shared risks'.[46] Since the
nation-state no longer sets the appropriate boundaries for the provision
of security, the Social Contract, citizenship and community must be
decoupled from the nation. Instead, they must rest solely on processes
of political opinion-formation. In this process citizens see themselves
as part of a community because of their access to and participation in
democratic self-government rather than their belonging to 'a quasi-
natural people' based on historical or social ties and cultural identities.
Cosmopolitan civic solidarity beyond national boundaries emerges from
transnational networks of communication and will-formation.

Two conditions can help to achieve this ideal. Firstly, the borders of
transnational communities have to coincide with perceptions of interdependence and common risks, and have to be stabilized by solidarity and reciprocity.[47] Instead of national or ethnic divisions, the scope
of a cosmopolitan community is defined by the answers to the questions: 'From whom can I expect help if and when necessary and to whom
will I have to give help in an emergency?'[48] Secondly, in spite of the
need to expand community beyond national borders, any community
or democratic body of politic requires closure.[49] Closure is necessary to
circumscribe the rights and obligations of citizenship, and the scope of
the democratic political decision-making process. It determines who
has a legitimate right to participate in political deliberations and who is
obliged to contribute to the common good of the community.

In spite of the resurgence of nationalist and ethnic conflict in Central
and Eastern Europe after the dissolution of the Warsaw Pact, the proponents of this model can point to several examples which suggest positive
developments towards the establishment of transnational communities
in Europe and North America. As early as the 1950s Karl Deutsch and
his co-authors observed the emergence of a transatlantic security community.[50] This community has been based on a sense of collective and

[46] J. Habermas, 'Kant's Idea of Perpetual Peace: A Two Hundred Years' Historical
     Remove', in *ibid.*, *The Inclusion of the Other* (Cambridge: Polity Press, 1999), p. 186.
[47] B. S. Turner, 'Cosmopolitan Virtue, Globalization and Patriotism', *Theory, Culture &*
     Society, 19, nos. 1–2 (2002) 59.
[48] Beck, 'The Cosmopolitan Perspective', p. 95.
[49] *Ibid.*, p. 91.
[50] K. Deutsch, S. A. Burrell and R. A. Kann. (eds.) *Political Community and the*
     North Atlantic Area: International Organizations in the Light of Historical Experiences
     (Princeton, NJ: Princeton University Press, 1957).

has been institutionalized through a number of overlapping organizations including NATO, the EU, the Western European Union (WEU) and the OSCE. While the end of the superpower confrontation has weakened the shared conventional security concerns of Europe and North America, vulnerability to transnational security threats such as terrorism, organized crime, refugee flows and environmental degradation have highlighted their interdependence in other areas. In particular in Europe, bilateral and multilateral security cooperation within these organizations has offered tangible benefits to their citizens. Notwithstanding debates over burden-sharing, all organizations have contributed to limiting national defence spending through mutual security guarantees and shared technologies and facilities. NATO's Article 5 'one for all – all for one' clause is still the main manifestation of the reciprocal security commitment among democracies in Europe and North America. It is complemented by a growing number of joint programmes ranging from NATO's multinationally staffed and owned Airborne Warning and Control System (AWACS) reconnaissance planes to the formation of joint military units by the three Baltic countries, Latvia, Lithuania and Estonia.

Empirical findings illustrate that contemporary transnational security communities are regional rather than global. NATO and the EU may have enlarged their membership and developed mechanisms, such as the Partnership for Peace and the Euro-Mediterranean Partnership, to collaborate with countries in their neighbourhood, but formal institutional and reciprocal security cooperation remains focused on the Euro-Atlantic region. Public opinion in Europe and North America shares this regional rather than global conception of their imagined transnational security communities. Thus, popular support for international interventions varies according to how distant the conflict is. In Germany, for instance, electoral acceptance of a peacekeeping mission in the Balkans, which had greater geographical proximity and closer social links to Germany, was considerably higher than for the mission in Afghanistan. Swedes, too, tend to favour interventions within Europe and are more sceptical towards humanitarian missions overseas. In particular, 'robust' military interventions with an increased likelihood of casualties are more likely to receive public support if they are closer to home and within an imagined security community.

In addition to recognizing the need for closure in order to enable democratic political deliberation, an acceptance of citizens' resistance towards accepting global security responsibilities is important because the emerging European and North American security policy processes have so far remained behind the expectations of Cosmopolitan Republicanism in terms of democratic control and accountability.

Since citizens are currently not able to directly participate in the political decision-making processes of most transnational security organizations in Europe and North America, their public deliberations on the definition of these security communities, their aims and policies have to serve as a substitute. To address this weakness, the advocates of Cosmopolitan Republicanism demand a reform of international organizations and their decision-making processes. They specifically envisage the transfer of decision-making capabilities and democratic participation from the national to the transnational level. Habermas, for instance, argues that the UN General Assembly 'must be transformed into a kind of upper house and divide its competencies with a second chamber. In this parliament, peoples would be represented as the totality of world citizens not by their governments but by directly elected representatives.'[51] While the UN is still far from this ideal, the EU has made some progress towards direct representation with the creation of the European Parliament in 1979 and the expansion of parliamentary participation in policy-making in the Treaty of Amsterdam, which came into force in 1999. Although the common European Constitution agreed in 2004 failed to be ratified by the necessary number of member states, it included additional efforts to strengthen the role of the European Parliament.

Some Cosmopolitan Republicans seem to believe that the creation of transnational democratic decision-making structures which facilitate equal access to the deliberative political process is sufficient for ensuring democratic accountability and control. Others, such as William Smith, suggest that cosmopolitan society also needs to revive civic virtue in order to assure the democratic character of transnational policy-making.[52] For classical Republicans the promotion of civic virtue was a requirement for a vigorous and participatory democracy. In this view, only a citizenry which is committed to ideals of solidarity, duty, community service and the common good is willing to invest itself personally in the political debate and share the burdens of the community. Most contemporary authors who have attempted to rejuvenate this view within the concept of civil society have focused on national democracy.[53] This does not mean that national and transnational civic virtues and obligations are conflicting. On the contrary, Maurizio Viroli

[51] Habermas, 'Kant's Idea of Perpetual Peace', p. 187.
[52] W. Smith, 'Cosmopolitan Citizenship. Virtue, Irony and Worldliness', *European Journal of Social Theory*, 10, no. 1 (2007), 37–52.
[53] M. Sandel, *Democracy's Discontent: America in Search of a Public Philosophy* (Cambridge, MA: Belknap Press of Harvard University Press, 1996); Pettit, *Republicanism*; Honohan, *Civic Republicanism*.

contends that 'love for one's country as a love for the republic does not
... rule out respect for other cultures and places. On the contrary, love
of country is merely a preparation for such respect.'[54]

Evidence for the argument that the development of civic virtue such
as a sense of responsibility for one's national community can facilitate
cosmopolitan notions of duty can be found in the emergence of cosmopolitan obligations towards 'strangers' in Europe. Countries which
hold on to Republican ideals such as duty, community and solidarity,
such as Germany, Sweden and Norway, also tend to justify their international security policies in terms of these ideals. The German government puts 'much emphasis upon cosmopolitan and humanitarian
causes, such as dying for peace, democracy, freedom, human rights, the
people of country X' when providing public justifications for a German
contribution to international humanitarian missions.[55] Contrary to
the US and the UK governments, the German government rarely uses
national interest as a primary argument for legitimizing military operations abroad.[56] National cultures emphasizing solidarity and collective welfare which translate into 'deepening senses of duty to distant
others' also characterize the Nordic states.[57] The populations of these
countries increasingly accept cosmopolitan responsibility for the lives
of peoples elsewhere, albeit primarily towards other Europeans.[58] This
notion of cosmopolitan responsibility extends towards accepting casualties among citizen-soldiers.[59]

Finally, the adaptation of the Cosmopolitan Republican model of
government to contemporary security challenges includes the juridification and civilianization of transnational relations. Although some
scholars such as David Held advocate less 'utopian' visions of overlapping national, regional and global spheres of common law, ultimately
the Cosmopolitan Republican ideal is that of a transnational Social
Contract.[60] The latter envisages an overarching legal authority and
monopoly on the legitimate use of force in the hands of a centralized

[54] M. Viroli, *For Love of Country: An Essay on Patriotism and Nationalism*
(Oxford: Clarendon Press, 1995) summarized by Turner, 'Cosmopolitan Virtue,
Globalization and Patriotism', p. 49.
[55] G. Kümmel and N. Leonhard, 'Casualties and Civil-Military Relations: The German
Polity between Learning and Indifference', *Armed Forces & Society*, 31, no. 4 (2005),
530.
[56] *Ibid.*, 531.
[57] A. Bergman, 'The Nordic Militaries: Forces for Good?' in L. Elliott and G.
Cheeseman (eds.) *Forces for Good: Cosmopolitan Militaries in the Twenty-first Century*
(Manchester: Manchester University Press, 2004), p. 169.
[58] Kümmel and Leonhard, 'Casualties and Civil-Military Relations', p. 518.
[59] *Ibid.*, p. 524.
[60] Held, 'Law of States, Law of Peoples', 1–44.

Table 8.3. *Revised models of the state*

Ideology	Neoliberalism (revised)	Cosmopolitan Republicanism
Geographical scope	local, national, transnational, regional, global	Regional, global
Functional scope	Fragmented provision of security functions by public and private actors at all levels	Centralized provision of security functions in international organizations and cosmopolitan forces
Resources	Fragmented financing, ownership and provision of military force by subnational and national public and private actors	Centralized financing, ownership and provision of military force by international organizations and cosmopolitan forces
Interests	Diverse individual security interests	Common and interdependent regional or global security interests
Norms	Individual sovereignty, self-responsibility, liberty	Regional or global sovereignty, mutual transnational responsibility, obligation
Decision-making	Horizontal, self-determination	Hierarchical, majority voting
Implementation	Transnationally fragmented, voluntary	Regionally or globally centralized, coercive
Control and Accountability	Limitation and fragmentation of control over military force among public and private actors, direct control of citizens over the hire of private security services through market choice and exit option	Citizen participation in transnational, regional or global government, civilianization of international security

regional or global government. The result is the creation of a new transnational 'domestic' space, within which citizens are subject to common laws and obliged to refrain from violence in return for collective protection. Within the EU this process of transnational juridification has progressed more than in other regional communities. Citizens can directly appeal to the European Court of Justice if they feel their basic rights are being compromised by national law. In addition, Cosmopolitan Republicanism can point to the expansion of international law and the creation of the International Criminal Court in 2002, which can prosecute individuals for genocide, crimes against humanity and war crimes, as examples for transitions towards transnational Social Contracts.[61]

According to Cosmopolitan Republicans these changes help to address the challenges faced by European and North American democracies in terms of the reconciliation of transnational security threats and problems with democratic control over the armed forces in several ways. Firstly, the creation of transnational security communities contributes to reducing the need for armed forces and, thus, the problem of their democratic control as the likelihood of violence decreases among its members. Secondly, the transnational scope of the new centralized 'government' allows it to combat security threats such as terrorism, crime and environmental degradation in a more effective and cost-efficient manner. Thirdly, the juridification of social relations across national boundaries 'de-securitizes' conflict and the internal use of force. It presents the use of violence as a breach of law rather than a military issue. Non-existential threats are, thereby, removed from the responsibilities and competencies of the armed forces and are instead tackled with political, economic and social instruments. Fourthly, by realigning representative government with the factual boundaries of contemporary security communities, Cosmopolitan Republicanism enhances democratic control and accountability. Giving citizens a representative voice in transnational security policy decision-making enhances parliamentary scrutiny, combats executive autonomy and contributes to fighting political apathy and encouraging civil society participation.

Redefining the soldier

In order to comprehensively address contemporary security challenges and improve democratic control over the use of collective violence, the revision of Neoliberal and Republican conceptions of the state must go hand in hand with a redefinition of their models of the soldier. One aspect of this redefinition is the democratic reform of the armed forces in accordance with the new tasks and identities of the soldier. Another is the realignment of these theoretical models with the changing roles of the state and the citizens in national and international security. Two competing ideological ideals emerge from these demands: the transnational private military contractor and the cosmopolitan citizen-soldier.

---

[61] International Criminal Court, at: www.icc-cpi.int.

Transnational private military contractors

While contemporary Neoliberal theorists have primarily based their argument on the state and the economy, the general principles of democratic control outlined in the preceding section are also applicable to the armed forces. The primary aim of these principles is to increase the ability of citizens to choose between competing security providers and to use market mechanisms to promote compliance with popular policy preferences and norms. Neoliberals, such as Friedman, have traditionally seen the professional soldier as the ideal embodiment of these principles.[62] Over the past decades, however, the private military contractor has increasingly emerged as a new Neoliberal model of the soldier. According to Neoliberal thought, the democratic control and accountability of this model rests on four characteristics: professionalism, private standard-setting, globalization, and specialization and civilianization.

The professionalization of private military contractors is an important condition for the emergence of a Neoliberal system of democratic control over the legitimate use of violence by private security providers. The transition from freelance mercenaries to incorporated private military companies has been the foundation for this development. While mercenaries operate outside the legal framework of the market, private military companies recognize and work within its formal and informal rules. The contemporary private military industry is a legitimate participant in the marketplace bound by business and contractual law and the mechanisms of competition, supply and demand. Private military companies have become subject to judicial prosecution for contractual obligations and to concerns about business reputation and industry best practice. Both mechanisms enable governments and citizens to exert direct control over the industry as consumers of private military services.[63] In addition, professionalization defines democratic standards of behaviour for the individual military and security contractor. According to Avant, military professionalism incorporates several core principles: civilian control of the military, abidance by the rule of law, respect for human rights and the laws of war.[64] With the entry of private military companies into the public marketplace the same professional principles play an important role in the social and democratic control of private military contractors. Private military firms have an interest in ensuring that their employees comply with these standards to protect their reputation and profits, and to prevent costly law suits.

---

[62] See Chapter 2. [63] Avant, *The Market for Force*, p. 61.
[64] *Ibid.*, p. 42.

For these reasons the professionalization of the industry has already progressed significantly. Contemporary private military companies are incorporated businesses with boards of directors, fixed headquarters and huge numbers of personnel. The largest and most well-known firms, such as KBR, CSC with its subsidiary DynCorp, and L-3 Communications with MPRI and Titan, are joint stock companies floated on stock markets. Many firms comply with professional industry management standards such as ISO 9001 and some companies have developed their own codes of conduct, such as Erinys, Control Risks and Triple Canopy.[65]

The professionalization of private military contractors is closely linked to private standard-setting and the self-regulation of the sector. As argued in the preceding section, they enhance democratic control and accountability since they facilitate the self-government of private firms and the transmission of consumer preferences regarding corporate standards and private business behaviour through market mechanisms. In terms of the private military contractor as the new model of the soldier, it means that individual behaviour has not only to comply with public law, but also a growing range of subsidiary regulations and standards. Since industry self-regulation frequently lacks convincing punitive measures, the socialization of employees becomes crucial for ensuring the effectiveness of these regulations. So far, private military businesses have largely relied on the professional standards many of their personnel have acquired through training within national armed forces. But some private military firms such as DynCorp are requiring employees to sign a pledge to their firm's code of conduct or to enrol in training courses before certain deployments.

The globalization of the market for private military contractors is another factor in the democratic control over armed force according to Neoliberal thought. Specifically, the globalization of personnel recruitment and industry competition increases the choice that states and citizens have between alternative security providers, thus exerting pressure to conform to public norms and expectations. In a global market consumers of private military services can easily replace contractors who do not abide by the law or professional standards with those who do. Moreover, globalization allows companies to use local personnel and expertise and, thus, work in a more cost-efficient and effective

---

[65] Erinys, 'Code of Ethics', at: www.erinysinternational.com; Control Risks, 'Code of Ethics', at: www.control-risks.com; Triple Canopy, 'Code of Conduct and Business Ethics', at: www.triplecanopy.com.

manner. Finally, global private military firms and contractors can be employed in international crisis management.[66] Transnational actors who lack armed forces, such as international organizations or NGOs, particularly benefit from a globalization of the market for private military contractors. The resulting ability of non-state actors to address transnational security threats where state action is slow or prevented by intergovernmental diplomacy contributes to the provision of security at subsidiary levels and receives its democratic legitimacy, at least partly, from the donations and personal participation of citizens who feel directly concerned about these security issues.

Owing to its advantages, a global market for private military personnel and firms has indeed been emerging over the past decades. As noted in the preceding chapters, in Iraq private military staff have come from a variety of countries, ranging from the USA and the UK to Fiji and Ukraine. In addition to states, international organizations and NGOs have gained from the growing competitive global market for private military contractors. The USA, the UN, the Economic Community of West African States (ECOWAS), the African Union and a range of NGOs have hired private military contractors to supply a variety of peacekeeping and peace support functions ranging from demining to logistics and personnel protection.[67]

Finally, the increasing specialization of private military personnel and the associated civilianization of their identity can enhance the democratic control over private contractors. In this view, specialization facilitates the reduction of state-controlled armed forces by separating combat from support functions and by limiting national militaries to the former. Specialization within the private military industry also contributes to differentiating between military and civilian means for combating contemporary security threats. The outsourcing of non-military tasks to private contractors highlights the civilian nature of a large section of contemporary security provision and can help to 'de-securitize' threats such as terrorism, crime and migration and move them from state to private security provision. In summary, specialization can facilitate democratic control and accountability through two developments. One is the further shrinking of national armed forces and the role of the state in the provision of national and international security. The second is the civilianization and privatization of contemporary security management.

---

[66] O. Bures, 'Private Military Companies: A Second Best Peacekeeping Option?' *International Peacekeeping*, 12, no. 4 (2005), 533–46.
[67] *Ibid.*, p. 538.

While there is some empirical evidence for such developments, their effectiveness can only be established in the long term. So far, cuts in the armed forces in the UK and the USA have been outweighed by the employment of private contractors. Moreover, efforts of the US and UK governments to include private military personnel within the rules and regulations of their national armed forces have blurred the boundaries between soldiers and contractors instead of civilizing security.

In conclusion, Neoliberalists suggest that a return to the theory's core principles can contribute to improving democratic control and accountability of contemporary armed forces in multiple ways. Firstly, professionalization, industry self-regulation and private standard-setting encourage the compliance of individual private military contractors with democratic norms, expectations and processes. Neoliberal forms of self-governance thereby aim to address the weaknesses of nation-states with regard to the transnational regulation of private military personnel. Secondly, the globalization of the market for private contractors gives states and citizens as customers a greater choice of security personnel and firms. Increased global competition promotes democratic control and accountability since consumers are less dependent upon individual contractors. Thirdly, the specialization of military and security contractors helps to distinguish between combat and civilian functions and, thus, can highlight the decreased utility of military means in combating present security threats.

Cosmopolitan citizen-soldiers

The Cosmopolitan Republican answer to the changing security environment and the challenges to the democratic control of the armed forces is the model of the cosmopolitan citizen-soldier. There are different versions of this model depending on whether it is based on Cosmopolitan Liberalism or Republicanism.[68] The Cosmopolitan Republican ideal of the cosmopolitan citizen-soldier differs from others by its reference to the three core principles: community, obligation and civic virtue. Aligned with the ideal of centralized regional or global government and policy-making processes outlined in the preceding section, the Cosmopolitan Republican model of the cosmopolitan soldier envisages transnational armed forces characterized by cosmopolitan

---

[68] L. Elliott and G. Cheeseman (eds.) *Forces for Good: Cosmopolitan Militaries in the 21st Century* (Manchester: Manchester University Press, 2004); T. Woodhouse and O. Ramsbotham, 'Cosmopolitan Peacekeeping and the Globalization of Security', *International Peacekeeping*, 12, no. 2 (2005), 139–56; M. Kaldor, *New and Old Wars: Organised Violence in a Global Era* (Cambridge: Polity Press, 2001).

norms, common standards and training, transnational military units, and civilianization and constabularization.

According to Cosmopolitan Republicanism, the subscription of the individual soldier to cosmopolitan norms and beliefs plays a crucial role in ensuring democratic control over collective force. Foremost among these norms and beliefs are the notions of 'solidarity with strangers', reciprocal obligation and transnational community.[69] The acts of violence perpetrated by cosmopolitan soldiers to defend citizens of other nationalities receive their legitimacy from the fact that both the soldiers and the 'strangers' belong to the same transnational security community. As argued above, the boundaries of this community are defined by interdependence and equal access to the political processes of deliberation. The democratic accountability of cosmopolitan soldiers and interventions is thus based on the political consent of those who are to be defended.

Although most Cosmopolitan Republican authors hesitate to explicitly proclaim a duty for the individual citizen to defend strangers, the ideal of the cosmopolitan citizen-soldier essentially represents a transposition of the model of the citizen-soldier from national to regional and global levels. By defending citizens of other nations but of the same transnational community, cosmopolitan soldiers protect their own society. Moreover, by drafting cosmopolitan soldiers from the same society Cosmopolitan Republicanism seeks to ensure the congruence between the norms and beliefs of the armed forces and the strangers whom they serve.

While critics see the extension of notions of solidarity and duty from the nation to transnational communities as one of the main obstacles to the continuation of conscription, multiple examples suggest that the ideal of cosmopolitan armed forces can indeed be reconciled with the model of the citizen-soldier. Several countries which regularly engage in international peacekeeping and humanitarian missions, such as Sweden, Norway, Germany and Austria, have conscripted armed forces. Interestingly, the support for cosmopolitan peacekeeping missions is greater among these conscript armies than among the professional militaries of the USA and the UK.[70] Whereas Germany has only recently

---

[69] Beck, 'The Cosmopolitan Perspective', p. 92. For another example of the use of the term see N. Wheeler, *Saving Strangers: Humanitarian Intervention in International Society* (Oxford: Oxford University Press, 2000).

[70] D. Avant and J. Lebovic, 'U.S. Military Attitudes toward Post-Cold War Missions', *Armed Forces & Society*, 27, no. 1 (2000), 37–56; M. Tomforde, 'Motivation and Self-Image among German Peacekeepers', *International Peacekeeping*, 12, no. 4 (2005), 576–85.

become actively engaged in international humanitarian interventions, Sweden has a long tradition of peacekeeping.[71] The cosmopolitan-mindedness of the Swedish citizen and military is illustrated by the fact that Sweden made international peace support operations a 'primary task' for its national armed forces in 1996, although it has a conscript army and relies on volunteers for peacekeeping.[72] Moreover, Sweden has tried to avoid the creation of 'professional peacekeepers' by limiting the number of missions that its citizen-soldiers can volunteer for in order to preserve a large democratic basis for international interventions.[73]

For the individual soldier in Germany and Sweden altruistic motives such as solidarity with strangers typically range below more personal objectives such as the desire for adventure or to save money as reasons for volunteering for peacekeeping missions. However, Eva Johansson finds that those with altruistic motives 'seemed to be more comfortable in their role and they more often perceived high confidence in commanders and peers as well as enjoyed their tasks'.[74] It seems, thus, that cosmopolitan-minded soldiers are more likely to volunteer for repeated postings. Moreover, conscripts usually have multiple reasons for joining up and cosmopolitan solidarity and obligation, while not their primary motivation, seems to be part of a general outlook created through the educational system and military training in Sweden.

Multinational integration, training and the development of common standards and rules of operation for cosmopolitan armed forces ideally reinforce normative and democratic controls over the uses and behaviour of cosmopolitan soldiers. Multilateral cosmopolitan armed forces require an international consensus in order to be deployed, and thereby facilitate the transnational democratic accountability of cosmo-politan interventions. The Scandinavian militaries serve as prototypes of Cosmopolitan Republican armed forces not only because of the beliefs of their citizen-soldiers, but also because of their integration and collaboration in international peacekeeping missions.[75] In 2003 Denmark, Finland, Norway and Sweden signed a memorandum for a common Nordic Pool of Forces Register to coordinate the training and deployment of soldiers for conflict management and peacekeeping.[76] Moreover, since the early 1990s a growing number of armed forces

[71] E. Johansson, 'A Portrait of the Swedish Peacekeeper at the Threshold of the 21st Century', paper presented at the IUS Seminar, 25–27 October 2002, Kingston, Canada, p. 4.
[72] Ibid., p. 4.   [73] Ibid., p. 10.
[74] Ibid., p. 21.
[75] Bergman, 'The Nordic Militaries: Forces for Good?', p. 169.
[76] Ibid., p. 174.

units within Europe have become part of multinational corps, includ-
ing the Allied Command Europe Rapid Reaction Corps (1991), the
German-French Brigade (1989), the German-Dutch Corps (1995), the
Eurocorps (1992), Eurofor (1995), the Multinational Corps North East
(1999), the Multinational Land Force (1998) and the Multinational
Peace Force Southeastern Europe (1998).[77]

Importantly, joint training and exercises within multinational forces
contribute to the creation of common professional standards, military
cultures and identities. The Nordic Peace exercises for instance serve
the explicit aim to 'establish an integrated approach to conflict prevention' among the Scandinavian countries, and their Nordcaps military training programme seeks to share the Scandinavian expertise in
peacekeeping with future military police, observers, delegates, logistics personnel and staff officers from other nations.[78] The promotion of
Republican ideals is one element of the programme, including teaching
peacekeepers 'to widen their perceptions of duty as well as transcend
their national community's "particularistic interests" to the benefit of
"the citizens of the emerging global community"'.[79]

Finally, the Cosmopolitan Republican ideal of expanding the scope
of the Social Contract from the national to the regional and global
levels is linked to a civilianization and constabularization of cosmopolitan armed forces. According to this model, the juridification of
international relations expands the boundaries of 'domestic' law and
the emergence of transnational security communities abolishes the use
of traditional military forces across national boundaries. In their place,
Cosmopolitan Republicanism envisages a cosmopolitan military which
is closer to a constabulary than a military force and more effective in
providing protection against non-state threats such as terrorism, transnational crime and ethnic conflict. The new cosmopolitan constabulary
forces are distinguished from conventional soldiers in terms of in their
rights, functions, equipment, training, operation and identity. Ideally,
the new constabularies use armed force only in self-defence, they are
not employed against collective armed forces, they do not normally use
large-scale weapons, they are trained to contain conflict, they engage
in small-scale operations and they maintain their civilian identities.
Again, the Scandinavian countries serve as an example of the growing

---

[77] S. B. Gareis, 'Wehrstrukturen und Multinationalität', in Ines-Jacqueline Werkner (ed.)
    Die Wehrpflicht und ihre Hintergründe (Wiesbaden: VS Verlag für Sozialwissenschaften,
    2004), p. 183.
[78] Bergman, 'The Nordic Militaries: Forces for Good?', p. 175.
[79] *Ibid.*, p. 175.

Table 8.4. *Revised models of the soldier*

Dimensions	Neoliberalism (revised)	Cosmopolitan Republicanism
Relationships with the state and society	Contracts at sub-state or transnational levels, e.g. with groups or individuals	Transnational reciprocal obligation
Motivation	Monetary gain	Solidarity with strangers and transnational self-defence
Identity	Individual-professional	Individual-civilian-constabulary
Democratic control and accountability	Professionalization, civilianization, self-regulation and global competition	Multinational training and standards; combination of transnational political and military roles; political and social representativeness of cosmopolitan armed forces

civilianization of cosmopolitan security provision. Their approach is based on the view that military force is not the only and not necessarily the most effective means to address contemporary insecurity, and that civil-military cooperation and integrated responses are required even in violent conflicts. In spite of strong commitments towards the defence of 'strangers', the Scandinavian countries are typically opposed to the large-scale use of military force in international operations. According to Bergman, this is not a result of aversion to military casualties, but part of a 'deep-rooted preference for rights-centered strategies of "criminalisation" over those of "warfighting"'.[80] Sweden has thus announced that it will provide larger contingents of military police, public prosecutors and judges to international peace operations rather than conventional soldiers.[81] By doing so, the Cosmopolitan Republican model expands the scope of functions subsumed under public security provision, thereby widening the usage and demand for citizen-soldiers and helping to restore the equity of conscription.

In summary, Cosmopolitan Republican reforms of the citizen-soldier and conscripted armed forces suggest that the perceived limitations of these models due to the growing inequality of conscription and the deployability of citizens in international interventions can be overcome. Moreover, these reforms promise to strengthen the efficiency, effectiveness and democratic control and accountability of contemporary

[80] *Ibid.*, p. 180.   [81] *Ibid.*, p. 172.

security provision. The approach specifically argues, and empirical examples confirm, that the notion of a civic duty to defend one's community and democratic accountability can be extended from the national to the regional or global levels through the promotion of common Republican values, and joint training and operations. In addition, Cosmopolitan Republicanism contends that civilian and constabulary cosmopolitan armed forces are not only more suited to the new security challenges, but also contribute to the equity of conscription by broadening the range of tasks under a comprehensive approach to national and international security.

Conclusion

The fundamental transformation of the transatlantic security environment since the end of the Cold War has served as one of the primary justifications and explanations for the privatization and outsourcing of military functions and services in Europe and North America. However, such arguments frequently do not take into account the full scale of the changes in the contemporary security context, characterized by the rise of non-military, transnational and non-existential threats. This chapter has argued that both Neoliberal and Republican models of the state, the citizen and the soldier have struggled to respond to these changes. In fact, the transformations in civil-military relations observed in this book pose serious problems for the efficient, effective and democratic use of armed force. In the UK, the USA and Germany reforms in the armed forces since the beginning of the 1990s have decreased public information and parliamentary scrutiny and have enhanced government-industry collusion and executive autonomy. Moreover, the changing roles and relations of the soldier have contributed to widening the gap between the armed forces and the citizens.

As in previous centuries, a key challenge lies in the revision of public ideologies in order to deal with changing circumstances and demands. Neoliberal scholars suggest that such a revision can proceed through a return to the key principles of Liberal democracy, namely the limitation of the state, competition and self-governance. Applied to the new security environment, they propose that transnational federalism can offer a model which enhances citizens' choice among alternative security providers. Neoliberals also believe that a globalization of the private security and military industry will provide the context for market competition and industry self-regulation to improve the compliance of private military contractors with the norms and interests of their customers.

Republican authors, conversely, contend that their ideological framework can be adapted to the changing security context not by reducing, but expanding the scope of government. They favour extending the notions of community and civic duty from national to cosmopolitan societies, and the juridification and civilianization of international conflict. The resulting Cosmopolitan Republican model envisages the centralization of democratic control over armed force within regional or global organizations and the creation of cosmopolitan armed forces and constabularies composed of citizen-soldiers.

Empirical evidence illustrates the practical potential of both ideological reforms. On the one hand, there has been an increasing transnationalization of the private security and military industry with a growing number of regional and global corporations. These companies have indeed made efforts to professionalize and enhance their 'democratic' accountability through codes of practice and industry self-regulation. Furthermore, industry claims that about 70–80 per cent of their customers are from the private sector suggests that citizens are seeing the democratic advantages of privately selecting and controlling their own security providers. On the other hand, the role and perceived responsibility of transnational organizations in national and international security has significantly expanded since the end of the Cold War. The number of UN interventions has more than doubled since the beginning of the 1990s and other regional organizations such as NATO, the EU, the OSCE and ECOWAS have also stepped up their contributions to regional and global security. Increasingly, these organizations and interventions rely on multinational armed forces which, albeit far from the ideal of cosmopolitan militaries, contribute towards the creation of common standards and identities. These developments demonstrate that both Neoliberalism and Cosmopolitan Republicanism hold the potential for providing new models of the state, the citizen and the soldier within a changing security environment. Yet they are in themselves not without dangers. The conclusion of this book turns to the question of whether there can be a conclusive answer to the problems of democratic control over the legitimate use of armed force.

9   Conclusion

Standing armies (miles perpetuus) shall be abolished in course of time.[1]

Immanuel Kant

The privatization and outsourcing of military services in Europe and North America are in the process of fundamentally transforming the relationships between the state, the citizen and the soldier in modern democracies. The changing security demands of the post-Cold War era have been an important impetus. However, these transformations also reflect the long-standing ideological dispute between Republicanism and Liberalism over how to ensure democratic control over military force. Republicanism and Liberalism agree that the state's monopoly on the use of collective violence can only be legitimate if it is democratically controlled by the citizens who are the ultimate source of the natural right to employ force in self-defence, but they disagree on how the latter can be achieved.

As this book has illustrated, Republicanism and Liberalism are still central to our understanding of the democratic control of the state and the armed forces. Nevertheless, the utility, relevance and legitimacy of both ideologies are constantly re-examined in the light of developments in the national and international political and security environments. Since the emergence of modern democracy in Europe and North America, governments have not only repeatedly shifted from one ideology and model of civil-military control to another, but have also revised them due to new demands, norms and values. This conclusion reviews the influence of both ideologies on contemporary models of democratic civil-military relations in the UK, the USA and Germany before discussing the potential contribution that both can make towards improving democratic control over the use of armed force in the new millennium.

[1] I. Kant, *Perpetual Peace. A Philosophical Essay* (London: Allen & Unwin, 1903).

Ideology, democracy and civil-military relations

Political theory is more than an abstract tool for analysing and understanding political institutions and processes. Through its conversion into public ideologies, endorsed and promoted by citizens, parties and governments, political theory has always also played a critical role in shaping the political organizations and practices which it has tried to explain. The legitimacy of the use of collective violence has been a central concern for political theorists through the ages ranging from Sun Zi's *The Art of War* to Machiavelli's *The Prince*.[2] By the seventeenth century Social Contract theorists, such as Hobbes, increasingly reasoned that there should be limits to the legitimate use of armed force. They first proposed that only sovereign governments should have the right to wield military force and subsequently argued that a government's monopoly on collective violence was only legitimate if it was democratically controlled by the citizens. Republican and Liberal theorists have offered alternative models of how citizens could achieve the democratic control and accountability of their governments and the armed forces. Republicans have advocated the centralization of political power and its control through the active participation of virtuous citizens in government and in armed forces composed of citizen-soldiers. Liberals have favoured the limitation and fragmentation of political power among public and private actors and the creation of non-political militaries based on volunteers.

During the past three centuries Republicanism and Liberalism have served as the predominant ideological foundations for distinct models of civil-military relations in the UK, the USA and Germany. Although the interpretation and implementation of these models have varied considerably in response to history, culture, institutional structures and processes as well as changing external circumstances, the core premises and principles of both ideologies have influenced politics and its public justifications. In the late eighteenth century the Republican writings of Rousseau affected the demands of the French Revolution, while Madison attempted to educate US citizens in the principles underlying their new constitution. In the mid nineteenth century the Liberal model of democracy and civil-military relations based, among others, on the works of the theorist and politician Mill increasingly influenced government policies in the UK and the USA. Although the two World Wars and the Cold War saw a revival of Republican ideals and their

---

[2] Sun Zi, *The Art of War* (New York: Columbia University Press, 2007); N. Machiavelli, *The Prince* (London: Penguin Books, 2004).

implementation in the warfare state model, by the 1980s the Neoliberal theory of Friedman provided a basis for Thatcher's and Reagan's 'rolling back' of the state in favour of increased public-private competition. Moreover, the extension and predominance of Neoliberalism in the post-Cold War era has contributed to the growth of private military contracting in the UK and the USA as well as in their international interventions, while the mixing of Republicanism and Neoliberalism in Germany has led to the development of new models of civil-military control based on public-private joint ventures for the provision of military services and the preservation of national conscription.

The interweaving of ideology and policy during the past three centuries suggests that the contemporary privatization and outsourcing of military services and the associated transformations in the roles and relations of the state, the citizen and the soldier in the UK, the USA and Germany are closely linked to their ideological justifications. While a multitude of other factors, such as the end of the Cold War, cuts in defence spending and the revolution in military technology, have contributed to these developments, Republicanism and Neoliberalism have played a critical role in defining and legitimizing governmental policies in response to these challenges. Some government leaders, such as Thatcher and Reagan, have made a virtue of the ideological nature of their reforms, emphasizing the theoretical credentials of radical institutional and policy changes. Others, such as Blair and Schröder, have attempted to present their policies as pragmatic, rational and unavoidable reactions to internal and external pressures. Whether explicit or implicit, any government decision is always inherently political and the ideological roots of recent changes in the models of the state, the citizen and the armed forces within Republican and Neoliberal thought are apparent in the content of these decisions and in the surrounding public debates. The promotion of the ideals of self-government, federalism and market competition fundamentally originates in Neoliberal theory, as do references to citizens as 'consumers' and increased 'choice' in UK and US government discourses.[3] By contrast, the commitment to partial state ownership of public-private joint ventures and the citizen-soldier model among the main political parties in Germany draws explicitly on the Republican traditions of the strong state, obligation and community.

The persistence or change of ideological models of the state, the citizen and the armed forces not only facilitates our understanding of the transformation of democratic civil-military relations over time, but also

---

[3] 'Gore Pushing Privatization', excerpts from speech by Al Gore on 14 January 1999, *PM*, 28, no. 2 (1999), pp. 18–22.

contributes to explaining the similarities and differences in the institutions and policies of democracies in Europe and North America. The widespread political and public support for the Neoliberal model of the small state, public-private competition and all-volunteer forces thus helps to account for the extensive scope of military outsourcing in the UK and the USA. Conversely, the persistence of Republican sentiments among the German public and post-war governments contributes to explaining why Germany has been more circumspect in its privatization of military services, although it faces similar functional pressures and security threats. Ideological differences also illuminate why the UK and the USA are increasingly willing to replace professional soldiers with private military contractors, while Germany so far remains committed to general conscription and the citizen-soldier model.

Ideology further helps to elucidate the problems of democratic control and accountability, created by particular models of the state, the citizen and the soldier. It shows that these problems typically stem either from the perceived or actual unsuitability of particular models for the existing security environment or from the inherent weaknesses of both Republican and Liberal theories of democratic civil-military relations. With regard to the former, the German model of the Republican citizen-soldier in particular has come under increasing pressure because it seems inappropriate for a security policy focused on international interventions rather than the defence of the national territory seems inappropriate. In addition, as Chapter 8 argues, the Neoliberal reforms of the armed forces in the UK and the USA have not been entirely successful in meeting contemporary security challenges because they remain premised on improving the availability and control of combat forces and fail to fully take into account the rise of transnational and non-military threats and actors. However, the preceding chapters have also demonstrated the inherent flaws of Republican and Neoliberal models of democratic control and accountability and the problems with their effective implementation. In the cases of the UK and the USA, the weaknesses of the Neoliberal model have been illustrated, among other areas, by the re-emergence of war profiteering in Iraq, the growing influence of a small number of private military contractors and the lack of public and parliamentary scrutiny. In Germany the Republican ideal of centralized state control over the provision of security has contributed to a merger of government and industrial interests in the form of public–private military service companies.

Finally, Republicanism and Liberalism offer competing visions of how democratic control over the legitimate use of armed force might be reformed in order to meet the changing security demands of a globalizing world. These visions can be summarized in terms of transnational Neoliberal security governance and Cosmopolitan Republican government. Both models are beginning to influence the practices and policies of Western democracies, ranging from the growing number of multinational cosmopolitan armed forces on the one hand to the expansion and transnationalization of private military contracting on the other. However, while these revisions of Republican and Liberal models of democratic control may address the demands of a security environment increasingly characterized by transnational and non-military threats and improve democratic control and accountability of the armed forces in contemporary militaries, they also contain some possible dangers. The following sections discuss these models and the need for additional analysis to understand their potential future implications. They highlight two issues for further empirical and theoretical research: the commodification of security within Neoliberalism and the limits of the Cosmopolitan Republican community and interventionism.

Neoliberalism and the commodification of security

As outlined in Chapter 8, the revised model of Neoliberal security governance seeks to address some of the problems caused by the increasingly transnational security environment and recent transformation of the armed forces in Europe and North America by returning to the Liberal principles of individualism, self-governance and competition. It argues that competition among multiple public and private security providers facilitates self-governance by increasing citizens' ability to influence security policy-making not only indirectly through elections, but also through a direct choice between different kinds of services and security providers. To do so Neoliberalism proposes the ideal of 'competitive federalism' which emulates the structures of the market by allowing citizens to opt out of unwanted policies. Competitive federalism works by permitting citizens to move and choose between competing public authorities, their policies and services at the subnational, national and international levels.

While the revised Neoliberal security governance holds the potential of increasing citizens' self-determination with regard to the provision of their own security, there are also a number of potential dangers to this model. Among them, the theoretical, practical and normative implications of treating security as a private commodity have so far been the least researched.[4] They may be observed in seven dimensions, including changes in the recipient, underlying values, degree and scope, threats, means, cost and duration of security services.[5] The focus of private military businesses on supplying security for profit, for instance, suggests that firms may seek to increase the number of potential customers by emphasizing individual as opposed to collective security interests. Private military companies may also attempt to encourage citizens to increase their private spending on personal security measures by inflating threat perception and highlighting future and unknown dangers. In addition, they are likely to shift attention from the collective prevention of conflict to individualized and reactive services such as personal protection. Finally, the commodification of security can contribute to inflating the cost of security since the expenses of security are no longer shared among all citizens.

In normative terms, attributing a greater role to the personal choice of citizens contributes to challenging key principles of national and international security. First among them is the state monopoly on the legitimate use of collective violence both domestically and in international affairs. Moreover, the monopoly of the state over the use of armed force is closely linked to other norms which have contributed to national and international stability such as national sovereignty and the laws of war. The commodification of security may also endanger the norm of non-pre-emption in military and security affairs if private firms seek to expand their markets by offering to address future security risks. Moreover, their focus on the individual citizen may contribute to undermining notions of community as the basis of national and international security along with normatively laden concepts such as the nation-state, public deliberation and burden-sharing. Lastly, the revised model of Neoliberal security governance may have serious implications for democracy itself, since it proposes a shift away from electoral process and parliamentary representation to market choices and individual consumption.

Cosmopolitan Republicanism, community and interventions

The Cosmopolitan Republican alternative to Neoliberal security governance is also not without potential problems. Building on the ideals of community, solidarity and obligation, Cosmopolitan Republicanism

[4] E. Krahmann, 'Security: Collective Good or Commodity?' *European Journal of International Relations*, 14, no. 3 (2008), 379–404; I. Loader, 'Consumer Culture and the Commodification of Policing and Security', *Sociology*, 33, no. 2 (1999), 373–92.
[5] Borrowed from D. Baldwin, 'The Concept of Security', *Review of International Studies*, 23, no. 1 (1997), 13–17.

advocates the expansion of democratic government, citizenship and collective security provision from the national to the regional and global
levels. According to the Cosmopolitan Republican model, the decoup-
ling of the Social Contract and security from the nation-state is the
key to addressing the challenges presented by transnational security
threats and the weakening of democratic control and accountability of
the armed forces. It believes that only by enlarging the scope of security policy-making structures to correspond with the newly emerging
transnational threats and interdependencies can citizens reassert their
democratic control over the provision of security. With regard to the
armed forces, this entails that citizens widen their conceptions of obligation and solidarity and replace national military service with multinational cosmopolitan armies.

The growing role of international organizations such as the UN,
NATO and the EU in providing national and international security
seems to illustrate the attractiveness of the Cosmopolitan Republican
model. However, Cosmopolitan Republicanism faces several problems
which are almost diametrically opposed to those of Neoliberal security governance. The idea of community, or civil society, and the question of whether political communities practically can and normatively
should be extended beyond national borders lie at the centre of these
problems. Doubts concerning the practicality of widening democratic
political communities from their current local and national levels to
regional and global organizations come from a number of directions.[6]
One concerns the psychological and social capacity of individuals to
feel solidarity with others and to construct common identities which
help to sustain the willingness of citizens to accept collective policies
which may not be in their personal interests.[7] Although Chapter 8
observed some evidence for the emergence of 'solidarity with strangers',
the persistence of national identities within the EU and the considerable opposition to further European integration among the citizens of
some member states seem to suggest that there may be inherent limits
to the size of social and political communities. Another problem derives
from a lack of homogeneity in transnational communities.[8] While many

---

[6] J. A. Scholte, 'Civil Society and Democracy in Global Governance', *Global Governance*,
8, no. 3 (2002), 289–92; C. Brown, 'Cosmopolitanism, World Citizenship and Global
Civil Society', *Critical Review of International Social and Political Philosophy*, 3, no. 1
(2000), 7–26.
[7] M. C. Nussbaum, *For Love of Country: Debating the Limits of Patriotism*, edited by
J. Cohen (Boston, MA: Beacon Press, 1996); W. Thaa, ' "Lean Citizenship": The
Fading Away of the Political in Transnational Democracy', *European Journal of
International Relations*, 7, no. 4 (2001), 503–23.

European and North American democracies have developed ways to protect the interests of minority groups, transnational cosmopolitan communities may only consist of minorities in the sense that differences of interests prevail over commonalities. Such political divisions may, at a minimum, require new political and institutional mechanisms to determine the public interest; at a maximum, they may undermine the potential for collective government. A third concern relates to the practical conditions for ensuring that all citizens have equal access to and a significant part to play in democratic deliberations and the political will-formation process. Since the weight of each citizen's voice, whether in the political discourse or representative elections, is inversely related to their total number, transnational communities and political organizations may simply be too large to make democratic participation meaningful. Already, electoral political participation in most European and North American democracies is decreasing due to a perceived inability to 'make a difference'.

Normatively, the extension of cosmopolitan community beyond the confines of the nation-state may hold a certain appeal. It suggests progress towards the ideals of cosmopolitan citizenship and cosmopolitan law which Immanuel Kant famously espoused in his essay 'Perpetual Peace' at the same time as Republicanism and Liberalism began to develop their theories of modern democracy and the democratic provision of national and international security. However, it raises the question to what degree cosmopolitan citizenship can build on shared definitions and norms as the bases for its laws and policies. The dangers of laws and policies which may represent the cultural understandings and ethical values of only a minority of citizens within a cosmopolitan democracy are particularly high with respect to the legitimate use of collective violence.[9] As Gerard Delanty notes, 'some of the greatest problems about violence concern its cultural definition: today there are deep divisions about exactly what constitutes violence.'[10] The issue of what makes a use of collective force 'legitimate' is even more controversial because it involves explicit value judgements. Finally, there is the problem of how to prioritize contradictory norms and values when it comes to fundamental concerns such as security.

[8] J. Bohman, 'Republican Cosmopolitanism', *The Journal of Political Philosophy*, 12, no. 3 (2004), 336–52.

[9] R. Fine, 'Cosmopolitanism and Violence: Difficulties of Judgement', *The British Journal of Sociology*, 57, no. 1 (2006), 49–67.

[10] G. Delanty, 'Cosmopolitanism and Violence: The Limits of Global Civil Society', *European Journal of Social Theory*, 4, no. 1 (2001), 42–3.

Recent 'cosmopolitan' military interventions serve well to illustrate these problems. NATO's bombing of Kosovo in response to the persecution of ethnic Albanians, for example, was fraught with divergent interpretations and value assessments in spite of the fact that it was conducted within what is typically regarded as a common transatlantic security community. For a start, there was considerable disagreement over how to define the violence: 'was it a "purge", a "genocide", a "war", a "civil war", "ethnic cleansing" or "forced expulsion"?'[11] In addition, different groups and individuals had divergent views on the legitimacy of the NATO response. Some interpreted NATO's intervention as a breach of international law and norms, manifested in the lack of a UN mandate; others considered it the defence of these laws and values, notably the Charter of Human Rights.[12] According to Beck, both interpretations represent the different hierarchies of norms characteristic of two distinct periods of modernity.[13] The first age of modernity placed international law over human rights. The second age of modernity has reversed this order. Whether this reversal is normatively superior is another question. While the aim of international law was collective peace, the protection of human rights prioritizes individual security.

Conclusion

Democratic control over the legitimate use of armed force is and has always been problematic. Since the advent of modern democracy, theorists and politicians have grappled with this problem, but neither of the ideal models of civil-military relations based on the mutual control of the state, the citizens and the armed forces proposed by Republican and Liberal theories, nor their practical implementation, have been without flaws. Some of these flaws are inherent in the nature of theoretical modelling based on a logical connection of premises and principles which is incapable of more than approximating the complexity and varying rationales of human behaviour and interaction. In Republican and Liberal theories this is prominently exemplified by their divergent emphasis on the community and obligations of citizens on the one hand, or their individuality and rights on the other. Other problems arise from the fact that pre-existing historical, political and social structures and

---

[11] *Ibid.*, p. 43.
[12] U. Beck, 'The Cosmopolitan Perspective: Sociology in the Second Age of Modernity', *British Journal of Sociology*, 51, no. 1 (2000), 82. See also U. Beck, 'War Is Peace: On Post-National War', *Security Dialogue*, 36, no. 1 (2005), 5–26.
[13] Beck, 'The Cosmopolitan Perspective', p. 83.

circumstances always distort any political representation and implementation of ideal-type models. Transitions from one set of models of civil-military control to another can cause such problems because they can lead to a mixing of contradictory principles, the elimination of core elements or the adoption of rules and regulations which undermine existing practices of democratic accountability and control. The privatization and outsourcing of military services in the UK, the USA and Germany have thus variously challenged the ability of governments and citizens to ensure the accountability of the armed forces. However, periodical revisions of the roles and relations of the state, the citizen and the military can also help to re-establish democratic control over the provision of national and international security by breaking up structures that have become corrupted. The widespread repulsion by private war profiteering during the First World War, for instance, increased public support for the centralization and nationalization of the defence sector during and after the Second World War. Moreover, the privatization and outsourcing of military production and services from the 1980s was partially a reaction to the rise of military-industrial complexes in Europe and North America which seemed shrouded in secrecy while increasing defence spending to previously unknown levels.

A look back over the past three centuries suggests that one of the most effective means of democratic control has been limiting the size of the military establishment, whether public or private. Since the end of the Cold War, several factors seem to have increased the possibility of pursuing such a policy within the transatlantic region, including the disappearance of major threats to national territories and the non-military nature of many contemporary security concerns. Both open the space for a return to the low levels of military spending and delimitation of standing armed forces characteristic of the eighteenth and nineteenth centuries. Again, however, Republican and Liberal theories disagree over how a reduction of the means and use of collective force could be achieved. Cosmopolitan Republicanism proposes the transnational integration of security provision within smaller, multinational armed forces, while Neoliberalism suggests that private military and security contractors can help to reduce or replace national and international armed forces. The preceding sections have argued that both models are also fraught with potential dangers. The Cosmopolitan Republican model may lead to the emergence of regional or global military-industrial complexes centred in international organizations which can decide on the use of military force without sufficient recourse to democratic will-formation processes. Neoliberalism may lead to the militarization of the private sphere and the ultimate loss of collective democratic oversight of the use of military force. A key towards resolving this dilemma may be one proposal on which both ideologies agree: a shift from military to civilian solutions. The answer to Kant's vision of the abolition of standing national armies might, thus, be found neither in their replacement with private military contractors nor in the rise of cosmopolitan militaries, but the civilianization of international conflict resolution.

Select Bibliography

Abrahamsson, B., *Military Professionalization and Political Power* (Beverly Hills, CA: Sage, 1972).

Adams, W., 'The Military-Industrial Complex and the New Industrial State', in C. W. Pursell, Jr. (ed.) *The Military-Industrial Complex* (New York: Harper & Row, 1972), pp. 81–94.

Alexandra, A., D.-P. Baker and M. Caparini (eds.), *Private Military and Security Companies. Ethics, Policies and Civil-Military Relations* (London: Routledge, 2008).

Altheide, D. L., and R. S. Michalowski, 'Fear in the News: A Discourse of Control', *The Sociological Quarterly*, **40**, no. 3 (1999), 475–503.

Anderson, D. G., 'British Rearmament and the "Merchants of Death": The 1935–36 Royal Commission on the Manufacture of and Trade in Armaments', *Journal of Contemporary History*, **29**, no. 1 (1994), 5–37.

Anderson, W. M., J. J. McGuiness and J. S. Spicer, *From Chaos to Clarity: How Current Cost-Based Strategies Are Undermining the Department of Defense* (Fort Belvoir, VA: Defense Acquisitions University Press, September 2001).

Aquina, H., and H. Bekke, 'Governance and Interaction: Public Tasks and Private Organisations', in J. Koiman (ed.) *Modern Governance: New Government-Society Interactions* (London: Sage, 1993), pp. 159–70.

Arnold, G., *Mercenaries: The Scourge of the Third World* (Basingstoke: Macmillan, 1999).

Avant, D. D., 'Privatizing Military Training', *Foreign Policy in Focus*, **5**, no. 17 (2000), 1–3.

   The Market for Force. The Consequences of Privatizing Security (Cambridge: Cambridge University Press, 2005).

Avant, D., 'From Mercenary to Citizen Armies: Explaining Change in the Practice of War', *International Organization*, **54**, no. 1 (2000), 41–72.

   'Privatizing Military Training: A Challenge to US Army Professionalism', in D. M. Snider and G. L. Watkins (eds.) *The Future of The Army Profession* (Boston, MA: Mc-Graw-Hill, 2002), pp. 179–96.

Avant, D., and J. Lebovic, 'U.S. Military Attitudes toward Post-Cold War Missions', *Armed Forces & Society*, **27**, no.1 (2000), 37–56.

Avant, D., and L. Sigelman, 'What Does Private Security in Iraq Mean for US Democracy at Home?', Research Paper, January 2008.

Baldwin, D., 'The Concept of Security', *Review of International Studies*, **23**, no. 1 (1997), 5–26.

Ball, N., 'Appendix 1: The United Kingdom', in N. Ball and M. Leitenberg (eds.) *The Structure of the Defense Industry* (London: Croom Helm, 1983), pp. 344–61.

Barnett, C., *Britain and Her Army, 1509–1970* (London: Allen Lane The Penguin Press, 1970).

Beaumont, R. A., 'Quantum Increase: The MIC in the Second World War', in B. F. Cooling (ed.) *War, Business, and American Society. Historical Perspectives on the Military-Industrial Complex* (Port Washington, NY: Kennikat Press, 1977), pp. 118–32.

Beaver, D. R., 'The Problem of American Military Supply, 1890–1920', in B. F. Cooling (ed.) *War, Business, and American Society. Historical Perspectives on the Military-Industrial Complex* (Port Washington, NY: Kennikat Press, 1977), pp. 73–92.

Beck, U., 'The Cosmopolitan Perspective: Sociology in the Second Age of Modernity', *British Journal of Sociology*, **51**, no. 1 (2000), 79–105.

'The Terrorist Threat: World Risk Society Revisited', *Theory, Culture & Society*, **19**, no. 4 (2002), 39–55.

'War Is Peace: On Post-National War', *Security Dialogue*, **36**, no. 1 (2005), 5–26.

Beckett, I., and J. Gooch, 'Introduction', in I. Beckett and J. Gooch (eds.) *Politicians and Defence. Studies in the Formulation of British Defence Policy 1845–1970* (Manchester: Manchester University Press, 1981), pp. vii–xv.

Belkin, A., '"Don't Ask, Don't Tell": Does the Gay Ban Undermine the Military's Reputation?' *Armed Forces & Society*, **34**, no. 2 (2007), 276–91.

Bell, M., 'Defence Industry Privatization: The British Case', *NATO Colloquium, Brussels*, 29–30 June 1994.

Bellamy, I., 'Accounting for Army Recruitment: White and Non-white Soldiers and the British Army', *Defence and Peace Economics*, **14**, no. 4 (2003), 281–92.

Berghan, V. R., *Der erste Weltkrieg* (Munich: C. H. Beck, 2003).

Bergman, A., 'The Nordic Militaries: Forces for Good?' in L. Elliott and G. Cheeseman (eds.) *Forces for Good: Cosmopolitan Militaries in the Twenty-first Century* (Manchester: Manchester University Press, 2004), pp. 168–86.

Bird, S. M., 'UK Statistical Indifference to its Military Casualties in Iraq', *The Lancet*, **367** (4 March 2006), 713–15.

Bishop, P., 'Competition and Collaboration in the Provision of Public Services: The Case of the UK Defence Sector', *Journal of Finance and Management in Public Service*, **3**, no. 1 (2003), 13–24.

Bohman, J., 'Republican Cosmopolitanism', *The Journal of Political Philosophy*, **12**, no. 3 (2004), 336–52.

Bolton, Jr., C. M., 'Providing the Soldier with the Right Stuff', *Army*, **55**, no. 10 (2005), 44.

Bondy, H. J., 'Postmodernism and the Source of Military Strength in the Anglo West', *Armed Forces & Society*, **31**, no. 1 (2004), 31–62.

Bontrup, H.-J., and N. Zdrowomyslaw, *Die Deutsche Rüstungsindustrie. Vom Kaiserreich bis zur Bundesrepublik* (Heilbronn: Distel Verlag, 1988).

Booth, B., M. Kestnbaum and D. R. Segal, 'Are Post-Cold War Militaries Postmodern?' *Armed Forces & Society*, **27**, no. 3 (2001), 319–42.

Bowling, K. B., 'Candid Voices – Military Readiness: Effects of Outsourcing Repairs', *Air Force Journal of Logistics*, 24, no. 4 (2000), 24–7.

Brereton, J. M., *The British Soldier. A Social History from 1661 to the Present Day* (London: The Bodley Head, 1986).

Broad, R., *Conscription in Britain 1939–1964* (London: Routledge, 2006).

Brooks, D. 'Messiahs or Mercenaries? The Future of International Military Services', *International Peacekeeping*, 7, no. 4 (2000), 129–44.

Brown, C., 'Cosmopolitanism, World Citizenship and Global Civil Society', *Critical Review of International Social and Political Philosophy*, 3, no. 1 (2000), 7–26.

Brzoska, M., 'The Erosion of Restraint in West German Arms Transfer Policy', *Journal of Peace Research*, 26, no. 2 (1989), 165–77.

'The Federal Republic of Germany', in N. Ball and M. Leitenberg (eds.) *The Structure of the Defense Industry* (London: Croom Helm, 1983), pp. 111–39.

Buchanan, J. M., 'Federalism and Individual Sovereignty', *Cato Journal*, 15, nos. 2–3 (1995), 259–71.

Bulmahn, T., *Bevölkerungsbefragung 2008: Sicherheits- und verteidigungspolitisches Meinungsklima in Deutschland* (Strausberg: SOWI, November 2008).

'Das sicherheits- und verteidigungspolitische Meinungsbild in Deutschland', *SOWI.NEWS*, no. 1 (2006), 1–11.

Bulmahn, T., R. Fiebig and W. Sender, *Sicherheits- und verteidigungspolitisches Meinungsklima in der Bundesrepublik Deutschland* (Strausberg: SOWI, April 2008).

Bures, O., 'Private Military Companies: A Second Best Peacekeeping Option?' *International Peacekeeping*, 12, no. 4 (2005), 533–46.

Burk, J., 'The Military Obligation of Citizens since Vietnam', *Parameters*, 31, no. 2 (2001), 48–60.

'Patriotism and the All-Volunteer Force', *Journal of Political and Military Sociology*, 12, no. 2 (1984), 229–41.

'Theories of Democratic Civil-Military Relations', *Armed Forces & Society*, Vol. 29, no. 1 (2002), 7–29.

Burroughs, P., 'An Unreformed Army? 1815–1868', in D. Chandler (ed.) *The Oxford History of the British Army* (Oxford: Oxford University Press, 1996), pp. 161–86.

Camm, F., *Expanding Private Production of Defense Services* (Santa Monica, CA: RAND, 1996).

Carter, A., 'Liberalism and the Obligation to Military Service', *Political Studies*, 46, no. 1 (1998), 68–81.

Cavadias, J., 'Contract Administration in a Performance-Based Acquisitions Environment Is Serious Business', *Defense Acquisition Review*, 39, no. 3 (2004–5), 325–35.

Cerny, P., 'Neomedievalism, Civil War and the New Security Dilemma: Globalisation as Durable Disorder', *Civil Wars*, 1, no. 1 (1998), 36–64.

Chandler, D. (ed.) *The Oxford History of the British Army* (Oxford: Oxford University Press, 1996).

Chesterman, S., '"We Can't Spy ... If We Can't Buy!": The Privatization of Intelligence and the Limits of Outsourcing "Inherently Governmental

Functions"', *The European Journal of International Law*, **19**, no. 5 (2008), 1055–74.

Chesterman, S., and C. Lehnardt (eds.) *From Mercenaries to Market: The Rise and Regulation of Private Military Companies* (Oxford: Oxford University Press, 2007).

Chung, R., 'The Cosmopolitan Scope of Republican Citizenship', *Critical Review of International Social and Political Philosophy*, **6**, no. 1 (2003), 135–54.

Cilliers, J., and P. Mason (eds.) *Peace, Profit or Plunder? The Privatisation of Security in War-torn African Societies* (Pretoria: Institute for Security Studies, 1999).

Clarke, M., 'Memorandum Submitted on the Foreign and Security Policy Aspects of the Strategic Defence Review', *Eighth Report: The Strategic Defence Review, Volume II – Minutes of Evidence & Memoranda*, HC 138-I (London: The Stationery Office, 10 September 1998).

Cohen, E. A., *Citizens and Soldiers. The Dilemmas of Military Service* (Ithaca, NY: Cornell University Press, 1985).

'Twilight of the Citizen-Soldier', *Parameters*, **31**, no. 2 (2001), 23–8.

Confederation of European Security Services, *Panoramic Overview of Private Security Industry in the 25 Member States of the European Union* (2004), at: www.coess.org.

Cook, F. J., 'The Warfare State', *Annals of the American Academy of Political and Social Science*, **351**, no. 1 (1964), 102–9.

Cooley, A., and J. Ron, 'The NGO Scramble: Organizational Insecurity and the Political Economy of Transnational Action', *International Security*, **27**, no. 1 (2002), 5–39.

Cooling, B. F. (ed.) *War, Business, and American Society. Historical Perspectives on the Military-Industrial Complex* (Port Washington, NY: Kennikat Press, 1977).

Crock, S., T. F. Armistead, A. Bianco, and S. A. Forest, 'Outsourcing War', *Business Week*, **3849** (15 September 2003), 68–78.

Cunningham, H., *The Volunteer Force. A Social and Political History 1859–1908* (London: Croom Helm, 1975).

Danchev, A., 'The Army and the Home Front 1939–1945', in D. Chandler and I. Beckett (eds.) *The Oxford History of the British Army* (Oxford: Oxford University Press, 1996), pp. 298–315.

Dandeker, C., 'On "The Need to be Different": Recent Trends in Military Culture', in H. Strachan (ed.) *The British Army. Manpower and Society into the Twenty-First Century* (London: Frank Cass, 2000), pp. 173–87.

'The United Kingdom: The Overstretched Military', in C. C. Moskos, J. A. Williams, and D. R. Segal (eds.) *The Postmodern Military* (Oxford: Oxford University Press, 2000), pp. 32–50.

Dandeker, C., and L. Freedman, 'The British Armed Services', *The Political Quarterly*, **73**, no. 4 (2002), 465–75.

Defense Contract Audit Agency, *Audit Report No. 3311–2002K11010001* (Houston, 13 May 2004).

Delanty, G., 'Cosmopolitanism and Violence: The Limits of Global Civil Society', *European Journal of Social Theory*, **4**, no. 1 (2001), 41–52.

Deutsch, K., S. A. Burrell, and R. A. Kann (eds.) *Political Community and the North Atlantic Area: International Organizations in the Light of Historical Experiences* (Princeton, NJ: Princeton University Press, 1957).

Deutscher BundeswehrVerband, *Umfrage zur Berufszufriedenheit – Zusatzbericht zur Mitgliederbefragung des Deutschen BundeswehrVerbandes*, Vol. I (Passau, 26 April 2007).

Dickinson, L. A., 'Public Law Values in a Privatized World', *The Yale Journal of International Law*, **31**, no. 1 (2006), 383–426.

Diedrich, H.-P., 'The Public-Private Partnership for NH90 Simulator-Based Flight Training', *RUSI Defence Systems* (2006), 104–6.

Dinter, H., 'Wehrpflicht, Freiwilligenarmee und allgemeine Dienstpflict – Aktuelle Argumentationslinien', in I.-J. Werkner (ed.) *Die Wehrpflicht und ihre Hintergründe. Sozialwissenschaftliche Beiträge zur aktuellen Debatte* (Wiesbaden: VS Verlag für Sozialwissenschaften, 2004), pp. 109–29.

Dorman, A., 'The United Kingdom', in L. Elliott and G. Cheeseman (eds.) *Forces for Good: Cosmopolitan Militaries in the Twenty-first Century* (Manchester: Manchester University Press, 2004), pp. 237–49.

Downes, C. J., 'To Be or Not to Be a Profession: The Military Case', *Defense Analysis*, **1**, no. 3 (1985), 147–8.

Drews, I.-I., 'Private Military Companies: The New Mercenaries? – An International Law Analysis', in T. Jäger and G. Kümmel (eds.) *Private Military and Security Companies. Changes, Problems, Pitfalls and Prospects* (Wiesbaden: VS Verlag für Sozialwissenschaften, 2007), pp. 331–43.

Driver, S., and L. Martell, *Blair's Britain* (Cambridge: Polity Press, 2002).

Edgerton, D., *Warfare State. Britain, 1920–1970* (Cambridge: Cambridge University Press, 2006).

Edmonds, M., 'Defense Privatisation: From State Enterprise to Commercialism', *Cambridge Review of International Affairs*, **13**, no. 1 (1999), 114–29.

Edmunds, T., and A. Forster, *Out of Step. The Case for Change in the British Armed Forces* (London: DEMOS, 2007).

Eighmey, J., 'Why Do Youth Enlist? Identification of Underlying Themes', *Armed Forces & Society*, **32**, no. 2 (2006), 307–28.

Elbe, M., 'Werte verwerten? Zum Spannungsverhältnis zwischen Führung und Ökonomisierung am Beispiel der Balanced Scorecard', in G. Richter (ed.) *Die ökonomische Modernisierung der Bundeswehr: Sachstand, Konzeptionen und Perspektiven* (Wiesbaden: VS Verlag für Sozialwissenschaften, 2007), pp. 33–50.

Elliott, L., 'Cosmopolitan Ethics and Militaries as "Forces for Good"', in L. Elliott and G. Cheeseman (eds.) *Forces for Good: Cosmopolitan Militaries in the Twenty-first Century* (Manchester: Manchester University Press, 2004), pp. 17–32.

Elliott, L., and G. Cheeseman (eds.) *Forces for Good: Cosmopolitan Militaries in the 21st Century* (Manchester: Manchester University Press, 2004).

Elsea, J. K., and N. M. Serafino, *Private Security Contractors in Iraq: Background, Legal Status and Other Issues* (Washington DC: CRS Report for Congress, 11 July 2007).

Engelbrecht, H. C., 'The Problem of the Munitions Industry', *Annals of the American Academy of Political and Social Science*, **174**, no. 1 (1934), 121–5.

Entwistle, T., and S. Martin, 'From Competition to Collaboration in Public Service Delivery: A New Agenda for Research', *Public Administration*, **83**, no.1 (2005), 233–42.

Erwin, S. I., 'Brass Ponders Mixed Blessings of Privatization', *National Defense*, **83**, no. 544 (1999), 12.

Farrar-Hockley, A., 'The Post-War Army 1945–1963', in D. Chandler and I. Beckett (eds.) *The Oxford History of the British Army* (Oxford: Oxford University Press, 1996), pp. 316–42.

Feaver, P., and R. H. Kohn (eds.) *Soldiers and Civilians: The Civil-Military Gap and American National Security* (Cambridge, MA: MIT Press, 2001).

Ferris, S. P., and D. M. Keithly, 'Outsourcing the Sinews of War: Contractor Logistics', *Military Review*, **81**, no. 5 (2001), 72–83.

Fine, R., 'Cosmopolitanism and Violence: Difficulties of Judgement', *The British Journal of Sociology*, **57**, no. 1 (2006), 49–67.

Flynn, G. Q., 'Conscription and Equity in Western Democracies, 1940–75', *Journal of Contemporary History*, **33**, no. 1 (1998), 5–20.

Foreign, and Commonwealth Office, *Private Military Companies: Options for Regulation*, HC 577 (London: The Stationery Office, 12 February 2002).

Foreman-Peck, J., 'The Privatization of Industry in Historical Perspective', *Journal or Law and Society*, **16**, no. 1 (1989), 129–48.

Forster, A., 'Breaking the Covenant: Governance of the British Army in the Twenty-first Century', *International Affairs*, **82**, no. 6 (2006), 1043–57.

Fraser, P., 'British War Policy and the Crisis of Liberalism in May 1915', *Journal of Modern History*, **54**, no. 1 (1982), 1–16.

Fredland, E., and A. Kendry, 'The Privatisation of Military Force: Economic Virtues, Vices and Government Responsibility', *Cambridge Review of International Affairs*, **13**, no. 1 (1998), 147–64.

Freiherr vom Stein Gesellschaft (ed.) *Der Fahneneid. Die Stellung des Soldaten in Staat und Gesellschaft. Ein Cappenberger Gespräch* (Cologne: Grote, 1970).

Friar, A., 'Why Training for Service Contract Management Is Mission Essential', *Defense Acquisition Review*, **39**, no. 2 (2004), 267–77.

Friedman, M., *Capitalism and Freedom* (Chicago: The University of Chicago Press, 1962).

Gansler, J. S., *The Defense Industry* (Cambridge, MA: MIT Press, 1980).

Garcia-Perez, I. K., 'Contractors on the Battlefield in the 21st Century', *Army Logistician*, **31**, no. 6 (1999), 40–3.

Gareis, S. B., 'Soldat für den Weltfrieden: Der Wandel der Bundeswehr von der Verteidigungs- zur Einsatzarmee', *SOWI.NEWS*, no. 2 (2005), 1.
    'Wehrstrukturen und Multinationalität', in I.-J. Werkner (ed.) *Die Wehrpflicht und ihre Hintergründe* (Wiesbaden: VS Verlag für Sozialwissenschaften, 2004), pp. 179–97.

Geis, A., 'Der Funktions- und Legitimationswandel der Bundeswehr und das "freundliche Desinteresse" der Bundesbürger' in B. Schoch, A. Heinemann-Grüder, J. Hippler, M. Weingardt and R. Munz (eds.) *Friedensgutachten 2007* (Berlin: LIT, 2007), pp. 39–50.

Geise, J. P., 'Republican Ideals and Contemporary Realities', *The Review of Politics*, **46**, no. 1, (1984), 23–44.

Gillard, E.-C., 'Business Goes to War: Private Military/Security Companies and International Humanitarian Law', *International Review of the Red Cross*, **88**, no. 863 (2006), 525–72.

Gimesi, T., R. Jindra, A. Siedschlag and T. Tannheimer, *National Threat Perception: Survey Results from Germany*, Garnet Working Paper No. 18.6 (May 2007).

Glassner, R., and C. Schetter, 'Der deutsche Beitrag zum Aufbau Afghanistans seit 2001: Bundeswehreinsatz und ziviles Engagement', in B. Schoch, A. Heinemann–Grüder, J. Hippler, M. Weingardt and R. Munz (eds.) *Friedensgutachten 2007* (Berlin: LIT, 2007), pp. 63–74

Gordon, M. R., and B. E. Trainor, *Cobra II: The Inside Story of the Invasion and Occupation of Iraq* (New York: Pantheon, 2006).

Gramm, C., 'Bekleidungsgesellschaft und öffentliche Vergabe – Zur Entscheidung des OLG Düsseldorf vom 30. April 2003', *Unterrichts blätter für die Wehrverwaltung (UBWV)*, no. **8** (2003), 281–5.

Graves, R. H., 'Seeking Defense Efficiency', *Defense Acquisitions Review*, **36**, no. 4 (2001), 47–60.

Großeholz, C., 'Die ökonomische Modernisierung der Bundeswehr im Meinungsbild der Soldatinnen und Soldaten', in G. Richter (ed.) *Die ökonomische Modernisierung der Bundeswehr: Sachstand, Konzeptionen und Perspektiven* (Wiesbaden: VS Verlag für Sozialwissenschaften, 2007), pp. 15–32.

Gunningham, N., and J. Rees, 'Industry Self-Regulation: An Institutional Perspective', *Law & Policy*, **19**, no. 4 (1997), 363–414.

Habermas, J., *The Inclusion of the Other* (Cambridge: Polity Press, 1999).
   'Kant's Idea of Perpetual Peace: A Two Hundred Years' Historical Remove', in J. Habermas, *The Inclusion of the Other* (Cambridge: Polity Press, 1999), pp. 165–201.

The Postnational Constellation (Cambridge: Polity Press, 2001).

Harmes, A., 'Neoliberalism and Multilevel Governance', *Review of International Political Economy*, **13**, no. 5 (2006), 725–49.

Hartley, K., 'Military Outsourcing: UK Experience', Research Paper, Centre for Defence Economics, University of York (undated).

Hartmann, W., *Geist und Haltung des Deutschen Soldaten im Wandel der Gesellschaft. Vom Kaiserheer zur Bundeswehr* (Limburg a.d. Lahn: C. A. Starke Verlag, 1998).

Hayek, F., *The Road to Serfdom* (London: Routledge and Paul Kegan, 1944).

Held, D., *Democracy and the Global Order: From the Nation State to Cosmopolitan Governance* (Oxford: Polity Press, 1995).
   'Law of States, Law of Peoples: Three Models of Sovereignty', *Legal Theory*, **8**, no. 2 (2002), 1–44.

Helwig, R. D., 'Privatization of Utility Systems', *The Air Force Comptroller*, **34** (2000), 14–17.

Herrera, R. A., 'Self–Governance and the American Citizen as Soldier, 1775–1861', *The Journal of Military History*, **65**, no. 1 (2001), 21–52.

HM Treasury, *Competing for Quality: Buying Better Public Services*, Cm 1730 (London: HMSO, 1991).

Hobbes, T., *Leviathan*, edited by R. Tuck (Cambridge: Cambridge University Press, 1991).

Hogan, M.J., *A Cross of Iron. Harry S. Truman and the Origins of the National Security State, 1945–1954* (Cambridge: Cambridge University Press, 1998), pp. 291–305.

Honohan, I., *Civic Republicanism* (London: Routledge, 2002).

Howe, H.M., 'Private Security Forces and African Stability: The Case of Executive Outcomes', *Journal of Modern African Studies*, **36**, no. 2 (1998), 307–31.

Huntington, S.P., *The Soldier and the State. The Theory and Politics of Civil–Military Relations* (Cambridge, MA: Belknap Press of Harvard University Press, 1957).

Huntington, S., 'The Defense Establishment: Vested Interests and the Public Interest', in O.L. Carey (ed.) *The Military–Industrial Complex and U.S. Foreign Policy* (Pullman: Washington State University Press, 1969), pp. 1–13.

Hussain, A., and M. Ishaq, 'Public Attitudes towards a Career in the British Armed Forces', *Defense & Security Analysis*, **21**, no. 1 (2005), 79–96.

Isenberg, D., *Shadow Force: Private Security Contractors in Iraq* (Westport, CT: Praeger, 2008).

Janowitz, M., 'The All–Volunteer Military as a "Sociopolitical" Problem', *Social Problems*, **22**, no. 3 (1975), 432–49.

The Professional Soldier. A Social and Political Portrait (New York: Free Press, 1960).

Jessop, B., 'The Changing Governance of Welfare: Recent Trends in its Primary Functions, Scale, and Modes of Coordination', *Social Policy & Administration*, **33**, no. 4 (1999), 348–59.

'Governance Failure', in Gerry Stoker (ed.) *The New Politics of British Local Governance* (Basingstoke: Macmillan, 2000), pp. 11-32.

'Post–Fordism and the State', in A. Amin (ed.) *Post Fordism. A Reader* (Oxford: Blackwell, 1994), pp. 251–79.

Kaldor, M., *New and Old Wars: Organised Violence in a Global Era* (Cambridge: Polity Press, 2001).

Rethinking British Defence Policy and its Economic Implications, Sussex European Institute, Working Paper, no. 8, February 1995.

Kamlet, M.S., D.C. Mowery and T.-T. Su, 'Upsetting National Priorities? The Reagan Administration's Budgetary Strategy', *The American Political Science Review*, **82**, no. 4 (1988), 1293–307.

Kant, I., *Perpetual Peace. A Philosophical Essay* (London: Allen & Unwin, 1903).

Karsten, P., 'The US Citizen–Soldier's Past, Present, and Likely Future', *Parameters*, **31**, no. 2 (2001), 61–73.

Keller, J., 'Streitkräfte und ökonomisches Kalkül: Top oder Flop? Grundsätzliche Überlegungen zu einer Ökonomisierung der Bundeswehr', in G. Richter (ed.) *Die ökonomische Modernisierung der Bundeswehr: Sachstand, Konzeptionen und Perspektiven* (Wiesbaden: VS Verlag für Sozialwissenschaften, 2007), pp. 51–64.

Kelty, R., and D. R. Segal, 'The Civilianization of the US Military: Army and Navy Case Studies of the Effects of Civilian Integration on Military Personnel', in T. Jäger and G. Kümmel (eds.) *Private Military and Security Companies: Chances, Problems, Pitfalls and Prospects* (Wiesbaden: VS Verlag für Sozialwissenschaften, 2007), pp. 213–39.

Kestnbaum, M., 'Citizenship and Compulsory Military Service: The Revolutionary Origins of Conscription in the United States', *Armed Forces & Society*, **27**, no. 1 (2000), 7–36.

Kier, E., 'Homosexuals in the U.S. Military: Open Integration and Combat Effectiveness', *International Security*, **23**, no. 2 (1998), 5–39.

Kinsey, C., *Corporate Soldiers and International Security. The Rise of Private Military Companies* (London: Routledge, 2006).

Kirkpatrick, D., 'Government and Industry: Problematic Partnering', *RUSI Defence Systems*, 7, no. 2 (2004), no pages, at: http://rusi.org/ go.php?structureID=articles_defence&ref=P4198C021618F9

Kitchen, M., *A Military History of Germany from the Eighteenth Century to the Present Day* (London: Weidenfeld and Nicolson, 1975).

Klingenberg, W., 'Mobilität der Streitkräfte', *Europäische Sicherheit*, **54**, no. 10. (2005).

Koistinen, P. A. C., *The Military–Industrial Complex. A Historical Perspective* (New York: Praeger, 1980).

Krahmann, E., 'Conceptualising Security Governance', *Cooperation and Conflict*, **38**, no. 1 (2003), 5–26.

'From State to Non-state Actors: The Emergence of Security Governance', in E. Krahmann (ed.) *New Threats and New Actors in International Security* (New York: Palgrave, 2005), pp. 3–19.

'National, Regional and Global Governance: One Phenomenon or Many?' *Global Governance*, **9**, no. 3 (2003), 323–46.

National Threat Perception: Survey Results from the UK, Garnet Working Paper No. 18.10 (May 2007).

'The New Model Soldier and Civil–Military Relations', in A. Alexandra, D.-P. Baker and M. Caparini (eds.) *Private Military and Security Companies. Ethics, Policies and Civil–Military Relations* (London: Routledge, 2008), pp. 247–65.

'Regulating Military and Security Services in the European Union', in A. Bryden and M. Caparini (eds.) *Private Actors and Security Governance* (Münster: LIT, 2006), pp. 189–212.

'Regulating Private Military Companies: What Role for the EU?' *Contemporary Security Policy*, **26**, no. 1 (2005), 1–23.

'Security: Collective Good or Commodity?' *European Journal of International Relations*, **14**, no. 3 (2008), 379–404.

'United Kingdom: Punching Above Its Weight', in E. J. Kirchner and J. Sperling (eds.) *Global Security Governance. Competing Perceptions of Security in the 21st Century* (London: Routledge, 2007), pp. 93–112.

Kümmel, G., 'The Winds of Change: The Transition from Armed Forces for Peace to New Missions for the Bundeswehr and Its Impact on Civil–Military Relations', *Journal of Strategic Studies*, **26**, no. 2 (2003), 7–28.

Kümmel, G., and N. Leonhard, 'Casualties and Civil–Military Relations: The German Polity between Learning and Indifference', *Armed Forces & Society*, **31**, no. 4 (2005), 513–36.

Langston, T. S., *Uneasy Balance: Civil–Military Relations in Peacetime America since 1783* (Baltimore, MD: The Johns Hopkins University Press, 2003).

Lapp, R. E., 'The Military–Industrial Complex: 1969', in O. L. Carey (ed.) *The Military–Industrial Complex and U.S. Foreign Policy* (Pullman: Washington State University Press, 1969), pp. 42–54.

Levi, M., 'The Institution of Conscription', *Social Science History*, **20**, no. 1 (1996), 133–67.

Loader, I., 'Consumer Culture and the Commodification of Policing and Security', *Sociology*, **33**, no. 2 (1999), 373–92.

Longhurst, K., 'Resisting Change: The Politics of Conscription in Contemporary Germany', in P. Joenniemi (ed.) *The Changing Face of European Conscription* (Aldershot: Ashgate, 2006), pp. 83–98.

'Why Aren't the Germans Debating the Draft? Path Dependency and the Persistence of Conscription', *German Politics*, **12**, no. 2 (2003), 147–65.

Macdonald, G., 'Reform of UK Defense Procurement and State/Industry Relationships during the 1980s and 1990s', *Defense Analysis*, **15**, no. 1 (1999), 3–29.

Machiavelli, N., *The Prince* (London: Penguin Books, 2004).

Majone, G., 'From the Positive to the Regulatory State: Causes and Consequences of Changes in the Mode of Governance', *Journal of Public Policy*, **17**, no. 2 (1997), 139–67.

Makin, K., 'UK MOD: Raising its Game as a PFI Customer', *RUSI Defence Systems*, **7**, no. 1 (2004), 97–9.

Mandel, R., *Armies without States: The Privatization of Security* (Boulder, CO: Lynne Rienner, 2002).

Manker, Jr., J. E., and K. D. Williams, 'Contractors in Contingency Operations: Panacea or Pain?' *Air Force Journal of Logistics*, **28**, no. 3 (2004), 14–16.

Mannitz, S., 'Weltbürger in Uniform oder dienstbare Kämpfer? Konsequenzen des Auftragswandels für das Soldatenbild der Bundeswehr', in B. Schoch, A. Heinemann–Grüder, J. Hippler, M. Weingardt and R. Munz (eds.) *Friedensgutachten 2007* (Berlin: LIT, 2007), pp. 98–109.

Markusen, A., 'The Case Against Privatizing National Security', *Governance*, **16**, no. 4 (2003), 471–501.

Matthews, R., and J. Parker, 'Prime Contracting in Major Defense Contracts', *Defense Analysis*, **15**, no. 1 (1999), 27–42.

Maynor, J., *Republicanism in a Modern World* (Cambridge: Polity Press, 2003).

McNaugher, T. L., 'Weapons Procurement. The Futility of Reform', *International Security*, **12**, no. 2 (1987), 63–104.

Meiers, F.–J., 'Germany's Defence Choices', *Survival*, **47**, no. 1 (2005), 153–65.

Melman, S., 'Pentagon Capitalism', in C. W. Pursell, Jr. (ed.) *The Military–Industrial Complex* (New York: Harper & Row, 1977), pp. 37–70.

Michaels, J. D., 'Beyond Accountability: The Constitutional, Democratic, and Strategic Problems with Privatizing War', *Washington University Law Quarterly*, **82**, no. 3 (2004), 1001–127.

Mill, J. S., 'Considerations on Representative Government', in *On Liberty and Other Essays*, edited with an introduction by J. Gray (Oxford: Oxford University Press, 1991).

Dissertations and Discussions: Political, Philosophical, and Historical, Vol. I (London: Parker, 1859).

On Liberty with The Subjection of Women and Chapters on Socialism, edited by S. Collini (Cambridge: Cambridge University Press, 1989).

Molander, E. A., 'Historical Antecedents of Military–Industrial Criticisms', in B. Franklin Cooling (ed.) *War, Business, and American Society. Historical Perspectives on the Military–Industrial Complex* (Port Washington, NY: Kennikat Press, 1977), pp. 171–87.

Moskos, C. C., 'Toward a Postmodern Military: The United States as a Paradigm', in C. C. Moskos, J. A. Williams and D. R. Segal (eds.) *The Postmodern Military* (Oxford: Oxford University Press, 2000), pp. 14–31.

'Towards a Postmodern Military?' in C. C. Moskos, J. A. Williams and D. R. Segal (eds.) *The Postmodern Military* (Oxford: Oxford University Press, 2000), pp. 3–26.

Moskos, C. C., J. A. Williams and D. R. Segal, 'Armed Forces after the Cold War', in C. C. Moskos, J. A. Williams and D. R. Segal (eds.) *The Postmodern Military. Armed Forces after the Cold War* (Oxford: Oxford University Press, 2000), pp. 1–13.

Moskos, C. C., 'What Ails the All–Volunteer Force: An Institutional Perspective', *Parameters*, **31**, no. 2 (2001), 29–47.

Myers, F., 'British Trade Unions and the End of Conscription: The Tripartite Committee of 1950–56', *Journal of Contemporary History*, **31**, no. 3 (1996), 509–20.

Navias, M. S. 'Terminating Conscription? The British National Service Controversy 1955–56', *Journal of Contemporary History*, **24**, no. 2 (1989), 195–208.

Nelson, K. L., 'The Warfare State: History of a Concept', in C. W. Pursell, Jr. (ed.) *The Military–Industrial Complex* (New York: Harper & Row, 1972), pp. 15–30.

Newbold, S. E., 'Competitive Sourcing and Privatization: An Essential USAF Strategy', *Air Force Journal of Logistics*, **23**, no. 1 (1999), 28–34.

Nussbaum, M. C., *For Love of Country: Debating the Limits of Patriotism*, edited by J. Cohen (Boston, MA: Beacon Press, 1996).

Padgett, S., 'Political Economy: The German Model under Stress', in S. Padgett, W. E. Paterson and G. Smith (eds.) *Developments in German Politics 3* (Basingstoke: Palgrave, 2003), pp. 121–42.

Parker, D., and K. Hartley, *Transaction Costs, Relational Contracting and Public–Private Partnerships: A Case Study of UK Defence*, 18 April 2001, Centre for Innovation Research, Ashton University, and Centre for Defence Economics, University of York.

Percy, S., *Mercenaries: The History of a Norm in International Relations* (Oxford: Oxford University Press, 2007).

Petersohn, U., 'Die Nutzung privater Militärfirmen durch US–Streitkräfte und Bundeswehr', SWP–Studie, no. 36 (Berlin, December 2006).

Pettit, P., *Republicanism: A Theory of Freedom and Government* (Oxford: Clarendon, 1997).

Pierre, A., *The Global Politics of Arms Sales* (Princeton, NJ: Princeton University Press, 1982).

Pierre, J., 'Conclusion: Governance beyond State Strength', in J. Pierre (ed.) *Debating Governance: Authority, Steering, and Democracy* (Oxford: Oxford University Press, 2000), pp. 242–6.

'Introduction: Understanding Governance', in J. Pierre (ed.) *Debating Governance: Authority, Steering, and Democracy* (Oxford: Oxford University Press, 2000), pp. 1–10.

Pilisuk, M., and T. Hayden, 'Is there a Military–Industrial Complex?', in C. W. Pursell, Jr. (ed.) *The Military–Industrial Complex* (New York: Harper & Row, 1972), pp. 51–80.

Pint, E. M., J. R. Bondawella, J. Cave, R. Hart, and D. Keyser, *Public–Private Partnerships Background Papers for the U.S.–U.K. Conference on Military Installations, Assets, Operations and, Services* (Santa Monica, CA: RAND, 2001).

Portugall, G. 'Das kontinuierliche Verbesserungsprogramm (KVP) in der Bundeswehr – Eine sozialwissenschaftliche Bestandsaufnahme', in G. Richter (ed.) *Die ökonomische Modernisierung der Bundeswehr: Sachstand, Konzeptionen und Perspektiven* (Wiesbaden: VS Verlag für Sozialwissenschaften, 2007), pp. 211–32.

Portugall, G., 'Die Bundeswehr und das Privatisierungsmodell der "Öffentlich–Privaten–Partnerschaft" (ÖPP)', in G. Richter (ed.) *Die ökonomische Modernisierung der Bundeswehr: Sachstand, Konzeptionen und Perspektiven* (Wiesbaden: VS Verlag für Sozialwissenschaften, 2007), pp. 141–58.

Qian, Y., and B. R. Weingast, 'Federalism as a Commitment to Preserving Market Incentives', *Journal of Economic Perspectives*, 11, no. 4 (1997), 83–92.

Rathmell, A., O. Oliker, T. K. Kelly, D. Brannan, and K. Crane, *Developing Iraq's Security Sector. The Coalition Provisional Authority's Experience* (Santa Monica, CA: RAND, 2005).

Rawls, J., *A Theory of Justice* (Cambridge, MA: Belknap Press of Harvard University Press, 1971).

Reeves, S. V., *The Ghosts of Acquisition Reform: Past, Present and Future* (Washington DC: The Industrial College of the Armed Forces, National Defence University, 1999).

Reppy, J., 'The United States', in N. Ball and M. Leitenberg (eds.) *The Structure of the Defense Industry* (London: Croom Helm, 1983), pp. 21–49.

Rhodes, R. A. W., 'Foreword: Governance and Networks', in G. Stoker (ed.) *The New Management of British Local Governance* (Basingstoke: Macmillan, 1999), pp. xii–xxvi.

Richter, G., 'Privatization in the German Armed Forces' in T. Jäger and G. Kümmel (eds.) *Private Military and Security Companies: Chances, Problems, Pitfalls and Prospects* (Wiesbaden: VS Verlag für Sozialwissenschaften, 2007), pp. 165–76.

Riedle, J., 'General–Instandhaltung für alle', *Instandhaltung*, no. 2 (2006), 20–1.

Roe Smith, M., 'Military Arsenals and Industry before World War I', in B. F. Cooling (ed.) *War, Business, and American Society. Historical Perspectives on the Military–Industrial Complex* (Port Washington, NY: Kennikat Press, 1977), pp. 24–42.

Rosenau, J. N., 'Change, Complexity, and Governance in Globalizing Space', in J. Pierre (ed.) *Debating Governance: Authority, Steering, and Democracy* (Oxford: Oxford University Press, 2000), pp. 169–200.

Rousseau, J.–J., *The Social Contract and Other Later Writings*, edited by V. Gourvitch (Cambridge: Cambridge University Press, 1997).

Rubin, G. R., 'United Kingdom Military Law: Autonomy, Civilianisation, Juridification', *Modern Law Review*, 65, no. 1 (2002), 36–57.

Sandel, M. J., 'Liberalism and Republicanism: Friends or Foes? A Reply to Richard Dagger', *The Review of Politics*, 61, no. 2 (1999), 209–14.

Sandel, M., *Democracy's Discontent: America in Search of a Public Philosophy* (Cambridge, MA: Belknap Press of Harvard University Press, 1996).

Sarkesian, S. C., J. A. Williams, and F. B. Bryant, *Soldiers, Society, and National Security* (Boulder, CO: Lynne Rienner, 1995).

Sassoli, M., 'Legislation and Maintenance of Public Order and Civil Life by Occupying Powers' *The European Journal of International Law*, 16, no. 4 (2005), 661–94.

Schaller, C., 'Private Security and Military Companies under the International Law of Armed Conflict', in T. Jäger and G. Kümmel (eds.) *Private Military and Security Companies. Changes, Problems, Pitfalls and Prospects* (Wiesbaden: VS Verlag für Sozialwissenschaften, 2007), pp. 345–60.

Schmid, J., 'Mehrfache Desillusionierung und Ambivalenz: Eine sozialpolitische Bilanz', in G. Wewer (ed.) *Bilanz der Ära Kohl: Christlich–liberale Politik in Deutschland 1982–1998* (Opladen: Leske + Budrich, 1998), pp. 89–111.

Scholte, J. A., 'Civil Society and Democracy in Global Governance', *Global Governance*, 8, no. 3 (2002), 281–304.

Segal, D. R., *Recruiting for Uncle Sam: Citizenship and Military Manpower Policy* (Lawrence, KS: University Press of Kansas, 1989).

Shields, P. M., 'The Burden of the Draft: The Vietnam Years', *Journal of Political and Military Sociology*, 9, no. 3 (1981), 215–28.

Simkins, P., 'The Four Armies 1914–1918', in D. Chandler and I. Beckett (eds.) *The Oxford History of the British Army* (Oxford: Oxford University Press, 1996), pp. 235–55.

Singer, P. W., *Corporate Warriors. The Rise of the Privatized Military Industry* (Ithaca, NY: Cornell University Press, 2003).
  'Corporate Warriors: The Rise of the Privatized Military Industry and Its Ramifications for International Security', *International Security*, 26, no. 3 (2001–2), 186–220.

Smith, R., 'Defence Procurement and Industrial Structure in the U.K,' *International Journal of Industrial Organization*, 8, no 2. (1990), 185–205.

Smith, W., 'Cosmopolitan Citizenship. Virtue, Irony and Worldliness', *European Journal of Social Theory*, 10, no. 1 (2007), 37–52.

Snider, D. M., and G. L. Watkins, 'The Future of Army Professionalism: A Need for Renewal and Redefinition', *Parameters*, **30**, no. 3 (2000), 5–20.

Snyder, R. C., 'The Citizen–Soldier Tradition and Gender Integration of the U.S. Military', *Armed Forces & Society*, **29**, no. 2 (2003), 185–204.

Citizen–Soldiers and Manly Warriors (Lanham, MD: Rowman & Littlefield, 1999).

Spackman, M., 'Public–Private Partnerships: Lessons from the British Approach', *Economic Systems*, **26**, no. 3 (2002), 283–301.

Spearin, C., 'American Hegemony Incorporated: The Importance and Implications of Military Contractors in Iraq', *Contemporary Security Policy*, **24**, no. 3 (2003), 26–47.

Sperling, J., and L. Tossutti, *National Threat Perception: Survey Results from the United States*, Garnet Working Paper no. 18.11 (May 2007).

Spiers, E. M., *The Late Victorian Army 1868–1902* (Manchester: Manchester University Press, 1992).

Stanhope, H., *The Soldiers. An Anatomy of the British Army* (London: Hamish Hamilton, 1979).

Starks, G. L., 'Public and Private Partnerships in Support of Performance–Based Logistics Initiatives – Lessons Learned from Defense Logistic Agency Partnerships', *Defense Acquisition Review*, **39**, no. 3 (2004–5), 305–15.

Stenning, P. C., 'Powers and Accountability of Private Police', *European Journal on Criminal Policy and Research*, **8**, no. 3 (2000), 325–52.

Strachan, H., 'The Civil–Military "Gap" in Britain', *The Journal of Strategic Studies*, **26**, no. 2 (2003), 47–8.

'Making Strategy: Civil–Military Relations after Iraq', *Survival*, **48**, no. 3 (2006), 59–82.

Sun Zi, *The Art of War* (New York: Columbia University Press, 2007).

Taulbee, J. L., 'Mercenaries, Private Armies and Security Companies in Contemporary Policy', *International Politics*, **37**, no. 4 (2000), 433–56.

Taylor, T., 'Contractor on Deployed Operations and Equipment Support', *Defence Studies*, **4**, no. 2 (2004), 184–98.

Taylor, T., and K. Hayward, *The U.K. Defence Industrial Base* (London: Brassey's, 1989).

Thaa, W., '"Lean Citizenship"': The Fading Away of the Political in Transnational Democracy', *European Journal of International Relations*, **7**, no. 4 (2001), 503–23.

The Commission on Global Governance, *Our Global Neighborhood* (Oxford: Oxford University Press, 1995).

Thomson, J. E., *Mercenaries, Pirates, and Sovereigns. State–building and Extraterritorial Violence in Early Modern Europe* (Princeton, NJ: Princeton University Press, 1994).

Thornton, R., 'A Welcome "Revolution"? The British Army and the Changes of the Strategic Defence Review', *Defence Studies*, **3**, no. 3 (2003), 38–62.

Tiron, R., 'Public–Private Ventures Could Ease the Pains of Privatization', *National Defense*, **85**, no. 570 (2001), 36.

Tomforde, M., 'Motivation and Self-Image among German Peacekeepers', *International Peacekeeping*, **12**, no. 4 (2005), 576–85.

Trebilcock, C., 'Legends of the British Armaments Industry 1890–1914: A Revision', *Journal of Contemporary History*, **5**, no. 4 (1970), 3–19.

Turner, B.S., 'Cosmopolitan Virtue, Globalization and Patriotism', *Theory, Culture & Society*, **19**, nos. 1–2 (2002), 45–63.

Ullmann, J.E., 'The Military Industrial Firm – Private Enterprise Revised', *Policy Analysis*, **29** (9 November 1983).

Uttley, M., *Civilian Contractors on Deployed Military Operations: United Kingdom Policy and Doctrine* (Carlisle, PA: Strategic Studies Institute, September 2005).

Contractors on Deployed Operations: United Kingdom Policy and Doctrine (Darby, PA: Diane Publishing, 2005).

'Private Contractors on Deployed Operations: The United Kingdom Experience', *Defence Studies*, **4**, no. 2 (2004), 145–65.

'Public–Private Partnerships in United Kingdom Defence', *RUSI Defence Systems*, **9**, no.2 (2006), 82–84.

Walker, W., and P. Gummett, 'Britain and the European Armaments Market', *International Affairs*, **65**, no. 3 (1989), 419–42.

Wallerstein, I., 'Foes and Friends?' *Foreign Policy*, **90** (1993), 149–50.

Walsh, K., 'Competition and Public Service Delivery', in J. Steward and G. Stoker (eds.) *Local Government in the 1990s* (Basingstoke: Macmillan, 1995), pp. 28–48.

Weber, M., *Political Writings*, edited by P. Lassman and R. Speirs (Cambridge: Cambridge University Press, 1994).

Weidenbaum, M.L., 'The Military–Industrial Complex: An Economic Analysis', in O.L. Carey (ed.) *The Military–Industrial Complex and U.S. Foreign Policy* (Pullman: Washington State University Press, 1969), pp. 29–41.

Werkner, I.–J., 'Die Wehrpflict – Teil der politischen Kultur der Bundesrepublik Deutschland?' in I.–J. Werkner (ed.) *Die Wehrpflicht und ihre Hintergründe. Sozialwissenschaftliche Beiträge zur aktuellen Debatte* (Wiesbaden: VS Verlag für Sozialwissenschaften, 2004), pp. 155–77.

Wheeler, N., *Saving Strangers: Humanitarian Intervention in International Society* (Oxford: Oxford University Press, 2000).

Williams, P.D., *British Foreign Policy under New Labour, 1997–2005* (Basingstoke: Palgrave, 2005).

Wochnik, L., 'Das kontinuierliche Verbesserungsprogramm (KVP) als Instrument der Gestaltung organisatorischen Wandels', in G. Richter (ed.) *Die ökonomische Modernisierung der Bundeswehr: Sachstand, Konzeptionen und Perspektiven* (Wiesbaden: VS Verlag für Sozialwissenschaften, 2007), pp. 191–210.

Woodhouse, T., and O. Ramsbotham, 'Cosmopolitan Peacekeeping and the Globalization of Security', *International Peacekeeping*, **12**, no. 2 (2005), 139–56.

Woodruff, T., R. Kelty and D.R. Segal, 'Propensity to Serve and Motivation to Enlist among American Combat Soldiers', *Armed Forces & Society*, **32**, no. 3 (2006), 353–66.

Woodward, R., and T. Winter, *Sexing the Soldier. The Politics of Gender and the Contemporary British Army* (London: Routledge, 2007).

Zamparelli, S.J., 'Competitive Sourcing and Privatization: What Have We Signed Up For?' *Air Force Journal of Logistics*, **23**, no. 3 (1999), 8–19.

Zangl, B., and M. Zürn, 'The Effects of Denationalization on Security in the OECD World', *Global Society*, **13**, no. 2 (1999), 139–61.

Zugbach, R. von, and M. Ishaq, 'Managing Race Relations in the British Army', *Defense Analysis*, **16**, no. 2 (2000), 185–202.

Index